BUDDHIST TEXT TRANSLATION SOCIETY'S

BUDDHISM A TO Z

www.drba.org

Buddhist Text Translation Society · Dharma Realm Buddhist University · Dharma Realm Buddhist Association
BURLINGAME, CALIFORNIA U.S.A.

Buddhist Text Translation Society's BUDDHISM A TO Z

Compiled by
RONALD B. EPSTEIN, PH.D.

In collaboration with
THE EDITORIAL COMMITTEE OF THE BUDDHIST TEXT TRANSLATION SOCIETY

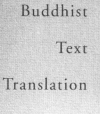

Buddhist Text Translation Society's Buddhism A to Z

Published by Buddhist Text Translation Society, 1777 Murchison Drive, Burlingame, CA 94010-4504. First edition.

07 06 05 04 10 9 8 7 6 5 4 3 2 1

Library of Congress Cataloging-in-Publication Data

Epstein, Ronald B.

Buddhist Text Translation Society's Buddhism a to z / compiled by Ronald B. Epstein in collaboration with the Editorial Committee of the Buddhist Text Translation Society.

p. cm.

Includes bibliographical references.

ISBN 0-88139-353-3

1. Buddhism—Dictionaries. I. Epstein, Ronald B. II. Buddhist Text Translation Society. Editorial Committee. III. Title.

BQ130 .E67 2003

294.3'03—dc21

2002001964

Cover and interior design by Buddhist Text Translation Society

Printed in Taiwan

CONTENTS

Introduction	vi
How to Use This Book	viii
List of Introductory Readings	ix
Technical Notes	x
Abbreviations of BTTS and Cited Non-BTTS Publications	x
Index of Entries: A to Z	xii
Illustrations	xxi
Buddhism A to Z Entries	2

Appendices

A	Additional Reference Material for Entries	224
B	The Buddhist Text Translation Society	238
C	Comparative Tables of Romanization: Pinyin/Wade-Giles/Yale	240
D	Sanskrit Pronunciation Guide	245
E	The Venerable Master Hsuan Hua Brings the Dharma to the West	246
F	On Translating Buddhist Texts and Speaking the Dharma	257
G	The Eighteen Great Vows of Venerable Master Hsuan Hua	265

Bibliographies

Bibliography of BTTS Publications in English	267
Bibliography of Cited Non-BTTS Publications	270

Indices

Index of Sanskrit Terms	273
Index of Pali Terms	277
Index of Chinese Terms (Pinyin)	279
DRBA Branch Monasteries	283

Introduction

This book is meant to provide basic information about Buddhism for students and others who have personal interest. It was especially designed as an aid for readers of the publications of the Buddhist Text Translation Society (BTTS), and the larger portion of the material presented consists of selections from BTTS publications. It is not meant to be a technical scholarly work.

The book is arranged in dictionary format and contains information on basic Buddhist concepts and lists. It can be used as a reference when reading Buddhist texts, and it can also function as an introduction to Buddhism. (See the "List of Introductory Readings" on page ix.)

Buddhism A to Z is by no means all-inclusive. For instance, very little historical information is provided. The most basic important terms and lists are found in it, but from time to time the reader will fail to find what he or she is looking for. In those cases, links to reference works listed on my website 'Resources for the Study of Buddhism' http://online.sfsu.edu/~rone/Buddhism/Buddhism.htm may be helpful.

The scope of the information found in the entries is not exhaustive. Many of the entries have an open-ended quality to them. The intent is to spur the interest of the reader to investigate further.

The following conventions have been adopted: All quotations from canonical works have been indented. Quotations not indented and indicated by quotation marks are from modern works. In quotations from canonical works, if the speaker is not indicated, it is the Buddha Śākyamuni. In modern works, if the speaker is not indicated, it is the Venerable Master Hsuan Hua, ninth patriarch of the Weiyang Chan lineage and founder and first chairperson of the Dharma Realm Buddhist Association.

Buddhism A to Z is by no means a finished work. Because of pressures to make it available, it has been decided to publish it in this preliminary form. The reader is cordially invited to participate in the development of the work for future editions by offering suggestions for its improvement and by providing information about errors and inaccuracies. Although many members of the editorial committee of BTTS have kindly contributed their suggestions and made additional and corrections, the errors that remain are solely my responsibility.

Ronald B. Epstein

Institute for World Religions
Berkeley, California

How to Use This Book

When using this book as a reference, look first under the term or list in question. If you do not find a list, then try under the key term in the list. If you still do not find the term, try either another translation, the Sanskrit, or a related term. Be sure to consult the Table of Contents.

When using this book as an introduction to Buddhist teachings, see the section on the next page entitled "List of Introductory Readings."

The Structure of the Entries

Most entries are structured following a pattern of going from easier to understand material to more difficult to understand material. Often the explanations progress according to level of teaching, culminating with the Mahayana teaching, but sometimes the progression is from less technical to more technical without regard to level of teaching.

Each entry includes some or all of the following elements: entry title, introductory quotation(s), definition of term or listing of members of list, short explanatory essay and/or quotations, alternate translations, and reference information for additional information in other entries.

ALTERNATE TRANSLATIONS: Lists other translations that have been used or proposed for the same term or list. Some of the alternate translations listed may not be accurate. They are given partly so that readers can be aware of equivalents found in other translations.

SEE ALSO: Indicates other entries that may give additional information on the topic or be of related interest.

Additional Information Concerning the Entries

The reader should consult the Illustrations listed on pages xxi-xxiii for the location of useful charts and illustrations that appear throughout the book.

List of Introductory Readings

For a general understanding of basic Buddhist teachings, start with the entries in Group I, then move on to Group II, and so forth. If you want information on a particular topic, read the specific entry that most closely approximates your topic, then check the entries listed after the "See also" symbol ☞ at the end of the entry, then check the sources listed for that entry in Appendix A: Additional Reference Material for Entries.

I karma
rebirth
enlightenment
Buddha
Thus Come One
Dharma/dharma

II Arhat
Four Holy Truths
Eightfold Path
Twelvefold Conditioned Arising
Bodhisattva
pāramitā
Six Pāramitās

III Six Spiritual Powers
Six Paths of Rebirth
Ten Dharma Realms
Five Skandhas
Eighteen Realms
Five Moral Precepts

IV meditation
mindfulness
Four Applications of Mindfulness
lotus posture
samadhi
Chan School
Four Dhyānas
Four Formless Realms

V Five Types of Buddhist Study and Practice
Mahayana and Hinayana Compared
Pure Land
Buddha Recitation
Eight Consciousnesses
One Hundred Dharmas
emptiness

VI demon
lineage

Technical Notes

Many passages from BTTS publications have been slightly edited and/or retranslated without each specific instance being indicated. In quoted passages some attempt, though not an exhaustive one, has been made to standardize terminology. The following conventions have been adopted:

1. Two slightly different conventions of romanization have been used for Sanskrit words depending upon whether or not they are treated as English. For those treated as English no diacritical marks will be used, and so the spelling is that English spelling closest to the pronunciation.
2. The following Sanskrit Buddhist terms have been treated as English words: Arhat, Bhikshu, Bhikshuni, Bodhisattva, Buddha, Dharma, Hinayana, karma, Mahayana, nirvana, Pratyekabuddha, samadhi, Sangha, stupa, sutra, Theravada.
3. Other Sanskrit words have been italicized to indicate that they have not yet become part of the English language, e.g. *asura, bodhi, dhyāna, kalpa, pāramitā, prajñā, śarīra, skandha, śramaṇa, śrāvaka, upāsaka, upāsikā, vajra*. Of course other less well-known non-English terms are also italicized. However, when such foreign terms occur in proper names, they are capitalized but not italicized, e.g. Ānanda, Avataṃsaka, Tathāgata.
4. Sanskrit terms are pluralized as though they were English, e.g. *asuras*, Six Pāramitās.
5. Pinyin is used for the romanization of Chinese words, except for some proper names which retain familiar romanizations. See Appendix C for Comparative Tables of Romanization: Pinyin/Wade-Giles/Yale.

Abbreviations of BTTS Publications

AS	*Amitābha Sutra*
BNS	*Brahma Net Sutra*
BRF	*Buddha Root Farm*
CL	*Cherishing Life*
CPL	*Ch'an and Pure Land Dharma Talks* (reprinted in LY, vol. 2)
DFS	*Dharma Flower Sutra*
DS	*Dhāraṇī Sutra*
EDR	Entering the Dharma Realm (FAS, ch. 39)
FAS	*Flower Adornment Sutra*
FASP	*Flower Adornment Sutra Prologue*
FASVP	*Flower Adornment Sutra Verse Preface*
FHS	*Filiality: The Human Source*

Abbreviations of BTTS Publications

HR	*Human Roots*
HS	*Heart Sutra*
LY	*Listen to Yourself, Think Everything Over*
NS	*Nirvana Sutra* (unpublished draft translation)
NTC	*News from True Cultivators*
OYE	*Open Your Eyes, Take a Look at the World*
PB	*Pictorial Biography of the Venerable Master Hsu Yun*
PDS	*Proper Dharma Seal*
PS	*Sixth Patriarch's Dharma Jewel Platform Sutra*
RH	*City of 10,000 Buddhas Recitation Handbook*
RHS	*Records of High Sanghans*
RL	*Records of the Life of the Venerable Master Hsuan Hua*
S42	*Sutra in Forty-two Sections*
SE	*Song of Enlightenment*
SM	*Śūraṅgama Mantra Commentary*
SPV	*Sutra of the Past Vows of Earth Store Bodhisattva*
SS	*Śūraṅgama Sutra*
SV	*Śrāmaṇera Vinaya and Rules of Deportment*
TD	*The Ten Dharma Realms Are not Beyond a Single Thought*
TS	*Three Steps One Bow*
TT	*Herein Lies the Treasure Trove*
UW	Universal Worthy's Conduct and Vows (FAS, ch. 40)
VBS	*Vajra Bodhi Sea*
VS	*Vajra Sutra*
WM	*Water Mirror Reflecting Heaven*
WOH	*With One Heart Bowing to the City of 10,000 Buddhas*
WPG	*World Peace Gathering*

Volume numbers are indicated by roman numerals.

Abbreviations of Cited Non-BTTS Publications

CWSL	Hsüan-tsang. *Ch'eng Wei-shih Lun; The Doctrine of Mere-Consciousness.*
DPPN	Malalasekera, G.P., ed. *Dictionary of Pāli Proper Names* (Pali Text Society).
EB	Malalasekera, G.P., ed. *Encyclopedia of Buddhism*
HYSC	*Huayan Shuchao* (National Master Qingliang's Commentary on the *Flower Adornment Sutra*)
PTSD	Rhys Davids, T. W., ed. *The Pali Text Society's Pali-English Dictionary.*
T.	Takakusu and Watanabe, eds. *Taisho shinshu Daizokyo.*

Index of Entries: A to Z

A

abbot 方丈 2
Abhidharma 阿毗達摩 2
Ajita ‹Bodhisattva› 阿逸多《菩薩》 2
Amitābha ‹Buddha› 阿彌陀《佛》 3
Amitābha Sutra 阿彌陀經 3
Ānanda ‹Venerable› 阿難《尊者》 4
anuttara-samyak-saṃbodhi 阿耨多羅三藐三菩提 6
Arhat 阿羅漢 6
Asaṅga ‹Bodhisattva› 無著《菩薩》 9
asaṅkhyeya / asaṃkhyeya 阿僧祇 10
asura 阿修羅 11
attachment 執著 11
Avalokiteśvara ‹Bodhisattva› 觀世音《菩薩》 12
Avataṃsaka Sutra 華嚴經 ☞ FLOWER ADORNMENT SUTRA 華嚴經 12
avīci hell 阿鼻地獄 12

B

Baozhi ‹Chan Master› ‹418-514 C.E.› 寶誌《禪師》 12
Bhikshu 比丘 13
Bhikshuni 比丘尼 14
blessings 福 14
bodhi 菩提 16
Bodhidharma ‹Patriarch› 菩提達摩《祖師》 16
Bodhi resolve, ‹bringing forth› 發菩提心 21
Bodhisattva 菩薩 22
bowing 拜 / 禮拜 / 頂禮 26
Brahma Net Sutra 梵網經 30
Budai ‹Venerable› ‹6th cent. C.E.› 布袋《和尚》 30
Buddha 佛 31
Buddhaland 佛土 32
Buddha-nature 佛性 33
Buddha-vehicle 佛乘 ☞ THREE VEHICLES 三乘 33

Buddhism / Buddhadharma 佛教 / 佛法 33
Buddhist sects 宗派 34

C

causation 因緣 35
certification 證得 37
Changren ‹Chan Master› ‹fl. early 20th cent.› 常仁《禪師》 37
Changzhi ‹Chan Master› ‹fl. early 20th cent.› 常智《禪師》 38
Chan School 禪宗 39
City of Ten Thousand Buddhas 萬佛城 41
☞ SAGELY CITY OF TEN THOUSAND BUDDHAS 萬佛聖城
compassion 慈悲 42
Consciousness-Only School 唯識宗 42
cosmology 宇宙論 43
creation ‹world and humans› 生 44
cultivation 修行 48

D

Daosheng ‹Venerable› ‹360-434 C.E.› 道生《法師》 48
demons 魔 50
Devadatta 提婆達多 52
dhamma 法 ☞ DHARMA 法 53
dhāraṇī 陀羅尼 53
Dhāraṇī Sutra 陀羅尼經 54
Dharma / dharma 法 54
Dharma body 法身 ☞ THREE BODIES OF A BUDDHA 佛之三身 55
Dharma-door 法門 55
Dharma-Ending Age 末法時代 55
Dharma Flower ‹Lotus› Sutra 法華經 59
Dharma Master 法師 59
Dharma-protector 護法 60
Dharma Realm 法界 60
Dharma-transmission 傳法 60

dhyāna 禪那 ☞ MEDITATION 坐禪, FOUR DHYĀNAS 四禪 60
dhyāna-meditation 禪定 ☞ SIX PĀRAMITĀS 六波羅蜜 / 六度 60

E

Earth Store ‹Bodhisattva› 地藏《菩薩》 61
Eight Consciousnesses 八識 62
Eighteen Realms 十八界 63
Eightfold Division of Ghosts and Spirits 天龍八部 64
Eightfold Path 八正道 65
Eight Winds 八風 67
Eighty-eight Deluded Viewpoints 八十八品見惑 69
Eighty-four Thousand Dharma-Doors 八萬四千法門 69
Eighty-one Cognitive Delusions 八十一品思惑 70
Eleven Benefits from Making Images of Buddhas 造像十一種功德 70
emptiness 空 71
enlightenment 悟 74
Esoteric School 密宗 76
☞ FIVE TYPES OF BUDDHIST STUDY AND PRACTICE 五大宗
expedient Dharmas 方便法 76

F

faith 信 77
false thinking 妄想 ☞ POLLUTED THOUGHTS 妄想 79
filial piety ‹respect for all› 孝《孝道》 79
Five Contemplations when Eating 食存五觀 80
Five Desires 五欲 81
Five Eyes 五眼 81
Five Moral Precepts 五戒 83
Five Skandhas 五陰 / 五蘊 85
Five Turbidities 五濁 89
Five Types of Buddhist Study and Practice 五大宗 90
Flower Adornment ‹Avataṃsaka› Sutra《大方廣佛》華嚴經 94
Four Applications of Mindfulness 四念處 97

Four Dhyānas 四禪 98
Fourfold Assembly 四眾 99
Four Formless Realms 四無色界 99
Four Great Elements 四大 100
Four Great Vows 四弘誓願 101
Four Holy Truths 四聖諦 102
Four Stations of Emptiness 四空處 ☞ FOUR FORMLESS REALMS 四無色界 103
Four Unlimited Aspects of Mind 四無量心 103

G

Gautama / Gotama ‹Buddha› 瞿曇《佛》 103
ghosts 鬼 103
God 上帝 / 天主 104
gods 天人 106
gongfu ‹kungfu› 功夫 107
Good and Wise Advisor 善知識 107
good roots 善根 108
Great Compassion Mantra 大悲咒 108
Great Vehicle 大乘 ☞ MAHAYANA AND HINAYANA COMPARED 大乘小乘比較 109

H

Hanshan and Shide ‹Bodhisattvas› ‹fl. 627-649 C.E.› 寒山拾得《大士》 109
Hearers 聲聞 ☞ ŚRĀVAKA 聲聞 111
Heart Sutra 心經 111
heavens 天 ☞ GODS 天人 112
hells 地獄 112
Hinayana 小乘 ☞ MAHAYANA AND HINAYANA COMPARED 大乘小乘比較 113
Huayan School 華嚴宗 113
Huineng ‹Chan Master / Patriarch› ‹638-713 C.E.› 惠能《禪師 / 祖師》 113
hungry ghosts 餓鬼 ☞ GHOSTS 鬼, SIX PATHS OF REBIRTH 六道輪迴 114

I

ignorance 無明 115
impermanence 無常 115

K

kalpa 劫 116

karma 業 117

Kṣitigarbha ‹Bodhisattva› 地藏《菩薩》 120

☞ EARTH STORE ‹BODHISATTVA› 地藏《菩薩》

Kumārajīva ‹Tripiṭaka Master› ‹344-413 C.E.› 鳩摩羅什《三藏法師》 120

L

liberating living beings 放生 122

lineage 宗派 / 法脈 124

living beings 眾生 124

lotus posture 雙跏趺坐 125

Lotus Sutra 法華經 ☞ DHARMA FLOWER ‹LOTUS› SUTRA 法華經 128

love 愛 / 貪愛 / 愛欲 128

M

Madhyamaka/Mādhyamika 中觀論《派》 129

☞ EMPTINESS 空, NĀGĀRJUNA ‹BODHISATTVA› 龍樹《菩薩》

mahā 摩訶 129

Mahākāśyapa ‹Venerable› 摩訶迦葉《尊者》 129

Mahāmaudgalyāyana ‹Venerable› 摩訶目犍連《尊者》 131

Mahāparinirvāṇa Sutra 大般涅槃經 ☞ NIRVANA SUTRA 涅槃經 132

Mahāsattva 摩訶薩 132

Mahayana Buddhism 大乘佛教 132

☞ MAHAYANA AND HINAYANA COMPARED 大乘小乘比較

Mahayana and Hinayana Compared 大乘小乘比較 133

Maitreya ‹Bodhisattva› 彌勒《菩薩》 134

maṇḍala 曼陀羅 136

Mañjuśrī ‹Bodhisattva› 文殊師利《菩薩》 136

mantra 咒 138

Māra 魔 ☞ DEMONS 魔 139

meditation 坐禪 139

merit / merit and virtue 功德 141

Middle Way 中道 142

mindfulness 念 142

moral precepts 戒 / 戒律 143

N

Nāgārjuna ‹Bodhisattva› 龍樹《菩薩》 144
namo 南無 146
nirvana 涅槃 146
Nirvana Sutra 涅槃經 147
no outflows 無漏 ☞ OUTFLOWS 漏 147
Northern Buddhism 北傳佛教 ☞ MAHAYANA BUDDHISM 大乘佛教 148
no self 無我 148

O

offerings 供 / 供養 149
One Hundred Dharmas 百法 152
One Thousand Hands and Eyes 千手千眼 152
ordination 受具足戒 154
outflows 漏 155

P

Pali 巴利文 157
pāramitā 波羅蜜多 157
polluted thoughts 妄想 158
prājñā 般若 158
Pratyekabuddha 辟支佛 160
precepts 戒 ☞ MORAL PRECEPTS 戒 / 戒律 161
pure land 淨土 161
Pure Land School 淨土宗 163
☞ FIVE TYPES OF BUDDHIST STUDY AND PRACTICE 五大宗

Q

Qingliang Chengguan ‹National Master› ‹738-840 C.E.› 清涼澄觀《國師》 163

R

ranking the teachings 判教 165

rebirth 生 / 再生 166
recitation of the Buddha's name 念佛 166
refuge with the Three Jewels 皈依三寶 168
relics 舍利 168
repentance 懺悔 169

S

Sagely City of Ten Thousand Buddhas 萬佛聖城 171
Śakra 帝釋 172
Śākyamuni ‹Buddha› 釋迦牟尼佛 172
samadhi 三昧 / 三摩地 / 定 174
Samantabhadra ‹Bodhisattva› 普賢《菩薩》 175
☞ UNIVERSAL WORTHY ‹BODHISATTVA› 普賢《菩薩》
saṃsāra 流轉 / 生死 / 輪迴 175
Sangha 僧伽 175
Sanskrit 梵文 176
Śāriputra ‹Venerable› 舍利弗《尊者》 176
śarīra / sharira 舍利 ☞ RELICS 舍利 178
śāstra 論 178
Shide ‹Chan Master› 拾得《禪師》 178
☞ HANSHAN AND SHIDE ‹BODHISATTVAS› 寒山拾得《大士》
Six Desire Heavens 六欲天 178
Six Pāramitās 六波羅蜜 / 六度 181
Six Paths of Rebirth 六道輪迴 183
Six Principles of the Sagely City of Ten Thousand Buddhas 萬佛聖城六大宗旨 183
Six Spiritual Powers 六神通 185
Sixth Patriarch's Dharma Jewel Platform Sutra 六祖法寶壇經 187
Small Vehicle 小乘 ☞ MAHAYANA AND HINAYANA COMPARED 大乘小乘比較 187
Sound Hearer 聲聞 ☞ ŚRĀVAKA 聲聞 187
Southern Buddhism 南傳佛教 ☞ THERAVADA BUDDHISM 南傳佛教 187
śramaṇa 沙門 187
śrāvaka 聲聞 188

suffering 苦 189
Śūraṅgama Mantra 楞嚴咒 191
Śūraṅgama Sutra 大佛頂首楞嚴經 192
sutra 經 193
Sutra in Forty-two Sections 四十二章經 193
Sutra of the Past Vows of Earth Store Bodhisattva 地藏菩薩本願經 193

T

Tathāgata 如來 ☞ THUS COME ONE 如來 194
tathāgatagarbha 如來藏 194
Ten Dharma Realms 十法界 194
Ten Grounds / Stages of the Bodhisattva Path 菩薩十地 195
Ten Titles of a Buddha 佛之十號 196
Ten Wholesome Deeds 十善 197
Theravada Buddhism 南傳佛教 199
Thirty-two Major Physical Characteristics of a Buddha 佛三十二相 199
Thousand Handed Thousand Eyed Dhāraṇī Sutra 千手千眼陀羅尼經 200
☞ DHĀRAṆĪ SUTRA 陀羅尼經
Three Aspects of Learning to Be without Outflows 三無漏學 200
Three Bodies of a Buddhas / Three Types of Buddha Bodies 佛之三身 201
Three Jewels 三寶 202
Three Poisons 三毒 202
Three Refuges 三皈 ☞ REFUGE WITH THE THREE JEWELS 皈依三寶 202
Three Realms 三界 ☞ THREE WORLDS 三界 202
Three Vehicles 三乘 202
Three Worlds 三界 203
Thus Come One 如來 203
Tiantai School 天台宗 203
time 時 204
transference of merit 迴向 206
transformation bodies 化身 207
Tripiṭaka 三藏 207

Tripiṭaka Master 三藏法師 207
Tuṣita Heaven 兜率天 ☞ SIX DESIRE HEAVENS 六欲天 207
Twelvefold Conditioned Arising 十二因緣 207
Two Vehicles 二乘 209

U

Universal Worthy ‹Bodhisattva› 普賢《菩薩》 209
upāsaka 優婆塞 210
upāsikā 優婆夷 210

V

vajra 金剛 210
Vajra ‹Diamond› Prajñā Pāramitā Sutra 金剛般若波羅密多經 211
Vasubandhu ‹Bodhisattva› ‹fl. 4th cent. C.E.› 世親《菩薩》 211
vegetarianism 素食主義 212
Vinaya 戒 / 毗奈耶 215
Vinaya School 律宗 215
vows 願 215

W

Way 道 ☞ MIDDLE WAY 中道 216
Way-place 道場 216
world systems 世界 216

X

Xuanzang ‹Tripiṭaka Master› ‹596-664 C.E.› 玄奘《三藏法師》 218
Xuyun ‹Chan Master› 虛雲《禪師》 220

Y

Yogācāra 瑜伽宗 ☞ CONSCIOUSNESS-ONLY SCHOOL 唯識宗 221
yojana 由旬 222

Z

Zen 禪 ☞ CHAN SCHOOL 禪宗 222
Zhiyi ‹Venerable› ‹538-597 C.E.› 智顗《法師》 222

Illustrations

NOTE: Color plates appear following page 102. Page numbers indicate where reduced size, black & white versions of the plates appear in the text.

COLOR PLATES

1	Amitābha Buddha	3
2	Arhats	7
3	Arhats	
4	Arhat	8
5	Bodhisattva Avalokiteśvara (with twelve hands)	12
6	Bodhisattva Avalokiteśvara (in white robes)	
7	Bodhisattva Avalokiteśvara (standing)	
8	Patriarch Bodhidharma	18
9	Venerable Budai	31
10	Life of the Buddha: Entering the womb	31
11	Life of the Buddha: Leaving home	32
12	Life of the Buddha: Becoming a Buddha	
13	Life of the Buddha: Turning the Dharma wheel	32
14	Life of the Buddha: Entering nirvana	
15	Śākyamuni Buddha and Many Jewels Buddha sharing a seat	59
16	The assembly of the future Buddha Maitreya	135
17	Earth Store Bodhisattva, who rescues beings from the hells	61
18	Eightfold Division of Ghosts and Spirits	64
19	Eightfold Division of Ghosts and Spirits	64
20	Scenes from the *Flower Adornment Sutra*	96
21	Flower Adornment Sea of Worlds	95
22	Bodhisattvas Hanshan and Shide	111
23	Beings receiving sentences and suffering retribution in the hells	112
24	The court of the First Lord of the Underworld	113
25	Beings suffering in the hells	113
26	The Buddha practicing extreme asceticism	173
27	Śarīra (relics)	168
28	Censer at the City of Ten Thousand Buddhas	
29	Vajradhātu *maṇḍala*	136
30	Garbhadhātu *maṇḍala*	136
31	Bodhisattva Mañjuśrī	136
32	Bodhisattva Mañjuśrī	137
33	Western Pure Land of Ultimate Bliss	161
34	Amitābha Buddha with Bodhisattvas Avalokiteśvara and Mahāsthāmaprāpta	162
35	Lotus pool in the Western Pure Land	163
36	Bodhisattva Avalokiteśvara with One Thousand Hands and Eyes	153

37 Śākyamuni Buddha 172
38 The Venerable Master Hua, founder of the City of Ten Thousand Buddhas
39 Ordination Hall
40 Bhikshunis walking to the Hall of Ten Thousand Buddhas 172
41 The entrance to the Sagely City of Ten Thousand Buddhas 171
42 Hall of Ten Thousand Buddhas (Guanyin Bodhisattva) 172
43 Hall of Ten Thousand Buddhas (statues of 10,000 Buddhas)
44 Universal Worthy Bodhisattva 209
45 Universal Worthy Bodhisattva 210
46 Tripiṭaka Master Xuanzang bringing sutras from India back to China 220

FIGURES

1 Woodblock depiction of Mount Sumeru rising above the seas 43
2 Chart of the Four Great Elements 87
3 Chart of the Eleven Form Dharmas 87
4 Emanation of Dharmas According to the ***Śūraṅgama Sutra*** FOLLOWING PAGE 47
5 Heaven of the Four Kings 179
6 Chart of the Three Worlds FOLLOWING PAGE 203
7 Chinese woodblock depiction of a world system 217
8 Chart of the Flower Treasury World System showing names and shapes of worlds 217
9 Chart of the Flower Treasury World System showing names of Buddhas 218

BLACK AND WHITE ILLUSTRATIONS

1 Chinese characters *fang zang,* "abbot" 2
2 Venerable Ānanda 4
3 Asuras 11
4 Venerable Baozhi 13
5 Master sculptor Wang, Taisheng crafting a Buddhist statue 15
6 Patriarch Bodhidharma 21
7 Avalokiteśvara Bodhisattva 24
8 A monk bowing 28
9 A scene from the *Brahma Net Sutra* 30
10 Venerable Budai 30
11 Chan Master Changren 38
12 Venerable Daosheng speaking Dharma to the rocks 49
13 Dharma protector Weituo Bodhisattva 60
14 Jiuhua Mountain, the Way-place of Earth Store Bodhisattva 61
15 Garudas 65

16 Filial piety 79
17 The realm of the *Flower Adornment Sutra* 94
18 Brahma god 106
19 Bodhisattva Hanshan 109
20 Bodhisattva Shide 110
21 Chan Master Huineng (Sixth Patriarch in China) 114
22 Tripiṭaka Master Kumārajīva 120
23 Liberating living beings 122
24 Lotus posture 125
25 Śākyamuni Buddha 129
26 Venerable Mahākāśyapa 129
27 Venerable Mahāmaudgalyāyana 131
28 Venerable Maitreya 134
29 Meditation 139
30 The figure 'O' 142
31 Bodhisattva Nāgārjuna 145
32 Offering of fruits, incense, and flowers 150
33 Offering of joined palms 151
34 Examples of polluted thinking: "Distractions of the Great" (cartoon) 159
35 National Master Qingliang 164
36 Repentance 169
37 Practicing meditation to attain samadhi 174
38 Venerable Śāriputra 177
39 One of the Four Heavenly Kings 180
40 The first *pāramitā* is giving to those in need. 182
41 Vasubandhu Bodhisattva 211
42 Bizarro / by Piraro (cartoon) 214
43 Tripiṭaka Master Xuanzang 218
44 Chan Master Xuyun 220
45 Chan Master Xuyun with Ven. Master Hua 221
46 Venerable Zhiyi 222

BUDDHIST TEXT TRANSLATION SOCIETY'S

Buddhism A to Z

abbot 方丈

fangzhang

The abbot is the head of a monastery. One Chinese term for abbot, *fangzhang,* 'ten feet square,' is a term used primarily in Chan monasteries and refers to the ideal size of the abbot's quarters. The great enlightened Buddhist layman Vimalakīrti, who lived during the time of the Buddha, was said to have lived in a stone room of that size. Another frequently used Chinese term for abbot, *zhuchi*, literally "dweller and upholder," is explained as meaning that an abbot is one who protects the Dharma while abiding peacefully in the world.

Abhidharma 阿毗達摩

The Abhidharma is the third of the three divisions or "baskets" of the Tripiṭaka or Buddhist Canon. Its Dharma is organized thematically and logically; it can be said to be a systematic exposition of Buddhist psychology of mind. The Abhidharma taught by the Buddha is in the seven books of the *Abhidharma-piṭaka*. Later Abhidharma includes systematic treatises by enlightened masters. The most well-known of the Hinayana Abhidharma treatises is the *Abhidharmakośa* by the Venerable ☞VASUBANDHU. Among the most widely studied of Mahayana Abhidharma treatises is the *Treatise on Consciousness Only* (*Cheng Weishi Lun*) by Tripiṭaka Master ☞XUANZANG. According to the *Abhidharmakośa*, "Abhidharma is the immaculate *prajñā* [i.e., wisdom] with its retinue" (Vasubandhu, 5). "In common use, the Abhidharma designates all *prajñā* that makes one obtain the Abhidharma in its proper sense" (Vasubandhu, 7).

> "Abhi" means "paired," and "dharma," which is variously translated, is of two types: one, Dharma in the supreme sense, that is, nirvana, which is both wholesome and permanent, and so is called "supreme"; two, dharma of dharma marks, which coincides with the Four Sagely Truths.... (FAS-PII 97)

> The paired Dharma Store has the special name "wisdom *śāstra*." The old translation [into Chinese] means "incomparable dharma." That is because it portrays wisdom as supreme. (FAS-PII 103)

☞ **paired dharma, incomparable dharma, special Dharma, higher knowledge**

☞ **Tripiṭaka, Dharma, dharma**

Ajita ⟨Bodhisattva⟩ 阿逸多《菩薩》

Another name for the Bodhisattva Maitreya. *Ajita* is Sanskrit and means "unconquerable."

☞ **Maitreya ⟨Bodhisattva⟩**

Amitābha 〈Buddha〉 阿彌陀《佛》

Amitābha Buddha (see plate 1)

Amitābha's body is the color of
gold;
The splendor of his hallmarks
has no peer.
The light of his brow shines
round a hundred worlds;
Wide as the sea are his eyes
pure and clear.
Shining in his brilliance by
transformation
Are countless Bodhisattvas
and infinite Buddhas.
His forty-eight vows will be
our liberation;
In nine lotus-stages we reach
the farthest shore.
Homage to the Buddha
of the Western Pure Land,
Kind and compassionate Amitābha.
(RH 137-138; UW 28)

The Buddha Amitābha is the Buddha of the Western Land of Ultimate Bliss. He is known as Amitābha, 'infinite light,' and also as Amitāyus, 'infinite life.' "Both Amitābha Buddha and Śākyamuni Buddha were people who became Buddhas...." (AS 11)

☞ **pure land, Five Types of Buddhist Study and Practice—Pure Land, recitation of the Buddha's name, Avalokiteśvara 〈Bodhisattva〉**

Amitābha Sutra 阿彌陀經

The complete title [translated from the Chinese] is *The Buddha Speaks of Amitābha Sutra.* Two sutras, the large and the small, have this title, both taking as their subject Amitābha Buddha, his pure Buddhaland to the West, and the means to rebirth therein. Sukhāvatī, or, as translated from the Chinese, Ultimate Bliss, is the name of this land. A third sutra also describes Sukhāvatī: the *Meditation on Amitābha Sutra (Amitāyurdhyāna-sūtra).* Together, these three sutras comprise the basic texts of the Pure Land School.

The large *Amitābha Sutra* explains the causal affinities resulting in the Pure Land of Ultimate Bliss. It relates Amitābha Buddha's vows made in a former life and their realization in the Land of Ultimate Bliss. The *Meditation on Amitābha Sutra* is concerned with quite another matter. It is a guide to cultivation and describes a series of sixteen meditations which lead to various grades of rebirth by transformation in the Land of Ultimate Bliss. Both sutras contain Dharmas preached in specific response to the requests of sentient beings: the large *Amitābha Sutra* at the request of Ānanda, "who had still to be advanced on the path of disciples"; and the *Meditation on Amitābha Sutra* at the request of Vaidehī, queen mother of the wicked Prince Ajātaśatru:

> "My only prayer," she continued, "is this: O World Honored One, mayest thou preach to me in detail of all the places where there is no sorrow or trouble, and where I ought to go to be born anew. I am not satisfied with this world of depravities, with Jambudvīpa, which is full of hells, full of hungry ghosts (*pretas*), and of the brute creation. In this world of depravities there is many an assemblage of the wicked. May I not hear, I pray, the voice of the wicked in the future; and may I not see any wicked person."

The small *Amitābha Sutra*, although the shortest of the three, is by no means unimportant. Nor is it just a summary recapitulation of the doctrine set forth in the other two. It is unique, because the entire sutra belongs to the "self-spoken division." In other words, the Buddha spontaneously preached the Dharma of this sutra, overstepping the usual practice of speaking Dharma only upon request. The very fact that no one in the great assembly knew to ask shows the extreme importance and inconceivability of the Dharma of this sutra. The Buddha proclaims in the text of the sutra: "You should know that I, in the evil time of the ☞ FIVE TURBIDITIES...for all the world speak this Dharma, difficult to believe, extremely difficult."

The sutra explains the causes and circumstances for rebirth in the Land of Ultimate Bliss.

"The essential message of this sutra is to teach us to recite the name 'Namo Amitābha Buddha.' Amitābha Buddha has a great affinity with living beings in the Sahā world. Before realizing Buddhahood, he made forty-eight vows and each one involved taking living beings to Buddha-hood. At that time, he was a Bhikshu named Dharma Treasury [Sanskrit: Dharmākara]. He said, 'When I realize Buddhahood, I vow that living beings who recite my name will also realize Buddhahood. Otherwise, I won't either....'

"By the power of his vows, Amitābha Buddha leads all beings to rebirth in his country where they realize Buddhahood. This power attracts living beings to the Land of Ultimate Bliss, just as a magnet attracts iron filings. If living beings do not attain enlightenment, he himself won't realize Buddhahood. Therefore, all who recite his name can realize Buddhahood." (AS 20)

☞ **Amitābha ⟨Buddha⟩, pure land, Five Types of Buddhist Study and Practice—Pure Land, recitation of the Buddha's name, sutra**

Ānanda ⟨Venerable⟩ 阿難《尊者》

One of the ten great disciples of the Buddha Śākyamuni.

the second patriarch, venerable ananda

"Ānanda was the Buddha's first cousin and his attendant. He also compiled and edited the sutras. His name means 'rejoicing,' because he was born on the day the Buddha realized Buddhahood. His father rejoiced and gave him that name. The entire country celebrated the Buddha's enlightenment on that day. With his flawless memory, Ānanda was able to remember all the sutras the Buddha spoke and was foremost among the Buddha's disciples in erudition." (DFS II 124)

"The *Śūraṅgama Sutra* was spoken for Ānanda's sake, precisely because he didn't have sufficient *samādhi*-power. He had not done the work of meditation required to develop it. When others were sitting investigating *dhyāna* [i.e., meditating], Ānanda would go read a book or write instead....Put another way, Ānanda hadn't cultivated real mark *prajñā*; he thought he could realize Buddhahood through literary *prajñā* alone. He thought that since he was the Buddha's cousin, the Buddha, who had realized Buddhahood, would certainly help him realize Buddhahood too, and so it didn't really matter whether he cultivated or not. He ended up wasting a lot of time.

"One day, as the *Śūraṅgama Sutra* relates, Ānanda went out begging for food by himself. He took his bowl and went from house to house, and while alone on the road he encountered the daughter of Mātaṅgī....Ānanda was particularly handsome, and when Mātaṅgī's daughter saw him, she was immediately attracted to him. But she didn't know how to snare him. And so she went back and told her mother, 'You absolutely must get Ānanda to marry me. If you don't, I'll die.'

"The mother, Mātaṅgī, belonged to the religion of the Kapilas, the 'tawny haired,' and she cultivated that religion's mantras and dharma devices, which were extremely effective. Since Mātaṅgī truly loved her daughter, she used a mantra of her sect—it was a mantra formerly of the Brahma heaven—to confuse Ānanda. Ānanda didn't have any *samādhi* power, and so he couldn't control himself. He followed the mantra and went to Mātaṅgī's daughter's house, where he was on the verge of breaking the precepts.

"The first five precepts prohibit killing, stealing, sexual misconduct, lying, and the taking of intoxicants. Ānanda was about to break the precept against sexual misconduct. The Buddha knew about it as it was happening. Realizing his cousin was in trouble, he quickly spoke the Śūraṅgama Mantra to break up the mantra, formerly of the Brahma Heaven of the Kapila religion. Ānanda's confusion had made him as if drunk or as if he had taken drugs—he was totally oblivious to everything. But when the Buddha recited the Śūraṅgama Mantra, its power woke Ānanda up from his confusion, and then he wondered how he had gotten himself into such a situation.

"He returned, knelt before the Buddha, and cried out in distress. 'I have relied exclusively on erudition and have not perfected any strength in the Way. I have no *samādhi* power. Please tell me how the Buddhas of the ten directions cultivated so that they were able to obtain *samādhi* power.' In reply the Buddha spoke the *Śūraṅgama Sutra*." (SS I 25-26)

The ☞DHARMA FLOWER SUTRA records the Buddha bestowing the prediction of future Buddhahood upon Ānanda:

> At that time the Buddha told Ānanda, "You in a future age shall become a Buddha by the name of King of Self Control and Penetrations with Wisdom like the Mountains and Seas Thus Come One. One Worthy of Offerings, One of Proper and Universal Knowledge, One Perfect in Clarity and Practice, Well Gone One, Unsurpassed One Who Understands the World, Hero Who Subdues and Tames, Teacher of Gods and Humans, Buddha, World Honored One. You shall make offerings to sixty-two million Buddhas, protecting and upholding their storehouses of Dharma. After that you shall obtain *anuttara-samyak-saṃbodhi*. You shall teach and transform Bodhisattvas as many as 20,000 myriads of millions of Ganges Rivers' grains of sand, causing them to accomplish *anuttara-samyak-saṃbodhi*. Your country shall be called Banner of Victory Always Raised. That land will be pure, with lapis lazuli for soil. The *kalpa* shall be called All Pervasive Wonderful Sound. Your life span as a Buddha shall be countless thousands of myriads of millions of *asaṃkhyeyas* of aeons. Were someone to attempt to reckon it through countless

thousands of myriads of millions of *asaṃkhyeyas* of aeons, they could not do so. The Proper Dharma shall dwell in that world for twice that length of time. The Dharma Image Age shall dwell twice the length of Proper Dharma. Ānanda, the merit and virtue of the Buddha King of Self-Control and Penetrations with Wisdom Like the Mountains and Seas shall be praised by all the Buddhas of the ten directions equal in number to the sands of countless thousands of myriads of millions of Ganges rivers." (DFS VIII 1500-1501)

☞ **Arhat**

anuttara-samyak-saṃbodhi 阿耨多羅三藐三菩提

This is a Sanskrit term referring to the perfect and universal enlightenment of a Buddha. It is variously translated as meaning "Utmost, Right and Perfect Enlightenment," "Supreme, Orthodox, and Equal Awakening," or the like. The commentarial traditions indicate that the term includes the levels of enlightenment of the Bodhisattva and Arhat within that of the Buddha.

> This Dharma is level and equal,
> with no high or low.
> Therefore, it is called
> *anuttara-samyak-saṃbodhi.*
> (FAS Ch16 22)

☞ **enlightenment, Buddha**

Arhat 阿羅漢

> Be careful not to believe in your own mind: your mind cannot be believed....Once you have become an Arhat, then you can believe your own mind. (S42 57)

In the Pali texts of the Theravada tradition (☞THERAVADA BUDDHISM) the standard formula for describing the Arhat is as follows: "Destroyed is (re-)birth, lived is the chaste life (of a student), done is what had to be done, after this present life there is no beyond." (PTSD)

"Arhat" is one of the four kinds of truly enlightened beings (☞ENLIGHTENMENT). It is a Sanskrit word, which can be interpreted in three ways:

> **1)** 'One worthy of offerings.' "Arhats are worthy of offerings from humans and gods. At the level of planting causes, a Bhikshu makes the alms round for his food, and as a result, as an Arhat he is 'worthy of offerings.'" (SS I 107).
>
> "If you make offerings to an Arhat, an enlightened sage who has been certified,...you thereby attain limitless and boundless blessings. There is no way to calculate how many." (S42 3-4)
>
> **2)** 'Slayer of thieves.' "The thieves referred to are not external thieves, but the thieves within you: the thieves of ignorance, the thieves of afflictions and the six thieves—the eyes, ears, nose, tongue, body, and mind. Unknown to you, they rob you....These six thieves steal your unsurpassed true treasures...." (SS I 107-108)
>
> **3)** 'Unproduced'/'Unborn.' "They have attained the patience with the nonproduction of dharmas. They do not have to undergo birth and death again.... Although they have not attained ☞ANUTTARA-SAMYAK-SAṂBODHI, the Unsurpassed, Proper and Equal Right Enlightenment, they will not fall into the ☞THREE REALMS." (SS I 108)

Those three aspects of being an Arhat are the result of causes created in cultivation as a Bhikshu.

> Constantly observing the 250 precepts, they enter into and abide in purity. By

practicing the four true paths [i.e., paths to the Four Stages explained below], they realize Arhatship. (S42 1)

"Having been certified as having attained the patience with the nonproduction of dharmas, the Arhat is beyond coming into being and ceasing to be. Wouldn't you agree that the state of the Arhat is really terrific? The Arhat isn't busy in the least. He is totally free and at ease, taking it easy, laid back, and not doing much, collecting unemployment. Do you recognize the Arhats? Their heads are bald and shiny, and so are their feet. That is, they don't wear shoes. Nobody supervises them and they don't pay any attention to anyone else. No ties, no cares, no hang-ups, no self, no others, no living beings, no life, no nothing. Ahhh...

"Their minds have attained self-mastery. They have no false thinking. Once they enter samādhi, they can sit (in meditation) for several thousand years. The First Patriarch ☞MAHĀKĀŚYAPA went to Jizu Mountain ['Chicken Foot' Mountain in Yunnan Province, China] and entered samādhi. He hasn't come out of it yet. That's because his mind has attained self-mastery." (DFS VIII 1449-1450)

"As killers of thieves, Arhats have killed the thief of ignorance. Ignorance is a thief who ruins one's karma for the Way. Why do people do things that are upside-down? It's out of ignorance. Why is it that, when one has no attachments, one deliberately looks for attachments? It's all out of ignorance. In spite of the fact that it is in our power to end birth and death, why do we fail to do so? It is because of ignorance. Ignorance is simply terrible!

"Arhats kill ignorance. While we say that they 'kill' ignorance, they haven't killed it entirely. They have killed coarse ignorance, but a subtle ignorance remains. Ignorance could be likened to a virus. Perhaps you break out with a sore. When you put some medicine on it, it clears up. But as soon as you quit applying the medicine, it breaks out again, and your skin itches like crazy. The Arhats have the medicine and put it on the sore, but they haven't gotten rid of the disease at its source. The only way to get rid of it entirely is to become a Buddha...." (DFS VII 1371-1372)

Arhats (see plates 2 & 3)

Four Stages of Arhatship

Strictly speaking, the term Arhat refers to the fourth stage only, but it is often used to refer to those of all four stages. The term can also include ☞PRATYEKABUDDHAS and is also employed in its more general meaning as one of the ☞TEN TITLES OF A BUDDHA.

First Stage

"The Arhat of the first stage is called one who has 'entered the stream' (*śrotaāpanna*). He has entered the stream of the Dharma nature of the sage, and he goes counter to the flow of the stream of the six senses of common people. He still has to undergo seven more rebirths among those in the heavens and among humans before he comes to the end of the Path." (DFS X 52)

> The *śrotaāpanna*...has seven deaths and seven births remaining, and then will be certified as an Arhat. Severing love and desire is like severing the four limbs; one never uses them again. (S42 1)

Second Stage

"The Arhat of the second stage is called a 'once-returner' (*sakṛdāgāmin*). He has one more birth to undergo in the heavens and one among humans." (DFS X 52)

> The *sakṛdāgāmin*...ascends once, returns once more, and thereafter becomes an Arhat. (S42 1)

Arhat (see plate 4)

Third Stage

"The Arhat of the third stage is called a 'never-returner' (*anāgāmin*). He does not have to undergo birth again in the human realm." (DFS X 52)

> At the end of his life, an *anāgāmin*'s vital spirit will rise above the nineteenth heaven [the highest heaven of the fourth *dhyāna*. ☞FOUR DHYĀNAS] and there he will be certified as an Arhat. (S42 1)

Fourth Stage

"The Arhat of the fourth stage is called 'unborn.' The fourth stage Arhat has attained patience with the nonproduction of dharmas. This means that he does not see the slightest dharma come into being or the slightest dharma cease to be. Such a vision is not easy to bear, but he has the patience to bear it...." (DFS X 52)

"What proof is there that someone has been certified as a fourth stage Arhat? A fourth stage Arhat's feet don't touch the ground. His feet are off the ground by three-tenths of an inch, and because of that, he never squashes worms or ants....Not only can one of the fourth stage do this, but one of the first stage can also do this." (S42 4)

> Arhats can fly and transform themselves. They have a life span of vast aeons, and wherever they dwell they can move heaven and earth. (S42 1)

"Wherever an Arhat dwells, the gods, dragons, and others of the ☞EIGHTFOLD DIVISION protect his Dharma, and it is very peaceful wherever he is. There aren't any hurricanes, tornadoes, earthquakes, volcanoes, tidal waves, or any such disasters, because the Dharma-protectors and good spirits are always protecting him and making auspicious things happen to him." (S42 5)

"People who have been certified as fourth stage Arhats have freedom over birth and death. They are truly free; no one can watch over them. If they want to live, they can live. If they want to die, they can die whenever they want. If they want to die standing up, they can die standing up. If they want to die sitting down, they can die that way. If they want to die walking, they can die walking. If they want to die sleeping, they can die sleeping. It's up to them...." (S42 5)

When the Venerable Master Daxiu decided it was time to leave, he chiselled a space out of the rock cliff next to where he lived and meditated and then fashioned some doors. He then sat down inside, arranged his body in full-lotus position, closed the doors, and entered the final stillness. Upon the doors he had inscribed this verse:

> There is no great, no small,
> no inside or out.
> Cultivate yourself, understand
> yourself, and
> Make your own arrangements.

The Non-Ultimacy of Arhatship

In the ☞DHARMA FLOWER SUTRA assembly the Buddha explained that the enlightenment of the Arhat is not ultimate. At that time five hundred Arhats in the assembly proclaimed:

> "World Honored One, we had always thought that we had gained the ultimate cessation [i.e., nirvana]. Now we know that we were like unknowing ones. Why is this? We should have obtained the Thus Come One's wisdom, but were content instead with lesser knowledge." (DFS VIII 1466)

> "Having attained the Way of the Arhat, we said of ourselves that we had gained cessation. In the difficulty of maintaining our livelihood, we were content with what little we had gained." [Commentary: The lifestyle of the Small Vehicle is like that of a very poor person.] "Still, our vows for All Wisdom remain; they have not been lost. Now the World Honored One has caused us to wake up, saying, 'Bhikshus! What you have obtained is not ultimate cessation!'" (DFS VIII 1475-1476)

Arhats are sometimes referred to as *śrāvakas*.

worthy, deserving and meritorious person, one worthy of offerings, destroyer of enemies, slayer of thieves

☞ **śrāvaka, enlightenment, Eighty-eight Deluded Viewpoints, Eighty-one Cognitive Delusions**

Asaṅga ⟨Bodhisattva⟩ 無著《菩薩》

Together with his teacher the Bodhisattva Maitreya, Asaṅga was the founder of the Yogācāra or Consciousness-Only School of Mahayana Buddhism. He was the oldest of three sons, all called Vasubandhu, born in Puruṣapura (Peshāwar) who were members of the Kauśika family of Indian Brahmins. All three became Buddhist Bhikshus. Asaṅga's youngest brother was known as Viriñcivatsa, while the middle brother was known merely as ☞VASUBANDHU.

> Asaṅga was a man who was endowed with the innate character of a Bodhisattva. He became a Bhikshu of the Sarvāstivāda School, but afterwards he practiced meditation and became free from desire. Though he investigated the doctrine of emptiness, he could not understand it. He was about to commit suicide. Piṇḍola, an Arhat, who was then in the eastern continent of Pūrvavideha, having perceived this, came to him from that region and expounded the doctrine of emptiness peculiar to the Hinayana. He arranged his thoughts according to what he was taught and at once comprehended it. Though he had attained the doctrine of emptiness peculiar to the Hinayana, he, nevertheless, did not find comfort in it. Thinking that it would not be right to drop the matter altogether, he went up to the Tuṣita

Heaven [☞ SIX DESIRE HEAVENS] using the supernatural power peculiar to the Hinayana and inquired of Maitreya, the Bodhisattva, who expounded for him the doctrine of emptiness belonging to the Mahayana. When he returned to Jambudvīpa, he investigated according to the methods explained to him and soon became enlightened. While he was engaged in investigation, the earth began to quake (of its own accord) in six ways. Since he understood the doctrine of emptiness, he called himself "Asaṅga," which means "without attachment." He afterwards often went up to the Tuṣita Heaven in order to ask Maitreya about the doctrines of the Mahayana sutras. The Bodhisattva explained them extensively for him. Whenever he acquired any new understanding, he would come back to Jambudvīpa and teach it to others. Most of those hearing him did not believe him. Asaṅga, Teacher of the Dharma, then prayed, saying, "I now intend to bring all beings to believe fully in the doctrine of the Mahayana. I only pray that you, O Great Master, come down to Jambudvīpa to expound the Mahayana so that all beings may become fully convinced of its truth." Maitreya, thereupon, in accordance with his prayer, came down to Jambudvīpa at night, flooding it with great rays of light, had a large assembly of those connected with the Dharma called in a lecture hall, and began to recite the *Saptadaśabhūmi-sūtra*. After having recited a passage, he would explain its purport. The seventeen *bhūmis* were finished during the nights of four months. Although all were together in one and the same hall listening to the discourse, it was, nevertheless, only Asaṅga, Teacher of the Dharma, who had access to the Bodhisattva Maitreya, while the others could merely hear him from afar. At night, all together heard the religious discourse by Maitreya, while in the daytime Asaṅga, Teacher of the Dharma, commented once again, for the sake of others, upon what had been taught by the Bodhisattva. In this way all the people could hear and believe in the doctrine of the Mahayana. Maitreya, the Bodhisattva, taught Asaṅga, Teacher of the Dharma, to learn the "sunlight" *samādhi*. As he learned according to what he had been taught, he subsequently attained entry into that *samādhi*. After he attained entry into that *samādhi*, what he formerly could not understand all became intelligible. Whatever he heard or saw was never forgotten, his memory having become retentive, whereas he formerly could not fully understand the sutras of the Mahayana, such as the *Avataṃsaka*, previously taught by the Buddha. Maitreya explained for him all these in the Tuṣita heaven; thus the Teacher of the Dharma became well-versed in them and remembered them all. Afterwards in Jambudvīpa he composed several *upadeśa* on the sutras of the Mahayana, in which he expounded all the teachings of the Mahayana taught by the Buddha. (Paramārtha, "The Life of Vasubandhu," J. Takakusu, tr. [with some editing], 273-275)

☞ **Maitreya ⟨Bodhisattva⟩, Vasubandhu ⟨Bodhisattva⟩, Consciousness-Only School**

asaṅkhyeya/asaṃkhyeya 阿僧祇

One of many Sanskrit words signifying an extraordinarily long or infinitely long period of time. The *Abhidharmakośa* states that an *asaṅkhyeya* is a period of time equal to 1 followed by 59 zeros, times the number of great *kalpas*. (For information of the length of a great *kalpa*, ☞ TIME.)

measureless, innumerable, incalculable, an immense period

☞ **time**

asura 阿修羅

Asuras have a violent nature,
Laden with blessings, lacking power.
Absolutely determined to fight,
They bob along in karma's tow. (TD 42)

The path of the *asuras* is one of the ☞SIX PATHS OF REBIRTH; *asuras* are also one of the ☞EIGHTFOLD DIVISION OF GHOSTS AND SPIRITS. *Asura* is a Sanskrit word that is explained as meaning either **1)** one without heavenly beer, **2)** ugly one, or **3)** not a god.

"They are without intoxicants because after drinking heavenly beer offered by Śakra, they became extremely drunk and were hurled out of heaven onto the slopes of Mount Sumeru on Śakra's command. Upon regaining their awareness, they vowed never again to drink the heavenly beer (*sura*). Therefore, they were called *asura*, 'without intoxicant.'" (DPPN 214-215)

Asura is said to mean 'not a god' because the *asuras* have the blessings to be reborn in the heavens but not the virtue of the gods and so are defeated by them.

"The category of *asuras* includes all beings who like to fight. *Asuras* who use their pugnacious natures beneficially join the armed forces and protect their countries. Asuras who use their propensity to fight in a bad way end up as thieves, robbers, and gunmen. *Asuras* may live in the heavens, among people, in the animal realm, or as ghosts...." (SS V 135)

"Male *asuras* are extremely ugly; the females are beautiful. It is the nature of the male *asura* to initiate fights. The female *asura* also is naturally fond of fighting, but wages covert wars, unlike the overt physical battles of the males. She uses weapons of the mind such as jealousy, obstructiveness, ignorance, and affliction....The world is full of *asuras* who are constantly battling one another, and they will keep on fighting forever. During the Age Strong in Fighting, that is, the present ☞DHARMA-ENDING AGE, we should vow not to fight. If we do that, every place we go to will become a place of genuine Dharma. If everyone fulfilled this vow, the Dharma-Ending Age would become the Age of Proper Dharma." (TD 43-44)

a fallen angel, a titan, a demi-god

☞ **Six Paths of Rebirth, Ten Dharma Realms**

attachment 執著

Attachments are what keep us turning on the wheel of rebirth. Becoming enlightened is nothing other than severing all our attachments. What is meant by "attachment" is the investing of mental or emotional energy in an "object." We can become attached to people, things, experiential states, and our own thoughts and preconceptions. In Buddhist teachings attachments are usually divided into two general categories: attachments to self and attachments to dharmas.

fetter, bond

☞ **ignorance**

Avalokiteśvara ⟨Bodhisattva⟩ 觀世音《菩薩》

Avalokiteśvara Bodhisattva (see plates 5-7)

One of the four Bodhisattvas of greatest importance in ☞MAHAYANA BUDDHISM, Avalokiteśvara is the Bodhisattva of Compassion and disciple and future successor of the Buddha ☞AMITĀBHA in the Western Pure Land. His name, which is Sanskrit, is often translated as Observer of the Sounds of the World. It can also be interpreted as meaning Contemplator of Self-Mastery.

Observer of the Sounds of the World, Contemplator of Self-Mastery

☞ **Bodhisattva, One Thousand Hands and Eyes**

Avataṃsaka Sutra 華嚴經

☞ **Flower Adornment Sutra**

avīci hell 阿鼻地獄

The 'lowest' hell, in which the suffering is the greatest and longest.

☞ **hells**

B

Baozhi ⟨Chan Master⟩ ⟨418*-514⟩ 寶誌《禪師》

Why should I look
  for treasure abroad?
Within yourself you have
  a bright pearl. (quoted in Watson,
tr. *Cold Mountain*, 73n)

Founder of the Pilu (Vairocana) lineage of ☞CHAN Buddhism.

"In Nanjing a woman named Zhu heard the sound of a small child's cries coming from an eagle's nest, went searching, and got him out. At age seven he left home. Later he went to Wan Mountain in the province of Sichuan at Jianshui ("Sword Water"), a treacherous area of the Yangzi River. He was commonly known as Zhigong ("Noble Zhi"). His face was rectangular and gleamed like a mirror, reflecting the faces of those who came before him. His hands and feet looked like birds' claws, and he ate minced fish. He would spit the fish meat back into the water where it would once again become living fish.

"Emperor Wu instructed a monk named Sengyou to paint the Master's portrait. The Venerable One scratched open his face with his talons, and from the gashes, one after another, emerged the twelve faces of

Bodhisattva ☞AVALOKITEŚVARA—too extremely beautiful to paint!

the venerable Bao-zhi of the Liang dynasty

"In the 13th year of the reign period Tianzhen (515 C.E.), he went unexpectedly to the emperor to announce his departure. The emperor was alarmed and asked, 'How long will I live?' Zhigong smiled and did not reply. He merely drew his finger across his throat and left." [*NOTE:* This ominous gesture was probably the Master's prophecy of the emperor's subsequent death by starvation. In a past life Emperor Wu had been a cultivator. Annoyed by a pesky monkey, he locked it in a cave. After a time he forgot about it, and the monkey died of starvation. In a later life, the cultivator had accumulated blessings enough to become emperor, but bandits, with the monkey reborn as their leader, locked him in a tower and left him to starve to death.] "Returning to his temple, he lit one candle and gave it to a secretary named Wuqing. Wuqing made this known to the emperor, who lamented, 'Does the great Master have nothing further to leave? Inform me of his death as soon as it happens.' Afterwards the emperor sponsored the construction of a five-story pagoda (stupa). On the day of his burial, the Master was seen standing among the clouds.

"His eulogy says:

Come forth from an eagle's nest,
He made strange tracks, impossible to fathom.
Ripping open his face, a body was disclosed.
There remains an image of purple sandalwood,
And, what is more, a standard of rules.
He stood alone above the clouds,
Leaving his traces in the void!"
(VBS #25 1-2)

*** Estimates of the date of his birth vary from 417 to 421.**

Bhikshu 比丘

Bhikshu is a Sanskrit word; it is the technical designation for a fully ordained Buddhist monk, one who leads a pure and celibate life and who upholds the basic 250 monastic regulations (227 in the Theravada tradition).

"*Bhikshu* has three meanings, and so it is not translated from Sanskrit. It means 'mendicant,' 'frightener of Māra' [the king of the heavenly demons], and 'destroyer of evil.' Above, a Bhikshu seeks the food of Dharma from all the Buddhas to nourish his Dharma body. Below, he seeks food from living beings to nourish the life of his wisdom. In making the alms round for food, he must seek alms from the rich and poor equally. What benefits does making the alms round for food bring? It gives living beings a chance to plant blessings. Living beings make offerings to the Triple Jewel in order to attain blessings and virtue. Unless they make offerings to the ☞TRIPLE JEWEL, their blessings thin out, and day by day they accordingly undergo more suffering. Many people don't know enough to make offerings on their own, and so the Bhikshus make the alms round for food to make them aware of this practice. Seeking alms helps the Bhikshus to reduce their greed. It also helps lay people give rise to charitable states of mind. When Bhikshus seek alms, they make the almsround in succession, from one house to the next; they can't skip over the poorer families and seek alms from the rich, hoping for better offerings. They must not discriminate in their seeking alms. They have to seek alms equally from all living beings, so that all will have an equal opportunity to plant blessings.

"The second meaning of the word Bhikshu is 'frightener of Māra.' When a person leaves the home-life to become a Bhikshu, the heavenly demons get upset. This is like your coming here to study the Buddhadharma: the demon kings use all their tricks to get you to quit studying, because they don't like it one bit. If you leave the home-life, the demons become even more unhappy. When a Bhikshu steps up on the Precept Platform for the [Bhikshu] Precepts to be transmitted, the three masters and seven certifiers (representing the Buddhas of the ten directions and the three periods of time), who administer and certify the precepts, ask him, 'Have you brought forth the Bodhi mind?' [☞ BODHI RESOLVE] And he says, 'Yes.' Then they ask him, 'Are you a great hero?' And he says, 'Yes, I am.' At that time, an earth-traveling *yakṣa* takes the news to a space-traveling *yakṣa*, and the space-traveling *yakṣa* flies up to the demon kings in the heavens and informs them that, among human beings, yet another one has left home to become a Bhikshu. When the demon king hears this, his palace quakes, as if there were an earthquake, and the demon king is afraid. Thus, Bhikshus are called 'frighteners of Māra.'

"Third, the word Bhikshu means 'destroyer of evil.' Bhikshus break through all the evils of the afflictions. People have afflictions which come to them at birth. When they are born, they lose their tempers and get angry and cry. Bhikshus break through afflictions, and just that is *bodhi*. They give rise to the Bodhi mind.

"Since the word Bhikshu includes these three meanings, it is not translated but is left in the Sanskrit." (DFS IX 1683-1685)

The three meanings of Bhikshu complement the three meanings of ☞ ARHAT.

✍ **⟨etymologically 'one who wishes to share or partake'⟩ almsman, mendicant, a Buddhist monk or priest**

☞ **śramaṇa, Bhikshuni, Sangha, moral precepts**

Bhikshuni 比丘尼

Bhikshuni is a Sanskrit term that designates a Buddhist nun. It is the feminine form of ☞ BHIKSHU.

The Buddha made the revolutionary move of establishing an organization, the Bhikshuni Sangha, for women who wanted to devote themselves exclusively to the Dharma. In doing so he recognized the inherent spiritual worthiness of women and indicated that they too could become enlightened. Later, as recorded in the ☞ DHARMA FLOWER SUTRA, the Buddha predicted that particular Bhikshunis would eventually become Buddhas.

✍ **Buddhist nun, female mendicant, almswoman**

☞ **Bhikshu, Sangha, moral precepts**

blessings 福

One who cultivates blessings
  but not wisdom
Is like an elephant wearing a
  necklace;
One who cultivates wisdom
  and not blessings
Is like a Arhat with an empty bowl.
(DFS 1080)

"How does one accumulate blessings? It is from a number of actions, not just one. There is a saying, 'Don't skip doing a good deed just because it is small, and don't do a bad deed just because you think it is insignificant....' For example, you should not think that a little lie is of no major importance. If you tell a lot of little lies, they become a big lie. In the same way, you should not think that killing an ant is a small and unimportant matter, because if one day you kill a person, it will have begun with your killing the ant. You should pay attention to little things and not follow your whims and wishes. To cultivate diligently the accumulation of blessings involves being very careful to do the deeds that should be done, even if they accumulate only a small amount of merit and virtue. Gradually they cause an accumulation of great merit and virtue. Mount Tai [a sacred mountain in Shandong Province in China] is made up of individual motes of dust, but even though motes of dust are small, many of them gathered together make up a mountain. So too is the creating of blessings." (UW 77)

> The Buddha, said, 'When you see someone practicing the Way of giving, aid him joyously, and you will obtain vast and great blessings.'
>
> A *śramaṇa* asked, 'Is there an end to those blessings?'
>
> The Buddha said, 'Consider the flame of a single lamp. Though a hundred thousand people come and light their own lamps from it so that they can cook their food and ward off the darkness, the first lamp remains the same as before. Blessings are like this, too.' (S42 23)

Sometimes a distinction is made between worldly 'blessings' (good karma) and world-transcending merit and virtue.

> Blessings attached to marks
> reap the result of the heavens.
> But just as an arrow shot into space
> falls as its velocity wanes,
> So, too, what you get in the life
> after that will make you unhappy.
> (FAS Ch24 44)

Building temples and giving sanction to the Sangha, practicing giving and arranging vegetarian feasts, are called 'seeking blessings.' Do not mistake blessings for merit and virtue. Merit and virtue are in the Dharma body, not in the cultivation of blessings. (PS 133)

Making Buddhist statues is one way to create blessings.

> A confused person will foster
> blessings,
> But not cultivate the Way, and say,
> 'To practice for the blessings
> is to practice the Way.'
> While giving and making offerings
> brings blessings without limit,
> It is in the mind that the three evils
> have their origin.
> By seeking blessings you may wish
> to obliterate offenses,
> But in the future, though you are
> blessed, offenses still remain.
> You ought to simply strike the evil
> conditions from your mind
> Through true repentance and
> reform within your own nature.
> (PS 194-195)

☞ **merit, karma**

bodhi 菩提

> If the mad mind stops, its very stopping is *bodhi.* (SS)
>
> All the things that exist in the world are the wonderfully bright inherent mind of *bodhi.* (SS III 196)

"*Bodhi* is Sanskrit. It is interpreted to mean 'awakening to the Way'.... Where does *bodhi* come from? *Bodhi* doesn't come from anywhere or go anywhere. Each of us is endowed with it. No one person has any more or less of it than anyone else. It neither increases nor decreases, neither comes into being nor ceases to be, nor is it defiled or pure." (SS I 180)

"The back of your hand is affliction, and the palm of your hand is *bodhi.* Realizing *bodhi* is just like flipping your hand from back to palm. When you turn affliction around, it's *bodhi.* Afflictions are the same as *bodhi.* Birth and death are the same as nirvana. If you understand, then afflictions are *bodhi.* If you don't understand, then *bodhi* is affliction. *Bodhi* isn't outside of afflictions, and there are no afflictions outside the scope of enlightenment. And so I very often cite the analogy of water and ice. If you pour a bowl of water over a person's body, even if you use a lot of force, you still won't hurt the person. However, if the bowl of water has turned into ice and you hit the person in the head with it, the person may very well die. *Bodhi* is like the water; afflictions are like the ice. If you melt ice, it becomes water; when you freeze water, it becomes ice." (FAS Ch24 63)

☞ **enlightenment, awakening**
☞ **enlightenment, nirvana**

Bodhidharma ⟨Patriarch⟩ 菩提達摩《祖師》

The twenty-eighth Indian patriarch and founder and first patriarch in China of the Chan School in a lineage traced back to the Buddha Śākyamuni. He was in China in the late fifth and early sixth centuries C.E.

"*The Patriarch was a native of Southern India, the third son of king Utmost Fragrance, of the Kṣatriya class. At first the king made offerings to Prajñātāra, because of being tested with a precious pearl. The Patriarch* Bodhidharma *became clear about the mind ground* Dharma-door. *Prajñātāra accordingly transmitted the Dharma to him.* Venerable Prajñātāra was the Twenty-seventh Indian Patriarch....

A verse says:

> *The mind ground produces all seeds.*
> *Because of specifics there further*
> *emerges principle.*
> *When the fruit is full,*
> *bodhi is perfected.*
> *When the flower blossoms,*
> *the worldly arises.*

"The specifics reveal the principle. But it can go either way, depending on what people do. The fruit can ripen into *bodhi* or it can flower into all kinds of worldly problems.

"*When the Patriarch had obtained the Dharma for a very long time, he called to mind that conditions in China were ripe, and so he sailed* by boat *to* see the reigning king Emperor Wu of the Liang dynasty. *When he reached Guangzhou* (Canton), a *subordinate envoy of the royal house of Xiao sent word to* Emperor *Wu* of the *Liang* dynasty, *who thereupon asked* him to come *to see him.*

"*He asked him, 'What is the sagely truth in the primary sense, the primary principle?'*

"*The Patriarch said, 'There simply isn't any sage.'*

"Emperor Wu of Liang didn't understand what he was talking about, and so he said, '*Then who is before me?* Who is it who is talking to me?' His meaning was, 'You're a sage, aren't you? You are talking to me, and so who is that?'

"*The Patriarch said, 'I don't recognize him.'* I don't recognize who he is.

"*The Emperor did not make the connection.* Emperor Wu of Liang did not understand that sages have no attributes of a self. He considered himself a sage and was very self-satisfied, but he basically was the same as any ordinary person. *Because of that, the Patriarch crossed the Yangzi* River and *passed through* the part of China that was under Wei reign. The Liang dynasty reigned in southern China with its capital at Nanjing. The north of China was at the same time governed by the Wei Dynasty with its capital at Loyang. This was during the Five Kingdoms period (386-581 C.E.), and so China was divided into many different countries with different rulers. *He arrived at Shaolin* Monastery on Song Mountain. *Afterwards he met Shenguang and transmitted the Great Dharma to him.* He transmitted the Patriarchs' Proper Dharma Eye Treasury to Shenguang. *And then accompanied him to Thousand Sages Monastery in Yunnan. He transformed himself while seated.* He sat down and went off to rebirth. That is what this account says. But many books say that Patriarch Bodhidharma did not enter the stillness (i.e., nirvana) at all. These are inconceivable events and are not subject to ordinary proofs and tests of truth. *He was buried at Bear's Ear Mountain.* Emperor *Taizong of* the *Tang* dynasty *conferred the posthumous title of 'Perfectly Enlightened Great Master' upon him. His* stupa *inscription reads: 'Contemplator of Emptiness.'*

"*A verse in praise says:*

When he first came to China,
He did not recognize who was before the emperor.
Overturning nest and bowl,
He beat emptiness until it bled.
He met a person who cut off his arm.
At Bear's Peak the path came to its end.
He divided his marrow and divided his skin,
Adding frost on top of snow.

"'Overturning nest and bowl' means he broke through the antiquated patterns, and so there wasn't any 'niche' for him. The Second Patriarch cut off his arm for the sake of the Dharma, and so Patriarch Bodhidharma transmitted the Dharma to him. Arriving at Bear's Ear Mountain, where he transmitted the Dharma, he had no further place he needed to go.

'He divided his marrow and divided his skin.' Some obtained the marrow of the Patriarch's teaching, some obtained the skin. The analogy is of frost added to snow. Snow is very cold to start with and when frost is added it is even colder still.

"*Another verse says:*

China's conditions were ripe, and so [Bodhi]dharma came.
He did not recognize who was before the emperor;
The potentials were not ready yet.
Shenguang at Bear's Ear knelt for nine years.
As 'able wisdom' [Huike], *he collected snow*
With one arm cut off.
Using the mind seal to seal the mind,
There was transmission of Great Dharma.
From the first patriarch to the second patriarch, the life-pulse continued.

Six times was he attacked, yet
not a hair of his was injured.
With one shoe he returned west,
to be remembered forever after.

"Patriarch Bodhidharma had been in India and all of a sudden it occurred to him that Buddhism ought to flourish in China where conditions were ripe. 'The Dharma came' means Patriarch Bodhidharma came to China, bringing the Dharma with him.

"When Emperor Wu of Liang saw Bodhidharma, he asked him, 'What's meant by Sagely Truth?' He was not just referring to the Four Sagely Truths, he was referring to the foremost truth—Truth in the Primary Sense. It is defined as being 'prior to the arising of a thought.'

The path of words and language
is cut off.
The place of the mind's workings
is extinguished.

Emperor Wu of Liang had heard a lot, had built a lot of temples, had sanctioned many people's wishes to leave home, and so he thought he had already obtained the Sagely Truth. He thought that his merit and virtue were plentiful. And so his aim in asking his questions was to get Patriarch Bodhidharma to praise him. He expected him to say things like, 'Great King, you are really good. You have a great destiny in advocating the Buddhadharma. You already have clearly seen the Sagely Truth.'

"But Patriarch Bodhidharma was the Twenty-eighth Indian Patriarch. How could he be vulgar and obsequious and play up to an emperor? He could not. He didn't say a single word of praise. He said, 'There simply isn't any sage. There isn't anything at all.'

"When Emperor Wu of Liang didn't get his praise, he tried giving Patriarch Bodhidharma a high hat to wear and said, in effect, 'You've come from India and are a member of the Sagely Sangha, someone who understands sagely truth, and so how can you say there simply isn't any sage?' And so still trying to get some praise from Bodhidharma, he said, 'Then who is before me? Who is talking to me?' His meaning was, 'You are a sage, and I too am a sage. Both of us have the skill that comes from realizing Truth in the Primary Sense.'

"Little did he expect that, far from agreeing with that, Bodhidharma would say, 'There simply isn't any sage,' thus sweeping away all dharmas and leaving all marks. 'There isn't anything at all.' If there is anything at all, there is attachment to marks. There is attachment to the mark of self, the mark of others, the mark of living beings, and the mark of life spans. But he was indicating that there is nothing whatsoever. And so Emperor Wu further asked him, 'Then who is before me?'

Patriarch Bodhidharma (see plate 8)

"Patriarch Bodhidharma's answer was even simpler than before. He said, 'I don't recognize who it is. I don't recognize who is before you, emperor.' On the one hand, that showed he wasn't self-satisfied, unlike we who feel that it is sweet as eating honey if someone praises us, and that getting that honey is the best thing there is. He 'didn't recognize who it was.' But the emperor didn't make the connection because his 'potentials were not ready yet.'

"'Shenguang at Bear's Ear knelt for nine years.' After Patriarch Bodhidharma finished his conversation with the emperor, he left. He could see that the emperor wasn't getting what he was saying—that he had only understood half a sentence of it at best. At Nanjing he encountered a Dharma Master who was lecturing on sutras. When Dharma Master Shenguang lectured, heavenly flowers showered down in profusion, and golden lotuses welled up from the earth. At the time, people who had opened the ☞FIVE EYES could see this state occur when he was lecturing. That was a big response! But when Patriarch Bodhidharma arrived on the scene to take a look, he asked Dharma Master Shenguang, 'Dharma Master, what are you doing here?'

"Shenguang replied, 'What am I doing! I'm lecturing on the sutras and speaking Dharma to teach and transform living beings!'

"Patriarch Bodhidharma replied, 'You say you are lecturing, but what is black is the words and what is white is the paper. How can that be used to teach and transform living beings?'

"When Dharma Master Shenguang heard that, he said, 'Now you are slandering the Buddha and the Dharma. You are a despicable barbarian! You are a great demon.' After scolding him like that, Dharma Master Shenguang took his recitation beads, which were made of iron, and struck Bodhidharma with them. He aimed at Bodhidharma's head, but the Patriarch threw his head back, and so he was struck on the mouth. The blow knocked two of his teeth loose. Bodhidharma thought, 'If I spit these two teeth out on the ground, this place will undergo a terrible drought for three years.' That is what happens if a sage's teeth are knocked to the ground—a great disaster will occur there. If it didn't rain for three years, a lot of people would starve to death. He didn't want that to happen, and so he swallowed his two teeth instead of spitting them out. That is how compassionate he was. Then he left.

"After Bodhidharma left, the Ghost of Impermanence arrived with a summons for Dharma Master Shenguang. The ghost said, 'Dharma Master, today your life should end. We have come to invite you to King Yama's for tea.'

"Dharma Master Shenguang said, 'I lecture on the sutras so well; I still have to die?'

"The ghost said, 'You lecture on the sutras just fine, but you haven't ended birth and death.'

"The Dharma Master asked, 'Is there anyone in this world that King Yama does not govern? Is there anyone who has ended birth and death?'

"The Ghost of Impermanence said, 'Yes, there is someone.'

"'Who?'

"'The Dharma Master whose two teeth you just knocked out, that ugly monk, is someone whom King Yama has no control over. Not only does King Yama not govern him, but when King Yama sees him, he bows before him.'

"'Oh! Then I must follow him and find him. I want to learn the method for becoming someone whom King Yama does not govern.'

"'Fine, I'll give you some time.' And with that, the Ghost of Impermanence let him go.

"Dharma Master Shenguang was in a terrible hurry. He didn't even take time to put on his shoes; he just grabbed them and ran barefoot.

"Meanwhile, Bodhidharma had met a parrot on the road. The parrot could talk. It said:

Mind Come from the West,
Mind Come from the West,
Please teach me the way
To escape from this cage.

"Bodhidharma thought, 'I came here to save people and it's not working out; at least I can save this parrot.' And so he taught him:

To escape from the cage,
To escape from the cage,
Stick both legs straight out.
Close both eyes tight.
That's the way to escape your cage.

"The parrot heard and understood. It pretended to be dead. It lay on the bottom of its cage with its legs still stuck out and its eyes closed tight, not moving, not even breathing. The owner found the parrot this way and took it out to have a look. He held the bird in his hand, peering at it from the left and right until he was convinced it was indeed dead. The only thing was that it was still warm. But it wasn't breathing. And so the owner opened his hand and in that instant the parrot fully revived. Phrtttt! It flew away and escaped its cage.

"Dharma Master Shenguang pursued Bodhidharma all the way to Bear's Ear Mountain (Xiong Er Shan), which was in the Song range, the middle range of China's five great mountain ranges. Bodhidharma was sitting there facing a wall, not speaking to anyone. Shenguang tried to talk to Bodhidharma, but the Patriarch completely ignored him. And so Shenguang knelt there. He knelt for nine years while Bodhidharma sat. After nine years of kneeling his skill was fairly well developed, but it had not yet been brought to realization. 'As "Able Wisdom"'—Huike—the name Bodhidharma gave Shenguang, 'he collected snow with one arm cut off.' How did his wisdom come to be 'able'? In the winter of the ninth year of kneeling, there was a great snowfall. The snow covered him as he knelt there. It reached clear up to his waist. He was probably shaking with cold and decided to try to speak to the Patriarch again. 'Patriarch, please be compassionate and transmit the Dharma to me. It was a terrible mistake I made when I knocked your two teeth out. I realize now that you have virtue in the Way, that you are One Who Has Obtained the Way.'

"Bodhidharma asked him, 'What is falling outside?'

"'Snow.'

"'What color is the snow?'

"'Snow is white.'

"'When the snow turns red, I will transmit the Dharma to you.' This was a test. But by that time Shenguang could figure out what to do.

"'Fine,' he thought, 'You want red snow?' And so he took his precept knife, which the ancients carried to use if a situation ever arose in which one would have to break a precept. Rather than break a precept, one would choose to use the knife to cut off one's own head. But now Shenguang grabbed the knife and sliced off one of his arms. The blood spurted out all over the place and colored the snow red. He took up a bunch of the red snow and went before Bodhidharma, holding it aloft to offer to him. 'See, the snow is red,' he said.

"Bodhidharma said, 'You have a bit of sincerity. My journey to China has not been in vain. Fine. I will transmit the Dharma to you.' Bodhidharma transmitted the Proper Dharma Eye Treasury, the Wonderful Mind of Nirvana, to Great Master Able Wisdom [Huike]. And so the First Patriarch and the Second Patriarch perpetuated the life-pulse of the Buddha's teaching.

the twenty-eighth patriarch, venerable bodhidharma

"'Six times he was attacked; not a hair of his was injured.' While Patriarch Bodhidharma was in China, people of various externalist cults and sects were jealous of him. They tried six times to poison him. The first five times he was not killed by it. The sixth time he was given poison, he spit it out on a rock, and it split the rock in two. And so he thought, 'People are so jealous, I'd best enter the stillness (i.e., nirvana).' And so he pretended to enter the stillness. Then people buried him. But just at that time, in Northern Wei there was a government official named Song. At Zongling, on Zhongnan Mountain, he encountered Bodhidharma. The Patriarch was carrying one shoe in his hand. He said to Officer Song, 'There is a lot of turmoil in your country. You should return there immediately.'

"Song didn't think there was any problem in his country, but he returned just the same and found that indeed the Wei dynasty was being overthrown. 'Ah,' he thought, 'Bodhidharma's words are really accurate.' When he related the Patriarch's advice to others, they asked him, 'Where did you see Bodhidharma?'

"'I saw him just two days ago at Zongling. He was carrying one shoe, and when I asked him where he was going, he said, "Back to India." He told me that our dynasty was in trouble, and he was right.'

"'You saw a ghost!' they told him. 'Bodhidharma has already been dead a long time.'

"'Where is he buried?' asked the official. 'Let's go see.' They opened the grave and there was nothing inside except for one shoe. 'With one shoe he returned West, to be remembered forever after.' He went back to India with one shoe. But the memory of him was left in China for people to hold ever after. They will never forget Patriarch Bodhidharma. His state was inconceivable." (VBS #169 (June 1984) 1-3, 12)

☞ **Chan School, lineage, Huineng ⟨Chan Master/Patriarch⟩**

Bodhi resolve ⟨bringing forth⟩
發菩提心

'Bringing forth the Bodhi resolve' means generating a true intention in your mind to become enlightened. That intention is a seed that can grow into a Buddha. Bringing forth the Bodhi resolve is the beginning of the Path to enlightenment.

"When you have your first thought of faith in the Buddha, that's bringing forth the Bodhi resolve. To want to cultivate is called bringing forth the Bodhi resolve. Bringing forth the Bodhi resolve is simply benefitting others. Not having selfish thoughts of benefitting oneself is bringing forth the Bodhi resolve." (FAS Ch17 2-3)

"The Bodhi resolve arises when, during the course of one's cultivation, one is most single-minded. One becomes a Buddha right here in the world, and it may occur at any time throughout several hundreds of thousands of myriads of aeons. Śākyamuni Buddha cultivated for three great ☞ASAṄKHYEYA *kalpas*. And how long is an *asaṅkhyeya kalpa*? It can only be described as a limitless length of time.... That means that Śākyamuni Buddha cultivated for three limitlessly vast expanses of time. Therefore, in the ☞FLOWER ADORNMENT SUTRA we are told how at the time of first bringing forth the resolve, one realizes Proper and Equal Enlightenment. When one is single-minded to the utmost, the Bodhi resolve suddenly comes forth, and one becomes a Buddha. It can also happen in one's mind in the course of walking the Path of Bodhi. In cultivating the ☞SIX PĀRAMITĀS and the myriad practices, one is also bringing forth the Bodhi resolve. When one is non-retreating to the point that one would never turn back, one is also bringing forth the Bodhi resolve. By being vigorous day and night, one is also bringing forth the Bodhi resolve. For example, those who live at the ☞WAY-PLACE here do Morning Recitation, work all day long, and then when evening comes, they forget about sleep—even after working so hard all day long. That's all part of bringing forth the Bodhi resolve. Therefore, you should all be attentive and not reject these aspects of bringing forth the Bodhi resolve—don't neglect them. Use whatever skill you have in cultivation, and consider the Bodhi resolve to be your personal responsibility and your responsibility toward others. In that way, you will be vigorous in your work. That is how one can be a superior and lofty person." (FAS Ch5 178-179).

> Good man, the Bodhi resolve brings to realization infinite merit and virtue.... You should know that it is entirely equal to all the merit and virtue of all Buddha-dharmas. Why? It is because the Bodhi resolve produces all Bodhisattva conduct. It is because the Tathāgatas of the three periods of time are born from the Bodhi resolve. Therefore, good man, if there are those who have brought forth the resolve for *anuttara-samyak-saṃbodhi*, they have already given birth to infinite merit and virtue and are universally able to collect themselves and remain on the Path of All-Wisdom. (EDR VIII 77-78)

> All Buddhas take a heart of great compassion as their substance. Because of living beings, they gave rise to great compassion. Because of great compassion, they brought forth the Bodhi resolve. Because of the Bodhi resolve, they realized the proper and equal enlightenment. (UW 101)

✍ **giving rise to/generating/developing the *bodhi*-mind, developing *bodhi* in one's heart, setting the mind on *bodhi*, developing the thought of enlightenment, the mental attitude which aspires to Buddhahood**

☞ **bodhi, Bodhisattva**

Bodhisattva 菩薩

"Bodhisattva (*bodhi* = enlightenment + *sattva* = being) is a Sanskrit word which can be interpreted in two ways:

"1) *Enlightener of sentient beings.* The Bodhisattva takes the enlightenment that he has been certified as having attained, the wisdom that he has uncovered, and uses that enlightened wisdom to enlighten all other sentient beings.

"2) *An enlightened sentient being.* The Bodhisattva is also a sentient being, but he is one who has become enlightened.

"Together these two meanings show that a Bodhisattva is an enlightened sentient being who enlightens other beings." (HD 13)

> Good man, you should know that what a Bodhisattva does is most difficult. It is difficult for him to appear (in the world) and difficult for one to encounter him. To be able to see a Bodhisattva is twice as difficult. A Bodhisattva is one on whom all living beings rely. He causes them to

grow and brings them to realization. He is the savior of all living beings, because he plucks them out of suffering and hardships. He is the refuge of all beings, because he protects and guards the world. He is the rescuer of all beings, because he delivers them from fear. (EDR II 70)

A Bodhisattva is someone who has resolved to become a Buddha (☞BODHI RESOLVE) and who is cultivating the Path to becoming a Buddha. Usually the term Bodhisattva is reserved for those who have reached some level of enlightenment. The term Bodhisattva Mahāsattva (great being), refers to Bodhisattvas who have gone beyond the seventh ground of the Bodhisattva Path (☞TEN GROUNDS).

"A Bodhisattva....is also called 'a living being with a great mind attuned to the Way.' No matter how badly people may act towards him, he doesn't hold it against them. He absolutely never becomes irritated, never loses his temper...." (SS I 107)

"Bodhisattva is an extremely spiritual and holy name....Some people claim they are Bodhisattvas, although they are not. Some people who are Bodhisattvas will not admit it. You see, it is very strange: those who are not Bodhisattvas say they are, while those who are don't say so. Ultimately, whether you say so or not, those who aren't, aren't, and those who are, are. There is no need to say so. Bodhisattvas don't put ads in the newspapers saying, 'Do you recognize me? I am a Bodhisattva.'" (HS 96)

"When the Bodhisattva walks the Bodhisattva Path, he does what is very difficult. From an ordinary point of view, a Bodhisattva practicing the Bodhisattva Path appears quite foolish. If he were not, then why would he choose to undergo suffering himself in order to come and teach and transform living beings? But no matter what kind of suffering there is, he can endure it. He undergoes intense suffering even to the point of enduring the suffering due other living beings. If the Bodhisattva weren't foolish, then why would he take such a big personal loss? He doesn't benefit himself in anything he does. But that isn't because he is foolish. A Bodhisattva has great wisdom. Because he has great wisdom, he wants to take across all living beings and cause all of them to have wisdom too. He wants to forsake himself for the sake of the multitudes. He forsakes his own small self in order to bring living beings' great selves to realization. When you walk the Path of the Bodhisattva, you benefit yourself and you benefit others. In doing this you shouldn't fear any kind of suffering. The Bodhisattva undergoes suffering just as if he were eating candy. He undergoes suffering as if there were no suffering to undergo. Furthermore, he wants to undergo suffering for the sake of all living beings. That is the one kind of suffering that's worthwhile. Moreover, the Bodhisattva thinks that:

> To endure suffering is to end
> suffering.
> To enjoy blessings is to exhaust
> blessings.

Because he thinks in that way, he undergoes suffering on behalf of living beings. He transfers all of his bliss to all living beings in the Dharma Realm (☞TRANSFERENCE OF MERIT). The merit from this kind of open and unselfish action is inexhaustible. It is completely public spirited, and it is intended for the benefit of all living beings." (FAS Ch9 44)

"A Bodhisattva is someone who likes to help other people. If you help others, then you are a Bodhisattva. If I help others, then I am a Bodhisattva. If you do not help others, then you are a *rākṣasa* ghost. If I do not help others, then I am a *rākṣasa* ghost....

"'But I have no power to help others,' you say. 'First of all I have no money, and secondly I don't know how to talk to people. How can I help people?'

"...Have a compassionate mouth, not one which scolds people. Have a skillful tongue that finds ways to reason with people, not a tongue which continually gossips. Find a way to lessen the strife and discord in the world. Then, whether or not you have money, you can foster merit. If you have money, you can use that too, but what is more important is to have good thoughts, do good deeds, and be a good person...." (DS 5-6)

Avalokiteśvara Bodhisattva

The Path of the Bodhisattva consists of practicing the ☞ SIX (or ten) PĀRAMITĀS and traversing the many stages of partial enlightenment leading to the perfect enlightenment of Buddhahood.

The Venerable Śāriputra Tries to Cultivate the Path of the Bodhisattva

"The Venerable ☞ ŚĀRIPUTRA, upon hearing the Buddha say that cultivating the Bodhisattva Way was the Great Vehicle practice, decided that he too would cultivate the Bodhisattva Way. When you are cultivating the Bodhisattva Path, if someone wants your head, you have to give them your head. If they want your hands, you have to give them your hands. If they want your feet, you have to give your feet away. In general, if living beings want your body, you are supposed to give it to them: head, eyes, brains, marrow—that's inner wealth. If someone needs those things of yours, and you're cultivating the Bodhisattva Path, you have to give them up.

"Śāriputra personally told the Buddha that he was going to cultivate the Bodhisattva Way, to cultivate Great Vehicle Dharma. The Buddha said, 'You'd better just try it first. It is not all that easy. Give it a preliminary three-month trial run. Then if you find you really can do it, you can set about cultivation of the Bodhisattva Way in earnest. In cultivating the Bodhisattva Way, you must have an attitude of there being no self, no others, no living beings, and no life span. You have to be able to stomach the most bitter things, and yield the most pleasant ones to others. You must sacrifice yourself for the sake of others.'

"Śāriputra said, 'I think I can do that. I imagine I could give my body away to someone if that person asked for it.'

"The Buddha said, 'Okay, go try it out.'

"Thereupon Śāriputra set out to cultivate the Bodhisattva Way. As he was walking the Bodhisattva Path, he saw a stone in the road and said to himself, 'I should move this rock away or else people with poor eyesight walking along this road could break a leg or have a spill and be injured.' And so he moved the rock away and thought to himself, 'I'm cultivating the Bodhisattva Way.' He kept on going and ran into a hole full of water. He said, 'I'd better fill this hole. It would be easy to walk here if there weren't any water. Filling the hole would prevent situations such as when Śākyamuni Buddha in a previous life had to spread out his hair to cover a mud puddle.' And so he found a pail and brought load after load of dirt until he had filled the hole so there was no more water. Then he said to himself, 'These are both ways of benefitting people. The road wasn't easy to travel on but I've repaired it, and that is cultivating the Bodhisattva Way.' He was very happy that he had cultivated the Bodhisattva Way twice that day. When he went back and sat in meditation that evening, he felt very comfortable and said, 'It's not strange that people cultivate the Bodhisattva Way. It's really fine. Today I have fewer false thoughts during my meditation. I'm certainly going to continue to cultivate the Bodhisattva Way.'

"The next day he set out for the mountains, where he found lots of dead trees. He said, 'I'm going to clear those dead trees off to one side, which will also be cultivation of the Bodhisattva Way.' Then he met an eyeless person who was walking down the road without a guide. He thought, 'I should cultivate the Bodhisattva Way and escort this blind person to his home.' And so he said, 'Mr Blindman, where do you want to go?'

"The eyeless person said, 'You are the blindman!'

"Śāriputra thought, 'What? He's the blindman, and he gets upset when I call him 'Mr. Blindman.' Oh well, when one cultivates the Bodhisattva Way, one has to be patient.' And so he said, 'Oh, you are Mr. Has Eyes.'

"To that the blindman retorted, 'What's it to you if I have eyes or not?' He was exploding with rage as he scolded him.

"Śāriputra said, 'I just want to help you. I'll guide you wherever you want to go.'

"The blind man said, 'I don't need any help from you,' and told him off.

"Śāriputra said to himself, 'The Bodhisattva Way is not easy to cultivate! I wanted to show him the road and he cursed me. But be patient, practice the *pāramitā* of patience and don't pay any attention to him. However, I think I'll take the Bodhisattva Way back with me for the day and let it rest a little. Tomorrow we'll see.'

He returned, and as he sat in meditation that evening he kept having false thoughts about what had happened. 'He was blind and when I wanted to guide him along the road, he cursed me! People in the world are really weird.' But he still didn't think of quitting, and hadn't decided it was too hard to cultivate the Bodhisattva Way. He still thought to himself, 'If he scolds me a bit it's not important. I can take it. I wouldn't have even cared if he had hit me!'

"The next day he set out again to cultivate the Bodhisattva Way. On the Bodhisattva Way he encountered a person who was walking along and crying, sobbing his heart out. Śāriputra asked him, 'What's wrong? No matter what kind of trouble you are in, you can tell me about it. You don't have to be so sad and in so much pain.'

"The crying person replied, 'You shouldn't even ask about my troubles! There's nothing you could do to help me.'

"Śāriputra said, 'Maybe there's something I can do for you. Give it a try and tell me.'

"The man said, 'It wouldn't do any good to tell you. Don't waste my time. I've got too much pain in my heart, so all I can do is cry.'

"Śāriputra said, 'I'm sure I can help you. Tell me what's wrong, and I'll find a way to help.'

"The man said, 'Do you really mean it? It's because my mother is sick. She went to see the doctor, who wrote her a prescription that says she needs the eye of a living person to cure her. I've gone the rounds of all the pharmacies trying to buy a live person's eye, but there are none for sale. That kind of medicine doesn't exist, so there's no way to cure my mother's illness, and all I can do is cry. At first I intended to take out my own eye to cure her, but I can't give it up. It's too painful. And so now there's nothing I can do but cry!'

"Śāriputra thought it over, 'I really should help him out of this painful dilemma. This is a Bodhisattva Way that I should cultivate! Also, he is very filial. I've found a friend in my cultivation of the Bodhisattva Way. This is excellent! I should practice this Bodhisattva Way!' He thought it over for not very long—maybe two minutes—and made up his mind, 'I'm going to do it!' Then he said, 'Don't cry. I'll give you my eye to help you out.'

"The man said, 'Really? Of course that would be wonderful! Can you really give up your eye to cure my mother's illness?'

"Śāriputra said, 'It's no big deal. I can give it up. I'm someone who wants to cultivate the Bodhisattva Way.'

"The person said, 'Fine. I'm going to bow to you first, bow to this Bodhisattva who wants to cultivate the Bodhisattva Way.'

"After the person bowed to him, Śāriputra couldn't get out of giving up his eye, and so he took a knife and gouged out his left eye. He was able to stand the pain and said, 'Okay, you can take this to cure your mother's illness.'

"The person took it, looked at it and said, 'Ugh, your eye stinks! And anyway it's a left eye, and I need a right eye. It's totally useless!' He slammed the eye to the ground and stamped it into the dirt with his foot, squashing it to bits.

"At that, Śāriputra's heart was filled with pain. Before, he had been able to bear the hurt from his eye, but now there was hurt from his eye and from his heart too, and he said, 'It's no wonder the Buddha said to give cultivating the Bodhisattva Way a trial run. It's really hard to cultivate the Bodhisattva Way! It's really hard!!!' He was in pain and regretted it; he didn't want to cultivate the Bodhisattva Way anymore.

"The crying person started to laugh and said, 'Oh, so that's how your Bodhisattva Way was all along. It was just a start without a finish. You could only manage to get started, but you couldn't keep it up. What kind of Bodhisattva Way were you cultivating anyway?' After saying that, he rose into empty space; it turned out that he was a god who had come to test him. Furthermore, Śāriputra hadn't lost his eye after all, but his Bodhisattva Way was finished." (FAS PI 51-54)

The Bodhisattva in Theravada Buddhism

That Theravada Buddhists do not recognize the Bodhisattva is a widespread misconception. In the Theravada both the Buddha Śākyamuni and the Buddhas of the past are referred to as Bodhisattvas. The reality of the Bodhisattva Path, which is the Path to becoming a Buddha, is acknowledged, but it is considered by Theravadins to be too difficult for all but a rare few to follow.

✍ **bodhi-being, Buddha-to-be, person destined for enlightenment**

☞ **Mahayana and Hinayana Compared, Bodhi resolve, enlightenment**

bowing 拜/禮拜/頂禮

"The Buddhist practice of bowing to the Buddha diminishes one's habits of self-importance, pride, and arrogance. It is also a good physical exercise that can make the body strong...." (WM 38)

"Bowing is an important practice in Buddhism. It involves a full prostration—the placing of the forehead, forearms, and knees on the ground in a total gesture of reverence and of worship. It is usually done before an image of the Buddha, Bodhisattva, sage, or before a holy text. It is a misconception, though, to think that the worshipper is bowing to a statue of the Buddha, to a wooden or stone or clay image. The Buddha we bow to is the Buddha inside our true minds, the pure, good, and perfect spiritual nature that has no shape or form. Images of the Buddha are simply symbols of the real thing." (PDS (Feb. 1984) 4)

Seven Ways to Bow

"There are seven different ways that people bow to the Buddha:

"**1**) The first is 'arrogant bowing,' and describes a person who, although he or she bows to the Buddha, still has a mark of a self. When someone like this bows to the Buddha, it is forced and is accompanied by thoughts like this: 'What am I doing bowing to the Buddha? Why do I have to bow to him?' A person like this becomes annoyed at being forced to put his head down. He sees everyone else bowing and feels that if he does not bow along with them, he will stand out, and so out of embarrassment he bows to the Buddha. Although he bows, his mark of self is still not empty; on the contrary, he is filled with arrogance....

"**2**) The second kind of bowing is called 'seeking fame.' This category describes one who hears others praising a cultivator saying, 'That person bows often and really cultivates vigorously; he bows to the Buddhas, he bows to sutras, and he bows repentance ceremonies. He is truly a diligent cultivator.' Upon hearing the praise of this cultivator, he also wishes to be recognized as a cultivator, and so he begins to vigorously bow to the Buddha. Although he finds pleasure in bowing, he does not truly bow to the Buddha; he is bowing for recognition. He is seeking recognition as a cultivator, and the pleasure he finds is in that recognition and in his dreams of fame....

"**3**) The third is called 'bowing with body and mind concurring'....This describes a person who bows when he sees others bowing. In mindless imitation, both his body and his mind go along with what everyone else is doing. He doesn't have the slightest concern as to whether bowing to the Buddha is beneficial or not, or whether it is reasonable or superstitious. Not seeking for recognition, he just follows along with everyone else, his body and mind concurring. This kind of bowing has no real benefits and no real faults.

"**4**) The fourth kind of bowing is called 'wise and pure.' 'Wise' refers to the functioning of wisdom, and 'pure' refers to the development of purity. This describes one who uses true wisdom to purify his body and mind. People who are wise use this method to bow to the Buddha, and by doing so, they purify the Three Karmas of body, mouth, and mind.

"When someone uses this fourth method to bow to the Buddha, his bodily karma is correct inasmuch as he does not kill, steal, commit sexual misconduct, and so in this way his bodily karma is purified. When he uses this method to bow to the Buddha, he entertains no thoughts of greed, anger, or delusion; rather he possesses the wisdom born from single-mindedly and respectfully bowing to the Buddha, and so his karma of mind also becomes pure. When someone bows to the Buddha, he also recites the Buddha's name, and by doing so, or by holding and reciting sutras and mantras, his mouth karma is also correct and devoid of any harsh speech, false speech, irresponsible speech or duplicity and is thereby purified. When the Three

Karmas of body, mouth, and mind are pure, this is called 'wise and pure bowing' with which one uses true wisdom to bow to the Buddha.

"5) The fifth kind of bowing is called 'pervading everywhere throughout the Dharma Realm'....It describes one who, when bowing, contemplates: 'Although I have not yet become a Buddha in body, the nature of my mind fills the Dharma Realm. As I bow before this one Buddha, I bow everywhere before all Buddhas. I am not just bowing before one Buddha; my transformation bodies bow before each Buddha, simultaneously making offerings to all Buddhas and Bodhisattvas.'

"Consider that 'everything is made from the mind alone,' and so one's mind totally pervades the ☞ DHARMA REALM. One's bowing practice totally pervades the Dharma Realm. What is the Dharma Realm? All of the Great World Systems of a Billion Worlds (☞ WORLD SYSTEMS) are contained within it. In fact, nothing is outside of the Dharma Realm. With this kind of bowing, you contemplate your respectful bowing pervading everywhere throughout the Dharma Realm....

"6) The sixth is called 'sincerely cultivating proper contemplation.' One who cultivates proper concentration is one who concentrates his mind and contemplates: 'Bowing to the Buddha is bowing to the Buddhas of the Dharma Realm; bowing to the Buddhas of the Dharma Realm is just bowing to one Buddha.' This is because 'all Buddhas of the ten directions and the three periods of time share one Dharma body in common, and all Buddhas' lands and ways are identical.' A concentrated mind must be used to bow to the Buddha, to contemplate the Buddha, and to cultivate, so that you will not have polluted thoughts.

A monk on a pilgrimage of bowing once every three steps

"It is not considered proper concentration if when you are bowing, your mind runs off to the movies, or to the race track, or goes off hunting, or to a dance hall, a bar, or a restaurant. You need not purchase a ticket for your mind to travel off in all directions. With no travel arrangements at all, suddenly it is in the heavens, and suddenly it is on earth. Sometimes your mind will fly off to New York and then for no apparent reason, it comes back to San Francisco. You think, 'Oh, I was here bowing to the Buddha and then I went to New York, only to fly back to San Francisco again. This must be a spiritual power!'

"In fact, that is not even a ghostly power, let alone a spiritual power. It is nothing more than polluted thought and is called deviant contemplation or improper contemplation. If you cultivate with proper contemplation, you will not have these polluted thoughts. You would bow to the Buddha with an undivided mind.

"'Sincerely cultivating' means that when you bow once, that surpasses one million bows made by someone who bows while having polluted thoughts. And so in cultivating, 'when you reach the gate, you enter.' You should understand this Dharma-door, because if you do not, then when you see others bowing to the Buddha, you will not bow the way they do but instead will think, 'As soon as I'm finished bowing, I'm going to have a cup of coffee, or perhaps I'll have a drink.' People like that have no control over their minds, and after they have finished bowing, they run off to have a drink.

"The problem is that not only do they themselves go out to have a drink, but they drag everyone else out with them. That is really pitiful. That is not 'cultivating purely with proper contemplation,' but is a form of deviant contemplation, because if you have false thoughts while you are bowing, your worship is devoid of any merit and virtue.

"7) The seventh is called the 'true mark of impartial bowing.' It describes a person who bows and yet does not bow; who does not bow while he bows. When I say this, some of you are thinking, 'You say we should bow and yet not bow, and not bow but yet bow. Therefore, if I don't bow to the Buddha, wouldn't I be bowing to the Buddha?' That is not what I mean. With this kind of bowing, although you bow to the Buddha, you are not attached to a mark of bowing to the Buddha. You cannot distort the meaning and say that while you are not bowing to the Buddha, it counts as bowing to the Buddha. One who speaks like that is mentally disturbed.

"For example, recently someone told me he had attained the void. That is an extremely foolish thing to say. What is more, people like that cannot be helped, and there is no way to save them because their heavy attachment makes them too ignorant.

"The 'true mark of impartial bowing' means that 'I am bowing to the Buddha, I am impartially bowing to the Triple Jewel; I am reverent to the Buddha, reverent to the Dharma, and reverent to the Sangha. Although I bow in this way, I, nevertheless, do not think that I am bowing. 'Not one thought is produced, nor is one thought destroyed.' This is the Dharma of the 'true mark of impartial bowing.' It is a Dharma that involves neither coming into being nor ceasing to be: 'When not even one thought arises, the entire substance appears.' When you bow to the Buddha to the point that not even one thought is produced, you cause your body to manifest throughout the entire Dharma Realm. Although your body is bowing here, it is the same size as the Dharma Realm. This is just the true mark that has no mark. You bow until there are no people, no self, no living beings, and no life span. You become identical to the Dharma Realm. Your body is the Dharma Realm; the Dharma Realm is your body.

"Isn't this wonderful? Before, your body was just a speck on Mount Sumeru, and Mount Sumeru was the size of a dustmote in the Dharma Realm. But when you reach the point of the 'true appearance which has no appearance,' Mount Sumeru is contained within your Dharma body. You now contain Mount Sumeru. Isn't this wonderful? You contain absolutely everything; everything in the universe is contained within your nature, and you understand everything. The true mark of impartial bowing is an inconceivable state. If you can reach this state while bowing to the Buddha, can you then explain all of its wonderful aspects? No, they are ineffable." (UW 19-23)

☞ **full prostration, worship, paying homage, making obeisance**

☞ **faith**

B

Brahma Net Sutra 梵網經

There are two sutras by this title: **a)** a Theravada text that explains the moral precepts and then lists the sixty-two deviant views, and **b)** a Mahayana text, which explains the ten major and forty-eight minor precepts of the Bodhisattva.

net of purity, perfect net

moral precepts, Bodhisattva

Budai 〈Venerable〉 〈6th cent. C.E.〉 布袋《和尚》

the cloth sack monk of the liang dynasty

"The Master was from Fenghua in Mingzhou, and, because of his propensity for sitting by a riverside, was known as Old Riverbank. No one knew his name, but because he always carried a cloth sack on his back, he was also known as Budai Heshang ("Cloth Sack Monk"). He always spoke strange and wonderful words, and could make anyone alternately laugh and weep. He was constantly chortling and was fond of playing with children.

"When he passed through a marketplace, he would beg for anything he saw in an attempt to get people to establish affinities with him. One day he slapped the back of a monk who was walking in front of him and said, 'Give me a coin.'

"The monk replied, 'Tell me the Way, and I'll give it.'

"The Master set down his cloth bag and stood with his hands firmly planted on his hips.

"Another time the monk Baofu asked, 'What is the great meaning of the Buddhadharma?'

"The Master then set down his cloth sack.

"Baofu replied, 'Is that all? Is there nothing bigger?'

"The Master then picked up the sack, flung it across his back, and left. Later on, at Yaolin Temple, he sat upright on a stone and spoke the following verse.

"Maitreya, truly Maitreya.
With a hundred million
transformations,
He constantly reveals himself
to the world,
But people do not understand.

"Although he then entered nirvana, he later was seen in another province, walking along with his cloth bag. His eulogy reads,

"Just as this cloth sack confuses
many men,
He begs from whomever he meets.
Whatever for?
Whenever he meets a test,
There's nothing you can do.
Don't miss the chance;
He is the future Buddha!"
(VBS #29 1-2)

Maitreya 〈Bodhisattva〉, transformation-bodies

Venerable Budai (see plate 9)

Buddha 佛

In the heavens above and on earth
below,
There is no one like the Buddha.
No one in the worlds of the ten
directions is equal to him.
I have seen everything in the world,
And nothing compares with the
Buddha. (UW 27)

Buddha means 'the awakened or enlightened one.' It is a title which is applied to those who have reached perfect enlightenment (☞ANUTTARA-SAMYAK-SAMBODHI) and who have perfect wisdom and universal compassion. The Buddha of the present historical period is known as the Buddha ☞ŚĀKYAMUNI. There were also Buddhas prior to his time; there were and are Buddhas in other ☞WORLD SYSTEMS; and there will be Buddhas in the future both in our world system and in others.

"Small Vehicle Buddhism (☞MAHAYANA AND HINAYANA COMPARED) only recognizes one Buddha, Śākyamuni [in the historical period], and does not acknowledge other Buddhas in the world systems of the other directions [but they do recognize Buddhas of the past]....Is it true that there are no other Buddhas since they say that there are none? No. If they recognize the other Buddhas throughout the ten directions, then those Buddhas exist, but if they do not recognize those Buddhas, those Buddhas nonetheless still exist. The Buddhas of the ten directions are one with Śākyamuni Buddha, and so it is said, 'The Buddhas of the ten directions and the three periods of time share a single Dharma body.'" (UW Ch40 25-26)

"Who is the Buddha? The Buddha is the Greatly Enlightened One. His great enlightenment is an awakening concerning all things, without a single bit of confusion. A true Buddha is without karmic obstacles and has transcended emotional responses. Living beings, on the other hand, are attached to emotions and worldly love." (AS 2) "You still don't know who the Buddha is? I will tell you. You are the Buddha. 'Then why don't I know it?' you ask. Your not knowing is just the Buddha. But this is not to say that you have already become a Buddha. You are as yet an unrealized Buddha. You should understand that the Buddha became a Buddha from the level of being an ordinary person. Living beings have the ability to cultivate and become Buddhas. A Buddha is an Enlightened One; therefore, when a human being becomes

Entering the womb (see plate 10)

fully enlightened, he will be a Buddha too." (AS 4-5)

"When someone heard it said that the Buddha is living beings and living beings are the Buddha, he was really delighted. After that, he told everyone to call him Buddha. 'Don't call me by my name, just call me Buddha, because living beings are Buddhas!' Then some people started calling him 'Buddha,' but because there were others who did not, he became irate and said, 'I told you to call me Buddha. Why aren't you calling me Buddha? I'm going to give you a hard time!' Then someone said to him, 'The Buddha is kind. In his heart there is compassion for all living beings; he doesn't get angry or afflicted. If you were a Buddha, you would not have a temper or any afflictions. Because you still have a temper and afflictions, you are still an ordinary living being.'" (FAS Ch7 33)

Eight Stages of the Path of Buddhas

In all world systems the careers of all Buddhas share the following eight stages:

1 Descending from the Tuṣita Heaven
2 Entering the womb
3 Emerging from the womb
4 Leaving the home-life
5 Subduing Māra
6 Becoming a Buddha
7 Turning the Great Dharma Wheel
8 Entering nirvana

In meditation (see plates 11 & 12)

"Śākyamuni Buddha,

"For three *asaṃkhyeya kalpas*
cultivated blessings and wisdom,
For a hundred *kalpas* perfected
marks and characteristics.

"It took him that long in the past so that in this life he could 'at midnight see a bright star and awaken to the Way.' If he hadn't cultivated before, he wouldn't have been able to do it." (FAS-PII(1) 234-5)

Turning the Dharma Wheel (see plates 13 & 14)

Awakened One, Fully Enlightened One

enlightenment, bodhi, Śākyamuni ⟨Buddha⟩, Ten Titles of a Buddha

Buddhaland 佛土

A Buddhaland is a land in which a Buddha dwells. In the Buddhist sutras many worlds are discussed, some with Buddhas and some without. Those that have Buddhas are Buddhalands. For example, the Buddhaland where our historical Buddha Śākyamuni lived is our own world, which in Buddhism is called the Saha World. The Buddhaland of Buddha Amitābha is called the Land of Ultimate Bliss.

Buddha-field

pure land, Amitābha ⟨Buddha⟩

Buddha-nature 佛性

When the Buddha Śākyamuni first realized Buddhahood, he proclaimed:

> How amazing! How amazing! How amazing! All living beings have the Buddha-nature; all can become Buddhas. Only because of their polluted thinking and attachments do they fail to realize this and to obtain certification.

The Buddha-nature is the innate, inherent potential to become a Buddha that resides in the mind of every living being.

> Buddha-nature in all beings dwells permanent and unalterable, throughout all rebirth, ever ready to develop itself as soon as the opportunity arises. (*Nirvana Sutra* Ch. 26, quoted Demieville, ed. *Hôbôgirin* II, 185ff, EB "Buddha-Nature")

> The supreme, pure bright mind originally pervades the Dharma Realm. It is not something obtained from anyone else. Why, then, labor and toil with marrow and joint to cultivate and be certified? This is to be like the person who has a wish-fulfilling pearl sewn in his clothing without realizing it. Thus he roams abroad in a state of poverty, begging for food and always on the move. Although he is indeed destitute, the pearl is never lost. Suddenly a wise person shows him the pearl: all his wishes are fulfilled, he obtains great wealth, and he realizes that the pearl did not come from somewhere outside. (SS IV 108-111)

"Showing him the pearl in his clothing represents pointing out to him his inherent Buddha-nature." (SS IV 111)

☞ **Buddha, Daosheng ⟨Venerable⟩**

Buddha-vehicle 佛乘

☞ **Three Vehicles**

Buddhism/Buddhadharma 佛教/ 佛法

> The Buddhadharma is subtle,
> wondrous, and difficult to
> measure.
> No words or speech can express it.
> Neither combined nor
> uncombined,
> It is still and quiet in nature,
> without any marks.
> (FAS Ch9 93)

> The Buddhadharma is here
> in the world:
> Enlightenment is not beyond
> the world.
> To look for *bodhi* beyond the world
> Is like looking for a hare with horns.
> (PS 121)

Buddhists do not call the teachings of the Buddha, which they follow, Buddhism; they call them the Buddhadharma, the Dharma of the Buddhas.

"Buddhism is a religion that teaches people to end birth and death, whereas other religions teach people to undergo birth and death. The difference between them is that of being able to ultimately end birth and death as opposed to ultimately not being able to, and so undergoing birth and death." (FAS-PII 128)

"What is the basic, fundamental character of Buddhism? It is simply instruction for people in how to recognize truth, how to eliminate selfishness and establish what is public, how to have a public-spirited, unselfish attitude, not setting up barriers of nations and lands, races or clans, and how not to make distinctions of self and others.

> "All under heaven is one family,
> And the ten thousand Buddhas
> are a single person." (FAS-PII 129)

"Buddhism is the teaching within the minds of all living beings. And so Buddhism can be called the Buddha's teaching or it can be called no teaching at all. Buddhism simply records what practices the Buddha engaged in to become enlightened. The Buddha didn't have the idea that he wanted to establish a religion. He is fundamentally one with all living beings. If he had wanted to establish a 'Buddhism,' wouldn't that have been setting himself apart from living beings? The Buddha said that the mind, the Buddha, and living beings are one, and undifferentiated. If he had professed to be teaching a 'Buddhism,' then there would also be non-Buddhism, and so it would be separate from other religions. However, Buddhism includes everything. Every religion is in Buddhism—Protestantism, Catholicism, Judaism, Islam, and all the others. Why? The Buddha said, 'All living beings have the Buddha-nature; all can become Buddhas.'

"No matter what religion you are, aren't you a living being? Even if you protest that you are a heavenly spirit, heavenly lord, or heavenly demon, you are still a living being. And so I say that whether you are Buddhist or not, I count you as part of Buddhism." (VBS #128 (January 1981) 2)

the law/methods of the fully awakened ones

☞ **Buddha, Dharma/dharma**

Buddhist sects 宗派

"Buddhism has neither school nor sect: no Mahayana, no Hinayana, no Caodong [Jap. Soto], Linji [Jap. Rinzai], Yunmen [Jap. Ummon], Fayan [Jap. Hogen], or Weiyang [Jap. Igyo] sect. There is no Chan [Jap. Zen], Teaching, Vinaya, Esoteric, or Pure Land School. The Buddha spoke of the ☞DHARMA REALM; he did not divide Buddhism into Chinese, Japanese, Thai, or Sri Lankan. Those divisions were all made by men who came after the Buddha who had nothing better to do than go out and look for trouble. Every school is a door, and where there was a unity, they created divisions, made walls and windows in the undivided, universal Buddhadharma. In the undivided Buddhadharma they built partitions by saying, 'My door is better than your window! I am from the Soto sect, the very best; the Buddhadharma is here.'

"'My window is better than your door!' some replied. 'Rinzai Zen is the highest. The Buddhadharma is here.' People are just people and they make trouble by bickering over who is number one and who is number two. What a headache! 'My window is not the same as yours,' each cries, showing off his spiritual powers and insisting that he is the best.

"Within the Buddhadharma, where is good and where is bad? The good comes from the bad, and the bad comes from the good. Don't split things up into high and low. The ☞VAJRA [DIAMOND] SUTRA says, 'This Dharma is level and equal with nothing above or below.' The Great Master the Sixth Patriarch said, 'If I said I had a Dharma to give people, I would be lying to you.' The Dharma absolutely cannot be spoken." (VBS #12 (March 1971) 32)

"Before the Buddha came into the world, there was no Buddhism. After the Buddha appeared, Buddhism came into being, but there was not as yet any division into sects or schools. Sectarianism is a limited view, a view of small scope, and cannot represent Buddhism in its entirety. The complete substance of Buddhism, the totality, admits no such divisions. When you divide the totality of Buddhism into sects and schools, you merely split it into fragments. In order to understand Budddhism in its totality, one must eliminate views of sects and schools and return to original and schools and return to original Buddhism. One must return to the root and go back to the source." (Tripiṭaka Master Hsuan Hua, "Back to the Source," *Shambala Review*, v. 5, nos. 1-2, Winter, 1976, 26)

☞ **Buddhist schools/lineages/houses, sectarian divisions**

☞ **Mahayana and Hinayana Compared, Five Types of Buddhist Study and Practice**

C

causation 因緣

Bodhisattvas fear the cause,
  not its result;
Living beings fear the result,
  not its cause.
(Ven. Master Hua)

Deep is this doctrine of events as rising from causes, and it looks deep too. It is through not understanding this doctrine, through not penetrating it, that this generation has become a tangled skein, a matted ball of thread, like to muñja-grass and rushes, unable to overpass the doom of the Waste, the Woeful Way, the Downfall, the Constant Round [of transmigration]. (*Dialogues of the Buddha* II 50)

Basic Teachings about Cause and Effect

"A cause refers to the cause you plant, from which you reap a corresponding result. If you plant a good cause, you will get a good result. And if you plant a bad cause, you will obtain a bad result....You plant a certain cause, myriad conditions assemble, and a certain retribution or result is brought about." (EDR VI 215)

Cause and effect "are not a matter of belief or disbelief. If you believe in it, there is such a thing as cause and effect; if you do not believe in it, cause and effect operate just the same. For example, if you go punch someone, you will certainly get hit back. Your initial punch is the cause, and your being beaten in return is the effect...." (SPV 128)

"The cause is the seed. What contributes to its growth is the conditions. Planting a seed in the ground is a cause. Conditions are the aiding factors which contribute to the growth—soil, water, sunlight, and other such things...." (SS II 112)

Causes and Effects Operate Over Many Lifetimes

From causes made in lives gone by
  comes your present life.
Results you'll get in lives to come
  arise from this life's deeds. (AS 30)

The Interwoven Net of Karmic Responses of Cause and Effect

"The Dharma Realm is not large; a mote of dust is not small. Why? All is one, and one is all. Yet there is something more wonderful, subtle, and difficult to believe than even this: the net-like interweaving of karmic responses and the wheel-like spinning of cause and effect.

"For example, the karmic influences between countries are interwoven; the causes and effects of their mutual debts and repayments compel them to ceaseless wars.

It becomes difficult to stop the murders and massacres which increase endlessly until the final destruction of the countries and the annihilation of all races when everything is eradicated and brought to an end. There is a saying, 'Plant good causes, reap good results; plant bad causes, reap bad results.' How true it is!

"There is also this interweaving of karmic influences as well as the causes and effects of mutual debts and repayments between families. When there is kindness, there is harmony, but when enmity arises there is revenge. The participants do not understand and continue to rail at each other for life. Who awakens from this?

"A sutra says, 'Even though a hundred thousand *kalpas* pass, karma which is created does not perish. When causes and conditions come together, retribution will still be personally undergone.' In all our actions, how can we possibly not be cautious and attentive, 'as if standing on the edge of a deep abyss, as if treading on thin ice!'" (WM 41 rev.)

The Buddha gave this advice in *The Buddha Speaks the Sutra of Cause and Effect in the Three Periods of Time*:

> Wealth and dignity come from one's destiny
> From causes planted in lives past.
> People who hold to this simple principle
> Will reap good fortune in future lives.
>
> Kind men and women, listen to the causes,
> Hear and remember this sutra's reminder
> Of the causes and effects of karmic deeds
> In the past, future, and present.
> Cause and effect are no small care.
> True are my words; don't take them lightly.
>
> ....
>
> Sometimes people have plentiful goods;
> The reason, again, is quite fair.
> In the past these people gave food to the poor.
> Others don't have food or drink.
> Who can guess the reason why?
> Before those people were plagued with a fault:
> Stingy greed made them squeeze every penny.
>
> ....
>
> Enjoying blessings and justly prosperous,
> Are people who reap a fitting reward.
> In the past they helped build temples
> And saw that the Sangha had huts and shelters.
>
> ....
>
> Some have long life spans; why are they lucky?
> Liberating creatures, they ransomed lives.
> Have you seen how many suffer short life spans?
> Their wanton slaughter of beings is why.
>
> ....
>
> Most cows and horses were humans before—
> People who didn't settle their debts.
> Many former people are now pigs or dogs
> Because they injured and cheated others.
>
> ....
>
> In our myriad deeds, whatever we do,
> We reap our own rewards, it's true.
> Who can we blame for our woe in the hells?

Who can there be to blame,
but ourselves?
Don't say that cause and effect
are unseen.
Look at you, your offspring, heirs,
and grandchildren.
If you doubt the good of pure
eating and giving,
Look around and find those
enjoying fortune.
Having practiced of old, they now
harvest abundance.
To cultivate now will bring
blessings anew.

....

To know of past lives' causes,
Look at the rewards you are reaping
today.
To find out about future lives,
You need only notice what you are
doing right now.
(FHS I 24-32)

☞ causes and conditions, conditioned cause, causal conditions, connections
☞ Twelvefold Conditioned Arising, karma, rebirth

certification 證得

According to the Buddhist teachings, all those who realize ☞ENLIGHTENMENT must have their enlightenment certified by a truly enlightened master. The master looks directly into the mind of the person seeking certification to see whether all traces of attachment to self have been eliminated. This practice ensures the proper continuation of the authentic teachings of the Buddha. It also makes clear why ☞LINEAGES of enlightened masters going back to the Buddha himself are essential to living Buddhism.

Very often, particularly in the West, people think they are enlightened when they are not, or simply do not understand what is meant by enlightenment. If someone mistakenly thinks that he or she is enlightened, that precludes their making further progress toward enlightenment. They may also seriously mislead others. The requirement of certification keeps these people from damaging themselves and others because of their ignorance. Of course there are also those who deliberately mislead others for their own selfish ends.

☞ verification
☞ enlightenment, lineage, Chan School

Changren 〈Chan Master〉 〈fl. early 20th cent.〉 常仁《禪師》

"The Venerable Changren was born near the end of the Qing Dynasty in the city of Turin, Jilin province, China. His family name was Wang. Although he had no formal schooling, he was endowed with an understanding of the principles of filiality and practiced the filial act of bowing to his parents every morning and evening. Both his parents passed away when he was twenty-eight years old, and at that time he began a six-year vigil beside their graves. During that period of time, he lived in a small grass hut and ate only uncooked rice or noodles. During the final three years of that time, he also practiced not speaking, remaining completely silent.

"The Venerable Changren had intended to travel to the Thousand Mountain Range for further cultivation after observing his six-year mourning period. But one day toward the end of that time, an old monk (who had been alive since the Ming dynasty) appeared at the door to his hut. In his mind the Venerable Changren asked the monk, 'Where has the Honorable One come from?'

"The monk answered aloud, 'I have come from Thousand Mountain Range especially for your sake. Your Dharma affinities lie not with the Thousand Mountain Range but with those in Shuangcheng ("Twin Cities").' After communicating this message, he went out the door and disappeared.

Chan Master Changren (center)

"On the day that the Venerable Changren came out of mourning, people from forty-eight villages in the surrounding area gathered to celebrate. They formed an organization dedicated to protecting the Triple Jewel. It was this group that built Three Conditions Monastery as an everlasting Way-place. Women and children, as well as high public officials, received his teaching and took refuge with the Triple Jewel under him.

"In 1949, at Beijing's Nanhua Monastery, at the age of seventy-two, the Venerable One manifested the stillness. Some of the many miraculous events that occurred in response to his cultivation are described in detail in the book *Water and Mirror Reflecting Heaven* (WM).

"A verse in praise says:

Endowed with natural genuineness,
He returned to the unvarnished truth.
Unable to read a single word,
He still, on his own, reached the myriad Dharmas.
With utmost virtue and filial piety,
He was righteous and humane.
He was just like the Big Dipper,
Which all the stars salute.

"Another verse says:

Very silent, of few words, he was slow to speak.
But when it came to practice, he let no chance slip by.
Sincere and earnest to the utmost, he was happy with simple fare.
His wholehearted filial reverence delighted his parents and elders.
For six years he practiced pure conduct
In a hut by his parents' graves.
His reputation continues on,
Seeking those who know his sound.
His tremendous virtue transforms beings who hear of him.
Once the faithful hear his Dharma, they are ever mindful of it.

(VBS #193 (June 1986) 12, 19)

Changzhi ⟨Chan Master⟩ ⟨fl. early 20th cent.⟩ 常智《禪師》

"The Master, whose family name was Meng, was a native of Shuangcheng County ('Twin Cities') in Manchuria. Although he never received a formal education, he was loyal, generous, unassuming, and honest. The Master was a farmer, and he treated people kindly and handled affairs in a public and fair manner. He believed in taking a loss, and so when employed to work, he always did more work but took less pay than was usual. His was the spirit of renouncing oneself for the sake of others.

"While Great Master ☞CHANGREN was observing the filial practice of living in a hut by one's parent's grave, the Master brought forth the resolve to protect his Dharma. During the first three years, he brought food to Master Changren every day, dauntless even in the wind and rain. During the final three years, Master Changren ate only uncooked rice flour, and Master Changzhi also provided him with that.

"When he was in his forties, the Master, inspired by Master Changren, decided to leave the home-life. His wife and children grasped his feet and wept bitterly, refusing to let him go. The Master said, 'If you do not let go of me now, by tomorrow you will be carrying me out in a coffin.' At that point, they had no other choice but to release him.

"He then left the home-life under Elder Master Xiuyun. He specialized in cultivating the Pure Land practice of reciting the Buddha's name. Later, he entered seclusion in the house of Layman Ran Yanming. He understood his own mind and saw his own nature. When he came out of seclusion, his wisdom was bright and apparent. He had unimpeded eloquence, and learned discourses would spontaneously flow from his tongue. The educated people of his time were astonished by his wisdom, and all admitted that they were not his equals. The Master departed while reciting the Buddha's name.

"A verse in praise says:

"Loyal, kind, and unassuming,
He had a sincere nature.
With fervor he practiced charity,
And labored in the fields and
gardens.
Earnestly he toiled, taking only half
the normal salary.
Thrifty and sparing towards
himself,
He was generous to others.
He found true happiness in helping
others succeed.
Supporting the filial one, he built a
shack for him.
Resolutely, he left the home-life
without any impediment,
Abruptly renouncing wearisome
defilements, love, and desire."
(VBS #204 (May 1987) 7)

Chan School 禪宗

The Dharma banner is raised;
The School's purport is established.
The Buddha very clearly directed
that it was to be at Cao Creek.
With Kāśyapa, the first, began the
transmission of the lamp.
Twenty-eight generations were
recorded in India.
The Dharma flowed east
and entered this land (China).
Bodhidharma was the first
Patriarch.
The robe was transmitted to the
sixth generation,
As all the world has heard.
How could one count the people
Who have realized the Way since
then?
(SE 56-60)

Chan is an abbreviation of *chan-na*; the Chinese characters sounded slightly different in the past and were used to represent the sound of the Sanskrit word ☞ DHYĀNA. The general meaning of *dhyāna* is meditation. In the Chan School the practice of meditation is foremost. The Japanese pronounce the character for *chan* as 'Zen.'

"The Chan School is foremost among the Five Great Schools of Buddhism [☞ FIVE TYPES OF BUDDHIST STUDY AND PRACTICE] in that it transmits the Buddha's Mind Seal, pointing directly to the mind so that one sees one's nature and becomes a Buddha. When the Patriarch ☞ BODHIDHARMA came from India, he widely propagated this method. At that time the practitioners of Buddhism were still very enamored of the language of ☞PRAJÑĀ, exerting their efforts in composition and phrasing, vying to outdo one another. Even in lecturing on the sutras they argued over each other's strong and weak points, and in speaking Dharma they would praise themselves and deprecate others. Different schools were set up, and doing battle with words was the mode of the times. Some resorted to individualism, and in an attempt to be unique, they set up theories that were distinctly different from the mainstream, and they perfected the art of unobstructed and clever debate. People wrote books and set up doctrines, disparaging others while promoting themselves. In this way they forsook what was fundamental and pursued superficialities; the theories of teaching schools flourished widely.

"[The four main enlightened teachers in China just prior to the introduction of the Chan lineage were the Venerable Daosheng, Vinaya Master Daoxuan, the Great Master ☞ZHIYI, and the Venerable Daoyuan. Each taught meditation in the context of the teachings of his own school.] When the Venerable ☞DAOSHENG was slandered, he retreated to Tiger Mountain and spoke Dharma to the rocks. From this came the saying that even 'insentient rocks nodded their heads in agreement.' The Vinaya Master Daoxuan hid his tracks on Zhongnan Mountain, where he enjoyed the food-offerings of the gods. The Great Master Zhizhe ("Wise One") [☞ZHIYI (VENERABLE)] proclaimed the Teachings, and the Master of Lu Mountain (Ven. Daoyuan) propagated the Pure Land method. Those to whom their teachings were transmitted held them in esteem, yet the scholars were confused by them. Everybody had a different opinion, and people were at a loss as to which way to follow. Standing perplexed at the crossroads, one didn't know which way to turn. Gazing out at the vast ocean of different teachings, one could only heave a big sigh.

"In light of such circumstances, the First Patriarch Bodhidharma made amends for such biased teachings and patched up the flaws. His compassionate instructions were apart from speech; his teachings were not imparted through words. He taught that this mind of ours is none other than the Buddha, that the precious pearl hidden within our robe is not something obtained from outside. One only needs to concentrate one's energy and refine one's mind to a single focus, then:

> One day suddenly all connects right through, and then the myriad substances are reached everywhere, whether external or internal, fine or coarse. The great functioning of the entire substance of the enlightened mind is nowhere without clarity.

One becomes open to the vast and ultimate enlightenment, returns to the source and plumbs the origin. At this time one can appreciate the subtlety behind this interchange: the World Honored One held up a flower, and ☞MAHĀKĀŚYAPA, the Golden-Hued Ascetic, smiled: originally it was like this!

"This method is one in which the mind seals the mind, a transmission [☞DHARMA-TRANSMISSION] outside of the teachings. One takes one's own nature across. And after one has made one's way across the river (of afflictions), one leaves the raft (of Dharma) behind. How can there be anything else but this?" (WM 70-71)

"As to the Dharma of our sect, when the Buddha ascended to his seat for the last time, he held up and showed to the assembly a golden flower of sandalwood, offered to him by the king of the eighteen Brahmalokas (*mahābrahmā devarājā*). All men and ☞GODS (*devas*) who were present did not understand the Buddha's (meaning). Only Mahākāśyapa (acknowledged it with a) broad smile. Thereupon the World Honored One declared to him: 'I have the treasure of the correct Dharma eye, nirvana's wonderful mind and the formless Reality which I now transmit to you.' This was the transmission outside the teaching, which did not make use of scriptures and was the unsurpassed Dharma-door of direct realization.

"Those who came afterwards got confused about it and (wrongly) called it Chan (*dhyāna* in Sanskrit and Zen in Japanese). We should know that over twenty kinds of Chan are enumerated in the *Mahāprajñāpāramitā Sutra*, but none of them is the final one.

"The Chan of our sect does not set up (progressive) stages and is, therefore, the unsurpassed one. (Its aim) is the direct realization leading to the perception of the (self-)nature and attainment of Buddhahood. Therefore, it has nothing to do with the sitting or not sitting in meditation during a Chan week. However, on account of living beings' dull roots and due to their numerous false thoughts, ancient masters devised expediencies to guide them. Since the time of Mahākāśyapa up to now, there have been sixty to seventy generations. In the Tang and Song dynasties (619-1278), the Chan sect spread to every part of the country, and how it prospered at the time! At present it has reached the bottom of its decadence (and) only those monasteries like Jinshan, Gaomin and Baoguan can still manage to present some appearance. This is why men of outstanding ability are now so rarely found and even the holding of Chan weeks has only a name but lacks its spirit." (Luk, tr. "Master Hsu Yun's Discourses and Dharma Words," *Ch'an and Zen Teachings*, Series One, 49-50)

"One sits (in meditation) to cultivate the Dharma of Chan inquiry in order not to have any thoughts....That which is called the Buddha is not even a single thought arising. But can you go without having a single thought arise? As you sit there, you think of all sorts of things you don't ordinarily think of, and a lot of long-forgotten circumstances that suddenly pop up again in your mind....Is that not having a single thought arise? Of course not. How do you do it? There is no way. There is no way to keep a single thought from arising—but you can keep a single thought from being destroyed. And if you prevent its destruction, you'll keep it from arising.... For example, in the one thought, 'Who is mindful of the Buddha?' you can keep the 'Who?' going nonstop. 'Who?' This is searching for the 'Who,' not reciting 'Who?' As long as you keep searching, that single thought isn't destroyed, and therefore it won't arise. A single thought not arising is the Buddha. That's the doctrine of the Chan School. If you can be such that not a single thought is produced or destroyed, then the light of your wisdom will appear." (LY II 15)

☞ **lineage, Five Types of Buddhist Study and Practice—Meditation, meditation, Mahākāśyapa, Bodhidharma**

City of Ten Thousand Buddhas 萬佛城

☞ **Sagely City of Ten Thousand Buddhas**

The entrance to the Sagely City of Ten Thousand Buddhas (see plate 41)

compassion 慈悲

Three Kinds of Compassion

An Attitude of Loving Compassion

"Average persons love and sympathize with those close to them, but not with strangers. Seeing relatives or friends in distress, they exhaust their strength to help them, but when strangers are suffering, they pay no heed to them. Having compassion for those you love is called an attitude of loving compassion.

"There is as well an attitude of loving compassion that extends to those of the same species, but not to those of other species. For example, not only do people have no compassion for animals such as cattle, pigs, chicken, geese, or ducks, but they even go so far as to eat animals' flesh. They snatch away animals' lives in order to nourish their own. This is not a true attitude of loving compassion. Fortunately, people rarely eat each other. They may eat pork, mutton, beef, chicken, duck, and fish, but they don't catch, kill, and eat each other, and so they are a bit better off than animals that turn on members of their own species for food. People may not eat each other, but they certainly have no true attitude of loving compassion towards animals.

Compassion through Understanding Conditioned Dharmas

"Those of the Small Vehicle have compassion which comes from understanding conditioned dharmas as well as the attitude of loving compassion discussed above. They contemplate all dharmas as arising from causes and conditions, and they know that:

> Causes and conditions
> have no nature;
> Their very substance
> is emptiness.

Contemplating the emptiness of conditioned dharmas, they compassionately teach and transform living beings without being attached to the teaching and transforming. They know that everything is empty.

Great Compassion through Understanding the Identical Substance of All Beings

"Buddhas and Bodhisattvas have yet another kind of compassion. The Buddha's Dharma body pervades all places, and so the Buddhas and Bodhisattvas are of one substance with all beings; the Buddha's heart and nature are all pervasive, and all beings are contained within it. We are living beings within the Buddha's heart, and he is the Buddha within our hearts. Our hearts and the Buddha's are the same, everywhere throughout the ten directions—north, east, south, west, the intermediary directions, above, and below. Therefore, the Buddha and living beings are of the same substance, without distinction. This is called the Great Compassion." (AS 7-8)

✍ **kindness, friendliness, benevolence, loving-kindness, love, sympathy**

☞ **love, Four Unlimited Aspects of Mind**

Consciousness-Only School 唯識宗

The starting point of the Consciousness-Only School is that everything is created from the mind as "consciousness-only." Everything, from birth and death to the cause of attaining nirvana, is based upon the coming into being and the ceasing to be of consciousness, that is, of distinctions in the mind. Consciousness-Only doctrine is characterized by its extensive and sophisticated inquiry into the characteristics of dharmas. For if we can distinguish what is real from what is unreal, if we can distinguish what is distinction-making consciousness and not mistake it for the originally clear, pure, bright enlightened mind, then we can quickly leave the former and dwell in the latter. Chan Master Hanshan Deqing (1546-1623 C.E.) has said, "When Consciousness-Only was made known to them (i.e., those of the Hinayana vehicles), they knew that [all dharmas] had no existence independent from their own minds. If one does not see the mind with the mind, then no characteristic can be got at. Therefore, in developing the spiritual skill necessary for meditative inquiry, people are taught to look into what is apart from heart, mind, and consciousness and to seek for what is apart from the states of unreal (polluted) thinking."

The founder of the Consciousness-Only School was the Bodhisattva Maitreya, who transmitted its teaching to the Venerable Asaṅga. The school was spread in China primarily because of the efforts of Tripiṭaka Master Xuanzang.

✍ **mere consciousness, ideation only**
☞ **Maitreya, Asaṅga, Vasubandhu, Xuanzang, One Hundred Dharmas**

cosmology 宇宙論

The Buddha proclaimed that on the highest level of understanding the entire cosmos is pure Mind. On the ordinary level of understanding, he painted a picture of a cosmos filled with countless ☞WORLD SYSTEMS with countless planets filled with living beings of every sort. Our particular world system is neither unique nor central in any way. Other world systems also have their Buddhas, who also teach the path to enlightenment.

The ☞FLOWER ADORNMENT *(Avataṃsaka)* SUTRA describes the universe as consisting of an infinitely large lotus-flower in which our world occupies the thirteenth tier. The lotus is suspended on various oceans of primal mind-energy forces called Great Elements.

Our particular world system, as is the case with all world systems, can be described in both 'horizontal' and 'vertical' directions. The 'horizontal' refers to its layout in space, while the 'vertical' dimension refers to the levels of consciousness of the various types of beings who inhabit it.

The center of our world is Mount Sumeru, which is surrounded by four great 'continents.' Earth is located in the southern continent, named Jambudvīpa. The continents are surrounded by seas and rings of iron mountains.

Within the Sahā world are ☞SIX PATHS OF REBIRTH, that is, six different types of living beings, each with its own distinctive kind of karma. The beings are generally categorized according to which of the ☞THREE WORLDS they abide in. The Three Worlds are the world of desire, the world of form, and the formless world. [See the chart under the entry THREE WORLDS.]

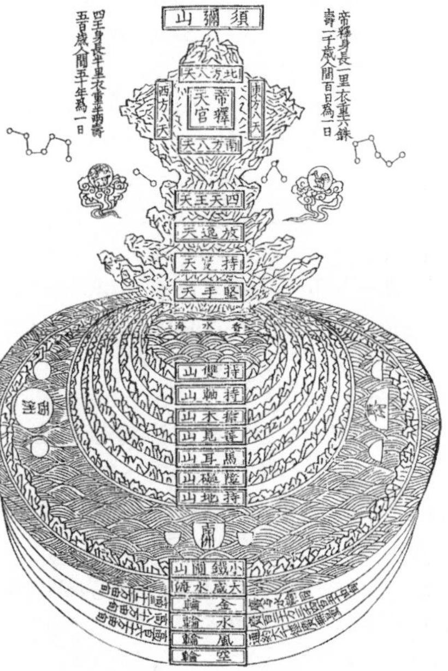

Mount Sumeru rising above the seas

☞ **Three Worlds, Six Paths of Rebirth, world systems, gods, ghosts, asura, Six Desire Heavens, Four Dhyānas, Four Formless Realms, creation, time**

C

creation ⟨world and humans⟩ 生

There is no creator and
There are no creations.
From karma and thoughts alone
Do things come to be.
How do we know this?
Because other than this,
There is nothing at all.
(FAS Ch14)

The Creation of the World

The Buddha taught that there is no creator god, and he never indicated that there was any beginning to the universe. Individual world systems do go through cycles of coming into being, developing, decaying and disappearing; however, the cycles are the direct result of the complex net of karmic causes planted by the living beings within the world systems.

Fundamentally, the entire conditioned world as such—seen as an endless series of transformations of matter-energy-mind taking place through time—is unreal. To talk about the coming into being of something that has no reality makes little sense. Therefore, the Buddha was not concerned with the question of whether the illusions of living beings had a beginning, since the whole question of 'beginning' belongs to the realm of illusion. He taught that the primary issue is the permanent ending of those illusions, so that they no longer arise.

In the ☞ŚŪRAṄGAMA SUTRA, when talking with his disciple Ānanda about the nature of seeing, the Buddha uses the analogy of a person afflicted with glaucoma to elucidate the true nature of our experience of the world:

What is meant by the false seeing based on individual karma? Ānanda, it is just like a person in the world with glaucoma of the eye. At night he alone sees around a lamp a circular image composed of the five colors and their various combinations. What do you think? Are the colors in the circle of light that appears around the lamp at night an aspect of the lamplight, or are the colors an aspect of the seeing? Ānanda, if the colors were an aspect of the lamplight, then why wouldn't they also be seen by someone without glaucoma? Why is it only the one with glaucoma who sees the circular image? If the colors were an aspect of the seeing, the seeing would already have created the colors; then how would we account for the fact that only the person with glaucoma sees a circular image? Further, Ānanda, if the circular image existed separately from the lamp, then when the person looked around him at a folding screen, a curtain, a table, or a mat, there would be circular images around them too. If the image existed separately from the seeing, it would not be seen by the eyes. How then would the person with glaucoma see the circular image with his eyes? Therefore, you should know that the colors are actually in the lamplight, while the diseased seeing makes an image out of them. The image and the seeing of it are both due to the glaucoma. What sees the glaucoma is not diseased. Thus you should certainly not say that the colors are an aspect only of the lamplight or that they are an aspect only of the seeing, nor yet that they are not an aspect only of the lamplight or that they are not an aspect only of the seeing. It is like the second moon, which is not a substance, and yet which is not an image. Why? The observation of the second moon is brought about by pressure.

A wise person would not say that what is derived from pressure on the eyes is the moon or is not the moon, nor that it is apart from the seeing or apart from the no seeing. The same is true of the image. It is brought about by the glaucoma of the eye. Can you say now that it is an aspect only of the lamplight or an aspect only of the seeing? You cannot. Even less can you distinguish it as neither an aspect of the I am plight nor an aspect of the seeing.... Ānanda, when the living being whose false seeing is based on individual karma sees the circular image appearing around the lamp, it seems to be an external object, but in fact what is seen is brought about by the glaucoma in the eyes. The glaucoma exerts a stress on the seeing. It is not created from the colors. But what sees the glaucoma is not defective. For example, you now make use of your eyes to look at mountains, rivers, countries, and all living beings: all are brought about, since time without beginning, by the disease in your seeing. (SS II 141-150, BTTS rev. tr.)

The Creation of Humans

According to the Buddha, human beings were not created by a creator god, nor are they the result of a long process of evolution, as suggested by Darwinian and Neo-Darwinian evolutionary theory. According to the Buddha's teaching, there have always been people, though not necessarily on this planet. The appearance of physical human bodies in any particular location begins with the mental generation of "human karma." Mind, not physical body, is primary in that process. Human beings are not independent of the other forms of sentient life in the universe and can be reborn in others of the ☞ SIX PATHS OF REBIRTH. Likewise, other sentient beings can be reborn as human beings. What is ultimately real about all living beings is their ☞ BUDDHA-NATURE, and that cannot be created or destroyed.

"At the very beginning, before heaven and earth came into being, there weren't any people. There was no earth, no living beings, nor anything called a world. Basically none of those things existed at all. And then, at the outset of the *kalpa* when things were coming into being, people gradually came to exist. Ultimately, where do they come from? Some say that people evolved from monkeys. But what do the monkeys evolve from? If people evolved from monkeys, then why are there no people evolving from monkeys right now? This is really strange. People who propagate this kind of theory basically don't have any understanding. They are just trying to set up some special theory. And so there is the theory of evolution which says that people came from monkeys. Why couldn't it be the case that people evolved from mice? Or caterpillars? Why couldn't we say the mice evolved from people or that caterpillars evolved from people? In general, there can be said to be four kinds of beings—flying, swimming, walking, and plants. Those with blood and breath are called animals, and plants refers to all kinds of grasses, trees, and flowers. Where do all those four kinds of beings come from? What is their origin? Their origin is the Buddha-nature. If there was no Buddha-nature, everything would be annihilated. The Buddha-nature is the only thing that passes through ten thousand generations and all time without being destroyed. From the Buddha-nature come Bodhisattvas, Hearers, Those Enlightened to Conditions, gods, *asuras*, people, animals, ghosts, and hell-beings. Those are the beings of the ☞ TEN DHARMA REALMS, and the Ten Dharma Realms are not apart from a single thought of the mind. This single thought of the mind is just the seed of the

Buddha-nature. One true thought is just another name for the Buddha-nature." (TT 149)

Genesis of the World

There comes a time...when sooner or later this world begins to re-evolve. When this happens, beings who had deceased from the World of Radiance, usually come to life as humans. And they become made of mind, feeding on rapture, self-luminous, traversing the air, continuing in glory, and remain thus for a long, long period of time.

Now at that time, all had become one world of water, dark, and of darkness that maketh blind. No moon nor sun appeared, no stars were seen, nor constellations, neither was night manifest nor day, neither months nor half-months, neither years nor season, neither female nor male. Beings were reckoned just as beings only. And to those beings...sooner or later after a long time, earth with its savour was spread out in the waters. Even as a scum forms on the surface of boiled milky rice that is cooling, so did the earth appear. It became endowed with colour, with odor, and with taste. Even as well made ghee or pure butter, so was its colour; even as the flawless honey of the bee, so sweet was it.

Then...some being of greedy disposition said: Lo now! What will this be? and tasted the savoury earth with his finger. He thus, tasting, became suffused with the savour, and craving entered into him. And other beings, following his example, tasted the savoury earth with their finger. They thus, tasting, became suffused with the savour, a craving entered into them. Then those beings began to feast on the savoury earth, breaking off lumps of it with their hands. And from the doing thereof the self-luminance of those beings faded away. As their self-luminance faded away, the moon and the sun became manifest, months too and half-months, the seasons and the years. Thus far then...did the world evolve again.

Now those beings..., feasting on the savory earth, feeding on it, nourished by it, continued thus for a long while. And in measure as they thus fed, did their bodies become solid, and did variety in their comeliness become manifest....(Rhys Davids, tr. *Dialogues of the Buddha* III, 82-83; cf. Jones, tr. *The Mahāvastu* I, 285).

The World as Created from Mind

Take the analogy of an artist,
Who spreads colors on canvas,
Grasping in vain at their different
forms,
While the great seed has no
distinctions.

There are no colors in the great
seed,
And no great seed exists in the
colors.
Yet apart from the great seed,
There are no colors to be found.

In the mind there are no paintings,
And in a painting there is no mind.
Yet apart from the mind,
There are no paintings to be
found.

That mind that never dwells
anywhere
Is infinite and inconceivable.
It reveals all colors, each oblivious
of the others.

As an artist is unaware of his own
mind,
Yet is directed by his mind as he
paints,
So too is the nature of all dharmas.

The mind is like an artist
Who can paint the entire world.

From this the five *skandhas* arise
As well as all dharmas.

As is the mind, so too is the
Buddha;
As is the Buddha, thus also are
living beings.
Know that the Buddha and the
mind
Are both essentially infinite.

One who knows that the mind's
activities create all in the world,
Sees the Buddha and understands
his true nature.

His mind dwells not in his body;
His body resides not in his mind.
Yet he does the Buddha's work
With unprecedented ease.

To understand all Buddhas
of the three periods of time,
Contemplate the nature of the
Dharma Realm:
Everything is created from the
mind alone.
(FAS Ch20, HYSC 30:54-70)

Generation of the Mental and Physical Worlds from the Three Fine and Six Coarse Characteristics

The Buddha said, 'Pūrṇamaitrāyaṇīputra, you have asked why the mountains, the rivers, and the great earth suddenly come into being within what is pure and fundamental. Have you not often heard the Thus Come One say that the enlightenment of the nature and beginning enlightenment are both wonderful understanding?...The enlightenment that is our nature is definitely understanding; it is wrong to consider realizing enlightenment a gaining of understanding. Enlightenment is not something understood.

When an understanding is posited, it must have an object. Where there is already an object wrongly posited, a false subject comes into being. Where there is not any sameness or differentiation, what is differentiated blazes forth. What differs from what is differentiated becomes sameness, because of the difference. Once sameness and differentiation appear, then what is neither the same nor differentiated is therefore also established. Thus from the turmoil of this interaction, stress comes into being, and the stress, when prolonged, produces defilement. Internal turbidity follows, and because of it there arises the defiling stress of afflictions.

What arises is the world; what is still is empty space. Empty space is what is the same, and the world is what is differentiated. What is neither undifferentiated nor differentiated is simply all other conditioned dharmas.

When there is understanding of enlightenment, then emptiness is obscured, and they interact to produce movement. Thus there are *maṇḍalas* of wind which support the world. Once movement has arisen in emptiness, the light created by the understanding of enlightenment becomes metal which is the precious essence of earth. Thus there are *maṇḍalas* of metal that support the land. Once there is metal, which is the solidifying of the understanding within enlightenment, and wind, which is the movement within the understanding, then friction takes place between mind and metal. Thus there is the light of fire, which by nature is mutable. The brightness of metal produces a moisture, which turns to vapor under the heat of fire. Thus there are *maṇḍalas* of water which contain the worlds of the ten directions. Fire ascends; water descends. Their interaction forms a solidity. What is moist becomes the oceans; what is dry becomes the continents and islands....The varying combinations of the false interactions become seeds that are the

ENLIGHTENMENT
('wonderful understanding)

▼

(ignorance)

▼

apprehension of the 'enlightened' mind as a gaining of 'understanding' ('bright and knowing'), a distinction leading to unknowing ▸ – **MARK OF COMING INTO BEING**

▼

= false subject
MARK OF EVOLVING

≡ (illusory) object
MARK OF APPEARANCE

THREE FINE MARKS

▼

'neither sameness nor differentiation'

▼

objective form

▼

clinging to names

▼

karmic activity

▼

suffering

▼

'beyond sameness and differentiation'

sameness — differentiation

Coming into Being ▸	– **Mark of Coming into Being** ▸	Self-Verifying Division	**THREE FINE MARKS (8th consciousness)**
Stasis ▸	= **Mark of Evolving** ▸	Perceiver Division	
	≡ **Mark of Appearance** ▸	Perceived Division	
	Mark of Worldly Wisdom	(subtle delusions of the 7th consciousness)	**FIVE OF THE SIX COARSE MARKS**
	Mark of Continuation		
Change ▸	**Mark of Grasping**	(coarse delusions of the 6th consciousness)	
	Mark of Clinging to Names		
Ceasing to Be ▸	**Mark of General Karma** ▸	(creation of delusion and suffering)	

EMANATION OF DHARMAS ACCORDING TO THE ŚŪRAṄGAMA SŪTRA

causes and conditions for the continuation of the world. (SS IV 13-27, BTTS rev. tr.)

☞ **cosmology, causation, time, God, gods**

cultivation 修行

'Cultivation' refers to putting the Buddha's teachings into practice on a continued and regular basis. The word itself brings to mind the agricultural metaphor.

> You should think of yourself as being like sprouting crops, and of the ☞ GOOD AND WISE ADVISOR as a dragon king. You should think of the dharma he speaks as seasonal rain, and you should think of cultivation as the process of ripening. (EDR VII 152-153)

Cultivation refers to the nourishing of the seeds of *bodhi* by the continual practice of whatever teachings of the Buddha one has been advised to follow.

"What does it mean to cultivate? Here it refers to cultivating precepts, samadhi, and wisdom and wholesome merit and virtue. To walk the other path means to do evil deeds, to involve oneself in greed, anger, and delusion." (TT 43)

> Cultivation is like climbing
> a hundred foot pole.
> It's easy to slide down,
> but hard to climb up.
> (EDR VII 152)

Although not Buddhist in origin, the following story from the *Mencius* provides us with a wonderful image of what cultivation means:

> ***The Man of Song***
>
> Among the men of Song there was someone who was sorry that his plants did not grow and pulled them higher. Having returned in a dull hurry, he said to his household, 'Today I am really tired! I have helped the plants grow!' His son went running to see them. The plants had withered.
>
> In the world those who do not help the plants grow are few indeed! Those who neglect the plants, considering helping them to be of no use, are those who do not weed the plants. Those who help them grow are those who pull the plants higher. Their help is not merely not beneficial, it is positively harmful! (*Mencius*, Bk II, Pt. I, Ch. 11)

☞ **practice, self-cultivation**

☞ **meditation, Eightfold Path**

Daosheng ⟨Venerable⟩ ⟨360-434 C.E.⟩ 道生《法師》

One of the foremost disciples of the Venerable Huiyuan, the Venerable Daosheng was a great enlightened master who is best known for his propagation of the teachings of the Mahayana and particularly the doctrine of the universality of the Buddha-nature, even in *icchantikas* ['those of insufficient faith'].

"At the time when only the first part of [the *Nirvana*] *Sutra* had been translated into Chinese, Dharma Master Daosheng was lecturing on it in Suzhou Province in China. When he came to the passage that said that *icchantikas* lack the Buddha-nature, he didn't explain it that way, but he said instead that they have the Buddha-nature. His reasoning went like this:

"'Why is it that *icchantikas* have the Buddha-nature? It is because all living beings have the Buddha-nature, and although *icchantikas* have insufficient faith, they are living beings. Therefore, how can one say they lack the Buddha-nature?'

"He lectured on the question in a way opposite to the reading in the first half of the sutra, which outraged the other Dharma Masters of his time. They protested, 'That's the talk of demon kings! The sutra that the Buddha spoke plainly says that *icchantikas* don't have the Buddha-nature, yet he says they do. That's really messed up.' No one would have anything to do with him after that, and when he lectured on the sutras, no one came. The Dharma Masters ganged up and told all the disciples and good people of faith, 'If Daosheng lectures, don't go. Anyone who listens to his sutra lectures will fall into the hells.'

Since the whole reason the good men and women of faith were studying the Buddhadharma was to avoid falling into the hells, when they heard they would fall into the hells if they went to Dharma Master Daosheng's sutra lectures, they didn't dare go to listen.

"Dharma Master Daosheng was not one to remain silent, but was determined to deliver sutra lectures. He said, 'Okay, you won't come to listen? Then I'll go lecture to the rocks and see what they do.' And so he went off to Huqiu [Tiger] Mountain and collected several hundred rocks from all over the area. He set them up in front of him and said, 'I invite you to a sutra lecture. Be good rocks and sit there nice and still.' It turned out that the rocks were very obedient. They didn't run off or roll away, but stayed right where he put them. When he got to the passage about *icchantikas* not having the Buddha-nature, he said, 'That isn't correct. *Icchantikas* have the Buddha-nature too. "Those with and without sentience identically perfect the wisdom of all modes." *Icchantikas* will become Buddhas too. I SAID *ICCHANTIKAS* DO HAVE THE BUDDHA-NATURE! DO YOU AGREE?'

"What do you think the rocks did then? Probably, although they were supposed to enter samadhi, they had not quite gotten into it and had not yet had a chance to fall asleep. When the rocks heard the Dharma Master ask that question, they all jumped to attention and started moving. This dull rock nodded its head, and that dull stone nodded its head. They all nodded in agreement, bumping into each other, because each would hit the rock in front of it.

"Someone might wonder who verified that really happened. It is not something that the Venerable Daosheng said himself. It was said by those who opposed him. How did they end up saying such a thing? The reason people were against him in the first place was that he lectured too well. His eloquence was unobstructed, as if lotuses were blooming on his tongue.

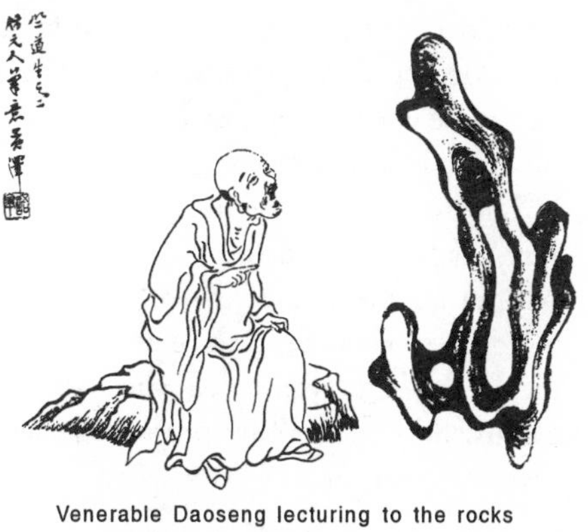

Venerable Daoseng lecturing to the rocks

Almost everyone was jealous of the way he could come up with explanations that never occurred to anyone else, and of how he could make the sutras come alive, as it were. That is the way people are. If someone is better than they are, they get jealous, and if they are better than someone else, they look down on that person. Living beings have that kind of knowledge and outlook. And so the people of his time formed a faction in opposition to Dharma Master Daosheng. When he went to the mountains to lecture to the rocks, some of them followed him on the sly to see what he was doing. Then, when he lectured there and all the rocks began to move, nodding their heads—without being blown by the wind or splashed by the rain—the Dharma Masters who were spying on him, those who believed in him and even those who were against him, all saw what occurred. That is the origin of the saying,

> When the Venerable Daosheng
> spoke the Dharma,
> Dull rocks nodded their heads.

"Afterwards, when the *Nirvana Sutra* had been fully translated, it turned out that the sutra itself says that *icchantikas* also have the Buddha-nature. That proved that Dharma Master Daosheng had fully understood the doctrine without having seen the entire sutra; it showed the extent of his wisdom and insight. After this incident, even those who had opposed him no longer did so and came to bow to him.

"The meaning of the dull rocks nodding their heads is that those who had no faith in him were the dull rocks—otherwise how could they have failed to believe in him? Yet, in the end, even those who had been jealous and opposed him prostrated themselves before him." (WM 71-73)

☞ **Nirvana Sutra, Buddha-nature**

demons 魔

> If one loses the Bodhi resolve, then even though one cultivates all good roots, one is still engaging in demonic deeds. (FAS Ch38(6))

> Deviant views and the three 'poisons' are the demon king. (PS 307)

> When one's inner fire departs,
> A demon takes possession.
> (Chinese saying)

In Buddhism the word translated as 'demon' is the Sanskrit *māra*, which means 'bringer of death.' The Chinese translation ***mo*** is often explained as meaning ***mo***, another character with the same sound which means 'to rub or polish.' Therefore, it has been said:

> Demons come to polish the Way,
> Those on the True Way
> have to endure demons.
> The more you get polished,
> the brighter you get;
> You'll be polished until you're like
> the autumn moon,
> Which illumines all the demon
> hordes in space.
> When the demon hordes disperse,
> The original Buddha manifests.
> (TT 66)

There are Four Kinds of Demons: **1)** demons which are afflictions, **2)** demons which are illnesses, **3)** the demon of death, and **4)** heavenly demons. The first three can be said to be internal demons and the fourth, external demons.

The head of the heavenly demons is Māra the Evil One, who rules over the Sixth Desire Heaven (☞ SIX DESIRE HEAVENS). The demons of that heaven derive their bliss from preying on the energies of other beings. They are particularly threatened by those who practice on the spiritual pathways that reach beyond their realms and finally lead to genuine enlightenment.

Māra, the king of demons, is the principal enemy of the Buddha and his Dharma. Buddha Śākyamuni himself related:

> On one occasion, Ānanda, I was resting under the goat herd's Nigrodha tree on the bank of the river Nerañjarā immediately after having reached the great enlightenment. Then Māra, the Evil One, came, Ānanda, to the place were I was, and standing beside me he addressed me in the words: 'Pass away now, Lord, from existence! Let the Exalted One now die! Now is the time for the Exalted One to pass away!'
>
> And when he had thus spoken, Ānanda, I addressed Māra, the Evil One, and said: 'I shall not pass away, O Evil One! until not only the brethren and sisters of the Order, but also the lay disciples of either sex shall have become true hearers, wise and well-trained, ready and learned, carrying the doctrinal books in their memory, masters of the lesser corollaries that follow from the larger doctrine, correct in life, walking according to the precepts—until they, having thus themselves learned the doctrine, shall be able to tell others of it, preach it, make it known, establish it, open it, minutely explain it and make it clear—until they, when others start vain doctrine, easy to be refuted by the truth, shall be able in refuting it to spread the wonder working truth abroad! I shall not die until this pure Dharma of mine shall have become successful, prosperous, widespread, and popular in all its full extent—until in a word, it shall have been well proclaimed among men!' (Rhys Davids, tr. *Dialogues of the Buddha II*, 120-121)

At another time, this encounter took place:

> And Māra the wicked one went to the place where the Blessed One was; having approached him, he addressed the Blessed One in the following stanza: 'Thou art bound by all fetters, human and divine. Thou art bound by strong fetters. Thou wilt not be delivered from me, O Samaṇa.'
>
> Buddha replied: 'I am delivered from all fetters, human and divine. I am delivered from the strong fetters. Thou art struck down, O Death.'
>
> (Māra said): 'The fetter which pervades the sky, with which mind is bound, with that fetter I will bind thee. Thou wilt not be delivered from me, O Samaṇa.'
>
> (Buddha replied): 'Whatever forms, sounds, odours, flavours, or contacts there are which please the senses, in me desire for them has ceased. Thou art struck down, O Death.'
>
> Then Māra the wicked one understood: 'The Blessed One knows me, the Perfect One knows me,' and, sad and afflicted, he vanished away. (Horner, tr. "Mahavagga" I, 11, 2)

The ☞ŚŪRAṄGAMA SUTRA gives a detailed explanation of the relation between failure to follow the fundamental Buddhist moral precepts and entrance into the realms of demonic experience and, subsequently, rebirth in those realms. The sutra also indicates that the following are fundamental ways people become susceptible to demonic influence: **1)** by mistaking that which is not enlightenment for enlightenment; **2)** by mistaking one who is not enlightened for one who is enlightened; **3)** by being overcome by one's own 'demonic' habits of mind; and **4)** by being overcome by external demonic forces that are attracted to one's own demonic tendencies.

Spiritual powers only become demonic when one becomes attached to them or when one takes them for a sign of enlightenment. They occur naturally on the meditational path as a by-product of cultivation. However, they also can occur as a sign of demonic possession. In the latter case the power is that of a demon and not that generated by the person's own mind.

The sutra also contains a most powerful mantra (☞ ŚŪRAṄGAMA MANTRA) for subduing all types of demonic forces.

killing, destroying, bringing death, the Evil One, the adversary and tempter, Death, evil spirit, hindrance to enlightenment

☞ **Devadatta, ignorance**

Devadatta 提婆達多

Devadatta is usually presented as the archetypical earthly enemy of the Buddha, in much the same fashion that Māra (☞ DEMONS) is portrayed as the Buddha's heavenly opponent. A cousin of the Buddha, Devadatta became a disciple shortly after the Buddha's enlightenment and eventually became one of the Buddha's foremost disciples, possessing great spiritual powers.

About eight years prior to the Buddha's nirvana, Devadatta succumbed to the demon of jealousy and turned against the Buddha. To that end he used his spiritual powers to impress Ajātaśatru, with whom he formed an alliance. Ajātaśatru would kill his father Bimbisara and become king himself and Devadatta would kill the Buddha. He made three attempts on the Buddha's life: sending archer-assassins, setting an avalanche, and loosing a drunken elephant. All failed. Afterwards Devadatta attempted to create a schism in the Sangha and set up his own sangha with slightly different monastic rules.

At the end of his life, Devadatta again wished to draw near to the Buddha, but the earth is said to have opened up and swallowed him as he was journeying there. At the moment of being swallowed up, he tried to declare his taking refuge with the Buddha, but before he could finish, he died and was reborn in the deepest of the hells, where he began to undergo one hundred thousand aeons of the most painful suffering because of the karma he had created.

"Devadatta was the Buddha's cousin, but he opposed everything the Buddha ever did. Some people say that he was the Buddha's enemy, but that is not the case. Devadatta actually helped the Buddha become a Buddha. Not only did he help him in one life, but in life after life. However, he did so in a backhanded way. He 'helped' Śākyamuni Buddha by 'opposing' him. How does that work? Say, for instance, someone resolves to cultivate the Way, but another person gives him trouble all day long, by either scolding him or ridiculing him or generally giving him a hard time. The opposition serves as a test to the cultivator's resolve. One of my disciples once asked, 'Is it okay to give people tests to help them out?' I said, 'No. If your attainment of the fruition has been certified and you know that your testing will help them realize the Way, then it is okay. If you haven't certified to the fruition, then don't test other people. If you test others, others will test you. If you test people and they fail, then they will fall. If people test you and you fail, then you will fall.'

"The situation with Devadatta was different, however. Devadatta's state was inconceivable. His spiritual powers were as great as those of the Buddha, and it was Devadatta's opposition that spurred the Buddha on to his attainment of the Way.... In the past Devadatta had lectured on the ☞ DHARMA FLOWER SUTRA to Śākyamuni Buddha, helping him to become a Buddha." (DFS X 1)

"How did Devadatta come to aid Śākyamuni Buddha in his realizing the Way? Let us look into the way it happened. Long ago there was a wealthy elder named Xutan whose fortune of the seven gems was impressively abundant. His eldest son was called Xu Moti. When his wife died, Xutan, although advanced in years, remarried and had another son named Xiu Piye. The elder passed away when his younger son was only about eighteen or twenty. The two sons proceeded to divide their father's riches, but Xu Moti, the elder brother, decided he didn't want to give his younger brother half. And so he took him up to Vulture Peak for a holiday barbecue, and when they got near the top, Xu Moti pushed his younger brother right off the edge! Then he threw rocks on top of him to bury him. And then he went home and took possession of all of his father's wealth.

"Xu Moti, surprisingly enough, was Śākyamuni Buddha in a former life. You shouldn't think that Śākyamuni Buddha never did anything wrong. The younger brother was Devadatta in a former life, and the elder was King Ajātaśatru, the one who locked his parents in jail. Life after life, Śākyamuni Buddha was involved with these people in varying combinations of affinities, and so even after he became a Buddha, they still came and gave him trouble." (DFS X 2)

Even though Devadatta kept trying to kill the Buddha, not only did Śākyamuni Buddha not seek revenge or harbor resentment or ill-will towards him, he expressed his gratitude toward his former teacher and bestowed upon him the prediction of Buddhahood. Of course Devadatta must first undergo the consequences of his own actions and then cultivate the proper Path to Buddhahood.

It is because of my good and wise advisor, Devadatta, that I have perfected the ☞ SIX PĀRAMITĀS, kindness, compassion, joy, and equanimity, as well as the ☞ THIRTY-TWO MAJOR PHYSICAL CHARACTERISTICS and Eighty Minor Characteristics, coloring of burnished purple-gold, the Ten Powers, the Four Fearlessnesses, the Four Dharmas of Attraction, the Eighteen Unshared Dharmas, the power of the way of spiritual penetrations, the realization of equal and proper enlightenment, and the rescue of vast numbers of living beings. All this came about because of my ☞ GOOD AND WISE ADVISOR, Devadatta. (DFS X 40)

I announce to the Four Assemblies that, after limitless aeons have passed, Devadatta will become a Buddha by the name of King of Gods Thus Come One. (DFS X 50)

☞ **demons**

dhamma 法

☞ **Dharma/dharma**

dhāraṇī 陀羅尼

Dhāraṇī is a synonym of mantra.

"*Dhāraṇī* is a Sanskrit word, interpreted to mean 'unite and hold.' *Dhāraṇīs*, sometimes called 'mantras,' unite all dharmas and hold limitless meanings. They are the chief, the head and the origin of all dharmas." (DS 1)

"A *dhāraṇī* also 'unites and holds the three karmas' of body, mouth and mind, so that there is no violation." (DS 73)

☞ **magic formula, incantation, the all-encompassing**

☞ **mantra**

Dhāraṇī Sutra 陀羅尼經

The full title of the work is *The Sutra of the Vast, Great, Perfect, Full, Unimpeded Great Compassion Heart Dhāraṇī of the Thousand-Handed Thousand-Eyed Bodhisattva Who Regards the World's Sounds.* This sutra tells of the past causes and conditions of the Bodhisattva of Great Compassion, Regarder of the World's Sounds [Avalokiteśvara], and of the various ways of practicing the Great Compassion Mantra. It is a fundamental text of the Esoteric School (☞ FIVE TYPES OF BUDDHIST STUDY AND PRACTICE—ESOTERIC).

☞ **dhāraṇī, mantra, Great Compassion Mantra, Avalokiteśvara 〈Bodhisattva〉**

Dharma/dharma 法

In Buddhism, Dharma no longer has its Hindu meaning of religious duty according to one's class. Instead it has several levels of meaning including: the teachings of the Buddha, which can be understood as **1)** methods (teachings) for becoming enlightened; **2)** the reality that one realizes at enlightenment; and **3)** the various divisions of the mental and physical world that are part of the teaching.

Dharma as Teaching

He turns the inconceivable,
  wondrous wheel of Dharma,
And reveals the conduct
  of the path to *bodhi*,
Which destroys the suffering
  of all living beings forever.
(FAS Ch1)

Dharma refers to all the methods of cultivation taught by the Buddha which lead to ultimate enlightenment. They are means to an end, not an end in themselves.

Monks, as a man going along a highway might see a great stretch of water, the hither bank dangerous and frightening, the further bank secure, not frightening, but if there were not a boat for crossing by or a bridge across for going from the not-beyond to the beyond, this might occur to him: 'This is a great stretch of water, the hither bank dangerous and frightening, the further bank secure and not frightening, but there is not a boat for crossing by or a bridge across for going from the not-beyond to the beyond. Suppose that I, having collected grass, sticks, branches and foliage, and having tied a raft, depending on that raft, and striving with hands and feet, should cross over safely to the beyond?' Then, monks, that man, having collected grass, sticks, branches and foliage, having tied a raft, depending on that raft and striving with his hands and feet, might cross over safely to the beyond. To him, crossed over, gone beyond, this might occur: 'Now this raft has been very useful to me. I, depending on this raft, and striving with my hands and feet, crossed over safely to the beyond. Suppose now that I, having put this raft on my head, or having lifted it on to my shoulder, should proceed as I desire?' What do you think about this, monks? If that man does this, is he doing what should be done with that raft?"

"No, Lord."

"What should that man do, monks, in order to do what should be done with that raft? In this case, monks, it might occur to that man who has crossed over, gone beyond: 'Now, this raft has been very useful to me. Depending on this raft and striving with my hands and feet, I have crossed over safely to the beyond. Suppose now that I, having beached this raft on dry ground or having submerged it under the water, should proceed as I desire?' In doing this, monks, that man would be doing what should be done with that raft. Even so, monks, is the Parable of the Raft *dhamma* taught by me for crossing over, not for retaining. You, monks, by understanding the Parable of the Raft, should get rid even of (right) mental objects, all the more of wrong ones." (Horner, tr. *Middle Length Sayings*, I 173-174)

The Dharma which I speak is like a raft. Even Dharmas should be relinquished, how much the more that which is not Dharma. (VS 49)

The raft of Dharma gives us something to hang onto as we eliminate our ☞ATTACHMENTS, which cause us to suffer and to be stuck on this shore of birth and death. The raft of Dharma refers to the methods of inward illumination; it takes us across the sea of our afflictions to the other shore, nirvana. Once there, "even Dharmas should be relinquished."

"The Dharma is spoken to break people's attachments. If people had no attachments, they wouldn't need the Dharma. But people have attachments because their consciousnesses take over, and so they give rise to distinctions and attachments. If you let your wisdom be in charge, you will have no attachments...." (VBS #179 6-9)

"There are no fixed, static dharmas. Because the Dharma is not fixed, it is alive. Dharma which is alive is separate from all attachments. It is said, 'One bestows the teaching for the sake of the individual and prescribes the medicine according to the illness.' In the same way the Dharma is spoken as an antidote to an individual's specific problems." (DFS I 7-8)

Dharma as Reality

In this sense Dharma refers to the reality which is realized through the application of Dharma as teaching. It is the world of total enlightenment (☞DHARMA REALM).

Divisions of the World as Dharma

Another use of the word dharma is any aspect or division of the teaching. Dharma in this sense is an expedient distinction made for the sake of greater understanding. For example, the ☞FIVE SKANDHAS, the ☞SIX PĀRAMITĀS, and the ☞EIGHTEEN REALMS are all dharmas (☞ONE HUNDRED DHARMAS).

✍ **method, law, factor (of existence), characteristic, quality, idea, category, state of existence, condition of being, truth, true ideal, the Teaching**

☞ **Dharma-door, Dharma Realm**

Dharma body 法身

☞ **Three Bodies of a Buddha/Three Types of Buddha Bodies**

Dharma-door 法門

A Dharma-door is an entrance to the Dharma, a teaching about a way or method of practice leading to enlightenment.

✍ **Dharma-entrance/approach, device, means of teaching the doctrine, religious discourse, entrance/door to doctrine/religion, introduction or way of entering the doctrine, discourse on Dharma**

☞ **Dharma/dharma, Eighty-four Thousand Dharma-doors**

Dharma-Ending Age 末法時代

Alas! In the evil time
Of the Dharma-Ending Age,
Living beings' blessings are slight;
It is difficult to train them.
Far indeed from the sages of the past!
Their deviant views are deep.

Demons are strong,
The Dharma is weak;
Many are the wrongs and injuries.
Hearing the door of the Thus Come
One's sudden teaching,
They hate not destroying it
as they would smash a tile.
The doing is in the mind;
The body suffers the calamities.
There's no need for unjust
accusations
That shift the blame to others.
If you don't wish to invite the karma
of the unintermittent [hell],
Do not slander the Thus Come One's
Proper Wheel of Dharma.
(SE 62-63)

The Dharma-Ending Age is the last of the Three Ages of Dharma, during which the understanding and practice of the Buddhadharma gradually decline and finally disappear. The Three Ages are:

1 The Orthodox Dharma Age
2 The Dharma-Image/Semblance Age
3 The Dharma-Ending Age

"The era when the Buddha dwelled in the world was called the Orthodox Dharma Age. At that time the Buddha taught the Dharma, and there were genuine Arhats and great Bodhisattvas; the sages were dwelling in the world. The Orthodox Dharma Age lasted for one thousand years. The Dharma-Image Age followed—after the Buddha entered nirvana. During this period, people who cultivated the Way were few; those who were attached to external appearances were many. People stressed the creation of Buddha-images and many were made, but genuine cultivators were few.

"After the Dharma-Image Age came the Dharma-Ending Age. The Orthodox Dharma Age lasted for one thousand years. The Dharma-Image Age lasted another one thousand years. That is two thousand years in all. The Dharma-Ending Age continues for ten thousand years. We are now living in the Dharma-Ending Age. What does the phrase 'Dharma-ending' mean? It means that the Dharma has nearly come to an end and is about to disappear. The 'disappearance' of the Buddhadharma involves disappearance of faith in the Buddha. In the Dharma-Ending Age living beings' faith in the Buddha is not firm. When the Buddha dwelled in the world, people's faith was so firm that if you held a person at knifepoint and threatened his life saying, 'Renounce your belief in the Buddha or I'll murder you,' he would rather die than surrender his belief....

"In the Dharma-Image Age things were different. If a person believed in the Buddha and someone said, 'If you believe in the Buddha, I'll kill you,' he would say, 'Fine, I won't believe in the Buddha.' People would change their minds because their faith was not firm.

"Now, in the Dharma-Ending Age, you don't even have to threaten a person with death. You merely have to say, 'Don't believe in the Buddha,' and they quickly reply, 'Fine'....It is very difficult to promote faith. Figure it out for yourself. How many people are there in the world? Among the entire human race, how many believe in the Buddha? You can lecture the sutras to those believers every day and they will still waver between doubt and faith. You can conduct a small experiment. Try this. Invite a person out to a movie. He'll accept on the spot and away you go. Then try asking him to a sutra lecture. He will say, 'Ohhh...sitting there for two hours is nothing but suffering and tedium. It's not half as much fun as a movie!' That is the Dharma-Ending Age for you." (BRF 17-18)

The Buddha Speaks the Sutra of the Ultimate Extinction of the Dharma

Thus I have heard. At one time the Buddha was in the state of Kuśinagara. The Tathāgata was to enter nirvana within three months and the Bhikshus and Bodhisattvas as well as the great multitude of beings had come to the Buddha to pay homage to the Buddha and to bow in reverence. The World Honored One was tranquil and silent. He spoke not a word and his light did not appear. Worthy Ānanda bowed and asked the Buddha, "O Bhagavān, heretofore whenever you spoke the Dharma, awesome light would naturally appear. Yet today among this great assembly there is no such radiance. There must be a good cause for this, and we wish to hear the Bhagavān's explanation."

The Buddha remained silent and did not answer until the request had been repeated three times. He then told Ānanda, "After I enter nirvana, when the Dharma is about to perish, during the Evil Age of the ☞ FIVE TURBIDITIES, the way of demons will flourish. Demonic beings will become ☞ ŚRAMAṆAS; they will pervert and destroy my teachings. Wearing the garb of lay persons, they will prefer handsome clothes and their precept sashes will be made of multicolored cloth. They will use intoxicants, eat meat, kill other beings, and they will indulge their desire for flavorful food. They will lack compassion and they will bear hatred and jealousy even among themselves.

"At that time there will be ☞ BODHISATTVAS, ☞ PRATYEKABUDDHAS, and ☞ ARHATS who will reverently and diligently cultivate immaculate virtue. They will be respected by all people and their teachings will be fair and egalitarian. These cultivators of the Way will take pity on the poor, they will be mindful of the aged, and they will save and give counsel to those people they find in difficult circumstances. They will at all times exhort others to worship and to protect the sutras and images of the Buddha. They will do meritorious deeds, be resolute and kind and never harm others. They will forsake their bodies for others' benefit. They will hold no great regard for themselves but will be patient, yielding, humane, and peaceful.

"If such people exist, the hordes of demonic Bhikshus will be jealous of them. The demons will harass them, slander and defame them, expel them from their midst and degrade them. They will ostracize the good monks from the monastic community. Thereafter these demons will not cultivate virtue. Their temples and monastic buildings will be vacant and overgrown with weeds. For want of care and maintenance their Way-places will drift into ruin and oblivion. The demonic Bhikshus will only be greedy for wealth and will amass great heaps of goods. They will refuse to distribute any of it or to use it to gain blessings and virtue.

"At this time, the evil monks will buy and sell slaves to till their fields and to slash and burn the mountain forests. They will do harm to living creatures and they will feel not the least bit of compassion. These slaves will themselves become Bhikshus and maidservants will become Bhikshunis. Totally lacking in virtue, these people will run amok, indulging in licentious behavior. In their turbid confusion they will fail to separate the men from the women in the monastic communities. From this generation on, the Way will be weakened. Fugitives from the law will seek refuge in my Way, wishing to become *śramaṇas* but failing to observe the moral regulations. The precepts will continue to be recited twice a month, but in name alone. Being lazy and lax, no one will want to listen any longer. These evil *śramaṇas* will be unwilling to recite the sutras in their entirety and they will make abbreviations at the beginning and at the end of the texts as they please. Soon the practice of reciting sutras will stop altogether. Even if there are people who recite texts, they will be unlettered, unqualified people who will insist, nonetheless, that they are correct. Bumptious, arrogant and vain, these people will seek fame and glory. They will display elegant airs in the hope of attracting offerings from other people.

"When the lives of these demonic Bhikshus come to an end their essential spirits will fall into the ☞ AVĪCI hells. Having committed the five evil sins, they will suffer successive rebirths as hungry ghosts and as animals. They will know all such states of woe as they pass on through aeons as numerous as sands on the banks of the Ganges River. When their offenses are accounted for they will be reborn in a border land where the Triple Jewel is unknown.

"When the Dharma is about to disappear, women will become vigorous and will at all times do deeds of virtue. Men will grow lax and will no longer speak the Dharma. Those genuine *śramaṇas* they see will be looked upon as dung and no one will have faith in them. When the Dharma is about to perish, all the gods will begin to weep. Rivers will dry up and the five grains will not ripen. Epidemic diseases will frequently take the lives of multitudes of people. The masses will toil and suffer while the local officials will plot and scheme. No one will adhere to principles. Instead, all people will be ever more numerous like the sands of the oceanbed. Good persons will be hard to find; at most there will be one or two. As the aeon comes to a close, the revolution of the sun and the moon will grow short and the life span of people will decrease. Their hair will turn white at the age of forty years. Because of excessive licentious behavior they will quickly exhaust their seminal fluids and will die at a young age, usually before sixty years. As the life span of males decreases, that of females will increase to seventy, eighty, ninety, or one hundred years.

"The great rivers will rise up in disharmony with their natural cycles, yet people will not take notice or feel concern. Extremes of climate will soon be taken for granted....

"Then there will be Bodhisattvas, Pratyekabuddhas, and Arhats who will gather together in an unprecedented assembly because they will have all been harried and pursued by hordes of demons. They will no longer dwell in the assemblies, but the ☞ THREE VEHICLES will retreat to the wilderness. In a tranquil place, they will find shelter, happiness, and long life. Gods will protect them and the moon will shine down upon them. The Three Vehicles will have an opportunity to meet together and the Way will flourish. However, within fifty-two years the ☞ ŚŪRAṄGAMA SUTRA and the *Pratyutpanna Samādhi*, the Standing Buddha Samadhi, will be the first to change and then disappear. The twelve divisions of the canon will gradually follow until they vanish completely, never to appear again. Its words and texts will be totally unknown ever after. The precept sashes of *śramaṇas* will turn white of themselves. When my Dharma disappears, it will be just like an oil lamp which flares brightly for an instant just before it goes out. So, too, will the Dharma flare and die. After this time it is difficult to speak with certainty of what will follow.

"So it will remain for the next ten million years. When ☞ MAITREYA is about to appear in the world to become the next Buddha, the planet will be entirely peaceful. Evil vapors will have dissipated, rain will be ample and regular, the crops will grow abundantly. Trees will grow to a great height and people will grow to be eighty feet tall. The average life span will extend to 84,000 years. It will be impossible to count all the beings who will be taken across to liberation."

Worthy ☞ĀNANDA addressed the Buddha, "What should we call this sutra and how shall we uphold it?"

The Buddha said, "Ānanda, this sutra is called *The Ultimate Extinction of the Dharma*. Tell everyone to propagate it widely; the merit of your actions will be measureless, beyond reckoning."

When the ☞FOURFOLD ASSEMBLY of disciples heard this sutra, they grieved and wept. Each of them resolved to attain the true Path of the Supreme Sage. Then bowing to the Buddha, they withdrew. (SS I xiv-xvi)

☞ **time**

Dharma Flower ⟨Lotus⟩ Sutra 法華經

The Buddhas Śākyamuni and Many Jewels sharing a seat (a scene from the Lotus Sutra) (see plate 15)

> Should I leave this burning house
> of ceaseless thought
> and taste the pure rain's
> single truth
> falling upon my skin?
> (Hirschfield and Aratani, tr. *The Ink Dark Moon* 84)

The complete title of the sutra is the *Sutra of the (White) Lotus Flower of the Wonderful Dharma*. It is one of the foremost Mahayana sutras, for it explains clearly and directly the central message of the Buddhadharma:

> Śāriputra, what is meant by 'All Buddhas, the World Honored Ones, appear in the world only because of the causes and conditions of the one great matter?' The Buddhas, the World Honored Ones, appear in the world because they wish to lead living beings to realize the knowledge and vision of the Buddhas and gain purity. (DFS III 416)

In this sutra the Buddha proclaims the ultimate principles of the Dharma that unite all previous teachings into one. The sutra is the major text studied by the Tiantai School of Buddhism in China and the Tendai and Nichiren-shoshu sects in Japan.

☞ **Tiantai School, Zhiyi ⟨Venerable⟩, Three Vehicles**

Dharma Master 法師

Dharma Master is a title of respect used to address a Buddhist ☞BHIKSHU (monk) or ☞BHIKSHUNI (nun). It implies that the person so addressed has mastered the Dharma and is qualified to teach it.

☞ **Good and Wise Advisor, Dharma/dharma, Tripiṭaka Master, Sangha**

Dharma-protector 護法

The term Dharma-protector has two meanings: **1)** it refers to those gods, spirits, and ghosts who protect the Dharma and those who cultivate it; **2)** it refers to human lay supporters of the Buddhist monastic establishment.

Weituo Bodhisattva

☞ **Dharma/dharma, Eightfold Divison of Ghosts and Spirits**

Dharma Realm 法界

The term Dharma Realm has at least three distinct meanings: **1)** the enlightened world, that is, the totality or infinity of the realm of the Buddhas, **2)** a particular plane of existence, as in the Ten Dharma Realms, and **3)** the eighteenth of the Eighteen Sense-fields.

The Enlightened World

The Dharma Realm is just the One Mind. The Buddhas certify to this and accomplish their Dharma bodies.... "Inexhaustible, level, and equal is the Dharma Realm, in which the bodies of all Thus Come Ones pervade"....

Going and returning without border,
Movement and stillness
  have one source;
Embracing multitudes of words,
  more remains,
Overstepping words and
  thoughts by far:
This can only be the Dharma Realm!
(EDR I 218)

A Particular Plane of Existence

"Dharma Realms pervade empty space to the bounds of the universe, but in general there are ten (☞ TEN DHARMA REALMS). There are four sagely Dharma Realms and six ordinary Dharma Realms....These Ten Dharma Realms do not go beyond the current thought you are thinking." (TD 57)

The Eighteenth Sense-field

In this technical sense of the term, dharma realm, or the field of dharmas, refers to 'object of mind' (☞ EIGHTEEN REALMS).

dharma field, dharma element, the ultimate principle of the Dharma, mental object considered as irreducible element, sphere of religion

☞ **Ten Dharma Realms, Eighteen Realms ⟨sense-fields⟩**

Dharma-transmission 傳法

The term Dharma-transmission has two meanings: **1)** It refers to authentic transmission of a certain teaching or Dharma from master to student or from master to master. **2)** It can also refer to the transmission of the responsibility for the life of the Buddhadharma from one enlightened master to another in a particular school or lineage of enlightened masters. The receivers of such transmissions are often called "patriarchs."

☞ **Dharma, lineage**

dhyāna 禪那

☞ **meditation, Four Dhyānas**

dhyāna meditation 禪定

☞ **Six Pāramitās**

Earth Store 〈Bodhisattva〉 地藏菩薩

Earth Store Bodhisattva (see plate 17)

"Earth Store Bodhisattva is named after the earth, which not only gives birth to things and makes them grow, but can store a great many things within itself as well. Because this Bodhisattva is like the earth, he can produce the myriad things and make them grow. Anyone who believes in him may obtain the treasures stored in the ground: gold, silver, lapis lazuli, crystal, mother-of pearl, red pearls, and carnelian....

"His Sanskrit name is Kṣitigarbha, "Earth Store." There are ten aspects of the earth: it is wide and extensive; it supports all living beings; it is impartial; it receives the great rain; it produces grasses and trees; it holds all planted seeds; it holds many treasures; it produces medicines; it is not moved by the blowing wind; and it does not tremble at the lion's roar." (SPV 20-21)

"You could say that Earth Store Bodhisattva is the dumbest of the Bodhisattvas, and also the most intelligent. Why is he dumb? It is because he does things no one else wants to do. He can bear what others can't bear and yield when others can't yield. When his parents were extremely mean to him, it didn't make any difference; he was filial just the same. That is why within Buddhism Earth Store Bodhisattva is known as the Bodhisattva of great filiality and also as the Bodhisattva of great vows.

He said, 'Until the hells are empty I will never become a Buddha.' Until every single living being is taken across, he doesn't want to attain proper and equal enlightenment. Take a look at that kind of vow-power: Doesn't it seem kind of dumb? On the other hand, we can also say he is the most intelligent Bodhisattva. That is because he stands out above everyone else. He transcends all his peers. Someone asks, 'Is he trying to be special?' No. He does what others don't want to do and are not able to do. And so we can say that he is the most intelligent Bodhisattva. In short, it can be said of Earth Store Bodhisattva that he has great vows, great conduct, great wisdom, and great compassion....Jiuhua Mountain [in Anhui Province in China] is the sacred Way-place devoted to Earth Store Bodhisattva." (SPV 136)

Jiuhua Mountain, the Way-place of Earth Store Bodhisattva

☞ **Bodhisattva Treasury/Womb of the Earth**
☞ **Bodhisattva, Sutra of the Past Vows of Earth Store Bodhisattva**

Eight Consciousnesses 八識

The eight consciousnesses are: **1)** eye-consciousness or seeing, **2)** ear-consciousness or hearing, **3)** nose-consciousness or smelling, **4)** tongue-consciousness or tasting, **5)** body-consciousness or tactile feeling, **6)** mind-consciousness or cognition, **7)** *manas*, the defiling mind-consciousness which is the faculty of mind, and **8)** *ālaya*, or storehouse, consciousness.

Consciousness is used exclusively in the sense of distinction-making activities of the mind, which include both the making of the distinctions and the distinctions made. Conscious awareness and what is normally unconscious are both considered aspects of consciousness in the Buddhist sense of the word.

The ☞CONSCIOUSNESS-ONLY SCHOOL describes the mind as a system of seven active consciousnesses (*vijñāna*) which all develop out of the eighth, or storehouse, consciousness. The latter is passive and contains the potentials, or "seeds" (*bīja*), for the development and activity of the first seven consciousnesses. The seventh consciousness acts as a communication link between the eighth consciousness and the first six consciousnesses. It contains the sense of self, of ego individuality, with which it defiles the communications to the first six consciousnesses. The sixth consciousness is a perceptual and cognitive processing center, while the first five consciousnesses are the perceptual awarenesses of eyes, ears, nose, tongue, and body.

Formal division is made among these seven consciousnesses after their emanation from the eighth, but division is totally based upon mental distinction. The eight are still basically "one." To use a simple analogy, let us think of a room with seven lightbulbs. You flick on the light switch and seven distinct lights shine. Turn the switch off and the lights disappear. Yet there is just one electric current; the electrical source is comparable to the storehouse consciousness, or, as it is understood after the transformation of consciousness, to the enlightened mind.

The system for describing the eight consciousnesses, and the mental dharmas (*caittas*) which arise out of them and are dependent upon them, was developed as an important part of a pragmatic psychology of mind. The system can be used to describe, in a manner that is accurate and practical, both mental functioning and the specific techniques employed on the Path to the enlightenment that is Buddhahood. It provides a way to account for mental processes without recourse to the notions of a real, permanent self (*ātman*) or of real, permanent external (and also internal) objects (*dharmas*). All actual and potential realms of experience are shown to be contained within the transformations of consciousness and appear as manifestations of the distinction-making mind.

Nevertheless, because of our attachment to and belief in the reality of self and the reality of the "objects" (dharmas) which we perceive and understand to be the external world, the true nature of ourselves and the world is obscured so that we are unaware of it.

"The *eye consciousness.* We say that eyes see, but it's not actually the eyes themselves that see. It is the eye consciousness which sees. The *ear consciousness.* We say the ears can hear, but if you sliced off your ears and laid them aside, would they be able to hear of themselves? If you gouged out your eyes and set them aside, would they be able to see? Could you say, 'I'm not going to the movies, but I'll send my eyes along, and they can take in the show? ' Obviously not. The eyes cannot see by themselves. It is the eye consciousness which does the seeing. And where does the eye consciousness come from? From the mind—the Mind King. The same is true for all the other consciousnesses as well, the *nose consciousness*, the *tongue consciousness*, the *body consciousness*, and the *mind consciousness*....

"The mind consciousness, the sixth or 'intellectual' consciousness, is not really the mind, properly speaking. The sixth consciousness is the function of the mind whose substance is the seventh consciousness, the *manas consciousness*, also called the 'transmitting' consciousness or the 'defiling' consciousness. It is the substance of the mind. It continually transmits the functions of the sixth consciousness to the eighth consciousness, the *ālaya consciousness*. The eighth consciousness is called the *ālaya*, which means 'storehouse,' because it stores all information transmitted to it by the seventh...." (HD 31-32)

"The human mind is an ever-spinning whirlpool in which mental activities never cease. There are four stages of production, dwelling, change, and decay in thought after thought. Often the seventh consciousness is described as a sea in which the currents of thought surge and seethe; meanwhile, the eighth consciousness is likened to a sea in which the apparent movement of waves has subsided, but underlying the placid surface is an uninterrupted rush of mental activity. The seventh consciousness is the 'transmitting' consciousness'; it relays sensory information from the sixth consciousness to the eighth (the storehouse or *ālaya* consciousness) and from the eighth back to the sixth and so forth. It takes for a self that which basically is devoid of a self. Because of a fixation to a false reckoning, thought movements rage on without stop. The wave patterns within the seventh consciousness are more apparent and forceful, whereas the movements of the eighth consciousness are still and imperceptible. Within the eighth consciousness are stored the seeds of all habit energies and impressions from beginningless time, and there are very subtle movements and a constant state of flux in that sphere." (EDR IV 27-28)

awareness, knowledge

☞ **Consciousness-Only School, One Hundred Dharmas, Five Skandhas—consciousness**

Eighteen Realms 十八界

The Eighteen Realms are comprised of the Six Organs, the Six Objects, and the Six Consciousnesses. The Six Organs are: **1)** eyes, **2)** ears, **3)** nose, **4)** tongue, **5)** body, and **6)** mind. The Six Objects are: **1)** sights, **2)** sounds, **3)** smells/odors, **4)** tastes/flavors, **5)** objects of touch, and **6)** dharmas (or objects of mind). The Six Consciousnesses are: **1)** eye-consciousness, **2)** ear-consciousness, **3)** nose-consciousness, **4)** tongue-consciousness, **5)** body-consciousness, and **6)** mind-consciousness.

The Six Organs and the Six Objects taken together are known as the Twelve Bases. They are the bases for the production of the Six Consciousnesses.

Like the ☞FIVE SKANDHAS, the Eighteen Realms are a way of analyzing the entire psycho-physical world as an aid to breaking attachments to it. Everything that we experience is included in the Eighteen Realms. The first five or the Six Objects include the entire external world. The first five of the Six Organs describe our physical bodies. Together they comprise the entire physical world. The mind organ, dharmas as objects of mind, and the Six

Consciousnesses comprise the world of mind. All mental experience is included within them. Since both mental and physical worlds are completely included, there is no need for recourse to a real, permanent self or soul to describe any experience.

According to the teachings of the ☞MAHAYANA, all dharmas are empty of any real, permanent, inherent identifying characteristics.

> Therefore, in emptiness there...[are] no eyes, ears, nose, tongue, body or mind; no sights, sounds, smells, tastes, objects of touch or dharmas; no field of the eyes, up to and including no field of mind-consciousness. (HS 56-57)

✍ **fields, sense-fields, constituents, element, factors, psycho-physical constituent elements, elements in sense consciousness**

☞ **Eight Consciousnesses**

Eightfold Division of Ghosts and Spirits 天龍八部

The Eightfold Division of Ghosts and Spirits includes: **1)** gods (*devas*), **2)** dragons (*nāgas*), **3)** *yakṣas*, **4)** *gandharvas*, **5)** *asuras*, **6)** *garuḍas*, **7)** *kinnaras*, **8)** *mahoragas*. All eight categories of beings are not ordinarily visible to the human eye; however, their subtle bodies can be clearly seen by those with higher spiritual powers. Gods are discussed in a separate entry (☞GODS). Brief descriptions of the other seven follow.

Dragons "can do all kinds of transformations; they can become big or small. They can appear and disappear. They are said to be 'spiritual,' that is, 'inconceivable.' How did they get to be dragons, that is, animals, if they have spiritual penetrations? When they were cultivating the Way, they were 'quick with the vehicle and slow with the precepts.' They cultivated the Great Vehicle Dharma with great vigor, but they did not keep the precepts. Because they cultivated the Great Vehicle Dharma, they gained spiritual penetrations. Because they failed to keep the precepts, they turned into animals....

"*Yakṣas* are 'speedy ghosts.' They get around very fast. There are ground-traveling *yakṣas* and space-traveling *yakṣas*. There are water-traveling *yakṣas*, too. *Yakṣas* are very fierce. Some specialize in sapping people of their energy. You may know some people who have very weak energy-systems. No matter what kind of good food they eat, they never have any energy. Most likely a *yakṣa* ghost is busy living off of their energy. Some *yakṣas* drink human blood; some absorb people's vitality. There are many varieties of *yakṣas*.

"*Gandharvas* are 'incense-inhaling spirits,' musicians in the court of the Jade Emperor. When the emperor wants some music, he lights some incense and the *gandharvas* all come to play.

"*Asuras* have big tempers. Take a look around you: whoever has a big temper is an *asura*. There are human *asuras*, ghost

Eightfold Division of Ghosts and Spirits (see plates 18-19)

asuras, and animal *asuras*. . . *Asura* is a Sanskrit word that means 'ugly.' It also means 'no *sura* (a beer-like alcoholic beverage).' They have the blessings of the gods but not the authority. They enjoy heavenly blessings, but they have no say in running things. Since they have no power, they are always fighting for power, battling with the heavenly armies.

"*Garuḍas* are great golden-winged *peng*-birds. They have a wingspan of three hundred sixty ☞YOJANAS. When they flap their wings, the ocean waters part and all the dragons at the bottom of the sea are exposed as potential meals. The dragons have no time to transform into anything. They are gobbled up on the spot by the *garuḍas*, who eat them with the same relish as we eat noodles. All gone!

"The dragons were getting very upset about this, because large numbers of them were being eaten, their species had become endangered. They went to the Buddha to complain, and the Buddha gave them each a thread from his precept sash, saying, 'You can wear this, and then you will be invisible to the *peng*-birds.'

"That worked fine for the dragons, but the *peng*-birds were then going hungry. And so they went to the Buddha and said, 'What about us? Dragons are our primary food supply. We're going to starve!' Śākyamuni Buddha said, 'Don't worry. I'll tell all of my disciples to set out some food for you when they eat lunch every day.' That is why left-home people set some food out for the *peng*-birds.

"*Kinnaras* are also musical spirits in the Jade Emperor's court. The Jade Emperor does a lot of entertaining and always has *kinnaras* play music so the gods can dance. The gods can dance! They dance because they are so happy they forget about everything.

Garudas

"*Mahoragas* are huge snake-spirits." (DFS IX 1677-1678)

eightfold pantheon, eight divisions of gods and ghosts, (lit.) gods, dragons, and [others of] the eight divisions

☞ **gods, ghosts, Ten Dharma Realms, Six Paths of Rebirth**

Eightfold Path 八正道

The Eightfold Path consists of **1)** Right Views, **2)** Right Thought, **3)** Right Speech, **4)** Right Conduct, **5)** Right Livelihood, **6)** Right Effort, **7)** Right Mindfulness, and **8)** Right Concentration. The Eightfold Path is one of the principal constituents of the Holy Truth of the Path (☞FOUR HOLY TRUTHS).

Right Views

Right views refers to understanding of the ☞FOUR HOLY TRUTHS. It also can refer to insight into the nature of the ☞DHARMA BODY of the Buddhas. Right views "refers to your manner of regarding something, your mental outlook and your opinions, not to what you view with your eyes. You practice the non-outflow [☞OUTFLOWS] conduct in contemplating yourself. Your own views and understanding must be proper." (AS 125)

Right Thought

Right thought means freedom from mental attachments, to have renounced thoughts of hatred and harm. It can also refer to the purification of the mind so that one no longer has any polluted thinking. It is sometimes translated 'right resolve' or 'right aspirations,' indicating the importance of mental intention. "If it is not in accord with propriety, don't listen to it.

Why would you think about it? Because you listened to it." (DFS IV 663)

Right Speech

Right speech means always speaking the truth, avoiding false speech, coarse speech, harsh speech, and frivolous speech. Right speech also means that because one realizes the emptiness of all dharmas, one can resolve all disputes.

"If it is not in accord with propriety, don't talk about it. Don't gossip." (DFS IV 663)

"If someone speaks improperly to you, you should think of it as proper. This is the pure karma of speech. Worldly people are of many kinds, and when they speak improperly, do not criticize them saying, 'Ah! He's speaking incorrectly!' On the other hand, be careful not to get too close to such people either." (AS 125-126)

Right Conduct

Right conduct means that one does not take life, steal, or engage in sexual misconduct.

"If it is not in accord with propriety, don't do it. Don't do deviant things like going into the gambling business and developing 'spiritual powers' in the numbers racket. That's deviant action.

"What is right action? Sitting in *dhyāna* meditation without any false thinking. Studying the Buddhadharma. That is the most proper form of action.

"'But,' you ask, 'if I study the Buddhadharma, where will I get food to eat?'

"You shouldn't worry about that. If you study well, you will naturally have food to eat." (DFS IV 664)

"Proper action refers to pure bodily karma. Use non-outflow wisdom to discard improper bodily karma, specifically sexual desire. I can't make it *too* clear; I can't say it *too* frankly. Many people say, 'Oh well, emptiness is form, and form is emptiness,' and they casually play around. That is improper action." (AS 126)

Right Livelihood

Right livelihood refers to having a correct lifestyle or way of life. One is content and has few wishes. One avoids karmically unwholesome occupations such as selling alcohol or drugs, selling firearms, being a butcher, or doing fortune-telling. It also refers to one's way of relating to others. For example, you should not dress or act eccentrically to call attention to yourself. You should not praise yourself, calling attention to your good deeds. You should not act in a loud or overbearing manner.

"'Look at me,' says the Great Vehicle monk dressed in Small Vehicle robes. 'I'm special. You should make offerings to me.'

"'He's special,' say the blind followers. 'He's probably a Buddha or a Bodhisattva,' taking the gaudy rickrack for a treasure." (AS 126)

Right Effort

Right effort means you should be vigorous in your practice, always thinking, saying, and doing what is right and not what is improper.

"Strangely enough, if you chat with someone, the more you chat, the more energy you have—talking, talking, too much talking. But of what use is all your vigorous talking? It's improper vigor." (AS 127)

"What is deviant vigor? Deviant dharmas harm other people. Those who cultivate deviant dharmas work very hard in the six periods of the day and night, cultivating all kinds of ascetic practices. Nevertheless, their ascetic practices are not beneficial. They may imitate the behavior of cows or of dogs, or practice being like chickens. They may imitate cows, eat grass, and say they are being vigorous because cows eat grass all day long. This happens because they saw that a cow was born in the heavens. They didn't realize it was because of the merit and virtue accrued from acts that the cow had performed in previous lives. They thought the cow had been born in the heavens because it ate grass! And so they take a cow for their teacher. The cow has no understanding of Dharma whatsoever, and so studying with a cow is called improper vigor." (DFS IV 665)

"Right vigor means to cultivate according to the Buddhadharma. One should not cultivate dharmas that the Buddha did not teach. That is called offering up your conduct in accord with the Buddha's instructions. Right vigor means vigor with the body and vigor with the mind. Mental vigor means recollecting the Three Jewels and not neglecting them for an instant. Vigor with the body means putting the teachings into actual practice...." (DFS IV 666)

Right Mindfulness

"This means mindfulness of the Buddha, the Dharma, and the Sangha (☞THREE JEWELS). Deviant mindfulness means mindfulness of deviant views, prejudiced views, love and emotion. Deviant mindfulness means always thinking about yourself first." (DFS IV 666)

Right Concentration

Right concentration refers to taking leave of one's desires and of unwholesome dharmas and then entering the first *dhyāna* and those succeeding (☞FOUR DHYĀNAS) in the correct fashion. Right concentration is the opposite of deviant concentration. What is deviant concentration? It's concentration that is an attachment, that you can't let go of. For example, some people like to drink, and although you tell them not to, they continue to drink with great concentration because they have deviant concentration. Or some people like to take drugs. The more they take, the more deluded they get. When you tell them not to, they say, 'I can get enlightened taking this stuff. When I take this, things really start happening. I go through changes. I see and hear differently. The world becomes adorned with the seven jewels. Isn't that a state?' It's deviant concentration, that's what it is! For example, one person came here to listen to a lecture, but not a word could get in because he had his deviant concentration going, and he was very attached: 'I'm right! I can't listen to you!' That's deviant knowledge, deviant views, and deviant concentration.

"Then what is right concentration? Right concentration is the cultivation of the ☞FOUR DHYĀNAS and the Eight Samadhis. Don't have a self at all. Cultivate these Dharmas, but forget your 'self.' If you have forgotten your 'self,' how could you still keep on drinking, taking drugs, and indulging yourself? Everyone looks for advantages for themselves, but people who cultivate...forget about advantages. That's right concentration." (DFS IV 669-670)

✍ **Proper Eightfold Path, Eight Sagely Way Shares, Aryan Eightfold Path**

☞ **Four Holy Truths, Four Applications of Mindfulness, mindfulness, samadhi**

Eight Winds 八風

The Eight Winds are **1)** praise/approval, **2)** ridicule, **3)** suffering, **4)** happiness, **5)** benefit, **6)** destruction/devastation, **7)** gain (or acclaim), and **8)** loss (or bad repute).

Su Dongpo (1037-1101), a famous Chinese poet, wrote the following poem to describe a state he had experienced in meditation:

I bow to the god among gods;
His hair-light illuminates the world.

Unmoved when the Eight Winds
  blow,
Upright I sit in a purple-golden lotus.

"He sent the poem to the Great Master Foyin (1011-1086), and the Master's reply was two words: 'Fart, fart.' As soon as Su Dongpo saw the Great Master Foyin's criticism, he couldn't get it out of his mind, and he rushed across the Yangtze—he lived on the south side of the river and Great Master Foyin lived on the north side—to find the Master and scold him. He wanted to tell the Master that he had written an enlightened poem, and so how could the Master possibly have replied, 'Fart, fart?'

"In fact, when Great Master Foyin criticized him, not only did Su Dongpo fart, he blazed forth and wanted to scorch Foyin to death. And so he rushed across the river and burst unannounced into the Master's quarters and shouted, 'How could you possibly scold someone and slander him that way by writing "fart, fart"?'

"Foyin replied, 'Who was I slandering? You said that you were unmoved by the Eight Winds, but just by letting out two small farts I've blown you all the way across the Yangtze. And you still say that the Eight Winds don't move you? You don't have to talk about eight winds; just my two farts bounced you all the way up here.'

"Then Su Dongpo thought, 'That's right. I said that I'm unmoved by the Eight Winds, but two words have been enough to make me burn with anger.' Realizing that he still didn't have what it takes, he bowed to the Master and repented....

"**1**) *Praise.* For example: '*Upāsaka*, you are really a good person; you really understand the Buddhadharma, and your wisdom really shines. Furthermore, your genius is unlimited and your eloquence is unobstructed.

"**2**) *Ridicule.* For instance: 'It's the scientific age now, and you are studying Buddhism. Why do you study that old, superstitious rubbish?' Really ridiculous ridicule and yet you think, 'They're right. How can I study Buddhism now in the scientific age? Cause and effect, no me and no you—how can such metaphysical theories be worth anything in the age of science? I am I, and people are people.' You become confused and are moved by the blowing of the wind.

"**3**) *Suffering.* The wind of ☞ SUFFERING makes you suffer. To be unmoved while ceaselessly performing ascetic practices is an example of being unmoved by the wind of suffering.

"**4**) *Happiness.* To eat well, to wear good clothes, to have a good place to live, and to be especially happy all day long, thinking, 'This certainly is good,' is to be moved by this wind.

"**5**) *Benefit.* You think, 'All I did is go to a lot of trouble cultivating. I don't even have any ☞ POLLUTED THOUGHTS. Consequently, people come to me and make an offering of a million dollars to build a temple, and they are very, very happy.' That is to be moved by the wind of benefit.

"**6**) *Destruction.* Perhaps the wind of benefit blew yesterday, but tomorrow people may come and ruin everything. They'll tell people, 'That monk is no good. Don't believe in him; he will do anything. Believe in me instead.'

"**7**) *Gain.*

"**8**) *Loss.*" (HS 18-20)

☞ **prosperity, decline, disgrace, honor, praise, censure, suffering, and pleasure**

Eighty-eight Deluded Viewpoints
八十八品見惑

"There are Eighty-eight Deluded Views, which are suddenly eradicated, and ☞EIGHTY-ONE COGNITIVE DELUSIONS, which are gradually eliminated.

"There are ten basic deluded views which manifest themselves in relation to the Four Holy Truths in each of the ☞THREE WORLDS—desire, form, and formless. The ten are greed, anger, delusion, arrogance, doubt, the view of (bodily) self, one-sided views, deviant views, the view of being attached to views, and the view of grasping (nonbeneficial) prohibitive precepts.

"In the world of desire, all ten operate in relationship to the Truth of Suffering, while seven (all except the view of self, one-sided views, and the view of grasping prohibitive precepts) operate in relation to the Truths of Accumulating and Cessation, and eight (all except the view of self and one-sided views) operate in relation to the Truth of the Path. In the form and formless worlds the relationship of the delusions to the Truths follows the same order with the exception of hatred in relation to all four Truths, since hatred must be eliminated before one can enter samadhi. Thirty-two deluded views in the world of desire, twenty-eight in the world of form, and twenty-eight in the formless world total eighty-eight....

"Upon eliminating the Eighty-eight Deluded Views, one becomes a first-stage Arhat (Skt. *śrotaāpanna*, Stream-winner)." (HS 123-124)

deluded views

☞ **Eighty-one Cognitive Delusions, Four Holy Truths, Arhat**

Eighty-four Thousand Dharma-doors
八萬四千法門

Eighty-four thousand is a symbolic number, which represents a countless number of Dharma-doors.

"In cultivation there are 84,000 Dharma-doors....Of those 84,000 Dharma-doors, ultimately which Dharma-door is number one? Of the 84,000 Dharma-doors, 84,000 are number one. What does that mean? It means, if a Dharma suits your potentials, then it is the number one Dharma. If it doesn't suit your potentials, then it is not number one for you. However, if it doesn't suit your potentials, it may suit someone else's potentials. Any Dharma that suits anyone's potentials is number one for that individual. Therefore, they are all number one Dharma-doors; all are nondual Dharma-doors. If you try to force a discrimination about which is best and say, 'This one is number one, that one is number two, and then there are the third, the fourth, counting up to 84,000,' no one would cultivate the 84,000th Dharma-door. Why not? Because it is the very last one. The way that people's minds work is that they want to be number one. Therefore, I don't pay attention to whether I'm right or not; I just call all the Dharma-doors spoken by the Buddha 'number one,' without any 'number two.' Whether you take a logical, psychological, philosophical, or scientific stance, all are number one. Each one is included in the 84,000 Dharma-doors. The same applies to each one of us. Each person is number one. There is no number two. For there to be a number two, you would have to tie two people together.

"You say, 'Now I understand! Now that you've spoken about this Dharma, Dharma Master, I have become enlightened. What have I become enlightened about? When a man and a woman marry, that counts as number two!'

"Not bad. Not only number two, it's even number three. A third one also appears. And so it would go, all the way up to 84,000. But if you don't count that way, then all are number one. Every single one is number one...." (TT 107-108)

☞ **myriad Dharma-doors**
☞ **Dharma-door**

Eighty-one Cognitive Delusions 八十一品思惑

"There are nine degrees of cognitive delusions, which manifest themselves on nine separate grounds. The nine degrees are simply the higher superior, the higher intermediate, and the higher inferior; the middle superior, the middle intermediate, and the middle inferior; the lower superior, the lower intermediate, and the lower inferior. The Nine Grounds are the Five Destinies [☞SIX PATHS OF REBIRTH minus *asuras*], which comprise the first ground, the Four Dhyānas, and the Four Formless Samadhis....Upon eliminating the first six degrees of the first ground, one becomes a second stage Arhat (Skt. *sakṛdāgāmin*, Once-Returner). Upon eliminating the final three degrees of the first ground, one becomes a third stage Arhat (Skt. *anāgāmin*, Never-Returner). When all the remaining seventy-two are eliminated, one becomes a fourth stage Arhat (Skt. *arhat*). Sometimes only the fourth stage is referred to as Arhatship." (HS 124)

☞ **Eighty-eight Deluded Viewpoints**

Eleven Benefits from Making Images of Buddhas 造像十一種功德

By making images of Buddhas a person plants karmic seeds, which are causes. The seeds will sprout and grow when conditions are appropriate, either in this life or future lives, and bear these eleven fruits or beneficial results.

"1) In every life you will have clear vision.

"2) You will not be born in evil places. Your friends and neighbors will all be good people. You won't meet up with evil people or evil beasts.

"3) You will always be born in a noble family. You will be born into a household that is wealthy and honored.

"4) Your body will be purple-golden in color.

"5) You will be very wealthy.

"6) You will be born in a worthy and good family.

"7) You can be born a king. Now there are no kings, but you could be President. It amounts to the same thing. Or if you insist on being a king, you can find a country with a monarchy and be born there.

"8) You can be a Wheel-turning Sage King. That is even higher than being President. If you cultivate while you are a Wheel-turning Sage King, you can become a Buddha.

"9) You can be born in the Brahma heavens and live for an aeon. You can be a king among the gods.

"10) You will not fall into the evil paths. Those who make images of Buddhas will not fall into the hells, the animal realm, or the realms of ghosts.

"**11**) In future incarnations you will still be able to revere the Three Jewels. You will not fall." (DFS III 470-471)

☞ **causation, karma, blessings**

emptiness 空

There are at least three ways in which the idea of "emptiness" can be understood: **a**) on the intellectual level, **b**) in practice, and **c**) as a description of enlightenment.

Intellectual Understanding of Emptiness

Technically, emptiness means that all dharmas have no independent existence of their own, apart from reliance on other dharmas. All dharmas have no real, individual essences that distinguish them from all other dharmas. In other words, everything in the world, both physical and mental, is interdependent with everything else in the world. The temporary existence of each is dependent on its relations with what it is not. There is no such thing as something existing entirely on its own, separate, and with no causal relation with anything else. That is, all dharmas are empty of individual inherent being, also called 'own-being,' 'intrinsic nature,' or 'self-nature' (Skt. *svabhāva*, Ch. *zi xing*).

A. The Logic of Emptiness

The Bodhisattva Nāgārjuna logically showed that all dharmas are empty in the following way:

"The own-being [of a dharma] (*svabhāva*) is a self-contradictory notion, so Nāgārjuna has little trouble demolishing any proposition whose terms are held to have. If it is real, it must exist. If it exists, it must be subject to change....

"The following abstract pattern expresses Nāgārjuna's standard strategy of refutation: You say that C relates A and B. A and B must be either completely identical or completely different. If they are completely identical, C cannot obtain, because two things that are completely different have no common ground and so cannot be related. Therefore, it is false that C obtains between A and B.

"The insistence that A and B must be completely identical or different rather than partly identical follows from the definition of *svabhāva* as not dependent on another. Qualifications such as 'some' and 'partly' are excluded because the discussion is concerned not with common sense assertions such as 'some fuel is burning and some is not,' but with concepts of own-being and essence. What pertains to part of an essence must pertain to the whole essence. A defining property is either essential or non-essential. If it is non-essential then it is not really a defining property of an essence. If it is essential, then the essence can never be devoid of the property." (Robinson, R.H., "Classical Indian Philosophy," 75-76; rpt. in Elder, Joseph W., *Chapters in Indian Civilization*)

B. The Five Types of Emptiness

Intellectually, we can also try to understand emptiness by the negative method—by understanding what it is not. Of the Five Types of Emptiness, it is only the fifth, true emptiness, which is the enlightened emptiness proclaimed by the Mahayana teachings:

"**1**) *Insensate Emptiness.* This kind of emptiness lacks any knowing consciousness; it has no awareness. This emptiness, the ordinary emptiness known to most people, is called insensate emptiness because it consists merely of the emptiness we can see with our eyes, and it lacks its own awareness. It is the false, insensate emptiness that people see in places where there is nothing at all. That lack of anything in a place is not the true emptiness.

"2) *Emptiness of Annihilation.* This is emptiness as it has been understood by those of certain external paths, none of whom understand the principle of true emptiness. They say that when people die they cease to exist, that is, they are annihilated. And so their version of emptiness is called the emptiness of annihilation.

"3) *Emptiness of Analyzed Dharmas.* This emptiness is a contemplation cultivated by those of the ☞SMALL VEHICLE. They analyze form as form, mind as mind, and sort them into their constituent dharmas without realizing that they are all empty. They only go so far as to say that because a perceptible characteristic can be analyzed as one of the form-dharmas, that because feeling, cognition, formations, and consciousness can be analyzed in terms of various mind-dharmas, they are empty. As a consequence, those of the ☞TWO VEHICLES are not certified as ones who have realized the wonderful meaning of true emptiness. They stop at the transformation city. They stand there, at that empty and unreal place, cultivating the contemplation of the emptiness of analyzed dharmas. That is what is called superficial *prajñā*, not profound ☞PRAJÑĀ....

"4) *Bodily Dharma Emptiness.* The fourth kind of emptiness is cultivated by the Condition-Enlightened Ones, the ☞PRATYEKABUDDHAS, who have the bodily experience of the emptiness of dharmas.

"5) *True Emptiness.* ☞BODHISATTVAS cultivate the contemplation of the emptiness of wonderful existence." (HS 21-23)

C. Emptiness and the New Physics

The lack of substantiality of matter according to the analysis of the New Physics is often wrongly compared to Buddhist emptiness. At most it can be used as an example to aid the understanding of the form *skandha* (☞FIVE SKANDHAS). The New Physics does not deal with the emptiness of the other four *skandhas*, which are categories of mind, not of matter-energy.

D. The Story of Master Deshan: Intellectual Understanding Is not Enough

This is a story about a monk who was a scholar of the ☞VAJRA (DIAMOND) SUTRA, which is perhaps the most well-known of the sutras that explain the meaning of emptiness.

"Master Teh Shan, [i.e., Deshan]...left home at the age of twenty. After being fully ordained, he studied the Vinayapiṭaka [☞TRIPIṬAKA] which he mastered. He was well-versed in the teaching of the noumenal and phenomenal as expounded in the sutras. He used to teach the Diamond [Vajra] Prajñā....

"Said he to his schoolmates:

When a hair swallows the ocean
The nature-ocean loses naught.
To hit the needle's point with
mustard seed
Shakes not the needle's point.
(Of) [learning] and [what is beyond
learning]
I know and I alone.

"When he heard that the Ch'an Sect was flourishing in the South, he could not keep his temper and said: 'All who leave home take a thousand aeons to learn the Buddha's respect-inspiring deportment and ten thousand aeons to study the Buddha's fine deeds; (in spite of this) they are still unable to attain Buddhahood. How can those demons in the south dare to say that the direct indication of the mind leads to perception of the (self-)nature and attainment of Buddhahood? I must (go to the south,) sweep away their den and destroy their race to repay the debt of gratitude I owe the Buddha.'

"He left Szu Ch'uan province with Ch'ing Lung's Commentary [on the *Diamond Sutra*] on his shoulders. When he reached Li Yang, he saw an old woman selling *tien hsin* (lit. mind refreshment) [a kind of Chinese hors d'oeuvres] on the roadside. He halted, laid down his load and intended to buy some pastries to refresh his mind. The old woman pointed at the load and asked him: 'What is this literature?' Teh Shan replied: 'Ch'ing Lung's Commentary.' The old woman asked: 'Commentary on what sutra?' Teh Shan replied: 'On the *Diamond Sutra*.' The old woman said: 'I have a question to ask you; if you answer it, I will offer you mind refreshment; if you cannot reply, (please) go away. The *Diamond Sutra* says: "The past, present and future mind cannot be found." What do you want to refresh?'

"Teh Shan remained speechless." (Charles Luk, tr. *Ch'an and Zen Teachings*, Series One, 58-60)

It took his encounter with the old woman to teach Deshan that intellectual understanding was not enough. He then went on to learn on another level from her teacher, the enlightened Chan Master Longtan, who showed him the way to a real understanding of the meaning of emptiness.

E. The Dangers of Misunderstanding Emptiness

> Emptiness, ill-conceived, destroys a stupid man as would a [poisonous] snake when handled improperly, or a spell badly executed. (Nāgārjuna, *Mūlamadhyamakakārikāḥ* XXIV:11)

In America, from the Beatniks to the present there have been many who have dangerously misunderstood the doctrine of emptiness as an invitation to self-indulgence: "Everything's OK." "Let it all hang out." "Morality is an uptight hang-up we have to get over." "Our feelings should be our guide." All these have involved wrong attempts to interpret the doctrine of emptiness in one way or another to deny cause and effect. In the long run the advocates of such positions drown in the sea of bad karma they themselves create, yet when they go under they are unable to see the suffering of their drowning as empty. For those who have truly realized emptiness, living in complete harmony with the moral precepts is the natural foundation of their being in the world.

Emptiness in Practice

A. Emptiness in Everyday Life

We can use emptiness as an indestructible sword of *vajra* to cut through our afflictions and doubts.

Rightly understood, 'emptiness' is not a concept to be understood intellectually; it is a way of life. It points to the emptying of our experience moment after moment. What do we mean by emptying experience? First we should remove 'me' and 'mine' from every thought that arises in consciousness. Emptiness is a tool that can extricate us from ego-centered experience and liberate us from the prison of selfishness. We learn to see ourselves and our concerns, both desires and fears, as empty—like a mirage or a dream, as ephemeral as a bubble or a flash of lightning. Emptying ourselves opens us up to the fullness of the world.

What is emptying experience? It is also eliminating the boundaries that we have drawn to cope with the world—the 'walls' we erect to protect ourselves, the 'turf' we stake out to rule, and the fantasies of future conquests that we map in our minds. Emptying ourselves must lead to the emptying of the 'other,' the 'not-self,' so that self and other are no longer two. When the line that divides them is erased, emptied, then there is no conflict, no longer anything to fear or gain.

True emptiness is identical to the fullness of wonderful existence. It can be reached through the hard work of becoming aware of every single thought and emptying them one by one.

B. The Wrong Understanding of Emptiness in Practice

When a practitioner of the Path wrongly assumes a particular samadhi or other meditational experience to be true emptiness, he or she is in great danger of blocking further progress or of falling. The *Śūraṅgama Sutra* mentions a Bhikshu who attained the Heaven of No Cognition and assumed that he had attained enlightenment. When his life span there came to an end, he slandered the Dharma and fell into the hells.

Emptiness as a Description of Enlightenment

This refers to the many passages in the sutras that are descriptions, as far as language will allow, of the true emptiness that is wonderful existence.

☞ **void/nothingness ⟨misleading⟩, transparency**

☞ **Mahayana and Hinayana Compared, Nāgārjuna ⟨Bodhisattva⟩**

---

enlightenment 悟

> The Way of enlightenment
> is ineffable,
> Surpassing the paths of language.
> All Buddhas are born from it.
> This Dharma is hard to conceive.
> (EDR I 96)

Of enlightened beings only the enlightenment of a ☞BUDDHA is perfect and complete. The less than perfectly enlightened beings are ☞BODHISATTVAS, ☞PRATYEKABUDDHAS, and ☞ARHATS.

All enlightened beings have the following in common:

1 They have seen through the illusion of self.

2 They have achieved permanent release from the cycle of rebirth.

3 As a byproduct of their enlightenments, they possess spiritual powers (☞FIVE EYES, SIX SPIRITUAL POWERS), including that of the extinction of outflows.

Becoming enlightened "is like opening a lock...on a door. You have to have a key to get it open. The key was made to fit the lock, and that's what opens it now. How do you find the key? It's by working hard at your cultivation, constantly keeping yourself at it, doing inquiry while sitting in meditation, reciting the Buddha's name, holding mantras, reciting sutras—in all of that, you're looking for the key. When you find it, you'll open the lock in your mind. What's the lock?...It's ignorance. It locks you up in the dark...." (FAS-PII(1) 232-233)

A Circumstance of Enlightenment

"One day the Buddha and his great Bhikshus left the Jeta Grove in the city of Śrāvastī, where they were living, and went to accept an offering of food, leaving behind only one small *śrāmaṇera* (novice monk) to watch the door. After the Buddha had departed, an *upāsaka* (Buddhist layman) came to the monastery to request that a member of the Sangha come and accept offerings at his home on behalf of the ☞THREE JEWELS. Finding that all the Bhikshus and the Buddha had all gone out, he said to the one small *śrāmaṇera* who was left, 'That's okay. I'll invite you, *śrāmaṇera*, to come and accept my offering. Come with me.' The small *śrāmaṇera* nervously consented to accompany him, nervously because he had never gone out by himself to accept an offering before. He'd always gone with Bhikshus. Once he found himself obligated to speak Dharma, he realized that he didn't have any idea what to say. Although this concern weighed on him, he accompanied the host who had so sincerely asked him to go and accept the meal offering. After they had eaten, the inevitable happened. The host very respectfully turned to the small *śrāmaṇera* and bowed deeply, requesting Dharma. As an expression of his sincerity, the host kept his head bowed as he knelt before the small *śrāmaṇera*, waiting for him to speak Dharma. There sat the small *śrāmaṇera* staring at his host prostrate before him. And then what do you suppose happened? Without uttering a word, he slipped off his chair, tiptoed outside and beat a hasty retreat back to the Jeta Grove. Naturally he felt ashamed at having eaten his fill and then having run away without speaking the Dharma.

"For a long time the host knelt with his head bowed, but finally, having heard nothing, he lifted his head to steal a peek. And he saw that there was no one on the seat before him. The small *śrāmaṇera* had disappeared. At the moment he saw the *śrāmaṇera* was gone, he became enlightened. He awoke to the emptiness of people and the emptiness of dharmas. 'Haaa! So that's the way it is!' he exclaimed, and wished immediately to seek certification of his enlightenment. Naturally he headed for the Jeta Grove in search of the small *śrāmaṇera*.

"Meanwhile the small *śrāmaṇera*, petrified that his host would pursue him in quest of the Dharma, had run back to the Jeta Grove, headed straight for his room, slammed the door, and locked himself in. Who would have guessed that not long after he had locked the door, he would hear a knock? The little *śrāmaṇera* stood frozen with fear, not making a sound, on the inside of the door. He was totally panic-stricken. After all, he had eaten the host's food, and now the host had come demanding the Dharma. His nervousness reached such an extreme that at the height of his anxiety, he suddenly became enlightened; he also awakened to the emptiness of people and the emptiness of dharmas.

"This story illustrates that it is not certain under what circumstances one will become enlightened.... Some hear the sound of the wind and become enlightened. Some listen to the flow of water and become enlightened. Some become enlightened upon hearing a windchime; others upon hearing a bell ring.

"'I have heard all those things many times. Why haven't I become enlightened?' you may ask.

"How should I know why you haven't become enlightened? You must wait for enlightenment until your time arrives, just as you must wait for food to be cooked before you can eat it. You must wait till you are ripe for the opportunity, then anything you encounter can cause you to become enlightened.... It is only necessary that you continue to cultivate and investigate the Buddhadharma with determined and concentrated effort." (SS I 38-39)

When someone becomes enlightened, an auspicious earthquake occurs. Although the earth moves in six ways, no one is injured. In order for enlightenment to be accepted as genuine, it must be certified (☞CERTIFICATION). In the ☞ŚŪRAṄGAMA SUTRA the Buddha said this about claims of enlightenment:

> I command the Bodhisattvas and Arhats to appear after my cessation in

response-bodies in the ☞DHARMA-ENDING AGE, and to take various forms to rescue those in the cycle of rebirth....

But they should never say of themselves, "I am truly a Bodhisattva'; or 'I am truly an Arhat"....

How can people who make such claims, other than at the end of their lives and then only to those who inherit the teaching, be doing anything but deluding and confusing living beings and indulging in gross false claims?" (SS VI 48-55)

✍ **awakening**

☞ **bodhi, no self, Five Eyes, Six Spiritual Powers, outflows, ignorance**

Esoteric School 密宗

☞ **Five Types of Buddhist Study and Practice—Esoteric**

expedient Dharmas 方便法

"Being 'expedient' means being un-attached. For example, once there was a child crawling toward a well which was flush with the ground. If the child had continued, it would have fallen into the well. The Buddha saw this, but he knew that if he had called the child back, it would not have listened, but would have continued to crawl forward. And so he made a fist with one hand, held it out, and called, 'Child, come back! I have candy in my hand for you! I have candy. Do you like candy?' When the child heard that there was candy, it turned around and came back. There was no candy in the Buddha's hand after all. But was the Buddha lying? No. That is an example of an expedient method. He used his empty fist to save the child because there was no other method that would have worked at that point. The doors of expedients are countless. In general, whatever method will save a person is the Dharma-door you should use." (SS V 194)

"Skill-in-means [an alternate translation of 'expedient Dharma'] refers to provisional teachings: clever, expedient devices. Skill-in-means can also be explained as meaning 'exclusive Dharmas.' They are not restrained by any fixed standards; therefore, they are 'expedient.' In teaching beings one has to devise different kinds of Dharma-doors. As it is said,

> One devises a method
> according to the event;
> One devises a method
> according to the time; and
> One devises a method
> according to the circumstances.

Because of the different situations that arise, one has to use methods suited to the particular time and place. 'Skill-in-means implies that the methods are not constant and unchanging, but rather impromptu methods set up for a special purpose. Through those means one can 'pervasively bring the seas of living beings to maturity.' This is:

> Observing the opportunity and
> enticing with the teaching;
> Speaking Dharma according to
> the person, and
> Dispensing the medicine based
> on the illness."
> (EDR V 220-221)

> Moreover, she emitted clouds of bodies of all kinds, equal in number to the realm of living beings, which arrived before all living beings everywhere, and according to those beings' needs, spoke Dharma for them using all kinds of forms of speech and modes of expression. Perhaps they spoke of the power of worldly blessings and of the spiritual penetrations. Or else they described how fearsome the three

realms are, causing them to no longer create the karma of worldly conduct, but to separate themselves from the three realms and to escape from the dense forest of views. Or else they lauded the path of all-wisdom, causing them to transcend the ground of the Two Vehicles. Or else they spoke of neither abiding in birth and death nor abiding in nirvana, causing them not to become attached to either the conditioned or the unconditioned. (EDR V 79-80)

device, stratagem, means, skill-in-means, skillful means, provisional dharmas, skill in expedients, able management/diplomacy

☞ **Bodhisattva**

F

faith 信

Faith is one of the Eleven Wholesome Dharmas of the ☞ONE HUNDRED DHARMAS; it is also one of the Five Faculties (faith, vigor, mindfulness, concentration, and wisdom).

"Faith is necessary in whatever it is one does. One needs to have a sense of belief, an attitude of faith. First, one needs to have faith in oneself. What kind of faith? One needs to have faith that one certainly can become a Buddha. One has to believe that there is no difference between the Buddha and oneself. Yet that lack of difference is in one's Buddha-nature. Cultivation is still required in order to actually become a Buddha. If one cultivates, one will become a Buddha. In order to do so, one must have an initial belief in this principle.

"Second, not only is it necessary to believe that one can become a Buddha oneself, but also to believe that all people can become Buddhas. Moreover, not only can all people become Buddhas, one should believe that all living beings have the Buddha-nature and are capable of becoming Buddhas. If one has that kind of faith, then one should begin by following the rules oneself. To follow the rules means to hold the moral precepts. First one holds the precepts, and then one can become a Buddha. One does it oneself and also encourages others to do so as well.

"Faith must be solid, like a rock, firm and sturdy. Faith shouldn't be like a pile of ashes which seems to have some substance to it but which crumbles at the slightest disturbance. Don't be too soft. One's faith must be strong and solid." (HD 44-45)

"Faith is the foundation of cultivation of the Way and the mother of merit and virtue, because it is capable of nourishing wholesome roots. The Buddhadharma is like a vast sea; only by faith can it be entered. Therefore, the single word 'faith' is the essence of escape from birth and death and is the wonderful means for returning to the source. It is a precious raft on the stream of affliction, a torch in the dark cave of ignorance, and a guide who leads us out of the path of confusion. It is a compass for those floundering in the waves on the sea of suffering, and a sagely teacher for those in the Three Paths [Arhat, Pratyekabuddha, and Bodhisattva] and Eight Difficulties [being born in the hells, being born as a hungry ghost, being born as an animal, being born in the northern continent, being born in the Long Life Heaven, being born before or after the time of a Buddha, being born with impaired faculties, and being endowed with worldly intelligence and argumentative skill]. It is the origin of awakening for the Four Kinds of Creatures born [from wombs, eggs, moisture, and transformation] within the ☞ SIX PATHS. Faith cannot be ignored. An author of ancient times said, 'If a man has no faith, I do not know what can be made of him.'

"Once two Bhikshus were traveling to see Śākyamuni Buddha, the World Honored One. As they traveled they became extremely thirsty but could not find any water. As they walked they happened upon a human skull containing water in which some small bugs were swimming, enjoying themselves tremendously. One of the Bhikshus picked up the water and offered some to his companion. The companion replied, 'This water contains bugs, and the moral precepts do not permit drinking such water. I would rather die of thirst than violate the precepts in order to stay alive.' After this incident he died of thirst.

"When the Bhikshu who had drunk the water reached the place where the Buddha was residing, he bowed and said to the Lord, 'Your disciple was traveling in the company of another Bhikshu who perished of thirst on the road. I hope the Buddha will be compassionate and rescue him.'

"The Buddha said to the Bhikshu who had drunk the water, 'Because he stringently maintained the moral precepts and was so firm in his faith that he would not violate them even in the face of death, he received the awesome power of the Buddhas and arrived here before you. He has already seen the Buddha and heard the Dharma before you. He is a Bhikshu who has true faith in the precepts." (WM 53-54; also S42 75-76)

Hymn of Faith

"Faith is the source of the Way.
Faith is the mother of merit
and virtue.
As they arise by faith,
All wholesome dharmas
must by faith be nurtured.
Faith cuts the tangled web of doubt,
Escaping loves delusive flow,
And opens wide to reveal the true
and unsurpassed nirvana's road.

"Faith has no stain or mar,
Bringing the turbid mind
purification,
Eradicating pride,
Of all respect and reverence
the foundation.
Within the Dharma Treasury
Faith's jewel outshines
the fairest gold;
Hence every conduct our hands
by faith made pure
Receive and surely hold.

"Faith is the healing source
By which our faculties
are cleansed and quickened.
Nothing can turn its force.
The solid power of faith
cannot be broken.
And when by faith forever
From all affliction we depart,
The Buddha's merit will thus become
the sole devotion of our hearts.

"With faith the mind's unmoved,
Free from attachment to
conditioned arising;
Disasters far removed,
In the tranquility of faith abiding.
The bliss of faith victorious!
Among the conducts of all worlds,

This faith alone is the one most rare
and precious wish-fulfilling pearl.

"Profoundly we believe:
Trusting the Buddhas and the
Buddhas' Dharma,
Treading the Bodhi Path,
Forever followed by all true disciples.
And to the Great Enlightenment
Our thoughts are joyfully inclined:
The Bodhisattvas with this deep heart
of faith produce the Bodhi Mind!"
(RH 235)

belief

One Hundred Dharmas, Five Types of Buddhist Study and Practice—Pure Land

false thinking 妄想

polluted thoughts

filial piety ⟨respect for all⟩ 孝《孝道》

"Of the ten thousand evil acts,
lust is the worst;
Of the hundred wholesome deeds,
(filial) piety is foremost.

"What makes people different from animals is that people understand how to be filial to their parents and respectful to their teachers and elders. People are different from animals, who do not understand filiality, yet even

"The lamb kneels to nurse;
The crow returns to feed its parents.

"Filial piety...is basic to being human. Those who are not filial to their parents do not have good roots, but one who is filial certainly does." (UW 115)

"To practice filial piety means to be filial to one's parents and thus to be a dazzling light over the entire world. Both heaven and earth are greatly pleased by filial piety, and so it is said, 'Heaven and earth deem filial piety essential; filial piety is foremost. With one filial son, an entire family is peaceful.' If you are filial to your parents, your children will be filial to you; if you are not filial to your parents, your children will treat you in the same manner.

"One may think, 'What is the point of being human? Isn't it merely to try to get by as well as possible?' It certainly is not! The first duty of human beings is to be filial to their parents. Father and mother are heaven and earth; father and mother are all the elders; and father and mother are all the Buddhas. If you had no parents, you would have no body, and if you had no body, you could not become a Buddha. If you want to become a Buddha, you must start out by being filial to your parents." (SPV 18)

The Buddha said, "Filial compliance is a Dharma of the ultimate Way." (BNS 60)

"If one is filial to his parents, he will naturally be pleasant in his voice and will not say crude and unreasonable things. This is the discipline for the mouth. He is forever solicitous and never disobeys: this is the discipline for the body. He is full of sincere love and his mind will not harbor disloyal thoughts: this is the discipline for the mind. Filial piety has the power to stop evil, for one fears to disgrace one's parents: this is the discipline for proper conduct. It can also induce the performance of good, for one wishes to glorify one's parents:

this is the discipline for good dharma. Finally, filial piety also has the power to save others. Because of one's love for one's parents, other people can often be moved to follow one's example. Thus, this is also the discipline for saving sentient beings. To sum up, as long as one can be filial, one's conduct will naturally be perfect. It is no wonder that the discipline is so interpreted. Aside from filial piety, is there any other discipline?" (Ven. Chu-hung, quoted in Yu, Chun-fang, *Renewal of Buddhism in China*, 90)

> If there were a person who carried his father on his left shoulder and his mother on his right shoulder until his bones were ground to powder by their weight as they bore through to the marrow, and if that person were to circumambulate Mount Sumeru for a hundred thousand *kalpas* until the blood that flowed out of his feet covered his ankles, that person would still not have repaid the deep kindness of his parents....
>
> If you wish to repay your parents' kindness,...repent of transgressions and offenses on their behalf. For the sake of your parents, make offerings to the Three Jewels. For the sake of your parents, hold the precept of pure eating. For the sake of your parents, practice giving and cultivate blessings. If you are able to do these things, you are being a filial child...." (*The Buddha Speaks the Sutra About the Deep Kindness of Parents and the Difficulty in Repaying It*, FHS II, 103, 105)

☞ **filial duty, respect for parents and elders**

Five Contemplations when Eating
食存五觀

The Five Contemplations are:

1 I think about where the food came from and the amount of work necessary to grow the food, transport it, prepare and cook it and bring it to the table.

2 I contemplate my own virtuous conduct. Is it sufficient to merit receiving the food as offering?

3 I guard my mind against transgression, the principal ones being greed and so forth.

4 I realize that food is a wholesome medicine that heals the sufferings of the body.

5 I should receive the food offerings only for the sake of realizing the Way.

"1) *Consider the amount of work involved to bring the food to where it is eaten.* Think it over. How much human labor was necessary to bring even a single grain of rice to the table? It first had to be planted, then tended, then harvested and stored. And so the ancients had a poem which reads:

> The farmer hoes in the midday sun;
> His sweat falls on the soil.
> Who can guess how much toil it
> took
> To bring the food to the bowl?

"2) *Consider whether one's own virtuous conduct is sufficient to enable one to accept the offering.* Again, think it over. Have you cultivated any virtuous conduct? Count it up. How much do you have? Is it sufficient? Is it lacking? Are you entitled to receive this offering of food?

"3) *Take as one's guiding principle the guarding of the mind against transgressions such as greed.* Take as your principle, as your doctrine, a mind free from greed, anger, delusion, pride, and doubt.

"4) *Properly taken, the food is like medicine, to keep the body from wasting away.* If you don't eat, you body grows weak. Therefore, it is only to prevent weakness that you receive the food.

"5) *This food is accepted only in order to accomplish the Way.* Think to yourself, 'I only take this food in order to cultivate and accomplish the karma of the Way.'" (SV 55-56)

Five Contemplations Performed while Eating

vegetarianism

Five Desires 五欲

The Five Desires are the desires for **1)** wealth, **2)** sex, **3)** fame, **4)** food, and **5)** sleep.

When I obtain the Five Desires,
I vow that living beings
Will pull out the arrow of desire,
And attain ultimate peace and
security.
(FAS Ch11 99)

The Buddha said, "Those on the Way are like dry grass: it is essential to keep it away from an oncoming fire. People on the Way look upon desire as something they must keep at a distance." (S42 60)

The Buddha said, "People who cannot renounce wealth and sex are like small children who, not satisfied with one delicious helping, lick the honey off the blade of the knife and so cut their tongues." (S42 48)

The Buddha said, "There are people who follow emotion and desire and seek for fame. But by the time their reputation is established, they are already dead. Those who are greedy for worldly fame and do not study the Way wear themselves out with wasted effort. It is just like a stick of burning incense which, however fragrant its scent, consumes itself. So, too, greed for fame brings the danger of a 'fire' which burns one up in its aftermath." (S42 47)

The Buddha said, "As to love and desire: no desire is as deep-rooted as sex. There is none greater than the desire for sex. Fortunately, it is one of a kind. If there were something else like it, no one in the entire world would be able to cultivate the Way." (S42 51)

There was once someone who, plagued by ceaseless sexual desire, wished to castrate himself. The Buddha said to him, "To cut off your sexual organs would not be as good as to 'cut off' your mind. Your mind is like a supervisor: if the supervisor stops, his employees will also quit. If the deviant mind is not stopped, what good does it do to cut off the organs?" The Buddha recited a verse for him:

"Desire is born from your will;
Your will is born from thought.
When both aspects of the mind are still,
There is neither form nor activity."

The Buddha said, "This verse was spoken by Kāśyapa Buddha." (S42 63)

An alternate list of the Five Desires is comprised of: **1)** forms, **2)** sounds, **3)** smells, **4)** tastes, **5)** tangible objects (EIGHTEEN REALMS).

sense desires and enjoyments plus their objects

ignorance, love

Five Eyes 五眼

The five eyes are **1)** the heavenly eye, **2)** the flesh eye, **3)** the Dharma eye, **4)** the wisdom eye, and **5)** the Buddha eye.

Those five noncorporeal 'eyes' are possessed by Buddhas and other enlightened beings. They can also begin to function to varying degrees in people who are not enlightened but are cultivating or who have cultivated in past lives.

The heavenly eye penetrates what is
without obstruction;

The flesh eye sees obstacles and
  does not penetrate.
The Dharma eye can contemplate
  only the relative truth;
The wisdom eye can contemplate and
  know true emptiness,
While the Buddha eye blazes forth
  like a thousand suns.
Although the Five Eyes' functions
  differ,
Their substance is of one source.
(SPV 69)

F

"Even though one may be able to use these powers, it is better not to do so; for whenever things are looked at, a thought is spent, and adding a thought is not as good as diminishing one. To use the Five Eyes is to indulge in thought, and although such thoughts differ from ordinary ones, they are still not beneficial. It is always better to have one false thought less than to have one more." (SPV 69)

Heavenly Eye

"With the Heavenly Eye you see without obstruction. You can see the Buddhas, spirits, ghosts, and gods in the heavens. You can see everything that they are doing. That is even better than the closed circuit TV that the international spies use. It's not as much trouble either, and the best part is, it's all internal. You don't need any external help to know what's going on." (SM II 89)

> A Bodhisattva wisely knows the Heavenly Eye of the gods, beginning with the Four Great Kings; but the gods do not wisely know a Bodhisattva's Heavenly Eye. With his perfectly pure Heavenly Eye he wisely knows, as it really is, the decease and rebirth of all beings in the world systems numerous as the sands of the river Ganges, in each of the ten directions....(Conze, tr. *Large Sutra on Perfect Wisdom*, 44)

Flesh Eye

"The Flesh Eye sees obstructions and doesn't penetrate. The Flesh Eyes sees things that have form. The Heavenly Eye can't see things with form. The Flesh Eye does not refer to the regular eyes in our physical body. It is another, different eye. The Heavenly Eye can't see physical things, but it can see ghosts, gods, and so forth. The Flesh Eye can see things with physical form and also things without physical form. If you open your Flesh Eye you can see the people in the room with you, and you can also see the people outside the room. Walls present no obstacle to your vision." (SM II 90)

> There is the fleshly eye of a Bodhisattva which sees for one hundred miles, for two hundred miles, across Jambudvīpa, a Four-Continent world system, a world system consisting of 1,000 worlds, a world system consisting of 1,000,000 worlds, a world system consisting of 1,000,000,000 worlds. (Conze, *ibid.*, 43-44)

Dharma Eye

"The Dharma Eye contemplates the common truth, which is also called the conventional, relative truth, or wonderful existence. If this eye is opened, there is no need to use books in order to read sutras, since the entire extent of space is seen to be full of limitless Dharma treasures." (SPV 69)

> Here a Bodhisattva knows, by means of the Dharma eye, that "this person is a Faith-follower, that person a Dharma-follower. This person is a dweller in Emptiness, that person a dweller in the Signless, that person a dweller in the Wishless. The five cardinal virtues will arise in this person by means of the emptiness-door to deliverance, in that person by means of the signless door to deliverance, in that person by means of the

wishless door to deliverance. By means of the five cardinal virtues this one gazes upon the unimpeded concentration. By means of the unimpeded concentration he will produce the vision and cognition of emancipation. By means of the vision and cognition of emancipation he will forsake three fetters, i.e., the view of individuality, the contagion of mere rule and ritual, and doubt. He then is a person who is called a Streamwinner. After he has acquired the path of development, he attenuates sensuous greed and ill-will. He is then the person who is called a Once-Returner. Through making just this path of development preponderant and developing it, he will come to the forsaking of sensuous greed and of ill-will. He is then the person who is called a Never-Returner. Through making just this path of development preponderant and developing it, he will forsake greed for the world of form, greed for the formless world, ignorance, conceit, and excitedness. He then is the person who is called an Arhat." This is the perfectly pure Dharma Eye of the Bodhisattva, the great being. Moreover, a Bodhisattva knows wisely that "whatever is doomed to originate, all that is also doomed to stop." Coursing in perfect wisdom, he attains the five cardinal virtues.... (Conze, *ibid.*, 44-45)

Wisdom Eye

"The Wisdom Eye contemplates true emptiness; one understands and certifies to the principle of true emptiness and is filled with the Dharma bliss of true emptiness." (SM II 90)

> A Bodhisattva who is endowed with that Wisdom Eye does not wisely know any Dharma—be it conditioned or unconditioned, wholesome or unwholesome, faulty or faultless, with or without outflows, defiled or undefiled, worldly or supramundane. With the Wisdom Eye he does not see any dharma, or hear, know or discern one. (Conze, *ibid.*, 44)

Buddha Eye

"The Buddha Eye is like a thousand suns, shining everywhere, illuminating the one substance underlying all diversity. It shines on different things, but underneath, they are all one substance. The Buddha Eye is the most perfect of the Five Eyes. It surpasses the other four. With it one can see people and ghosts, spirits, and everything else, both physical and nonphysical." (SM II 90)

> The Bodhisattva, when immediately after the thought of enlightenment he has, with a wisdom conjoined with one single thought-moment, entered on the adamantine concentration, reaches the knowledge of all modes. He is endowed with the ten powers of a Tathāgata, the four grounds of self-confidence, the four analytical knowledges, the 18 special Buddha-dharmas, the great friendliness, the great compassion, the great sympathetic joy, the great evenmindedness, and the unhindered deliverance of a Buddha. And that Eye of the Bodhisattva does not meet with anything that is not seen, heard, known or discerned—in all its modes. (Conze, *ibid.*, 46)

☞ **five superior qualities of vision**
☞ **Six Spiritual Powers**

Five Moral Precepts 五戒

The Five Moral Precepts are prohibitions against **1)** killing, **2)** stealing, **3)** sexual misconduct, **4)** false speech, and **5)** taking intoxicants.

"The Five Precepts prohibit killing, stealing, sexual misconduct, lying, and taking intoxicants. Why should one keep the Five Precepts? In order to:

Do no evil, yet
Reverently practice good deeds.

"Do not kill; do not steal; do not commit sexual misconduct; do not engage in false speech; do not take intoxicants. If you observe the Five Precepts, you do not do these five kinds of evil deeds and you instead practice good acts.

"Why should one refrain from killing? It is because all living beings have a life; they love their life and do not wish to die. Even one of the smallest creatures, the mosquito, when it approaches to bite you, will fly away if you make the slightest motion. Why does it fly away? Because it fears death. It figures that if it drinks your blood you will take its life. From this you can see that all living beings love life and do not wish to die. Especially people. Everyone wants to live and no one wants to die. Although people sometimes commit suicide, ordinarily people do not seek death. Suicide is a special exception to the principle. That is why we should nurture compassionate thoughts. Since we wish to live, we should not kill any other living beings. That explains the precept against killing.

"Stealing. If you don't steal, no one will steal from you. Many of you have heard this verse I wrote:

If in this life you don't cage birds,
In future lives you will not sit in jail.

If in this life you do not fish,
In future lives you will not beg for
food.
If in this life you do not kill,
In future lives you'll suffer no
disasters.
If in this life you do not steal,
In future lives you won't be robbed.
If in this life you commit no sexual
misconduct,
In future lives you will not be
divorced.
If in this life you do not lie,
In future lives you will not be
deceived.
If in this life you do not take
intoxicants,
In future lives you will not
go insane....

"Some people say, 'Of the Five Precepts, the four which prohibit killing, stealing, sexual misconduct, and lying are very important. But taking intoxicants is a very commonplace thing. Why prohibit that?' When you consume intoxicants, it becomes very easy to break the other precepts. Thus, we ban such things as drinking alcohol, smoking tobacco, and taking any kind of intoxicating drugs.

"Some people say, 'The Five Precepts don't specifically prohibit smoking tobacco or taking drugs. Doing those things is not in violation of the precepts.' Those people are wrong. The precept against intoxicants also prohibits smoking tobacco, taking drugs, and using all intoxicating substances—including marijuana and opium." (BRF 59-60)

"The Five Precepts are extremely important. Strict adherence to them will insure rebirth in the realm of humans. If you cultivate the Five Precepts, you won't lose the opportunity to be born a person.

"Someone may say, however, 'I understand why one should not kill. After all, all living beings have the ☞ BUDDHA-NATURE, all can become Buddhas, and so every living being's life should be spared. I also understand why stealing is not good and that it is important to refrain from indulging in sexual misconduct and lying, but why are intoxicants included within the Five Precepts? I always enjoyed drinking and smoking. Everybody drinks. Everybody smokes. What's wrong with it? In fact I'm seriously considering dropping my study of the Buddhadharma just because of this prohibition against intoxicants.'

"You should stop and think about it, instead of just following the crowd. Others enjoy smoking, and so you join them; others enjoy drinking, and so you drink too. You get caught up in such company and do the things they do until eventually you get the habit as well. Most people don't have grave illnesses, rather merely slight sicknesses and little problems. But just on account of those slight problems you would consider cutting short your study of the Buddhadharma. How foolish that would be! Do you want to know why there is a prohibition against alcohol? I'll tell you a true story which should clarify this point.

"There once was a man who liked to drink. He took the Five Precepts, but afterwards he didn't keep them....One day he thought, 'Perhaps I'll have a little drink of wine.' He took out a bottle and had a few swallows. He was accustomed to having something to eat with his drink, so he set the bottle down and went outside to look for something to eat. He noticed that his neighbor's chicken had strayed over into his yard. 'Good,' he thought, 'it will make a good chaser,' and he snatched up the pullet. At that point he broke the precept against stealing. Once he'd stolen it, he had to kill it before he could eat it, and so he broke the precept against killing. Once the chicken was cooked, he used it to chase down his wine, and soon he was roaring drunk, thus breaking once again the precept against the use of intoxicants. About that time there was a knock at his door. It was the neighbor lady in search of her chicken. 'I haven't seen it,' he blurted out, thereby breaking the precept against lying.

"A second glance at the neighbor lady revealed her beauty to him and, aroused by an overpowering sexual desire, he raped her.

"Afterwards he was met with litigation. All that came about because he wanted to drink. Just because he had a few drinks, he broke the other four precepts and got into a lot of trouble. Intoxicants cause one to become confused and scattered, and so they are the object of one of the Buddhist prohibitions. A person who is drunk lacks self-control. With no forewarning he can find himself suddenly in the heavens, suddenly on earth. He mounts the clouds and drives the fog—he'll do anything....

"If you receive the Five Precepts and do not violate them, then you are protected by good Dharma-protecting spirits, who are connected with each precept. If you break the precepts, the good spirits leave and no longer protect you. That is why receiving the precepts is extremely important in Buddhism." (SS I 46-47)

☞ **moral precepts, Ten Wholesome Deeds**

Five Skandhas 五陰/五蘊

The five *skandhas* are **1)** form, **2)** feeling, **3)** cognition, **4)** formations, and **5)** consciousness.

> The mind is like an artist
> Who can paint the entire world.
> From this the five *skandhas* arise
> As well as all dharmas.
> (FAS Ch20, HYSC 30:63)

When the Bodhisattva ☞AVALOKITEŚVARA was practicing the profound *prajñā-pāramitā*, he illuminated the five *skandhas* and saw that they are all empty. (HS 1)

The Meaning of "Skandhas"

Skandha is a Sanskrit word meaning 'heap, pile, or aggregate.' The Buddha illustrated his teaching about the *skandhas* by using five small piles—heaps—of different grains. The *skandhas* are general divisions for categorizing all phenomena in the conditioned world. Because they include within them all transitory, impermanent phenomena, they are an important tool for understanding the Buddhist doctrine of ☞NO SELF. If one analyzes all aspects of what one feels to be one's "self," one finds that all fall within the scope of the Five Skandhas.

"The Five Skandhas as they are found in your body:

1 The body is the *form skandha*.
2 Once you have the form *skandha*, you then have *feelings* of enjoyment and pleasure.
3 You want pleasure, and so you give rise to polluted thinking, which is *cognition*. How can I get what I want? How can I actually indulge in pleasure?
4 You have to go and do it. That is *formations*.
5 Acting requires a certain amount of wisdom, a *consciousness* which is a kind of small intelligence, a minute amount....

"Your body achieves its aims. 'Oh, enjoyment! Ahhh!' The enjoyment lasts about five minutes. Because of the excessive exertion, your blood vessels rupture and then death comes....What was it all about? It was just the Five Skandhas.

"The Five Skandhas are just five ways of uniting, of working together to open a company. The company, once opened, opens again and again....The *skandha*-company grows everywhere like a wild vine that is never cut. Once opened, the Five Skandhas, Inc. always stays open, always feeling that there is hope. What hope? 'Ah! This life I didn't make money, but wait until next life and I will be able to make some.' Who can know whether there will be even less capital in the next life?" (HS 46-47)

"When you break through all five *skandhas*, and are no longer deluded by them, you can 'cross beyond all suffering.' You can then put an end to all bitterness. Seeing that the Five Skandhas are all empty is getting rid of the attachment to self." (LY II 104)

Form

> And why, brethren, do ye say body [i.e., form]? One is affected, brethren. That is why the word "body" is used. Affected by what? Affected by touch of cold and heat, of hunger and thirst, of gnats, mosquitos, wind and sun and snakes. One is affected, brethren. That is why we say "body." (Rhys Davids, tr. *Kindred Sayings* III 72-73)

"What is *form*? The body is included among the form-dharmas; since it is form, it is called the "form body." Your form body has an appearance, but when you seek for its origin you will find that it is empty.... When the Four Great Elements, namely earth, water, fire, and wind, unite, the body comes into being. This is what is meant by having a form. Working together the elements establish a corporation. The corporation comes into being from the four conditioned causes: earth, which is characterized by solidity and durability; water, which is characterized by moisture; fire, which is characterized by warmth; wind, which is characterized by movement. When the four conditioned causes disperse, each has a place to which it returns; therefore, the body becomes empty." (HS 44-45)

"Once you break through the form *skandha*, 'all the mountains, rivers, and great earth are seen as empty.'" (LY II 103)

Form includes the Four Great Elements and the eleven derived types of form known as the Eleven Form Dharmas. When they are in equilibrium, the Four Great Elements together produce a pure form that is not detectible by the ordinary senses. That pure form is the inner substance of the five perceptual organs and the medium of their actual functioning. When the Four Great Elements are out of equilibrium, different combinations of them produce both the coarse material aspect, or "sheaths," of the perceptual organs and also their objects (what they perceive).

Four Great Elements

NAME	STATE	ACTIVITY
earth	solidity	produced by repulsion
water	liquidity or fluidity	produced by attraction
fire	temperature	produced by heat
air/wind	expansion, lightness, and mobility	produced by motion

Eleven Form Dharmas

ORGANS	OBJECTS
1 eyes	6 sights
2 ears	7 sounds
3 nose	8 smells
4 tongue	9 tastes
5 body	10 tangible objects
	11 subtle traces

*** The subtle traces are mental residue of verbal and physical action. They can be understood as the "seeds" of future retribution.**

Feeling

And why, brethren, do ye say "feeling"? One feels, brethren. That is why the word "feeling" is used. Feels what? Feels pleasure and pain; feels neutral feelings. One feels, brethren. That is why the word "feeling" is used. (*Kindred Sayings* III 73)

"Once the body manifests, it likes pleasurable *feelings*. There are three kinds of feelings, which correspond to the three kinds of suffering: feelings of suffering; feelings of happiness; feelings which are characterized by neither suffering nor happiness." (HS 45)

"A state arises and you perceive it; you feel it is pleasurable. Eating good things, putting on a fine garment, feeling warm and being greatly delighted—these feelings of contentment, as well as feelings of displeasure and pain, are all grouped under the feeling *skandha*." (LY II 103)

Feelings are pleasant, unpleasant or neutral. They arise from contact of organ, object, and consciousness. Feeling includes both the primary sensation and the primary affective categorization of it.

Cognition

And why, brethren, do ye say "perception [another translation of *saṃjñā*]"? One perceives, brethren. That is why the word "perception" is used. Perceives what? Perceives blue-green, perceives yellow, or red, or white. One perceives, brethren. That is why the word "perception" is used. (*Kindred Sayings* III 73)

When you are awake, your mind thinks. When you are asleep, you dream. Thus your thinking [another translation of *saṃjñā*] is stirred to perceive false situations . (SS VIII 377)

"As for *cognition*, you certainly must have (the need for) false thoughts if you want enjoyment. You can't be without it. 'How can I think of a way to buy a car? How can I buy a beautiful home? How can I think of a way to buy a yacht? An airplane?' Your false thoughts fly back and forth and your hair turns white. Why? It turns white from false thinking." (HS 46)

Cognition is the differentiation and identification of objects both physical and mental. Therefore, it includes both higher perceptual functions and thinking processes, including those of language.

Formations

In many of the passages below the alternate translation 'activities' is used.

> And why, brethren, do ye say "the activities-compound"? Because they compose a compound. That is why, brethren, the word "activities-compound" is used. And what compound do they compose? It is the body that they compose into a compound of body. It is feeling that they compose into a feeling-compound. It is perception that they compose into a perception compound; the activities into an activities-compound; consciousness into a consciousness-compound. They compose a compound, brethren. Therefore, the word (activities)-compound is used. (*Kindred Sayings* III 73)

> These activities never stop. They progress through subtle changes: your nails and hair grow, your energy wanes, and your skin becomes wrinkled. The processes continue day and night and yet you never wake up to them. (SS VIII 378)

"When you lie in bed at night, you have a thousand plans....Sometimes you get up early and act on them. Sometimes sleeping seems nice, and you just sleep. *Formations* are basically the acting out of karma, that is, really acting upon your false thinking." (HS 46)

"Activities mean movement. They are ceaseless. People are first young, and they become middle-aged, and then old, and then they die. Thought after thought arises and is extinguished, thought after thought without cease. This is the *skandha* of activities." (SS III 22)

Formations refer to both conscious and unconscious volitional forces, including:

1 conscious intentions or acts of will, the most important category of this *skandha*
2 innate predispositions (karma from past lives)
3 unconscious forces having to do with basic life functions, nourishment, and growth

Consciousness

> And why, brethren, do ye say consciousness? One is conscious, brethren. Therefore, the word "consciousness" is used. Conscious of what? Of (flavours) sour or bitter; acrid or sweet; alkaline or non-alkaline; saline or non-saline. One is conscious, brethren. That is why the word "consciousness" is used. (*Kindred Sayings* III 74)

> It is like rapidly flowing water that appears to be still on the surface. Due to its speed you don't perceive the flow, but that does not mean it is not flowing. (SS VIII 384)

> "The *skandha* of consciousness involves the making of distinctions. It discriminates, considers, and seeks advantages from circumstances." (SS III 22)

Consciousness is the subtle basis of feeling, cognition, and formations. It consists of a subtle distinction-making awareness that distinguishes awareness from the objects of awareness. It is a flux of constantly changing, knowing activity.

The Five

> Body [i.e., form], brethren, is impermanent. What is impermanent, that is suffering. What is suffering, that is not the Self. What is not the Self, "that is not mine, that am not I, that is not the Self of me." This is the way one should regard things

> as they really are, by right insight. So likewise with regard to feeling, perception, the activities, consciousness. So seeing, brethren, the well-taught Ariyan [i.e., noble] disciple feels disgust at body, at feeling, perception, the activities and consciousness. Feeling disgust he is repelled: by repulsion he is released; by that release set free, knowledge arises: "in the freed man is the free thing," and he knows: 'destroyed is rebirth; lived is the righteous life; done is the task; for life in these conditions there is no hereafter." (*Kindred Sayings* III 68-69)

The *skandha* of form is like a mass of foam, because, when taken hold of, it cannot be kept together (in the hand); feeling is like a bubble because, as lasting only for a moment, it is impermanent; perception (cognition) is like a mirage, because it is misled by the thirst of craving; the impulses (formations) are like a plantain tree because, when (the leaf-sheaths) are taken away, no core remains; consciousness is like a dream, because it takes hold of what deceives. Therefore, the five *skandhas* have no self, (and they contain) no person (*pudgala*), no living being, no living soul, no personality and no manhood (*puruṣa*).... (Conze, tr. *Ārya-prajñā-pāramitā-hṛdaya-ṭīkā* 54)

☞ *SKANDHAS* : heaps, aggregates, agglomerations
***FORM* : material qualities, materiality**
***FEELING* : sensation and feeling, primary (initial perception), initial perceptual input, reception, sense perception, sense reception**
***COGNITION* : perception, thinking**
***FORMATIONS* : activities, coefficients of consciousness, impulses, compositional factors, volitional and karmic formations and forces, motivational dispositions, processes**
***CONSCIOUSNESS* : subjective discriminative awareness**

☞ Dharma/dharma

Five Turbidities 五濁

The Five Turbidities are **1)** the turbidity of *kalpa*, **2)** the turbidity of views, **3)** the turbidity of afflictions, **4)** the turbidity of beings, and **5)** the turbidity of life span.

"What are the Five Turbidities? The first is the turbidity of the ☞KALPA. KALPA is a Sanskrit word that is interpreted as a 'division of time.' How does the *kalpa* become turbid? At the time of the five evil realms, the evil karma of living beings makes the *kalpa* turbid.

"The second turbidity is views. In the past, people saw everything as clean. But when the turbid *kalpa* arrives, people see things as unclean. The turbidity of views is composed of the Five Quick Servants: a view of the body, prejudiced views, views of prohibitions, views of views, and deviant views.

"The first is the *view of a body:* all living beings are attached to having bodies. They love their bodies. 'I certainly have to take care of myself. I can't let anything happen to me.' They look upon their own bodies as extremely important. They want to wear good clothes, eat good food, live in a good place. They always look upon their bodies as priceless gems. Right, your body is a priceless gem, but if you misuse it, your priceless gem turns into something not even as good as excrement. Why? Because you tend only to its superficial aspects, and don't discover the true gem of your self-nature. All you know is that your body is yours, and you can't put it down. From morning to night you are busy on behalf of your body. That's the view of a body.

"*Prejudiced views* favor one side or the other. If you don't favor emptiness, then you favor existence. In general, it means not being in accord with the Middle Way.

"The third 'quick servant' is the *view of prohibitions*. Precepts can turn into something bad when they are based on mistaking for a cause something that is not a cause. Such a mistake leads to the cultivation of unbeneficial ascetic practices. I explained earlier how some people imitate the habits of cows or dogs, or sleep on beds of nails, or undertake other unbeneficial ascetic practices. People who do this have a view of prohibitions. 'See me,' they think, 'I hold precepts. None of you can do what I do; you can't compare to me.' They always have this arrogance in their minds.

"The fourth is the '*view of views*,' or '*grasping at views*.' This is to mistake for an effect something that is not an effect. People with this problem think that they have obtained effects which they have not obtained.

"The fifth is *deviant views*. People with deviant knowledge and views are always thinking about things in an improper way. These are the Five Quick Servants, which comprise the turbidity of views.

"The third turbidity is the turbidity of the afflictions, which is composed of the Five Slow Servants: greed, anger, delusion, arrogance, and doubt. 'Greed' refers to an insatiable greed for pleasant experiences. You are greedy for the things you like. 'Anger' is the dislike of unpleasant situations. 'Delusion' means deluded false thoughts. 'Arrogance' refers to pride and self-satisfaction—the feeling that 'I am the greatest' and 'no one is equal to me.' Arrogant people have no courtesy towards others.

"'Doubt' refers to doubt of the genuine Dharma and preference for improper dharmas instead. Such people doubt the true and rely on the false. They doubt the proper Dharma and believe deviant dharmas.

"These are the Five Slow Servants, which comprise the third turbidity, that of afflictions. The existence of these five dull servants creates a lot of affliction.

"The fourth turbidity is that of living beings—let's not even try to express it. Why? Living beings are just too filthy, too unclean, too impure. You shouldn't think of yourself as being so terrific. Living beings are murky and turbid; there's nothing so good about them. But living beings think of themselves as something really special, despite the fact that they comprise the fourth kind of turbidity.

"The fifth turbidity is the turbidity of a life span. Our mundane lives, our destinies, are impure." (SS III 205-207)

five turbid realms, evil world of the five turbidities, five periods of turbidity, impurity or chaos of decay

time, Five Skandhas

Five Types of Buddhist Study and Practice 五大宗

The Five Types of Buddhist Study and Practice are **1)** Study and Practice of the Teachings, **2)** Study and Practice of the Moral Regulations (Vinaya), **3)** Study and Practice of the Esoteric Dharmas, **4)** Study and Practice of Meditation (Chan), **5)** Study and Practice for Rebirth in the Pure Land.

"The Buddha's teachings are taught in Five [Types of] Schools: the Teachings Schools, the Vinaya School, the Esoteric School, the Chan School, and the Pure Land School. There are many who like to say that these are five sects, or types of Buddhism, which leads to all kinds of doctrinal squabbling. It is not accurate; the schools might better be called five basic approaches to cultivation. Each of these Dharma-doors has special appeal to certain types of people, but only one can be said to be equally easy for all to cultivate, and that is the Pure Land Dharma-door." (WM 17-18)

Teachings

The Teachings include the Buddhist doctrinal schools, such as the eighteen Hinayana schools, the ☞MĀDHYAMIKA and ☞YOGĀCĀRA schools of the Mahayana, and sutra-based Mahayana schools such as ☞TIANTAI and ☞HUAYAN.

"The Teachings Schools emphasize using skillful expedients, and therefore capitalize on beautiful expression and elegant phraseology. Adherents to these schools are well-versed in terminology and characteristics. They determine the different periods of the teachings and divide them into categories. Thus, the sea of meanings billows, and the Dharma's principles run deep. They serve to focus the audience's rambling thoughts, and to gather in stray mental activities that leak out through seeing and listening. When this occurs, it's as if one has entered the hall of samadhi, and ascended the six heavens of the desire realm. Layer upon layer one bores in; step by step one ascends. Even if one wanted to stop, it would be nearly impossible, and it's hard to fathom the very source.

"Regarding the teachings of the Teachings Schools—such as the Four Teachings of Tiantai, the Five Esoteric Meanings of Xianshou (i.e., Huayan), the Dharma-mark propagated by ☞CONSCIOUSNESS-ONLY—each has its strengths. Although each of these schools may not be extremely biased, nevertheless, on occasion they extol themselves at others' expense.

"Whenever clear-eyed ☞GOOD AND WISE ADVISORS see such incidents, they feel greatly pained at heart. Since the foundation of the Teachings has not flourished, and true talent is scarce, these good advisors are willing to act personally as models, practice ascetic discipline, and cultivate the door of the ☞SIX PĀRAMITĀS. In the face of a hundred oppositions they do not bend, and they are glad to undergo ten thousand vicissitudes, to the point that even if their bodies had to be smashed to pieces and their bones pulverized, they would not begrudge such a sacrifice. Supported by magnanimous vows, they are courageous and vigorous. Renouncing themselves for others, they take across everyone with whom they have causal connections. Observing the opportunities, they entice with the teachings and dispense medicine according to the illness. Not avoiding weariness or toil, they would offer up their heads, eyes, brains and marrow, give away their bodies and minds, all with the sole intention of causing living beings to turn away from confusion and return to enlightenment, to cast out the deviant and come back to what is proper. They want living beings to quickly attain *bodhi* and perfect the sagely fruition. Therefore, they employ both provisional and actual means, and bestow both sudden and gradual teachings. With kindness they draw in those with whom they have no affinities; with compassion they embrace all things and become one with them. Revealing a vast and long tongue, they take great pains to exhort with earnest words, sparing no efforts. They teach and admonish without tiring, while always conducting themselves in accord with strict discipline. In such ways they act as the 'dragons and elephants' at the Dharma's entrance, also as teachers of gods and people. Throughout long *kalpas* they practice the Bodhisattva Way and never rest." (WM 74-75)

"The cultivation of the Teachings Schools, while serving as an excellent cure for the disease of ignorance, does demand certain qualifications. It cannot, for example, be cultivated by the illiterate, by those who do not know the languages in which the teachings are written, or by the very ignorant. And so, although the teachings are universal and there is not a single being who cannot benefit from them, in their literary form there is a definite group of people to whom they are best suited." (WM 18)

Moral Regulations

"The Vinaya School stresses the study of precepts, the rules and regulations. In the four comportments of walking, standing, sitting, and lying down, one has to be stern and dignified, and the three karmas of body, mouth and mind have to be pure. *Upāsakas* and *upāsikās* [laymen and laywomen], the two lay assemblies, may maintain the ☞FIVE PRECEPTS and the Eight Precepts, as well as the Ten Major and Forty-eight Minor Bodhisattva Precepts. *Srāmaṇeras* and *srāmaṇerikās* [male and female novices] take the Ten Novice Precepts.

☞BHIKSHUS [monks] have 250 precepts, and ☞BHIKSHUNIS [nuns] have 348 precepts. One should maintain each and every one of those precepts without ever violating them and believe in them, accept them, and offer up one's conduct. One should be mindful of the agony of revolving in birth and death. If we lose this human body, it will be hard to recover it in ten thousand aeons. Therefore, at all times, we should strictly cultivate the *vinaya* and never be lax." (WM 75-76)

"The Vinaya, or 'Rules and Regulations' School, requires not only that one be literate, but also that one be living a monastic life. There is no way for the worldly man to perfect cultivation of the ☞VINAYA. Pure maintenance of this Dharma-door serves as a supremely efficacious cure for greed, desire, and arrogance. Much of it, however, can be practiced by men and women in the world, and it can be an immense help in cultivation. All real practicers of Buddhadharma, Sangha members or lay people, formally maintain precepts, ranging from the five for lay people to the more than three hundred for Bhikshunis. There are few more awesome people in the world than the masters of Vinaya, perfect in the three thousand rules of deportment." (WM 18)

Esoteric

"The Esoteric School specializes in the holding of ☞MANTRAS and maintains that one can realize Buddhahood in this very life. And yet, if practitioners are the slightest bit reckless, they can easily fall into the Dharma Realm of ☞ASURAS. That is because the majority of those in these practices have not subdued the anger in their minds, and their tendency to seek revenge is extremely strong. They lack thoughts of kindness and compassion, and rarely practice the art of patience. Many of them are prone to be arrogant, and their pride and conceit are deeply rooted. In holding secret mantras they dare to slight others, and wielding their *vajras* they are not afraid of bullying people. However, if one can be rid of the bad habits described above, then one's practice of samadhi can become successful, and one can go on to achieve the fruition that is ☞BODHI. In that case, this Dharma-door is also a skillful expedient for cultivators of the Way." (WM 76)

"The Esoteric School requires among other things both a good memory to hold its many mantras and ☞DHĀRAṆĪS, plus a good deal of money to carry out its elaborate and splendid rituals. A fully adorned *bodhimaṇḍa* (☞WAY-PLACE) is required as well as a profusion of images and various Dharma instruments. Also essential are numbers of Dharma Masters well-trained and conversant with the esoteric lore of this school. They are hard to find. Without them and without special instruction, it is not possible to be successful with the teachings of the Esoteric School." (WM 19)

> I have preached the truth without making any distinction between exoteric and esoteric doctrine; for in respect of the truths, Ānanda, the Tathāgata has no such thing as the closed fist of a teacher who keeps some things back. (Rhys Davids, tr. *Dialogues of the Buddha* II 107)

Meditation ⟨Chan⟩

"The ☞ CHAN (Zen) or Dhyāna-meditation School stresses the practice of meditation, and its cultivation requires a special set of circumstances. First, it is essential to have an advisor, one of great wisdom and skill, who can teach the student by all manner of expedient means. Without such a teacher, there is no way for ordinary people to have any success in Chan ☞ MEDITATION. They may achieve some measure of attainment, but due to lack of wise counsel, they will be turned by their experience; thinking that they are like the great Chan Masters of old, they will go around committing all sorts of deluded and even dangerous or immoral acts. Such so-called 'enlightened masters' and 'patriarchs' are too often well-meaning practicers of Chan who have either not met or not submitted to the teaching of a ☞ GOOD AND WISE ADVISOR. Too many of them have entered into the various demonic states that the Buddha discussed in the ☞ ŚŪRAṄGAMA SUTRA. Anyone who professes to be a follower of the Buddha should act in accordance with his teachings and find a capable advisor, one whose experience and lineage are unquestioned.

"In addition to the above qualifications, Chan cultivation requires a certain temperament which is rarely found. While some immediately get a response in Chan cultivation, there are many for whom it represents unbearable difficulty. If this is the only means of cultivation presented to them, many people will flee from the Buddhadharma as a small child screams upon seeing a tame but incredibly fierce-looking tiger on a leash." (WM 18-19)

Pure Land

"The Pure Land School Dharma is the most perfect and the most instantaneous, the simplest and the easiest. It is a Dharma that everyone can cultivate; one and all can practice it. Hence it is described as 'universally including the three types of faculties (superior, average, and inferior capabilities), and gathering in both the keen and the dull.' One only has to single-mindedly uphold the great name 'Namo ☞ AMITĀBHA BUDDHA,' that of the teaching host of the Land of Ultimate Bliss of the West [☞ PURE LAND]. When one recites this name and arrives at the point of single-minded concentration, then one will definitely be reborn in the West from a lotus flower. When that lotus blooms, one will see the Buddha, awaken to a forbearance with the not coming into being of dharmas, and attain irreversible ☞ ANUTTARA-SAMYAK-SAṂBODHI. Therefore, if all cultivators only become replete with deep faith and earnest vows, and actually realize the three requisites—faith, vows, and practice—they all will most certainly reach their destination. It is my hope that all of you good people will exhort each other onwards." (WM 76-77)

"Recitation is the central practice of the Pure Land Dharma-door. 'Namo Amita Buddha.' 'Namo' means 'to return in reliance,' 'to take refuge.' 'Amita' means 'limitless' and refers to the fact that this Buddha has both 'Limitless Light' (Amitābha) and 'Limitless Life' (Amitāyus). 'Buddha' means 'Enlightened One.' And so 'Namo Amita Buddha' means 'I take refuge with and return my life in worship to the Buddha of

Limitless Light and Life.' The constant repetition of this Buddha's name is the core of the Pure Land Dharma-door....

"The Pure Land Dharma-door requires no great learning. Many illiterates attain inconceivable spiritual benefit through it. Many, too, are the high and learned masters who praise this door. The Pure Land Dharma-door shows us how to purify our minds, and as such it is identical with the Teachings Schools, whose complex and learned systems serve to keep the mind from wandering off on useless excursions. To be able to hold (in one's mind) the elaborate systems of the Teachings Schools requires prolonged concentration on the Buddhadharma. Concentrating on what is pure is fundamentally identical with recollection of the Buddha. The Pure Land Dharma does not require that one lead a monastic life and perfect the three thousand awesome deportments. This Dharma-door can be cultivated right in the midst of the most ordinary life. Lay people and *vinaya* specialists alike can cultivate this Dharma. Nor does it require elaborate rituals and expensive ceremonies, or secret, esoteric lore to be learned from specialized teachers. The secret of the Pure Land School—and there is indeed a great secret to it—lies in the response. It is a secret clothed not in elaborate ritual and ceremony but in the simplicity of ☞FAITH and sincerity. Its secret, which is right out in the open, is in fact the highest secret." (WM 19)

"The Five [Types of] Schools were created by Buddhists who had nothing to do and wanted to find something with which to occupy their time. The Five Schools all issued from Buddhism. Since they came forth from Buddhism, they can return to Buddhism as well. Although the Five Schools serve different purposes, their ultimate destination is the same. It is said:

"There is only one road back to the source.
But here are many expedient ways to reach it."
(*Shambala Review*, v.5, nos.1-2, Winter, 1976, 26)

five basic approaches to cultivation, five schools

☞ **Consciousness-Only School, Tiantai School, Huayan School, Vinaya School, Chan School, recitation of the Buddha's name, pure land**

Flower Adornment ⟨Avataṃsaka⟩ Sutra 《大方廣佛》華嚴經

The infinitely multi-layered realm of the Flower Adornment

The complete title of the sutra is the *Great Means Expansive Buddha Flower Adornment Sutra*. Known as the 'King of Kings' of all Buddhist scriptures because of its profundity and great length (eighty-one rolls containing more than 200,000 Chinese characters), this sutra contains the most complete explanation of the state of the Buddhas and of the ☞BODHISATTVA path to Buddhahood.

"The *Flower Adornment Sutra* is the sutra of the ☞DHARMA REALM and the sutra of empty space. To the exhaustion of the Dharma Realm and empty space there is no place where the *Flower Adornment Sutra* is not present. Wherever the *Flower Adornment Sutra* is found, the Buddha is to be found, and also the Dharma and the Sangha of worthy sages. That is why, when the Buddha realized proper enlightenment, he wished to speak the *Great Flower Adornment Sutra* to teach and transform the great masters of the Dharma body [i.e., Bodhisattvas]. Since this sutra was a sutra of inconceivable wonder, it was then concealed within the dragon's palace for the dragon king to protect. Afterwards ☞NĀGĀRJUNA ('dragon-tree') BODHISATTVA went to the dragon's palace, memorized it, and brought it back.

"The *Flower Adornment Sutra* is like an auspicious cloud in empty space, which extends throughout the Three Thousand Great Thousand World System [☞WORLD SYSTEMS], raining down the sweet dew of Dharma rain to moisten all living beings. The *Flower Adornment Sutra* is also like the sun, which everywhere illumines the Three Thousand World system, bringing warmth to every single living being. The *Flower Adornment Sutra* is also like the great earth, which can produce and grow the myriad existing things. Therefore, it can be said that any period in which the *Flower Adornment Sutra* exists is a period in which the proper Dharma long remains.

"Consequently, in our daily investigation and lecturing of the *Flower Adornment Sutra*, it is essential to rely upon the sutra's principles to cultivate and to use the sutra as a cure for our own personal faults. Those who are greedy, after hearing the *Flower Adornment Sutra*, should rid themselves of greed. People who are angry, upon hearing the sutra, should give up their anger; and those who are deluded should stop being deluded. The principles discussed in the sutra are designed to correct our faults and bad habits. It is absolutely not the case that the sutra was Dharma spoken for Bodhisattvas with no relation to us, or that it was Dharma spoken for Arhats with no relevance for us. Don't think, 'All I, as an ordinary person, can do is listen to the sutra. I could never aspire to the states of a sage.' To think that way is to forsake yourself, to separate yourself from the sages.

"From the beginning to the end of the *Flower Adornment Sutra*, every phrase of the sutra is an unsurpassed Dharma jewel. If we are able actually to apply the principles and cultivate according to the principles of the sutra, then we are certain to become Buddhas. For that reason the *Flower Adornment Sutra* can be called the mother of all Buddhas. The *Flower Adornment Sutra* is the ☞DHARMA BODY of all Buddhas. The Buddha praised the ☞VAJRA SUTRA saying:

> "Wherever the sutra text is found,
> There is the Buddha.

"Wherever the *Flower Adornment Sutra* is, there is the Buddha. The Buddha is right there. It is just that your karmic obstacles are so deep and heavy, so although you are face to face, you do not see the Buddha....

Flower Adornment Sea of Worlds (see plate 21)

"We ☞ ŚRAMAṆAS should diligently cultivate precepts, samadhi, and wisdom, and put to rest greed, anger, and delusion. In every move we make, we should return the light and look within. If you cultivate that way, you will make progress. If we listen to the *Flower Adornment Sutra*, lecture on the *Flower Adornment Sutra*, and recite the *Flower Adornment Sutra*, but fail to practice according to the principles of the *Flower Adornment Sutra*, the sutra remains the sutra, you remain you, I remain myself, and others remain themselves, and we cannot unite as one. If we ourselves can become one with the sutra by acting according to its principles, that is actual union with the sutra. If you are unable to truly practice in accord with the sutra, but instead are deficient in kindness and compassion with a dearth of joy and giving, having ignorance and afflictions as your only companions, then you have failed to understand the sutra and lack the ability to listen to the sutra.

"Upon hearing one phrase of the sutra, we should ask ourselves, 'How should I act? Should I run after my faults and bad habits, or should I rely upon the principles of the sutra and cultivate?' If you can constantly ask yourself that question, you will certainly obtain great benefit. The reason you have not obtained great benefit is simply that you look upon the sutra as the sutra, having no connection with yourself. Actually, when the Buddha spoke the *Flower Adornment Sutra*, it was spoken for all living beings including you, me, and everyone else present. The Buddha is speaking it for us in person from his golden mouth. When we listen to the sutra, it is the same as having the Buddha take us by the ear and speak the principles right to our faces, telling us to use the sutra's Dharma-doors to cultivate.

"When the sutra discusses the ten kinds of Dharma-doors or ten samadhis, none of the Dharma-doors or samadhis goes beyond the self-nature of each one of us. Our self-nature, too, exhausts empty space and the Dharma Realm. Therefore, if you can expand and enlarge the measure of your mind, you will unite with the *Flower Adornment Sutra*, being two and yet not two. If all people can make the states of the *Flower Adornment Sutra* their own states and receive the *Flower Adornment Sutra*'s limitless principles and infinite wisdom as their own, how vast and great that will be! As it is said:

> "Roll it up, it secretly hides away.
> Let it go, it fills the whole universe.

"That is ineffably wonderful!" (FAS-VP xv-xvii)

flower ornament, flower garland, flowering-adornment

☞ **Huayan School, Qingliang Chengguan ⟨National Master⟩**

Scenes from the Flower Adornment Sutra (see plate 20)

Four Applications of Mindfulness
四念處

The Four Applications of Mindfulness are **1)** contemplation of the body as impure, **2)** contemplation of feeling as suffering, **3)** contemplation of thoughts as impermanent, and **4)** contemplation of dharmas as devoid of self.

The Four Applications of Mindfulness are part of the Thirty-seven Wings of Enlightenment (i.e., Seven Wings of Bodhi, ☞EIGHTFOLD PATH, Five Faculties, Five Powers, Four Bases of Psychic Power, Four Applications of Mindfulness, Four Types of Upright Diligence) that comprise the traditional description of Path, the last of the ☞FOUR HOLY TRUTHS.

"The Four Applications of Mindfulness were given by the Buddha as a dwelling place for the Bhikshus after his departure into nirvana." (DFS IV 760)

Contemplation of the Body as Impure

"Our bodies are unclean things.... Perspiration flows from the entire body, and once you perspire, you smell. Tears and matter flow from the eyes. Wax oozes from the ears and mucus flows from the nose. Saliva and phlegm flow from the mouth. These seven orifices are always leaking unclean substances. Then add the eliminatory orifices and you have nine holes which constantly ooze with impurities. Everyone is familiar with these impurities. In our flesh and blood there are many kinds of bacteria as well which are impure. Someone may not believe this at all, but in the future advances in science will without a doubt prove that the flesh and blood are unclean. It's all very complex, especially when people eat a lot of strange things which get into their systems and do strange things. The matter in the digestive system is also unclean. Therefore, why should you be so caught up in working for your body? First of all, contemplate the body as impure.

Contemplation of Feeling as Suffering

"Secondly, contemplate feelings as suffering. Pleasurable sensations are enjoyable at first, but one soon grows tired of them, and they become disagreeable. It's a very obvious principle that there is nothing much to pleasure in itself.

Contemplation of Thoughts as Impermanent

"Thirdly, contemplate thoughts as impermanent. Thought after thought changes and moves on. Thoughts are like waves on the sea. When one thought passes, another takes its place. Coming into being and ceasing to be, coming into being and ceasing to be, thoughts do not stop.... Past, present, and future—none of the three phases of thought can be got at. Therefore, contemplate thought as impermanent. We are never aware of where our thoughts have gone off to. Mencius said, 'If people's chickens and dogs run off, they go after them. But if their thoughts run off, they don't know to go after them....' When you have polluted thinking, that is just your mind running off....

Contemplation of Dharmas as Devoid of Self

"Not only is there no self, there are no dharmas either! Make empty both people and dharmas. Empty emptiness as well." (DFS IV 608-610)

☞ **Dwellings in Mindfulness, Applications of Mentality Awareness**
☞ **Four Holy Truths—Path, mindfulness**

Four Dhyānas 四禪

The Four Dhyānas are:

1. First Dhyāna: Bliss Born of Separation
2. Second Dhyāna: Bliss Born of Samadhi
3. Third Dhyāna: Wonderful Happiness of Being Apart from Bliss
4. Fourth Dhyāna: Clear Purity of Casting Away Thought

The Four Dhyānas are higher states or realms of consciousness (levels of ☞SAMADHI) reached in two ways: **a**) temporarily, through correct meditation, and **b**) on a lifetime basis through rebirth as a god in the *dhyāna*-heavens (☞GODS).

One enters the First Dhyāna by abandoning "examination" (*vitarka*), which refers to coarse polluted thinking. One is thus separated from one's afflictions. In the First Dhyāna a more subtle kind of polluted thinking called "investigation" (*vicāra*) still remains, as do "bliss" (*prīti*) and "happiness" (*sukha*). *Prīti* is a type of blissful light ease associated with the body, and *sukha* is a more subtle and pure happiness or joy. When one enters the Second Dhyāna, *vicāra* is eliminated, and a finer experience of bliss from one's meditational state remains. In the Third Dhyāna *prīti* is eliminated, so that only the pure happiness of *sukha* remains. And in the Fourth Dhyāna *sukha*, a very subtle cognitive function of the mind, is also eliminated, leading to an even purer state of mind.

"*Dhyāna* is a Sanskrit word meaning 'meditation,'....the purifying and quieting of cognitive considerations....When you reach the First Dhyāna, your pulse stops, and you can sit for seven days at a time without getting up from your seat, eating or drinking....There is no happier experience in the world—it is the happiness of the heavens, not that of the human realm. When you reach the Second Dhyāna, you can sit for forty-nine days at a time without getting up, eating or drinking. While in that samadhi, the joy is far greater than that of the First Dhyāna. When you reach the Third Dhyāna, you have no thought, and can sit for three years at a sitting. And so you claim that you've...become enlightened? Can you even sit for three days at a time?... When one reaches the state of the Fourth Dhyāna, one can sit for nine years without getting up, eating or drinking. At that time, one doesn't merely stop having thoughts; the thought process stops altogether, and one's consciousness is unmoving. Although without movement, consciousness still exists...." (FAS-PII(1) 35-39)

"In the First Dhyāna (the Ground of Bliss Born of Separation), one's pulse stops, but this doesn't mean one is dead. This brings a particular happiness which is unknown to those in the world.

"The Second Dhyāna is called the Ground of Bliss Born of Samadhi....In the Second Dhyāna, one's breath stops. There is no detectible breathing in and out, but at that time an inner breathing takes over.

"The Third Dhyāna is the Ground of the Wonderful Happiness of Being Apart from Bliss. One renounces the *dhyāna*-bliss as food and the happiness of the Dharma that occurs in initial samadhi. One goes beyond that kind of happiness and reaches a sense of wonderful joy. It is something that one has never known before, that is inexpressible in its subtlety, and that is inconceivable. At the level of the Third Dhyāna, thoughts also stop. There is no active thought process—not a single thought arises.

"When not a single thought arises,
The entire substance manifests.
When the six organs suddenly move,
There is a covering of clouds.

"At the point when not one thought arises, the entire substance and great function (of your Buddha-nature) are in evidence. But once your six organs suddenly move, then it is obscured. It just takes a slight movement by the eyes, ears, nose, tongue, body, or mind to cause this to happen. Then one is covered over by the clouds of the ☞FIVE SKANDHAS.

"The Fourth Dhyāna is called the Ground of the Clear Purity of Casting Away Thought. In the Third Dhyāna thoughts were stopped—held at bay—but they still had not been renounced altogether. In the heavens of the Fourth Dhyāna, not only are thoughts stopped, they are done away with completely. There basically are no more cognitive considerations. This state is extremely pure, subtly wonderful, and particularly blissful.

"However, reaching the Fourth Dhyāna is simply a preliminary, expedient state of meditational inquiry reached by beginners. Having reached this state is of no use at all in itself. It is not certification of sagehood. You shouldn't make the mistake of thinking that reaching these four levels makes you somehow very special.... You've only experienced a bit of the flavor of Chan." (LY II 75-76)

trances, initial levels of correct meditation, concentrations
☞ **samadhi, meditation**

Fourfold Assembly 四眾

The fourfold assembly originally referred to those who gathered to hear the Buddha teach the Dharma: Bhikshus, Bhikshunis, *upāsakas*, and *upāsikās*, in other words, monks and nuns, and laymen and laywomen. It now also refers in general to those four categories of Buddhists.

☞ **Bhikshu, Bhikshuni, upāsaka, upāsikā**

Four Formless Realms 四無色界

The Four Formless Realms are **1)** the Realm of Infinite Space, **2)** the Realm of Infinite Consciousness, **3)** the Realm of Nothing Whatsoever, and **4)** the Realm of Neither Cognition Nor Non-Cognition.

The Four Formless Realms are states which are experienced temporarily in meditation. They lie beyond the ☞FOUR DHYĀNAS, and are so subtle they are difficult to talk about using ordinary language and even difficult to conceptualize.

They also correspond to the Four Formless Heavens, the homes of the formless gods (☞GODS). In other words the states can be experienced for a relatively short time by humans who have reached them in the course of their meditation, or they can be experienced as states of rebirth for those reborn as gods in the formless heavens.

Although the experiences of these realms are of rare and subtle states of bliss, none is considered enlightenment.

Infinite Space

> Those who dwell in the thought of renunciation and who succeed in renunciation and rejection realize that their bodies are an obstacle. If they thereby obliterate the obstacle and enter empty space, they are among those in the realm of (infinite) space. (SS VII 230-231)

"These gods accomplish renunciation of bliss and rejection of suffering. They know that physical bodies are an obstruction.... They don't want to be hindered by anything, and so they contemplate their bodies as being just like empty space...." (SS VII 231)

> ...[H]aving surpassed all notion of materiality, neglecting all cognition of resistance, one penetrates the realm of endless space. (*Dhyāna-sūtra*, quoted in DZDL (Lamotte, tr.) II 1032)

Infinite Consciousness

"For those who have eradicated all obstacles, there is neither obstruction nor extinction. Then there remains only the *ālaya* consciousness (i.e., eighth consciousness) and half of the subtle functions of the *manas* (i.e., seventh consciousness) (☞ EIGHT CONSCIOUSNESSES). These beings are among those in the realm of infinite consciousness." (SS VII 231)

"The *manas* is functioning at only half its capacity, and so the defilement that remains is extremely subtle." (SS VII 232)

At this stage one abandons empty space as an object and also abandons the feelings, cognitions, formations, and consciousness that are associated with it. The only attachment that remains is to a consciousness that is immense and infinite.

Nothing Whatsoever

> Those who have already done away with empty space and form eradicate the conscious mind as well. In the extensive tranquility of the ten directions there is nowhere to go at all. These beings are among those in the realm of nothing whatsoever. (SS VII 232)

"All the worlds of the ten directions throughout the entire Dharma Realm have disappeared. A stillness pervades. There is nowhere to go. Nor is there anywhere to come to....Although there is nothing whatsoever, nonetheless, the nature of these beings still remains. Their nature is the same as empty space." (SS VII 233)

One contemplates nothing whatever in order to break one's attachment to and to abandon the state of infinite consciousness.

Neither Cognition Nor Non-Cognition

> When the nature of consciousness does not move, within cessation they exhaustively investigate. Within the endless they discern the end of the nature. It is as if it were there and yet not there, as if it were ended and yet not ended. They are among those in the realm of neither cognition nor non-cognition. (SS VII 233-234)

This is the highest state or heaven within the conditioned world. At this stage, although there is still very subtle cognition, it does not function.

"Consciousness is practically nonexistent, and so it is said that there is no thought. However, a very fine trace of thought still exists and so it is called neither cognition nor non-cognition." (SPV 60)

> Because this cognition is subtle and difficult to be aware of, it is called non-cognition. But because it is cognition, it is called not non-cognition. (cf. DZDL (Lamotte, tr.) II 1034)

stations of emptiness, formless samadhis, samāpattis, formless absorptions

☞ **Four Dhyānas, meditation**

Four Great Elements 四大

The Four Great Elements are **1)** earth, **2)** water, **3)** fire, and **4)** wind.

While you are in your body, what is solid is of earth, what is moist is of water, what is warm is of fire, and what moves is of wind. (SS IV 144)

four primary elements

☞ **Five Skandhas—Form**

Four Great Vows 四弘誓願

The Four Great Vows are:

1 Living beings are countless; I vow to take them all across.

2 Afflictions are inexhaustible; I vow to eliminate them all.

3 Dharma-doors are innumerable; I vow to learn to enter them all.

4 The Way of the Buddhas is unsurpassed; I vow to realize it.

The Four Great Vows are basically a Mahayana reinterpretation of the ☞ FOUR HOLY TRUTHS. In addition to ending one's own suffering, one vows to end the suffering of all living beings. In addition to eliminating one's own afflictions, one vows to end the inexhaustible afflictions of all living beings. In addition to learning only the single Dharma-door necessary for one's own enlightenment, one vows to learn all the Dharma-doors, so that one can teach all living beings appropriately. Rather than being satisfied with reaching the stage of the Arhat, one vows to become a Buddha.

"It is not enough just to recite [the vows]. You have to return the light and think them over: The vow says that I will save a countless number of beings. Have I done so? If I have, it should still be the same as if I had not saved them. Why? It is said that the Thus Come One saves all living beings, and yet not a single living being has been saved.

"'Well,' you say, 'if my saving them is the same as not saving them, then is my not saving them the same as saving them?'

"No. You can say that you save them, and yet are not attached to them; not attached means that you are not attached to the mark of saving living beings. But you can't fail to save them and claim to have saved them. It doesn't work that way. You can say that you save them without saving them because you are not attached to them. But you can't say that you have saved them when you have not saved them.

"The Buddha leads all beings to nirvana, and yet not a single being is led to nirvana. We have not yet become Buddhas or saved living beings, and so it is not all right for us to say that we have done so." (DFS IV 788-789)

> "I vow to save the limitless living beings of my own mind.
> I vow to cut off the infinite afflictions of my own mind.
> I vow to study the immeasurable Dharma-doors of my own mind.
> I vow to realize the supreme Buddha Way of my own nature.
>
> "Good Knowing Advisors, did all of you not just say, 'I vow to take across [to the other shore of nirvana] the limitless living beings'? What does it mean? You should remember that it is not ☞ HUINENG who takes them across. Good Knowing Advisors, the 'living beings' within your minds are deviant and confused thoughts, deceitful and false thoughts, unwholesome thoughts, jealous thoughts, vicious thoughts: all these thoughts are 'living beings.' The self-nature of each one of them must take itself across. That is the true crossing over...." (PS 178)

Four Vast Vows, Four Universal Vows

☞ **Bodhi resolve, Bodhisattva, living beings**

Four Holy Truths 四聖諦

Soon after the Buddha's enlightenment he taught the doctrine of the Four Holy Truths: **1)** suffering, **2)** the origin of suffering, **3)** the cessation of suffering, and **4)** the Path to the cessation of suffering. The Truth of Suffering is the understanding that all of human experience is unsatisfactory, because it is inextricably tied up with the notion of self and because it is impermanent. Birth, old age, sickness, and death all involve suffering. Even happiness is seen as suffering, the suffering of decay, because it is impermanent and inevitably leads to a less happy state. Moreover, even the greatest self-based bliss is suffering compared to enlightenment. In the Truth of the Origin of Suffering the Buddha taught that basic ignorance leads to desire and other afflictions, which are the cause of suffering. In the Truth of the Cessation of Suffering, that is, enlightenment, we are given an alternative to suffering as our fundamental mode of being. The Truth of the Path indicates how to get to enlightenment.

Suffering

> This, O Bhikkhus, is the Noble Truth of Suffering: Birth is suffering; decay is suffering; illness is suffering; death is suffering. Presence of objects we hate is suffering; separation from objects we love is suffering. Briefly, the fivefold clinging to existence is suffering. (Rhys Davids, tr. *Vinaya Texts* I, 95)
>
> ...[T]he Holy Truth of Suffering is either called offenses, or called oppression, or called flux and change, or called grabbing onto conditions, or called conglomeration, or called horns, or called relying on the root, or called vain and deceptive, or called carbuncles and sores, or called the conduct of ignorant people. (FAS Ch8 14)

Origin of Suffering

> This, O Bhikkhus, is the Noble Truth of the Cause of suffering: Thirst, that leads to rebirth, accompanied by pleasure and lust, finding its delight here and there. (This thirst is threefold), namely, thirst for pleasure, thirst for existence, thirst for prosperity. (*Vinaya Texts* I, 95) [*NOTE:* The usual list has nonexistence, referring to nonexistence after death, instead of prosperity.]
>
> ...[T]he Holy Truth of the Accumulation of Suffering is either called being bound up, or called decay and ruin, or called the meaning of love and attachment, or called false awareness and thoughts, or called tending toward and entering, or called definiteness, or called a net, or called idle speculation, or called following along, or called the root of inversion. (FAS Ch8 17)

Cessation of Suffering

> This, O Bhikkhus, is the Noble Truth of the Cessation of suffering: (it ceases with) the complete cessation of this thirst—a cessation which consists in the absence of every passion—with the abandoning of this thirst, with the doing away with it, with the deliverance from it, with the destruction of desire. (*Vinaya Texts* I, 95)

Path

> This, O Bhikkhus, is the Noble Truth of the Path which leads to the cessation of suffering: that holy eightfold Path, that is to say, Right Belief, Right Aspiration, Right Speech, Right Conduct, Right Means of Livelihood, Right Endeavor, Right Memory, Right Meditation. (*Vinaya Texts* I, 95-96) [For an alternate translation and explanation, ☞ EIGHTFOLD PATH.]

...[T]he Holy Truth of the Way Leading to the Extinction of Suffering is perhaps called the one vehicle, or called tending toward stillness, or called instructing and guiding, or called ultimately without difference, or called equality, or called setting down one's burden, or called without tendencies, or called according with the sagely intent, or called the conduct of the immortals, or called the ten treasuries. (FAS Ch8 19)

Four Truths, Four Noble Truths, Fourfold Truth of Sages

suffering, causation, enlightenment, Eightfold Path, Eighty-eight Deluded Viewpoints

Four Stations of Emptiness 四空處

Four Formless Realms

Four Unlimited Aspects of Mind 四無量心

The Four Unlimited Aspects of Mind are **1)** kindness, **2)** compassion/sympathy, **3)** joy, and **4)** equanimity/renunciation.

Herein a monk lets his mind pervade one quarter of the world with thoughts of benevolence, compassion, sympathetic joy and poise...and so the second, the third and fourth quarter; and thus the whole world, above, below, around and everywhere does he continue to pervade with heart free from anger and ill-will. (quoted from EB "Brahmavihara," 333)

infinitudes, divine states. Individual: benevolence, compassion, sympathetic joy, poise

Bodhisattva, compassion

G

Gautama/Gotama ⟨Buddha⟩ 瞿曇《佛》

The family name of Śākyamuni Buddha. His full name was Siddhartha Gautama. Upon becoming a Buddha, he was known by the name Śākyamuni, 'the sage of the Śākyas.'

Śākyamuni ⟨Buddha⟩, Buddha

ghosts 鬼

"Still, still, barren waste—a dream.
Then, now, triumph, loss—
  lazy thought measures.
Wild grass, idle flowers—
  picked how many?
Bitter rain, sour wind—
  how many broken hearts?

At night with firefly light,
  come and go.
At dawn the cock crows;
  I hide away my form.
Regret from the first
  not tilling the mind-ground:
Two streams are caused to fall—
  green mountain tears." (PS 83)

"Some people say they don't believe in ghosts. Why do they say that? It is because they are ghosts themselves, and they are afraid others will recognize them as such. And so they are always telling others not to believe in such things as ghosts. I often say, "Basically there is no real difference between Buddhas and ghosts. If you are evil to the ultimate point, then you are a ghost. If you are good to the ultimate point, then you are a Buddha. If you cultivate to the point of becoming enlightened, then you are a Buddha. If you don't get enlightened and keep being deluded, then you are a ghost. Basically there is no difference.

"Some people believe in the Buddha and say that Buddhas exist....But they don't believe there are ghosts....'I haven't seen any ghosts,' they argue, 'and so I don't believe any such things exist.'

"I ask them, 'Well, have you seen Buddhas?' I can safely ask them that because if they haven't seen ghosts, they haven't seen Buddhas. And so I say to them, 'You have never seen Buddhas either, so why do you believe in them?...

"They say, 'I have seen Buddha-images.' Well, there are pictures of ghosts around too. If you see Buddha-images and, therefore, believe in Buddhas, then when you see pictures of ghosts, shouldn't you believe in ghosts?...I'll tell you right now that those who don't believe in ghosts are that way because they don't have the wisdom to believe ghosts exist. They don't have the genuine, perfectly interpenetrating and unobstructed wisdom to understand this principle. If you don't believe in ghosts, you shouldn't believe in the Buddha either. There just won't be anything at all. How will that be? Of course, originally there isn't anything at all. Basically, there is no self and also no people, no Buddhas, no ghosts, nothing at all. But you have to reach that state. You must truly have achieved the level of no self. It can't be that you talk about having no self, but when it comes time to eat, you eat more than anyone else...." (HD 83-84)

"The ghostly crew delights in hate,
Deluded by effects,
confused about causes.
Their ignorance and delusion
Grow greater each day,
deeper each month." (TD 50)

"Ghosts are masses of *yin* energy which have shadow and no form or form and no shadow. Perhaps you have seen a dark shadow, but when you looked closer, it disappeared. Or perhaps you've seen what seemed like a person, but which vanished in the blink of an eye. This phenomenon is difficult to understand.

"There are as many different kinds of ghosts as there are grains of sand in the Ganges River. Some ghosts are affluent and reign as kings over the realms of ghosts; some ghosts are poverty-stricken and devoid of authority—it is often the poor ghosts who bother people. If you want to investigate ghosts in detail, work hard at cultivation,open the Five Eyes and develop the Six Spiritual Powers, and then explore for yourself." (TD 51)

☞ **hungry ghosts, dead departed spirits**
☞ **Six Paths of Rebirth**

God 上帝/天主

According to Buddhist teachings, the God of Judaism, Christianity, and Islam is not the One God, the Creator, nor is he omnipotent and omniscient. However, Buddhism does not deny his existence or the existence of his heaven.

There is no creator and
there are no creations.
From karma and thoughts alone
do things come to be.
How do we know this?

Because other than this,
There is nothing at all.
(FAS Ch14)

[The reader can decide for himself or herself whether or not the following commentarial selection applies to the God of the Abrahamic religions.] "Most religions say that there is a ruler who rules over all the ten thousand things between heaven and earth, who is the creator, and that the ten thousand matters and things are his creation. But in actual fact there is no one who can control all the ten thousand matters and things. Therefore, the ☞FLOWER ADORNMENT SUTRA says, 'There is no creator and there are no creations.' How does it all come about then? 'From karma and thoughts alone do things come to be.' Everything exists because one becomes deluded, creates karma, and undergoes retribution. From where does karma arise? It is created from ☞FALSE THINKING. The very beginning, the lack of enlightenment, is ignorance. Because of ignorance, confusion and doubt arise. If there were no ignorance, there would be no confusion and doubt. Having confusion and doubt, one produces false thought. Having false thought, one creates all kinds of ☞KARMA. In creating karma, if you plant good causes, you reap good effects. If you plant bad causes, you reap bad effects. If you plant causes which are neither good nor bad, you reap a retribution which is neither good nor bad. And so of all things which happen to people, there is none which is not of their own creation. No one tells them to create these things. No one controls them. They create them all themselves. Therefore, the reason you cannot get off the turning wheel of birth and death is that you follow the karma you create. According to your karma you receive your retribution. Birth after birth, death after death, death after death, birth after birth.

"'How do we know this? Because other than this, there is nothing at all.' If you depart from this doctrine, there isn't another doctrine which can explain the way things are. For instance, if it were as other religions explain it, that we are controlled by a God, since there is a God in control, it has nothing to do with us at all. If in every situation we are being controlled by someone, then whether we do good or bad has nothing to do with us. But when the time comes to undergo the retribution, it is we ourselves who must undergo it. That does not make sense.

"That is why it is explained as being our own karma. For instance, if there is a person who goes and tells another person to commit a murder, although the murderer commits an offense, half the offense lies with the one who told him to do it. If we say that God controls us, that in all matters it is God who rules, then half of the karmic offenses we create should be God's. If it is not like that, and instead, of the things he tells us to do, those with merit belong to him and those with offenses are ours, that would be unreasonable.

"What one creates has nothing to do with anyone else. If you yourself do good deeds, then you receive a reward. If you do bad things, then you undergo retribution. That is reasonable. And so in every move we make we are certainly not controlled by any God. If we really were controlled by God, then he should not make us do all kinds of evil things. It would only make sense for us to do all kinds of good things, because God does not want people to do evil. If he doesn't have the ability to govern right and wrong, and yet the offenses we create are ours and the merit we accrue reverts to him, that is totally illogical.

"And so it follows that we are not controlled by any other person nor by any God. We are controlled only by our karma and our false thinking. What proof is there of this? Take a look. If there were someone controlling us, then what we did every day would be decided for us, but on the contrary we are able to do whatever we want. If people had a God controlling them, then all living beings should have a God controlling them. And in controlling them, he should teach them to do good things; he should not teach them to do bad things. And so why would God make a cat? Why would he make a mouse? Why does the cat like to eat mice? Why does the mouse like to steal things? From this it can be seen that it is all their own karma that has caused them to undergo the retributions.

"Take fish for example. They can swim wherever they want in the water. They are also very independent. But fish in the water are not aware of the water. They consider it their world. People in the air are not aware of the air. People live in the air, but they don't even see it. To them it is invisible. That is the same way fish are in water. This is all because whatever karma you create causes you to undergo that retribution. It certainly is not the case that there is a God controlling you. Nor is there a Buddha telling you what to do. Buddhas don't pay attention to such small matters. Bodhisattvas don't pay attention either. How much the less would a God be able to watch over you." (FAS Ch14 ms.)

☞ **Heavenly Lord**
☞ **gods, creation, Six Desire Heavens—Trayastriṃśa**

gods 天人

The Six Desire Heavens have
the Five Signs of Decay.
The Third Dhyāna Heaven
suffers the disaster of wind.
No matter how you cultivate, even up
to the Heaven of Neither Cognition
Nor Non-Cognition,
It's still better to be born in the
Western Pure Land
and then come
back again.
(FAS Ch11 69-70)

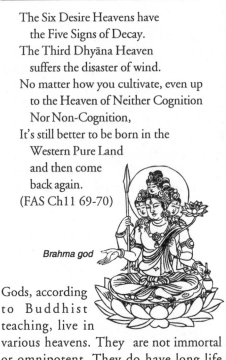

Brahma god

Gods, according to Buddhist teaching, live in various heavens. They are not immortal or omnipotent. They do have long life spans and various spiritual powers. Anyone can be reborn as a god by generating the appropriate good karma; however, gods are not enlightened. They eventually die and are reborn in lower realms according to their karma.

The Six Desire and Brahma gods,
With Five Precepts and
Ten Good Acts,
Plant seeds that have outflows,
And so the turning wheel
is hard to stop. (TD 39)

The Buddha said:

Ānanda, each and every being in all these heavens is ordinary [and not a sage]. They are still answerable for their karmic retribution. When they have answered for their debts, they must once again enter rebirth. (SS VII 236-237)

The gods constitute one of the ☞SIX PATHS OF REBIRTH and are one of the ☞TEN DHARMA REALMS. The heavens in which the gods reside are divided into three basic categories: **1)** the Desire Heavens, of which there are six (☞SIX DESIRE HEAVENS), **2)** Form Heavens, also called the Four Dhyāna Heavens (☞FOUR DHYĀNAS), and **3)** Formless Heavens, of which there are four also (☞FOUR FORMLESS REALMS).

angels, heavenly spirits, celestial beings, devas

☞ **God, Six Desire Heavens, Four Dhyānas, Four Formless Realms, Six Paths of Rebirth, Ten Dharma Realms, creation, cosmology, time**

gongfu ⟨kungfu⟩ 功夫

Gongfu is a Chinese word that means 'skill' or 'ability.' It can be used in the ordinary sense or to apply to spiritual ability, or as is currently popular, to refer to ability in the martial arts.

Good and Wise Advisor 善知識

> Good man, in seeking a good and wise advisor, you should not grow weary. In seeing a good and wise advisor, do not give rise to a sense of satiation or boredom. In inquiring from a good and wise advisor, do not shrink from toil and suffering. In drawing close to a good and wise advisor, do not harbor thoughts of retreat. In making offerings to a good and wise advisor, do not rest. In receiving teachings from a good and wise advisor, do not distort his teachings. In studying a good and wise advisor's principles, do not give rise to doubts. In hearing a good and wise advisor explain the doors to liberation, do not be hesitant.... Toward a good and wise advisor, produce a mind of deep faith and veneration, without changing. (EDR VII 142)

"If you want to have some realization, it is essential to meet a clear-sighted good and wise advisor, who can instruct you in methods for increasing your skills. Then you can make progress day by day....

"How are you to know who is a good and wise advisor? A good and wise advisor would never plaster a sign on his forehead saying, 'Do you recognize me?... I am a clear-sighted good and wise advisor.' If someone did in fact advertise and claim to be a good and wise advisor, he wouldn't be a genuine one. As to a genuine good and wise advisor, if you recognize him, then you recognize him; but if you don't recognize him, he won't put any pressure on you by saying, 'You should draw near to me.'... A true good and wise advisor wouldn't act like a patent medicine man selling tonics. He wouldn't praise himself. If you recognize him, that's fine; if you don't recognize him, that's all right, too. He won't introduce himself.

"Since that's the way it is, how are you to know who really is a good and wise advisor. It is not easy to know.... As a matter of fact, in the entire world there are very, very few good and wise advisors.... A good and wise advisor teaches people to walk on the right road. He does not teach people to take deviant paths. What is meant by the right road? He teaches people not to kill, not to steal, not to engage in sexual misconduct, not to lie, and not to take intoxicants. He would be a bad advisor if he said, 'Wine is no problem. When the Buddha included the prohibition against alcohol in the Five Precepts, he was talking to people who were as fond of alcohol as they were of their very lives. He wasn't referring to ordinary people.'

To speak that way is teaching deviant knowledge and deviant views....

"The bad advisor also says to you, 'As to your sexual desire, although the Buddha said that desire and lust are not good things, if you can employ sexual desire to an extreme, you can become enlightened too.' That is also an example of deviant knowledge and deviant views. And so when the bad advisor goes on and continues to tell you to do what is improper, he is indicating to you that he is not a good and wise advisor....

"One who is without greed, anger, and delusion is a good and wise advisor. One who can actually cultivate precepts, samadhi, and wisdom is a good and wise advisor. If you are observing to see if someone is a good and wise advisor, see if he is selfish. If he is, he is not a good and wise advisor. If he is after profit for himself, he is not a good and wise advisor. The person who isn't selfish and has no desire to benefit himself is a good and wise advisor." (LY I 49-51)

> Good man, the good and wise advisor is like a kind mother, in that he gives rise to the seed of Buddhahood. He is like a kind father in that he vastly benefits (all beings). He is like a nurse in that he protects one and stops one from doing evil. He is like a teacher in that he shows one what a Bodhisattva should learn. He is like a good guide in that he can open up the path of the ☞PĀRAMITĀS. He is like a skilled physician in that he can heal the sickness of the afflictions. He is like the snowy mountains in that he makes grow the medicine of all-wisdom. He is like a valiant general in that he banishes all terror. He is like a ferryman in that he enables one to get out of the torrent of birth and death. He is like a boat captain in that he can take one to the jeweled continent of wisdom. Good man, you should, with proper mindfulness, reflect upon all good and wise advisors in this way. (EDR VII 147)

wise counsel, good friend, counselor, someone with knowledge, wisdom, experience; intimate friends, good mentor, ⟨clear-sighted⟩ knowing one, spiritual guide/advisor, good companion, honest and pure friend

good roots 善根

"Good roots are another name for your Dharma body and your wisdom. Good roots are the firm foundation which comes from cultivation. A good foundation causes your Dharma body to manifest, your wisdom to increase, and your originally existent real mark ☞PRAJÑĀ to function.

"It is essential, however, that you plant good roots before the Triple Jewel in order to reap the fruit of ☞BODHI. If you plant good roots with non-Buddhist religions, you will not be able to reap any ultimate benefit, no matter how many good roots you plant or how long you nurture them." (VS 50)

wholesome faculties, the basis or root of goodness or merit

☞ **karma, causation**

Great Compassion Mantra 大悲咒

One of the most widely used and most efficacious of all Buddhist mantras, the Great Compassion Mantra is a Dharma taught by the Bodhisattva Who Regards the World's Sounds (☞AVALOKITEŚVARA ⟨BODHISATTVA⟩). The teachings on the Great Compassion Mantra are found in the ☞DHĀRAṆĪ SUTRA. [The text of the mantra can be found in the *Dhāraṇī Sutra*, pp. 40-43, and in the *City of Ten Thousand Buddhas Recitation Handbook*, pp. 30-33.]

The Bodhisattva Who Regards the World's Sounds again addressed the Buddha, saying, "World Honored One, if humans and gods recite and hold the phrases of the Great Compassion Mantra, then when they approach the end of life, all the Buddhas of the ten directions will come to take them by the hand to rebirth in whatever Buddhaland they wish according to their desire."

He further said to the Buddha, "World Honored One, should any living being who recites and holds the spiritual mantra of great compassion fall into the three evil paths, I vow not to realize the right enlightenment. Should any living being who recites and holds the Spiritual Mantra of Great Compassion not be reborn in any Buddhaland, I vow not to realize the right enlightenment. Should any living being who recites and holds the Spiritual Mantra of Great Compassion not obtain unlimited samadhis and eloquence, I vow not to realize the right enlightenment. Should any living being who recites and holds the Spiritual Mantra of Great Compassion not obtain the fruits of whatever is sought in this very life, then he cannot have been making proper use of the Dhāraṇī of the Great Compassion Heart." (DS 30-31)

☞ **Dhāraṇī Sutra, mantra, dhāraṇī, Avalokiteśvara 〈Bodhisattva〉**

Great Vehicle 大乘

☞ **Mahayana and Hinayana Compared**

h

Hanshan and Shide 〈Bodhisattvas〉 〈fl. 627-649 C.E.〉 寒山拾得《大士》

Great Master Han-shan

"No one knows what sort of man Han-shan was. There are old people who knew him: they say he was a poor man, a crazy character. He lived alone seventy li west of the T'ang-hsing district of T'ien-t'ai at a place called Cold Mountain. He often went down to the Kuo-ch'ing Temple. At the temple lived Shih-te, who ran the dining hall. He sometimes saved leftovers for Han-shan, hiding them in a bamboo tube. Han-shan would come and carry it away; walking the long veranda, calling and shouting happily, talking and laughing to himself. Once the monks followed him, caught him, and made fun of him. He stopped, clapped his hands, and laughed greatly—Ha Ha!—for a spell, then left.

"He looked like a tramp. His body and face were old and beat. Yet in every word he breathed was a meaning in line with the subtle principles of things, if you only thought of it deeply. Everything he did had a feeling of the Tao in it, profound and arcane secrets. His hat was made of birch bark, his clothes were ragged and worn out, and his shoes were wood. Thus men who have made it hide their tracks: unifying categories and interpenetrating things. On that long veranda calling and singing, in his words of reply—Ha Ha!—the three worlds revolve. Sometimes at the villages and farms he laughed and sang with cowherds. Sometimes intractable, sometimes agreeable, his nature was happy of itself. But how could a person without wisdom recognize him?

"I once received a position as a petty official at Tan-ch'iu. The day I was to depart I had a bad headache. I called a doctor, but he couldn't cure me and it turned worse.

GREAT MASTER SHR-DE

Then I met a Buddhist Master named Feng-kan, who said he came from the Kuo-ch'ing Temple of T'ien-t'ai especially to visit me. I asked him to rescue me from my illness. He smiled and said, 'The four realms are within my body; sickness comes from illusion. If you want to do away with it, you need pure water.' Someone brought water to the Master, who spat it on me. In a moment the disease was rooted out. He then said, 'There are miasmas in T'ai prefecture, when you get there take care of yourself.' I asked him, 'Are there any wise men in your area I could look on as Master?' He replied, 'When you see him you don't recognize him, when you recognize him you don't see him. If you want to see him, you can't rely on appearances. Then you can see him. Han-shan is a ☞MAÑJUŚRĪ hiding at Kuo-ch'ing. Shih-te is a ☞SAMANTABHADRA. They look like poor fellows and act like madmen. Sometimes they go and sometimes they come. They work in the kitchen of the Kuo-ch'ing dining hall, tending the fire.' When he was done talking he left.

"I proceeded on my journey to my job at T'ai-chou, not forgetting this affair. I arrived three days later, immediately went to a temple, and questioned an old monk. It seemed the Master had been truthful, so I gave orders to see if T'ang-hsing really contained a Han-shan and Shih-te. The District Magistrate reported to me: 'In this district, seventy li west, is a mountain. People used to see a poor man heading from the cliffs to stay awhile at Kuo-ch'ing. At the temple dining hall is a similar man named Shih-te.' I made a bow and went to Kuo-ch'ing. I asked some people around the temple, 'There used to be a Master named Feng-kan here. Where is his place? And where can Han-shan and Shih-te be seen?' A monk named Tao-ch'iao spoke up: 'Feng-kan the Master lived in back of the library. Nowadays nobody lives there; a tiger often comes and roars. Han-shan and Shih-te are in the kitchen.' The monk led me to Feng-kan's yard. Then he opened the gate: all we saw was tiger tracks. I asked the monks Tao-ch'iao and Pao-te, 'When Feng-kan was here, what was his job?' The monks said, 'He pounded and hulled rice. At night he sang songs to amuse himself.' Then we went to the kitchen before the stoves. Two men were facing the fire, laughing loudly. I made a bow. The two shouted HO! at me. They struck their hands together—Ha Ha!—great laughter. They shouted. Then they said, 'Feng-kan—loose-tongued, loose-tongued. You don't recognize ☞AMITĀBHA, why be courteous to us?' The monks gathered round, surprise going through them. 'Why has a big official bowed to a pair of clowns?' The two men grabbed hands and ran out of the temple. I cried,

'Catch them'—but they quickly ran away. Han-shan returned to Cold Mountain. I asked the monks, 'Would those two men be willing to settle down at this temple?' I ordered them to find a house, and to ask Han-shan and Shih-te to return and live at the temple.

"I returned to my district and had two sets of clean clothes made, got some incense and such and sent it to the temple—but the two men didn't return. So I had it carried up to Cold Mountain. The packer saw Han-shan, who called out in a loud voice, 'Thief! Thief!' and retreated into a mountain cave. He shouted, 'I tell you man, strive hard!'—entered the cave and was gone. The cave closed of itself and they weren't able to follow. Shih-te's tracks disappeared completely.

"I ordered Tao-ch'iao and the other monks to find out how they had lived, to hunt up the poems written on bamboo, wood, stones, and cliffs—and also to collect those written on the walls of people's houses. There were more than three hundred. On the wall of the Earth-shrine Shih-te had written some *gāthā*. It was all brought together and made into a book.

"I hold to the principle of the Buddha-mind. It is fortunate to meet with men of Tao, so I have made this eulogy."

Lu Ch'iu-Yin, Governor of T'ai Prefecture (Snyder, tr.*Riprap, and Cold Mountain Poems,* 33-36)

Bodhisattvas Hanshan and Shide (see plate 22)

The place where I spend my days
Is farther away than I can tell.
Without a word the wild vines stir,
No fog, yet the bamboos
  are always dark.
Who do the valleys sob for?
Why do the mists huddle together?
At noon, sitting in my hut
I realize for the first time
  that the sun has risen.

Han-Shan
(Watson, tr. *Cold Mountain*, 64)

Have I a body or have I none?
Am I who I am or am I not?
Pondering these questions,
I sit leaning against the cliff
  as the years go by,
Till the green grass grows
  between my feet
And the red dust settles on my head,
And the men of the world,
  thinking me dead,
Come with offerings of wine and fruit
  to lay by my corpse.

Han-Shan
(*ibid.*, 114)

☞ **Cold Mountain and Pick Up**

Hearers 聲聞

☞ **śrāvaka**

Heart Sutra 心經

The full title of this sutra is *Heart of Prajñā Pāramitā Sutra*. Probably the most popular sutra in the world today, the *Heart Sutra* explains the meaning of *prajñā pāramitā*, the perfection of wisdom that enables one to perceive clearly the emptiness of self and of all phenomena. The *Heart Sutra* is the heart of the perfection of wisdom; it is also the heart of the entire family of *prajñā pāramitā* sutras.

☞ **sutra, emptiness, Six Pāramitās—Wisdom**

heavens 天

The heavens are the dwelling places of the ☞GODS.

hells 地獄

Beings receiving sentences (see plate 23)

"With each cry, in hell there is a small dark room." (FAS-VP 24)

> "The hells' anxiety and suffering
> is devoid of doors,
> Yet one bores right in.
> Delusin arises, and deeds are done.
> The retribution is borne
> in due accord." (TD 52)

"The term 'hell' is a translation of two Chinese characters which literally mean 'ground prison.' Just as there are prisons made by governments to punish offenders in the human realm, so too are there prisons in the shadowy places within the ground. Those prisons, or hells, differ from those among human beings in that they are not prepared by a governmental authority to await the arrival of criminals. The hells have no concrete form, only names. When a being is due to fall into one, however, it is manifested as a result of that being's powerful karma." (SPV 141)

> Within the three seas are hundreds of thousands of great hells, each one different. There are eighteen that are specifically known as great hells. In succession there are five hundred with unlimited cruel sufferings, and further there are over one hundred thousand with limitless sufferings. (SPV 84-85)

"The word 'sea' represents a large quantity and does not necessarily denote an actual body of water. Here it symbolizes the powerful karma of living beings, as vast as a boundless sea. The three seas represent the deeds done by the bodies, mouths, and minds of living beings.

"There are hundreds of thousands of tens of thousands of hells, each one with its own attributes, each hell corresponding to an evil deed done by a living being. Hells are not prepared before living beings fall into them; rather they are manifestations of the various particular karmas of beings. Whatever evil deed a being has done elicits a corresponding hell.

"For example, in the roasting hell there is a large hollow brass pillar full of fire. Those guilty of sexual misconduct fall into this hell and see the roasting pillar as a person. Men, for example, see it as a beautiful woman who they rush to embrace, only to find themselves burned so badly that they cannot pull their seared flesh away from the pillar. A woman sees the pillar as her most beloved partner in life and rushes to him only to be seared to death.

"As soon as death occurs in the roasting hell, a wind called the 'Clever Breeze,' a wonderful dharma, blows and revives the dead, who then forget the painful consequences of their behavior, recalling only its pleasurable aspects. Driven by this memory, they rush to the pillar again, only to find the cycle repeated. The roasting

The court of the underworld (see plate 24)

Beings suffering in the hells (see plate 25)

hell is only one of the many hells, and each one is unique. Eighteen are called great, and within each of these eighteen there are eighteen subsections." (SPV 85-86)

purgatory, a place of torment for the deceased
☞ **Six Paths of Rebirth**

Hinayana 小乘

☞ **Mahayana and Hinayana Compared**

Huayan School 華嚴宗

A school of Mahayana Buddhism founded in China, based on the teachings of the ☞FLOWER ADORNMENT SUTRA. *Huayan* means 'Flower Adornment' and is the standard Chinese translation of the Sanskrit *avataṃsaka*. The school is also often referred to as the Xianshou School after its influential third patriarch (see below).

The Venerable Master Dushun (557-640) is traditionally regarded as the first patriarch of the school. The second patriarch was the Venerable Ziyan (602-668), the third, Fazang (643-712), the fourth ☞QINGLIANG CHENGGUAN (738-840?), and the fifth, Zongmi (780-841), who was also a Chan Master in the lineage of Chan Master Shenhui.

In addition to its propagation of the fundamental teachings of the *Flower Adornment Sutra*, the school is best kown for: **1)** its system of analysis of the Buddha's teachings (☞RANKING THE TEACHINGS) which was developed by the school's third patriarch, the Venerable Fazang, and **2)** its system for lecturing on Buddhist sutras, called the Ten Doors of the Xianshou School.

☞ **Flower Adornment Sutra, Qingliang Chengguan ⟨National Master⟩**

Huineng ⟨Chan Master/Patriarch⟩ ⟨638-713 C.E.⟩ 惠能《禪師/祖師》

The great Master was named Huineng. His father's family name was Lu; his personal name was Xingtao. His mother's maiden name was Li. The Master was born during the Tang dynasty between between 11 PM and 1 AM on the eighth day of the second Chinese month in 638 C.E. At that time a beam of light ascended into the sky and an unusual fragrance filled the room. At dawn two exotic-looking Bhikshus came to visit. They addressed the Master's father saying, "Last night a son was born to you, and we have come with the sole purpose of naming him. In his name, the Chinese character 'hui' ("to benefit") can come first, the character 'neng' ("able") second."

His father said, "Why shall he be called Huineng?"

The monks replied, "'Hui' means he will benefit living beings with the Dharma.

‘Neng’ means he will be able to do the Buddha’s work. Having said this, they left. No one knows where they went.

the thirty-third patriarch, great master hui neng

The Master did not drink his mother’s milk. At night, spirits appeared and poured sweet dew over him.

He grew up, and at the age of twenty-four he heard a sutra and awakened to the Way. He then went to Huangmei to seek certification [from the Fifth Patriarch}.

In 661 C.E. the Fifth Patriarch gauged his capacity and transmitted the robe and Dharma to him, so that he inherited the position of patriarch. He then returned south and went into hiding for sixteen years.

In 676 [677?] C.E., on the eighth day of the first Chinese month, he met Dharma Master Yinzong. Together they discussed the profound and mysterious. Yinzong had an awakening and was in harmony with the essential meaning of what the Master had said.

On the fifteenth day of that month, at a gathering of all of the Four Assemblies, the Master’s head was shaved. On the eighth day of the second month, all those of well-known virtue gathered to administer the complete precepts to him....

In the spring of the following year, the Master took leave of the assembly and returned to Baolin[1] (Forest of Jewels). Yinzong, together with more than a thousand black-robed monks and white-robed laypeople, accompanied him directly to Cao Creek[2]. (*Platform Sutra*, unpubl. tr.)

What is preserved of the Sixth Patriarch’s teachings at Baolin in Caoxi, the present northern Guangdong Province, is contained in the ☞SIXTH PATRIARCH’S DHARMA JEWEL PLATFORM SUTRA.

On the third day of the eighth month of the year Guichou, the second year of the Xintian reign [713 C.E.], after a meal in Guoen Temple, the Master said, ‘Each of you take your seat, for I am going to say goodbye.... [After giving final instructions to his disciples], the Master sat upright until the third watch, when suddenly he said to his disciples, ‘I am going!’ In an instant he changed, and a rare fragrance filled the room. A white rainbow linked with the earth, and the trees in the wood turned white. The birds and beasts cried out in sorrow....The Master’s springs and autumns were seventy-six. The robe was transmitted to him when he was twenty-four, and when he was thirty-nine his hair was cut. For thirty-seven years he spoke Dharma to benefit living beings. Forty-three men inherited his Dharma, and an uncountable number awoke to the Way and overstepped the common lot....(PS 305-314)

☞ **Chan School, Sixth Patriarch’s Dharma Jewel Platform Sutra**

NOTES:

1 Baolin is both the name of a mountain and the name of a monastery.

2 Cao Creek is both a place name and the name of a creek running through the area.

hungry ghosts 餓鬼

☞ **ghosts, Six Paths of Rebirth**

1

ignorance 無明

Ignorance is the fundamental cause of our non-enlightenment. "Ignorance is merely a false mark. It is not real, and so it is subject to production, extinction, increase, decrease, defilement, purity, and so on. Ignorance is empty and unreal. It has no real substance. It is only a name and corresponds to nothing in reality. It cannot be grasped or seen. It causes us to undergo birth, old age, sickness, and death, worry, grief, and misery." (DFS II 374) Ignorance is the first link in the Twelvefold Conditioned Arising.

lack of knowledge, nescience

Twelvefold Conditioned Arising, attachment

impermanence 無常

In Chinese Buddhist monasteries at the end of the final ceremonies of the evening, this verse is chanted:

> This day is already done.
> Our lives are that much less.
> We're like fish in a shrinking pond;
> What joy is there in this?
> We should be diligent and vigorous,
> As if our own heads were at stake.
> Only be mindful of impermanence,
> And be careful not to be lax.
> (Universal Worthy Bodhisattva's
> Verse of Exhortation, TT 111)

The Buddha taught about impermanence in order to help living beings sever their attachment to the ideas of permanence and the eternal, particularly those taught by non-Buddhist religions.

> The Buddha said to the king [Prasenajit], "May I ask, is your body as indestructible as *vajra*, or is it subject to decay?"
>
> "World Honored One, this body of mine will continue to change until in the end it will perish."
>
> The Buddha said, "Your majesty, you have not perished yet. How do you know that you will?"
>
> "World Honored One, my impermanent body, though subject to decay, has not perished yet, but now, upon reflection, I can see that my every thought fades away, to be followed by a new thought which also does not last, like fire turning to ash, constantly dying away, forever perishing. This convinces me that my body must also extinguished."
>
> The Buddha said, "So it is. Your Majesty, you are in your declining years. How do you look now, compared to when you were a boy?"
>
> "World Honored One, when I was a child, my skin was fresh and smooth. When I reached the prime of life, I was full of life and energy. But now in my later years, as old age presses upon me, my body has become withered and weary. My vital spirits are dull, my hair is white, my skin is wrinkled, and I haven't much time remaining. How can this be compared to the prime of life?"

The Buddha said, "Your Majesty, your body's decline cannot have occurred suddenly."

The king said, "World Honored One, the change has been so subtle that I have hardly been aware of it, since I reached this point only gradually through the passage of the years. Thus when I was in my twenties, though I was still young, I already looked older than I did when I was ten. My thirties marked a further decline from my twenties, and now, at two years past sixty, I look back on my fifties as a time of strength and health.

"World Honored One, as I observe these subtle transformations, I realize that the changes wrought by this descent toward death are evident not only from decade to decade; they can also be discerned in smaller increments. If I consider them more closely, I see that the changes occur by the year as well as by the decade. In fact how could they occur merely year by year? There are changes every month. And how could they occur only by the month? These changes happen day after day. If one contemplates this in depth, one can see that there is ceaseless change from instant to instant, from thought to thought. Thus I can know that my body will continue to change until it has perished...."

The Buddha said, "...What changes will perish. What does not change does not come into being and does not perish. How could it be subject to your birth and death? You no longer need be concerned...that after the death of this body, there is annihilation."

The king believed the words he had heard, and he knew now that when we leave this body, we go on to another.... (SS II 25-35, BTTS rev. tr.)

Whatever flourishes must decay.
Every union entails separation.
The prime of one's life
  does not last long.
Health is encroached upon
  by illness.
Life is swallowed up by death.
There are no dharmas
  that last forever.
Kings attain to sovereignty,
With power that has no equal.
Yet all of it declines and perishes,
And our lives are that way too.
The wheel of sufferings
  has no bounds.
It keeps turning without cease.
All three realms are impermanent,
And none of the existences is bliss.

(NS Ch2 #25, BTTS draft tr.)

Impermanence together with suffering and no-self are called the Three Characteristics of the Conditioned World. In the third of the ☞FOUR APPLICATIONS OF MINDFULNESS, the impermanent nature of the mind is contemplated.

☞ **suffering, no self, Four Applications of Mindfulness**

k

kalpa 劫

An Indian unit of time, an aeon.

☞ aeon, cosmic cyclical period
☞ time

karma 業

The myriad things you do to others
Will return for you yourself to
undergo.
(Sutra on Cause and Effect, FHS I 30)

According with the karma
that is done,
That is the way
the retribution is borne.
The doer is nonexistent.
All Buddhas speak thus.
(FAS Ch10)

Who plants mangoes,
mangoes shall he eat.
Who plants thornbushes,
thorns shall wound his feet.
(Indian proverb, quoted in Keyes, *Karma*, 49)

Because of ignorance, living beings create karma. The word 'karma' means activity, activity that is based upon desire and governed by the law of cause and effect (☞ CAUSATION). For every good and bad act of the body, of speech, and of thought performed in the present, there is a corresponding result which is experienced in the future. In every moment, we experience the results of our past body-, speech-, and thought-karma and simultaneously create new karma which will bear fruit in the future. Thus karma is the primary force which keeps us in the cycle of rebirth, continually being reborn in the various realms of existence (☞ SIX PATHS OF REBIRTH).

The law of karma clearly explains why people undergo seemingly unwarranted rewards and retributions. Everything that happens to us, whether good or bad, has a reason, a cause, in the past.

> Ānanda, these living beings who do not recognize the fundamental mind all undergo rebirth for limitless aeons. They do not attain true purity, because they keep getting involved in killing, stealing, and lust, or because they counter them and are born according to their not killing, not stealing, and lack of lust. If these three kinds of karma are present in them, they are born among the troops of ghosts. If they are free of these three kinds of karma, they are born in the destiny of the gods. The incessant fluctuation between the presence and absence of these three kinds of karma gives rise to the cycle of rebirth. (SS VII 244)

"Karma is a Sanskrit term that refers to that which is made by the activity of body, speech, or mind. What is the difference between 'cause' and 'karma'? Cause refers to a single incident; karma is a long accumulation of causes. There are many causes and conditions that constitute karma, and each being has his own karma. Therefore, the states encountered by living beings differ. Some encounter great joy because they planted good seeds long ago, while others must endure a great deal of hardship, always living in difficult situations, because they have only sown bad causes. In general, if you plant good seeds, you reap good fruit; if you plant bad seeds, you reap bad fruit.

"Good deeds and bad are done by you alone, and no one forces you to do either. Even the work of becoming a Buddha is something to which you alone must apply effort; no one else can make you do it, and nobody can do it for you. If you do the work, you will plant the seeds of Buddhahood....If you do the deeds, the karma, of Buddhas, you will be a Buddha in the future; if you do the deeds of demons, you will become a demon." (SPV 101-102)

To know of past lives' causes,
Look at the rewards you are reaping today.
To find out about future lives,
You need but notice what you are doing right now.
(Sutra on Cause and Effect, FHS 32)

"Living beings' ignorance leads them to act in upside-down ways, and their various upside-down acts create various kinds of karma. According to their various kinds of karma, they undergo various retributions. Why do people do evil things: it is because of their ignorance, their lack of understanding, their delusions. Their delusions lead to the creation of bad karma, and since they create bad karma they undergo the retribution of suffering. It is a three-part process: delusion, leading to the creation of bad karma, which leads to the retribution of suffering.... You can't say which precedes the other; they follow after one another in continuous revolution, life after life, aeon after aeon. Where would you say it all began? There is no beginning. It's an endless cycle on the spinning wheel of the six paths of rebirth.

"Each of us born here in the world is like a mote of dust which suddenly rises high, suddenly falls low, suddenly goes up and suddenly descends. When your actions are good and meritorious you are born higher. When you do things which create offenses, you fall. Therefore, we people should do good things and perform meritorious deeds. Don't do things which create offenses, because this world runs on the principle of cause and effect, the law of karma. And 'the seeds of karma naturally run their course': you undergo a (reward or) retribution for whatever you do...." (SS I 172-173)

"You Can't Take It With You"

"Once there was a fabulously wealthy old man who had a beautiful wife and three fine, intelligent sons. But from the time this man had been born, he didn't pay any attention to anything but money. He ignored his father, his mother, and his brothers and sisters. The only thing he didn't ignore was money. He knew money like the back of his hand. It was his best friend and closest relative. He even wrote a verse about it:

"What heaven has conferred is called 'money.' According to this money it is called 'money.' Money...ah...may not be left for a moment.

"Actually, this is a rather perverted take-off on the first chapter of the Chinese classic, *The Doctrine of the Mean*, which reads, 'That which has been conferred by heaven is called the nature; according with the nature is called the path....The path may not be left for a moment.'

"He named his oldest son 'Gold.' His second son he named 'Silver.' He decided to give his third son an unusual name and called him 'Karmic Obstacle.' When his third son had grown up and he himself was already old, he got sick. He was completely bedridden and couldn't walk. Although he was very rich, after he was sick for some time, no one looked after him. His beautiful wife kept her distance, and his intelligent sons never came to visit him. He gritted his teeth and thought, 'I hope I hurry up and die. But being dead alone in King Yama's den will be very lonely. I should take someone with me.' He called for his wife and said, 'I'm not going to recover from this lingering illness. I hope to die soon. Won't you go with me?'

"'How can you ask a thing like that?' she said. 'Nobody can die for anyone else. How could you expect me to want to go along with you? Are you sure you haven't lost your marbles?'

"And so the old man called his eldest son. 'Gold,' he said, 'I have always loved you the most. Did you know that?'

"'Yes, father,' said his son. "I know you love me the most.'

"'Well, son, I'm going to die. Would you go along with me?'

"'You old blockhead!' came the reply. 'You're an old man. I'm young. How can you ask me to do something like that? And you claim to be fond of me. If you were, you wouldn't ask me to die with you!' And he ran off.

"Then the old man spoke to his second son, 'Silver, won't you die with me?'

"'You're really messed up,' said his son. 'How can you expect me to die just because you are dying?'

"There was nothing the man could do but call for his youngest son, Karmic Obstacle. 'You are the youngest,' he said. 'I love you the most. I could die, but I can't bear to part with you. What am I going to do?' He didn't dare ask outright for his son to go with him, but the boy caught on right away.

"'If you love me so much, I'll go with you,' said his son. The old man was delighted.

"'You haven't let me down,' he said. 'I always liked you best, and now I know you are my most filial son.'

"His pretty wife wouldn't go with him, and his sons Gold and Silver wouldn't go. The only one who went with his father to the hells was his young son Karmic Obstacle. And so it is said:

> "You can't take your gold and silver
> With you on your dying day;
> But your karmic obstacles
> Stick with you all the way!..."
> (DFS I 48-50)

No One Can Escape His/Her Karma

> And there was the mighty King Crystal....
> Crystal exterminated the Gautama clan.
> [He] sank into the unintermittent hell
> while still alive. (SS VII 86)

"King Crystal and the Buddha were supposedly relatives, though in fact they were not. King Crystal's father, also a king, wanted to marry into the Gautama clan. Since the Gautama clan was more honorable one than the king's, the members of the Gautama clan did not like the idea. No one wanted to give a daughter to the king in marriage, but they didn't dare refuse outright, because the king was powerful. A refusal might have resulted in a lot of trouble. Finally they decided among themselves to send one of their servant girls, a particularly beautiful one, and pretend she was of the Gautama clan. King Crystal was an offspring of that marriage.

"Once, while the king was still a child, someone built a temple for the Buddha, complete with an elaborate Dharma Seat. When the seat was finished, but before the Buddha himself had ascended the platform to sit on it and speak Dharma, the child who was to become King Crystal climbed up and sat on it. The Buddha's disciples and the donors who saw him all scolded him, saying, 'You're the son of a slave; how dare you sit in the Buddha's seat?' Hearing them call him that, he was outraged, and he said to his attendant, 'Wait until I am king, and then remind me of what was said here today, lest I forget it. People from the Gautama clan say I'm the son of a slave. Remind me of that. I intend to get even.'

"Later, when he was king, his attendant did remind him, and the king issued an edict that the entire Gautama clan was to be exterminated, including the Buddha himself. When ☞ MAHĀMAUDGALYĀYANA got wind of this, he went to the Buddha to report. 'We have to think of away to save them,' he said. But the Buddha didn't say anything. And so Maudgalyāyana loosed his spiritual powers, put five hundred members of the Gautama clan into his precious bowl, and sent them to the heavens. He thought they would be safe there. When the king had completed the extermination, Maudgalyāyana told Śākyamuni Buddha, 'I've got five hundred Gautamans in a bowl stashed away in the heavens, and so the clan isn't totally gone after all. I'll bring them down now and let them go.' But when he had recalled them and took a look at his bowl, he found nothing there but blood. "Why was I unable to save them?' asked the puzzled Maudgalyāyana. He wanted the Buddha to explain the causes and conditions.

"'Ah, you don't know,' said the Buddha, "At the level of planting causes, a long time ago, at a place where the weather was hot, there was a pool with schools of fish in it. The two leaders of the schools were named Bran and Many Tongues. The water in the pool evaporated in the intense heat, and since the people in the area didn't have anything else to eat, they ate the fish. In the end there was just a mud-hole, but even then they noticed a movement in the mud. Digging in, they found the two big fish-kings—Bran and Many Tongues. At that time, I, Śākyamuni Buddha, was a child among these people, who were later to become the Gautama clan. Seeing that the two fish were about to be devoured alive, I beat them over the head three times with a club to knock them out first.' That is why in his life as a Buddha he had to endure a three-day headache as retribution. 'Further, the fish Bran was the present King Crystal, and the fish Many Tongues was his attendant who reminded him of the words spoken by the Gautama clan to the king as a child. And so it was fated that he would exterminate the Gautama clan.' Even though Śākyamuni had become a Buddha, he could not rescue his people from the fixed karma they were destined to repay."

☞ **action, deeds, occupation**
☞ **rebirth, causation, God**

Kṣitigarbha ⟨Bodhisattva⟩ 地藏《菩薩》

☞ **Earth Store ⟨Bodhisattva⟩**

Kumārajīva ⟨Tripiṭaka Master⟩ ⟨344-413 C.E.⟩ 鳩摩羅什《三藏法師》

the venerable kumarajiva of yao qin

"Kumārajīva's father, Kumārāyaṇa, was the son of a prime minister. He should have succeeded his father, but, instead he left his home and went everywhere looking for a teacher. Although he hadn't left the home-life in the formal sense by taking the complete precepts, he still cultivated the Way, and in his travels, went to the country of Kucha in central Asia. The king of Kucha had a little sister, and when she saw Kumārāyaṇa, she said to the king, 'I really love this man.' The king gave his sister in marriage to Kumārāyaṇa and she soon became pregnant.

"When Kumārajīva was still in his mother's womb, it was much like the situation with ☞ŚĀRIPUTRA and his mother. Kumārajīva's mother could defeat everyone in debate. At that time, an Arhat said, 'The child in this woman's womb is certainly one of great wisdom.'

"When Kumārajīva was seven years old, his mother took him to a temple to worship the Buddha. Kumārajīva picked up a large bronze incense urn and effortlessly lifted it over his head. Then he thought, 'Hey, I'm just a child. How can I lift this heavy urn?' With that one thought, the urn crashed to the ground. From that, he realized the meaning of the doctrine, 'Everything is made from the mind alone,' and he and his mother left the home-life.

"Kumārajīva's mother had difficulty leaving the home-life. Although Kumārajīva's father had previously cultivated the Way, he was now too much in love with his wife to permit her to leave home. Thereupon, she went on a strict fast. 'Unless you allow me to leave home,' she said, 'I won't eat or drink. I'll starve myself.'

"Then don't eat or drink, if that's what you want,' said her husband, 'but I'll never let you leave home.'

"For six days she didn't eat or drink, not even fruit juice, and she became extremely weak. Finally, Kumārāyaṇa said, 'This is too dangerous. You're going to starve to death. You may leave home, but please eat something.'

"'First call in a Dharma Master to cut off my hair,' she said, 'and then I'll eat.' A Dharma Master came and shaved her head, and then she ate. Shortly after leaving home, she was certified as having become a first stage Arhat.

"Soon after that, Kumārajīva, her son, also left the home-life. Everyday he read and recited many sutras, and once he read them, he never forgot them.... Because of his faultless memory, he defeated all non-Buddhist philosophers in India and became very well-known.

"His reputation spread to China, and when Fuqian, emperor of the Former Qin Dynasty, heard of him, he sent the great General Lü Guang and seventy thousand troops to Kucha to capture Kumārajīva and bring him back to China. Kumārajīva said to the king of Kucha, 'China is sending troops, but do not oppose them. They don't wish to take the country. They have another purpose and you should grant their request.'

"Kumārajīva's uncle, the king, wouldn't listen to him, but went to war with the general from China, Lü Guang. As a result, the king of Kucha was put to death, the country defeated, and Kumārajīva captured.

"On the way back to China, General Lü Guang one day prepared to camp in a low valley. Kumārajīva, who had spiritual powers, knew a rain was coming which would flood the valley. He told the general, 'Don't camp here tonight. This place is dangerous.'

"But Lü Guang had no faith in Kumārajīva. 'You're a monk,' he said. 'What do you know about military affairs?' That night there was a deluge and many men and horses were drowned. General Lü Guang then knew that Kumārajīva was truly inconceivable.

"They proceeded until they heard that there had been a change in the Chinese government. Emperor Fuqian had been deposed, and Yaochang had seized the throne. General Lü Guang maintained his neutrality and did not return to China. Yaochang was emperor for several years, and when he died, his nephew Yaoxing took the throne. It was Yaoxing who dispatched a party to invite Kumārajīva to China to translate sutras. A gathering of over eight hundred Bhikshus assembled to assist him in this work.

"We have proof that Kumārajīva's translations are extremely accurate. When he was about to complete the stillness, that is, die, he said, 'I have translated numerous sutras during my lifetime, and I personally don't know if my translations are correct. If they are, when I am cremated, my tongue will not burn; but if there are mistakes, it will burn.' When he died, his body was burned, but his tongue remained intact.

"The Tang Dynasty Vinaya Master Daoxuan once asked the god Lu Xuanchang, 'Why does everyone prefer to read and study Kumārajīva's translations?' The god replied, 'Kumārajīva has been the Translation Master for the past seven Buddhas and so his translations are accurate.'" (AS 45-47)

L

liberating living beings 放生

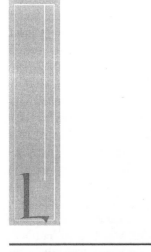

Liberating living beings is just liberating ourselves. Why? Because we and all living beings are basically of one substance.

A Buddhist practice of rescuing animals, birds, fish and so forth that are destined for slaughter or that are permanently caged. They are released to a new physical and spiritual life. The practice exemplifies the fundamental Buddhist teaching of compassion for all living beings.

> A disciple of the Buddha must maintain a mind of kindness and cultivate the practice of liberating beings. He should reflect thus: 'All male beings have been my father and all females have been my mother. There is not a single being who has not given birth to me during my previous lives, hence all beings of the Six Destinies (☞ SIX PATHS OF REBIRTH) are my parents. Therefore, when a person kills and eats any of these beings, he thereby slaughters my parents. Furthermore, he kills a body that was once my own, for all elemental earth and water previously served as part of my body and all elemental fire and wind have served as my basic substance. Therefore, I shall always cultivate the practice of liberating beings and in every life be reborn in the eternally abiding Dharma and teach others to liberate beings as well.'
>
> Whenever a Bodhisattva sees a person preparing to kill an animal, he should devise a skillful method to rescue and protect it, freeing it from its suffering and difficulties.... (BNS I 162)

In China this practice was made popular by the Venerable ☞ ZHIYI and has continued to the present day.

Developing our Compassion by Liberating Living Beings

"Once a month at the ☞ CITY OF TEN THOUSAND BUDDHAS, we liberate animals destined for slaughter. We purchase them from the wholesalers, bring them to some appropriate place, and let them go free. We recite mantras, sutras, and praises on their behalf, so that they can hear them, and so that the merit of our recitation can be transferred to them. This traditional Buddhist practice, called 'liberating living beings,' has always been praised and honored by the sages and high masters.

"By liberating living beings, we also nurture compassion in our hearts. By not killing, we cultivate compassion. In letting living creatures go, we also cultivate compassion. The compassion in our hearts grows greater every day until it becomes as great as that of the greatly compassionate Bodhisattva Observer of the World's Sounds [☞ AVALOKITEŚVARA].

"Bodhisattva Observer of the World's Sounds did not kill living beings; she always liberated them, and so she has a greatly compassionate heart. We should imitate the great kindness and compassion of Bodhisattva Observer of the World's Sounds and liberate living beings. The principle is very logical: If you liberate life, you increase your compassion. Liberating living beings is just liberating ourselves. Why? Because we and all living beings are basically of one substance. We should think this way: 'If someone put me in a cage, wouldn't I be uncomfortable? Wouldn't I wish that someone would let me go? If I were put in jail, I would not want to stay there. Likewise, I don't like to see birds put in cages. This is because living beings and I are of one substance. Since I feel this way, I want to liberate living beings.

"What is more, you don't know which living being was related to you in a past life. One might have been your father, or your brother, or your sister. You can't know for sure. Perhaps they were your children, or your friends. Right now you haven't gained the use of the Heavenly Eye or the Penetration of Past Lives [☞ SIX SPIRITUAL POWERS], and so you don't know what kinds of causes and effects belong to each animal; and yet, when you see these creatures, you feel uncomfortable and want to set them free. Setting them free isn't a stupid thing to do by any means, as some people might think. It is an aspect of cultivation. There isn't just one way to cultivate. There are eighty-four thousand Dharma-doors in cultivation, and every single door leads to the realization of supreme enlightenment. Liberating living beings is one of them. We must be careful not to think of it as 'stupid.' If we have that kind of attitude, we will obstruct our own cultivation.

"I just said that we wouldn't want to be locked in jail. I will tell you the truth. This is not an analogy. Your own body is, in fact, a cage! You are stuck in your own body and you are not yet able to get out of it. Until we have gained a very high level of spiritual practice and wisdom, we will remain stuck in the cages that are our bodies. Only then will we have liberated our own lives. That's the real liberation of the living. If we want to liberate our own lives, we must first liberate the lives of those little creatures. The one kind of liberating the living helps the other kind.

"Liberating living beings is a very important aspect of Buddhist practice. But if one hasn't understood this yet, one might think it a very ordinary affair. If we don't cultivate the one kind of liberating the living, we won't be able to obtain the other kind. There are many changes and transformations, and so don't look upon this lightly. Liberating the living brings returns on one's own efforts." (Venerable Master Hsuan Hua, PDS, May, 1985)

"Why do we liberate...[living creatures]? It is because if we ransom creatures that were destined to be slaughtered for food and then set them free, then they can live out their natural life spans. This in turn enables the people who liberate the living to enjoy a long life.

"Why are there wars in the world? It is because our collective killing karma is so heavy. If in this life I kill you, in the next life, you'll kill me, and in the life after that I'll come back to kill you. This cycle of killing continues forever. People kill animals and in their next life they become animals. The animals which they once killed now return as people to claim revenge. This goes on and on. There is endless killing and bloodshed. When incidents of slaughter multiply until the resentment can no longer be contained, they explode into massive world wars, with the resultant huge massacres and horrendous destruction. On the battlefield, people are propelled by resentment and enmity that has accumulated during many lifetimes, and they go absolutely berserk, lashing out at one another like savages. 'You kill one person? I'll kill ten!' They take revenge on one another like that. Wars are the painful results of killing karma created in our past lives.

"Therefore, we liberate the living to diminish our killing karma. The more people engage in liberating the living, the less killing they will do. Wars will proportionately decrease. We who cultivate these compassionate practices do not oppose war: we just don't go to war. We don't kill but instead we set living creatures free. This is the true and ultimate way to eliminate war. It is also a gateway to long life and health and to the eradication of disasters and illnesses. The merit and virtue that one accumulates from liberating animals is boundless. It enables you to cause living beings to live out the full extent of their natural life spans. In addition, you benefit personally because illnesses are averted. As a result you enjoy good health and are able to peacefully cultivate the Way.

"The purpose of liberating the living is to protect the lives of creatures. It is a Dharma-door that exemplifies the Buddha's compassion. Everyone should protect living creatures and not abuse or slaughter them." (FAS Ch8 76-77)

> In liberating the living, you yourself
> will live long.
> Health, riches and blessings will
> descend upon you, never-ending.
> (CL II 15)

☞ **living beings, vegetarianism, compassion**

lineage 宗派/法脈

Lineage refers to the unbroken chains of enlightened masters stretching back to the Buddha Śākyamuni. These masters are the real foundation of the living tradition of Buddhist teaching and practice. True lineage insures that the Buddha's original message is preserved undistorted and in its essentials.

The most well-known, as perhaps the most important, of all Buddhist lineages are the Chan lineages (☞CHAN SCHOOL), which began with the transmission of the Mind Seal from the Buddha ☞ŚĀKYAMUNI to the First Patriarch ☞MAHĀKĀŚYAPA.

☞ **Chan School, Dharma-transmission**

living beings 眾生

Living beings refer to all creatures that possess life-force. Each individual living being comes into being as the resultant matrix of a variety of different causes and conditions.

"Even the smallest of ants is also a living being. The tiniest mosquito, too, is a living being. Even all the tiny germs and so forth are all living beings. Since this is the case, we should not look outwardly in our search to save living beings. Countless living beings for us to save can be found right within our own natures. Inside our own bodies there are countless living beings. Recent progress in the science of medicine gives proof to the fact that human beings are all like big bugs and within our bodies live countless smaller bugs. How many? No scientific method can be used to count them accurately. Why? Because they are countless! Who knows how many living beings are inside our blood, our flesh, and our internal organs? Why are there so many living beings? Some people even eat living beings! They eat the flesh of pigs, cows, sheep, fish, chickens, and ducks. When you eat the flesh of living beings, inside it are hidden the germs particular to that living being. When you eat it, that kind of living being's organisms go into you. Whichever kind of meat you eat the most of, you have a majority of that kind of living being's germs. That makes it very easy to become a member of the family of that kind of living being. You turn into one of his clansmen; because you have causal conditions with him that are just too deep, you can't get away from him. If you eat mostly pork, you have an opportunity to turn into a pig. If you eat mostly beef, you may turn into a cow.

"'I eat rice. Will I turn into a plant?' you ask.

"No, because rice is not generally considered sentient in the way that animals are. If you eat sentient beings, you can turn into that kind of living being. If you eat insentient things, you will not turn into plants or grasses or the like, but you will be truly helping the wisdom-life of your Dharma body. And so don't worry about turning into a rice-plant if you eat rice.

"Sentient beings have blood and breath, and when you eat them, you turn into that kind of living being. You could even say that by not eating a particular kind of living being, you are saving that living being. If you do not eat beef, you are saving cows. If you do not eat mutton, you are saving sheep. By not eating pork, you are saving pigs...." (DFS IV 789-790)

There are various categories of living beings, including lists of four, ten, and twelve kinds. The Four Kinds of Living Beings are those born from: **1)** wombs, **2)** eggs, **3)** moisture, and **4)** transformation.

being, creature
liberating living beings, Ten Dharma Realms

lotus posture 雙跏趺坐

> When sitting in the full-lotus posture,
> I vow that living beings
> Will have solid good roots
> And attain the Unmoving Ground.
> (FAS Ch11 127)

"When you sit down (to meditate), you take your left leg and put it on top of your right thigh, and then take your right leg and put it on top of your left thigh. That's the full-lotus posture. It is also called the jeweled *vajra* sitting position. It is also called the *bodhi* position. Although there are many names, they all refer to this one position. If you sit in this position it is easy to enter samadhi. It is also easier not to doze off. On the other hand, you can also sleep in this position. However, if you don't want to sleep, you don't have to. Why? It is because everything is made from the mind alone.

"When you sit, your body should be held upright. Don't lean back with your neck cocked backwards. Don't lean backwards or forwards or slouch to the right or left. Sit straight but not stiff as a board. Don't sit so stiffly that it seems you are hemmed in on all sides by stiff boards or iron bars. I say this because I know there are certain people who, when they sit, immediately sit up as stiff as boards. They pose like wooden statues. It takes a tremendous amount of effort to maintain yourself like that. That is not the way to subdue your body and mind. Subduing the body and mind should be very natural. Don't display some special style.... When meditation is done naturally, there is not any force at all about it. You just sit there very relaxed, and you feel quite comfortable....

"When you are sitting, you want to make your breath even. For instance, you don't want to make a point of taking very deep breaths...like a cow.... On the other hand, you shouldn't breathe like a mosquito—so shallowly that it's barely audible.... You breathe in when you need to breathe in, and you breathe out when you need to breathe out. It's very natural and you make your mind pure and don't have any false thinking.

"Put the tip of your tongue on the roof of your mouth. That way the saliva in your mouth will flow directly into your stomach. That is why it is best for people who meditate to refrain from smoking, drinking, and taking other intoxicants. Don't rely on external conditions to aid you. If you don't smoke and you don't drink, then your saliva won't be scorched and bitter, and you will be able to swallow it into your stomach, where the saliva helps in harmonizing the energy and the blood.

"When you are sitting, don't be afraid of the pain. Perhaps you can sit for half an hour before the pain starts, but when it does begin you should be patient. It is at that point when patience is of the utmost importance. The more it hurts, the more you are patient, just as if you were raising a child. You should say, "Come on, child, don't cry. Wait a bit and I will give you some candy." You can tell your legs, "Don't lose your temper; don't get angry. Wait a bit until I've mastered this sitting, and then you won't hurt anymore. Then we will have ended birth and death." Tell your legs that the very best thing to do would be to go to sleep and not get angry. ...When your legs hurt, you should bear it, and then pretty soon you will be able to sit for an hour, two hours, three hours. You will sit there in a state of unmoving suchness, and there in that unmoving state several hours will pass very quickly. That means you have experienced a little bit of 'light ease,' and you should continue with your cultivation. If you continue with your cultivation, then you can obtain genuine samadhi power.

"Some people are really worried.... They say, 'Well I'd like to investigate Chan, but I can't sit in full-lotus posture, so it is useless.' Don't worry; if you can't sit in full lotus you can sit in half lotus. That's putting your left leg on top of your right thigh. Why does the left leg go on the right leg?...The left leg is *yang* and the right leg is *yin*. The left leg represents heaven and the right leg represents earth. And so heaven is on top and the earth is on the bottom. You can sit that way. And if you can't manage half lotus, you can sit in any way that is comfortable. Subdue your body and mind. Cause the body and mind not to lose their tempers, so that no matter how long you sit there is no fear of pain, and they don't get angry...." (TD 66)

> To sit still for a single moment,
> Is worth more than building as many
> pagodas of the seven gems
> As there are grains of sand in the
> Ganges River. (TD 67)

On Sitting in Full-Lotus Posture: An Historical Account

"A long time ago in China, there was a monk who recited sutras for dead people. He always recited sutras for others' sake, but not for his own sake. He created merit and virtue for other people, but not for himself. One day he came back from creating merit and virtue for others. It was dark on his way back home. While he went through a village, a dog barked at him. It woke some people, and he heard a woman inside a house say, 'Do you hear the dog barking so loudly? Maybe there is a thief. We'd better take a look.' Her husband replied, 'It cannot be.' The dog then barked more fiercely, so he looked outside through the window.

"'Is that a thief?' his wife asked.

"'No, it's only a sutra-reciting ghost!'

"When the monk heard himself called him a sutra-reciting ghost instead of a sutra-reciting god, he was upset. 'Ha! What's the matter with reciting the sutras? How dare you call me a sutra-reciting ghost? If I were a real ghost, I'd give you a headache.' And so he had such thoughts as he passed through the village.

"As he was walking across a bridge it started to rain, so he quickly ran down under the bridge to get out of the rain. He had heard that if one sat in full-lotus posture the result was not bad, and so he tried it out. ...Suddenly he saw two ghosts. They didn't bother him; instead they bowed to him.

"They said, 'This golden stupa [i.e., reliquary monument, pagoda] must contain the Buddha's ☞ŚARĪRA [i.e., relics]. We should respect it and bow to it.'

"Because he sat in full-lotus position, he looked like a golden stupa in the eyes of those two ghosts. The monk saw the two ghosts bow to him. He probably also saw ghosts when he 'took across' dead people....He was not afraid of them. After sitting in full-lotus position for a while, he felt pain. It became so intense that he could no longer endure it, even if he clenched his teeth. And so he put down the leg on top and sat in the half-lotus position instead. When the two ghosts raised their heads from bowing, they were surprised: 'Why has this golden stupa become a silver stupa?' The full-lotus position is a golden stupa, and the half-lotus position is a silver stupa, viewed from the eyes of ghosts.

"One ghost said, 'Whether it's a golden stupa or a silver stupa, it still has the Buddha's *śarīra*, and so we should still keep on bowing to eradicate our karmic offenses!' Therefore, they kept on bowing to him.

"Probably he overheard the conversation between these two ghosts. Yet after another hour he could no longer endure the pain from sitting in half-lotus position. Because he was used to reciting sutras for dead people to make his living, he couldn't endure sitting in full lotus for half an hour and then half-lotus for another hour. And so he put down his other leg and just sat casually.

"When the two ghosts stood up from bowing, they saw him and said, 'Now this is neither a golden stupa nor a silver stupa. It's only a pile of mud!' They wanted to hit him and kick him.

"The monk was so scared that he quickly went back to the full-lotus position. When the ghosts were just about to hit him, they saw the mud pile had become a golden stupa again! They said, 'This is certainly an inconceivable state; we had better quickly bow. And so the ghosts continued to bow.

"After this experience, the monk didn't dare put down his legs. No matter how painful his legs felt, he endured the pain....He sat in meditation and recited the Buddha's name until the next morning. Then his two legs didn't hurt any more. He thought, 'I was called a sutra-reciting ghost before, because I recited sutras for others. But when I sat in full-lotus position, I was a golden stupa. And when I sat in half-lotus position, I was a silver stupa. But when I sat casually, I was just a pile of mud. When one sits in full-lotus position, even ghosts come to pay their respects. This is really inconceivable!'

"After this experience, he no longer dared merely to recite sutras for others, but resolved to sit in full lotus to help his own cultivation. After cultivating for a period of time, he got enlightened and was certified as such. After his enlightenment, he realized that the source of his enlightenment was the two ghosts who had forced him to resolve to cultivate. And so he gave up his former name and replaced it with a very strange one: 'Pressured-by-Ghosts.' Thereafter, everyone called him Meditation Master Pressured-by-Ghosts...." (FAS Ch11 127-131)

L

☞ **meditation**

Lotus Sutra 法華經

☞ **Dharma Flower ⟨Lotus⟩ Sutra**

love 愛/貪愛/愛欲

The single word 'love' can be used in many different ways. Buddhism teaches that it is extremely important to distinguish among its various meanings. 'Love' as craving or sexual desire is one of the major causes of our suffering and continued rebirth. On the other hand 'love' as totally selfless benevolence and compassion is one of the essential qualities of the minds of the Buddhas and Bodhisattvas (☞COMPASSION). The passages that follow speak of love as craving or sexual desire. The *Sutra in Forty-two Sections* says of love:

> People who cherish love and desire do not see the Way. It is just as when you stir clear water with your hand; those who stand beside it cannot see their reflections. People who are immersed in love and desire have turbidity in their minds, and because of it they cannot see the Way. ...When the filth of love and desire disappears, the Way can be seen. (S42 40)

> ...not satisfied with one delicious helping, [they] lick the honey off the blade of the knife, and so they cut their tongues. (S42 48)

Nine Analogies for Love

"**1**) Love is like an unpaid debt....
"**2**) Love is like a *rakśaṣa*-ghost woman....
"**3**) Love is like a wonderful lotus-flower whose roots are hiding a poisonous snake....
"**4**) Love is like disagreeable food....
"**5**) Love is like a prostitute....
"**6**) Love is like a *mleccha* [i.e., 'barbarian']....
"**7**) Love is like an infected sore....
"**8**) Love is like a destructive wind....
"**9**) Love is like a comet...." (FAS Ch9 32-33)

☞ **thirsting, craving, sexual desire**
☞ **compassion, Twelvefold Conditioned Arising—karmic activity, Five Desires—sex**

M

Madhyamaka/Mādhyamika 中觀論《派》

☞ **emptiness, Nāgārjuna**

mahā 摩訶

A Sanskrit word meaning 'great.'

Mahākāśyapa 〈Venerable〉 摩訶迦葉《尊者》

Mahākāśyapa was the eldest of the Buddha's great disciples. He was foremost in ascetic practices and first patriarch of the Meditation (Chan) School.

shakyamuni buddha

"*Mahā* means great, many, and victorious. The Sanskrit word *kāśyapa* means 'great turtle clan,' because Mahākāśyapa's ancestors saw the pattern on the back of a giant turtle and used it to cultivate the Way. *Kāśyapa* also means 'light drinking clan,' because his body shone with light which was so bright it seemed to drink up all other light.

"Why did his body shine? Seven Buddhas ago, in the time of the Buddha Vipaśyin, there was a poor woman who decided to repair a ruined temple. The roof of the temple had been blown off and the images inside were exposed to the wind and rain. The woman went everywhere and asked for help, and when she had collected enough money she commissioned a goldsmith to regild the images. By the time he was finished, the goldsmith fell in love with her and said, 'You have attained great merit from this work, but we should share it. You may supply the gold and I will furnish the labor, free.' And so the temple was rebuilt and the images regilded. The goldsmith asked the woman to marry him, and in every life for ninety-one *kalpas*, they were husband and wife and their bodies shone with purple and golden light.

"Mahākāśyapa was born in Magadha in India. When he was twenty, his father and mother wanted him to marry, but he said, 'The woman I marry must shine with golden light. Unless you find such a woman, I won't marry.' Eventually they found one, and they were married. As a result of their good karma their bodies shone with golden light, and they cultivated together and investigated the doctrines of the Way. When Mahākāśyapa left home to become a Bhikshu [monk], his wife became a Bhikshuni [nun] called Purple and Golden Light.

the first patriarch, venerable mahakashyapa

"Mahākāśyapa's personal name was Pippala, because his parents prayed to the spirit of a *pippala* tree to grant them a son.

"As the first patriarch, Mahākāśyapa holds an important position in Buddhism. When Śakyāmuni Buddha spoke the

Dharma, the Great Brahma Heaven King presented him with a golden lotus and Śakyāmuni Buddha held up the flower before the assembly. At that time hundreds of thousands of gods and men were present, but no one responded except Mahākāśyapa, who simply smiled. The Buddha said, 'I have the Right Dharma-Eye Treasury, the wondrous mind of nirvana, the reality beyond appearance. The Dharma-door of mind to mind transmission has been entrusted to Kāśyapa.' Thus Mahākāśyapa received the transmission of Dharma and became the first Buddhist patriarch.

"The Venerable Mahākāśyapa is still present in the world. When he left home under the Buddha, he was already one hundred sixty years old. At the time Śakyāmuni Buddha had spoken Dharma for forty-nine years in over three hundred Dharma assemblies, Kāśyapa was already over two hundred years old. After Śakyāmuni Buddha entered nirvana, Kāśyapa went to Southwestern China, to Chicken Foot [Jizu] Mountain in Yunnan Province. It has been over three thousand years since the Buddha's nirvana, but Mahākāśyapa is still sitting in samadhi in Chicken Foot Mountain waiting for ☞MAITREYA BUDDHA to appear in the world. At that time he will give Maitreya the bowl which the Four Heavenly Kings gave Śakyāmuni Buddha and which Śakyāmuni Buddha gave him, and his work in the world will be finished.

"When cultivators travel to Chicken Foot Mountain to worship the Patriarch Kāśyapa, on the mountain there are always three kinds of light: Buddha-light, golden light, and silver light. Those with sincere hearts can hear a big bell ringing inside the mountain. It rings by itself, and although you can't see it, you can hear it for several hundred miles. It is an inconceivable experience." (AS 75-76)

In the ☞ŚŪRAṄGAMA SUTRA, Mahākāśyapa explained the method he used to become enlightened:

> I contemplated that the world's six sense-objects change and decay; they are but empty stillness. Based on this, I cultivated cessation. Now my body and mind can pass through hundreds of thousands of *kalpas* as though they were a finger snap.
>
> Based on the emptiness of dharmas, I became an Arhat. The World Honored One says that I am foremost in *dhūta* [ascetic] practices. Wonderful Dharma brought me awakening and understanding, and I extinguished all outflows. The Buddha asks about perfect penetration. As I have been certified to it, dharmas are the superior means. (SS V 42-43)

Also in the *Śūraṅgama Sutra*, the Buddha commented on Mahākāśyapa's enlightened mind:

> There is also Mahākāśyapa in this assembly, dwelling in the samadhi of cessation, having obtained the stillness of a Sound Hearer. He has long since ceased using the mind-organ, and yet he has a perfectly clear knowledge which is not due to the mental process of thinking. (SS IV 198)

In the ☞DHARMA FLOWER (LOTUS) SUTRA, the Buddha bestowed upon Mahākāśyapa the prediction of future Buddhahood:

> My disciple, Mahākāśyapa, in a future age will serve and behold three hundred billion Buddhas, World Honored Ones, making offerings, paying reverence, venerating and praising them; he will broadly proclaim the limitless Great Dharma of all the Buddhas.
>
> In his final body he will become a Buddha by the name of Light Brightness Thus Come One, One Worthy of Offerings, One of Proper and Universal

Knowledge, One Perfect in Clarity and Practice, a Well Gone One, an Unsurpassed One Who Understands the World, Hero Who Subdues and Tames, Teacher of Gods and Humans, Buddha, World Honored One. His country will be called Light Virtue and his aeon will be called Great Adornment. His life span as a Buddha will last for twelve minor aeons. The proper Dharma will dwell there for twenty minor aeons. The Dharma Resemblance Age will also dwell there for twenty minor aeons. His realm will be adorned and free of any filth or evil, tiles or stones, thorns or brambles, excrement or other impurities. The land will be flat, without high or low places, gullies or hills. The land will be made of lapis lazuli, and set about with rows of jeweled trees. The roads will be bordered with golden ropes. Precious flowers will be scattered about, purifying it entirely. The Bodhisattvas in that land will number in the limitless thousands of millions, the assembly of Sound Hearers will likewise be uncountable. No deeds of Māra will be done there, and although Māra and his subjects will exist there, they will all protect the Buddhadharma. (DFS VI 1104-1109)

In the ☞ MAHĀPARINIRVĀṆA SUTRA the Buddha stated:

> Kāśyapa will be a great source of reliance for you. Just as the Thus Come One is the place of reliance for living beings, so too will Mahākāśyapa be the place of reliance for you. It is the way when a great king who rules many territories goes on a tour of inspection, he entrusts all affairs of state to a great minister. The Thus Come One, in the same way, has completely entrusted all his proper Dharma to Mahākāśyapa. (NS Ch3)

☞ **Chan School**

Mahāmaudgalyāyana 〈Venerable〉 摩訶目犍連《尊者》

One of the great enlightened disciples of the Buddha, Mahāmaudgalyāyana was foremost among the Arhats in spiritual powers. He was and had been for many lifetimes a close friend of the Venerable ☞ ŚĀRIPUTRA.

"Maudgalyāyana is Sanskrit and means 'descendant of a family of bean gatherers.' His name also means 'turnip root,' because his ancestors ate turnips when they cultivated the Way. He is also called Kolita after the tree where his father and mother prayed to a tree-spirit for a son.

"This Venerable One was the foremost in spiritual penetrations [☞ SIX SPIRITUAL POWERS]....When Mahāmaudgalyāyana first obtained these penetrations, he looked for...his mother. Where was she? His mother was in the hells. Why? Because she had not believed in the Three Jewels: the Buddha, the Dharma, and the Sangha; and what is more, she had slandered them. She had also eaten fish eggs and flesh, and thereby had killed many beings.

"Seeing her in the hells, Maudgalyāyana sent her a bowl of food. She took it in one hand and hid it with the other because she was afraid the other hungry ghosts would see it and try to steal it from her. Being greedy herself, she knew that other hungry ghosts were greedy too, and so she covered it over stealthily.

"Although it was good food, her heavy karmic obstacles prevented her from eating it. When the food reached her mouth it turned to flaming coals which burned her lips. Maudgalyāyana's spiritual powers could not prevent the food from turning into fire, so he asked the Buddha to help him.

"The Buddha told him to save his mother by arranging an Ullambana offering. Ullambana means 'releasing those who are hanging upside down.' The Buddha told Maudgalyāyana that, on the fifteenth of the seventh lunar month, the day of the Buddha's delight and the monks' *pravāraṇa* [the last day of the monks' rainy season retreat], he should offer all varieties of food and drink to the Sangha of the ten directions. In this way he could rescue his mother so she could leave suffering and obtain bliss.

"Maudgalyāyana followed those instructions, and his mother was reborn in the heavens. Not only was his mother saved, but all the hungry ghosts in the hells simultaneously left suffering and obtained bliss." (AS 73-75)

In the ☞DHARMA FLOWER SUTRA the Buddha bestows the prediction of future Buddhahood upon Mahāmaudgalyāyana:

> I now tell you that Mahāmaudgalyāyana will in the future, with various articles, make offerings to eight thousand Buddhas, honoring and venerating them. After the nirvana of those Buddhas, he will erect for each of them a stupa one thousand ☞YOJANAS in height and five hundred *yojanas* in breadth, and made of the seven jewels—gold, silver, lapis lazuli, mother of pearl, carnelian, pearls, and agate. He will make offerings to it of many flowers, beaded necklaces, paste incense, silk canopies and banners. After that, he will further make offerings to two hundred myriads of millions of Buddhas in the same manner.
>
> He will then become a Buddha called Tamālapattracandana Fragrance Thus Come One, One Worthy of Offerings, One of Proper and Universal Knowledge, One Whose Understanding and Conduct Are Complete, a Well Gone One Who Understands the World, an Unsurpassed Lord, a Taming and Regulating Hero, Teacher of Gods and Humans, Buddha, World Honored One.
>
> His aeon will be called Full of Joy. His country will be called Delighted Mind. His land will be flat and even with crystal for soil, and jeweled trees for adornments. Real pearl flowers will be scattered about, purifying it entirely, so that those who see it rejoice. There will be many gods, humans, Bodhisattvas and Sound Hearers, limitless and uncountable in number. His life span as a Buddha will last for twenty-four minor aeons. The Proper Dharma will dwell there for forty minor aeons. The Dharma Resemblance Age will dwell also for forty minor aeons." (DFS VI 1146-1154)

☞ **karma—"No One Can Escape His/Her Karma," Śāriputra ⟨Venerable⟩**

Mahāparinirvāṇa Sutra 大般涅槃經

☞ **Nirvana Sutra**

Mahāsattva 摩訶薩

A Sanskrit word meaning 'great being.' It is the title of a great Bodhisattva.

☞ **Bodhisattva**

Mahayana Buddhism 大乘佛教

☞ **Mahayana and Hinayana Compared**

Mahayana and Hinayana Compared
大乘小乘比較

'Mahayana' means 'Great Vehicle'; 'Hinayana' means 'Small Vehicle' or 'Lesser Vehicle.' The modern representatives of the Hinayana belong to the Theravada School of Buddhism, which is found in Sri Lanka and most of Southeast Asia. Because Hinayana is a pejorative term, it is sometimes referred to as Southern Buddhism, while Mahayana is called Northern Buddhism because it came to be found in China, Korea, Japan, and Tibet.

Mahayana and Hinayana began not as separate schools but as alternative goals which were a matter of personal choice. The adherents of each lived and practiced together. Over the centuries they developed into different schools and eventually spread into different geographic areas.

What then are the different goals? The goal of the Hinayana is that of ending attachment to self and, thereby, becoming an Arhat, who undergoes no further rebirth. The Mahayana teaches that Arhatship is not an ultimate goal; its adherents follow the Path of the Bodhisattva, which leads to Buddhahood. The Bodhisattva is reborn voluntarily in order to aid all living beings to become enlightened. The realization of Buddhahood includes not only realization of the emptiness of self but also of the emptiness of dharmas, that is, of the entire psycho-physical world (☞ EMPTINESS).

The Mahayana accepts all of the teachings of the Hinayana; however, the Hinayana rejects the Mahayana sutras and does not recognize the "expansive" teachings of the Mahayana about Bodhisattvas and about the Buddhas of the other directions.

"In Buddhism we find an attachment to the Great and Small Vehicles, and much opposition between them. Those of the Small Vehicle won't admit there is a Great Vehicle. And in the Great Vehicle, the attitude toward the Small Vehicle is condescending.

"Within the Buddhadharma itself this difficulty arises. You say I'm false, and I say you're false; as a result, it's become the case that both are false; neither is true. That's because the Buddha's disciples didn't listen to the Buddha's instructions and made the divisions of Great and Small.

"An expression says that one must enter as the master and come out as the servant. If you are a Great Vehicle person, then the Great Vehicle is the master, the lord, and the Small Vehicle is the servant. If you're of the Small Vehicle, then you say the Small Vehicle is the master and the Great Vehicle is the servant. All this struggle occurs right in the basic substance of the Buddhadharma....

"Those of the Small Vehicle should take a step forward and not be so attached. And those of the Great Vehicle should take a step backward and not be so attached. When the two, those of both the Great and the Small Vehicles, don't have any attachments, they can become one. When they become one, then they can benefit one another and not indulge in mutual slander.

"In the ☞ DHARMA-ENDING AGE Buddhists work on a superficial level. They don't apply their effort on the real, fundamental level. It is a very painful situation....Is it not strange that people nowadays make discriminations and say there are only Arhats, that there aren't any Bodhisattvas or any Buddhas in the ten directions? They still argue ceaselessly, and that's really too bad....In Buddhism there shouldn't be any Great Vehicle and

Small Vehicle; there is only the Buddha Vehicle. There is no other vehicle. If you look at it this way, you won't be able to be so attached. Also, for the sake of the Dharma you should forget yourself. For the sake of seeking the Buddhadharma, you should spare neither body nor life. It is said that to the ends of space throughout the Dharma Realm, there isn't a place as small as a mote of dust which is not a place where all the Buddhas and Bodhisattvas of the past, the present, and the future have given up their lives. All Buddhas and Bodhisattvas have renounced their lives for the sake of the Buddha-dharma in order to seek true principle, to seek the unsurpassed Way.

"Nowadays people not only don't seek true principle; they also indulge in slander of one another. Those of the Small Vehicle slander the Great Vehicle; those of the Great Vehicle slander the Small Vehicle. Evolving in this way Buddhism has developed a lot of discriminations: right and wrong, us and them, mine and yours. Such Buddhists don't understand in the least that the practices which the Buddhas of the past cultivated were without self and others, were beyond right and wrong. They concentrated on cultivating many ☞ DHARMA-DOORS and did not criticize the Dharma-doors cultivated by others as being wrong." (LY I 146-150)

a) Greater Vehicle, b) Small/Lesser Vehicle
☞ **Bodhisattva, Arhat**

Maitreya ⟨Bodhisattva⟩ 彌勒《菩薩》

Maitreya, also known as Ajita, is one of the great Bodhisattva-disciples of the Buddha. He is foremost in the perfection of patience, and in a future age he will become the next Buddha. He is also the founder of the ☞ CONSCIOUSNESS-ONLY (Yogācāra, Vijñānavāda) School of Mahayana Buddhism.

"Maitreya Bodhisattva is also known as Ajita. Maitreya is his family name. Ajita is his given name. Maitreya means 'compassionate clan.' Ajita means 'invincible.' Perhaps you have seen images of a fat monk in the dining hall in Buddhist temples. Maitreya is that monk. Maybe this Bodhisattva liked to eat good things and got fat that way. He also liked to laugh, but his laugh was not a coarse "ha ha ha!" Rather he always had a big smile on his face. He enjoyed playing with children, and so the children were all fond of him. He was always surrounded by them. After ☞ ŚĀKYAMUNI BUDDHA retires as the teaching host of this world, Maitreya Bodhisattva will take over that position. Śākyamuni Buddha is known as the Red-Yang Buddha. When Maitreya Bodhisattva becomes a Buddha, he will be known as the White-Yang Buddha. This means that when Maitreya Bodhisattva comes to the world as a Buddha, people's blood will be white, not red. People are red-blooded now because of the Red-Yang Buddha." (SS V 112)

As to Maitreya Bodhisattva's perfection of patience, "if someone scolded him, he pretended he hadn't heard it. How did he do that? His face was like rubber, as thick as an automobile tire. If someone scolded him he paid no attention. If someone hit him, he just pretended it didn't happen. He knew how to be patient....

"Maitreya Bodhisattva's stomach was like the sea; you could float a boat in it. His heart was the heart of a Buddha, extremely compassionate.

1

Amitābha Buddha
Artist / Chiang, Yi-Tze

2 & 3

Arhats

Anonymous / Yuan Dynasty
Collection of the
National Palace Museum,
Taipei, Taiwan,
Republic of China

4

Arhat
Artist / Ding, Guan-peng, Qing Dynasty
Collection of the National Palace Museum, Taipei, Taiwan, Republic of China

5 (OPPOSITE)

Bodhisattva Avalokiteśvara (Guanyin)
Anonymous / Ming Dynasty
Collection of the National Palace Museum, Taipei, Taiwan, Republic of China

6 (OPPOSITE)

Bodhisattva Avalokiteśvara
Artist / Chiang, Yi-tze

7

Bodhisattva Avalokiteśvara

8 (OPPOSITE)

Patriarch Bodhidharma
Artist / Chiang, Yi-tze

9

Venerable Budai
Artist / Chiang, Hong,
Ming Dynasty
Collection of the
National Palace Museum,
Taipei, Taiwan,
Republic of China

10 (ABOVE)

Entering the womb
Before giving birth to the Buddha, Lady Māyā dreams that a white elephant enters her womb.
Pakistan (ancient Gandhara), 2nd-3rd centuries

11 (BELOW LEFT)

Leaving home
The Buddha practices extreme asceticism after leaving home.
Pakistan (ancient Gandhara), 2nd-3rd centuries

12 (BELOW RIGHT)

Becoming a Buddha
A huge serpent shields the Buddha from a storm as he meditates and becomes enlightened under the Bodhi tree.

13 (ABOVE)

Turning the Dharma wheel
Anonymous / Ming Dynasty
Collection of the National Palace Museum, Taipei, Taiwan, Republic of China

14 (BELOW)

Entering nirvana
All beings grieve when the Buddha enters nirvana.

15

Śākyamuni Buddha and Many Jewels (Prabhūtaratna) Buddha sharing a seat

A scene from the Dharma Flower (Lotus) Sutra. Clay sculpture, Cave No. 80, Maijishan, Northern Wei Dynasty

16

The triple assembly of the next Buddha Maitreya

17

Earth Store Bodhisattva, who rescues beings from the hells
Artist / Chiang, Yi-tze

18 & 19

Eightfold Division of Ghosts and Spirits

Anonymous / Song Dynasty
Collection of the National Palace Museum, Taipei, Taiwan, Republic of China

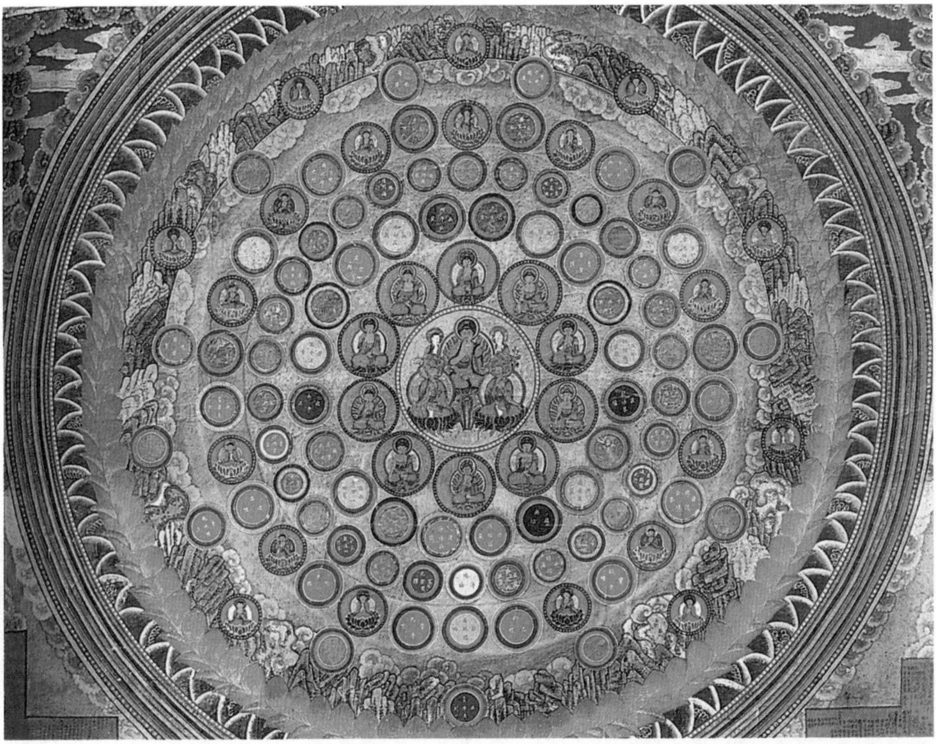

20 (OPPOSITE)

Scenes from the *Flower Adornment Sutra*
Chaoxian period (1770) (Korea)

21 (ABOVE)

Flower Adornment Sea of Worlds
Chaoxian period (Korea)

22 (RIGHT)

Bodhisattvas Hanshan and Shide
Artist / Chiang, Yi-tze

23 (LEFT)

Beings receiving sentences and suffering retribution in the hells
Chaoxian period (1884) (Korea)

24 (BELOW RIGHT)

The court of the First Lord of the Underworld
Chaoxian period (1775)

25 (ABOVE RIGHT)

Beings suffering in the hells
Chaoxian period (1775)

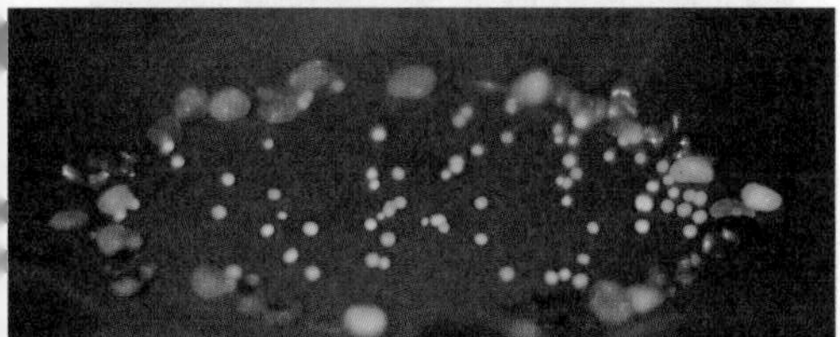

26 (ABOVE LEFT)

The Buddha practicing extreme asceticism
3rd c. Gandhara

27 (BELOW LEFT)

Śārira
(relics left after cremation)

28 (RIGHT)

Censer at the City of Ten Thousand Buddhas

29

Vajradhātu maṇḍala
9th c., Kyoto, Japan

30

Garbhadhātu maṇḍala
9th c., Kyoto, Japan

31 (OPPOSITE)

Bodhisattva Mañjuśrī

Artist / Ding, Guan-peng,
Qing Dynasty
Collection of the
National Palace Museum,
Taipei, Taiwan,
Republic of China

32

Bodhisattva Mañjuśrī

Artist / Yao, Wen-han,
Qing Dynasty
Collection of the
National Palace Museum,
Taipei, Taiwan,
Republic of China

33

Western Pure Land of Ultimate Bliss

Artist / Ding, Guan-peng, Qing Dynasty
Collection of the National Palace Museum, Taipei, Taiwan, Republic of China

34 (OPPOSITE ABOVE)

Amitābha Buddha with Bodhisattva Avalokiteśvara on his left and Bodhisattva Great Strength (Mahāsthāmaprāpta) on his right (detail of plate 30)

35 (OPPOSITE BELOW)

Lotus pool in the Western Pure Land (detail of plate 30)

36

Bodhisattva Avalokiteśvara with One Thousand Hands and Eyes

Artist / Chiang, Yi-tze

37 (RIGHT)

Śākyamuni Buddha
Artist / Chiang, Yi-tze

38 (LEFT)

Venerable Master Hsuan Hua, founder of the City of Ten Thousand Buddhas

39 (BELOW LEFT)

Precept masters (left) transmit precepts to monks in the Ordination Hall

40 (BELOW RIGHT)

Bhikshunis (nuns) walking to the Hall of Ten Thousand Buddhas

41
(OPPOSITE ABOVE RIGHT)

The entrance to the Sagely City of Ten Thousand Buddhas

42 & 43
(BELOW RIGHT & OPPOSITE LEFT)

Hall of Ten Thousand Buddhas
Guanyin Bodhisattva and some of the more than 10,000 Buddhas that line the halls and ceiling

41
43
40 42

44

Bodhisattva Universal Worthy (Samantabhadra)
Artist / Chiang, Yi-tze

45

Bodhisattva Universal Worthy (Samantabhadra)
Anonymous / Qing Dynasty
Collection of the National Palace Museum, Taipei, Taiwan, Republic of China

46

Tripiṭaka Master Xuanzang
bringing sutras from India back to China

He has a short verse which...[I] will repeat for you now:

"The Old Fool wears a tattered robe,
and fills his belly with plain food.
He mends the rags
to keep his body warm,
And lets the myriad affairs
just take their course.
Should someone scold the Old Fool,
the Old Fool just says, 'Fine.'
Should someone strike the Old Fool,
he just lies down to sleep.
'Spit right in my face,' he says,
'and I'll just let it dry.
That way I save energy
and you don't get afflicted.'
This kind of *pāramitā*
is the most wondrous treasure.
Now that you know this news,
How can you worry about not
attaining the Way?"
(DFS II 350-351)

The assembly of the future Buddha Maitreya (see plate 16)

In the ☞ŚŪRAṄGAMA SUTRA Maitreya explains the method of cultivation he used to realize enlightenment:

I remember when, as many *kalpas* ago as there are fine motes of dust, a Buddha named Light of Sun, Moon and Lamp appeared in the world. Under that Buddha I left the home-life; yet I was deeply committed to worldly fame and liked to fraternize with people of good family. Then that World Honored One taught me to cultivate consciousness-only concentration, and I entered that samadhi. For many aeons I have made use of that samadhi as I performed deeds for as many Buddhas as there are sands in the Ganges River. My seeking for worldly fame and fortune ceased completely and never recurred. When Burning Lamp Buddha appeared in the world, I finally realized the unsurpassed, wonderfully perfect samadhi of consciousness. I went on until, to the ends of empty space, all the lands of the Thus Come Ones, whether pure or defiled, existent or nonexistent, were transformations appearing from within my own mind.

World Honored One, because I understand consciousness-only thus, the nature of consciousness reveals limitless Thus Come Ones. Now I have received the prediction that I will be the next to take the Buddha's place. The Buddha asks about perfect penetration. I was intent upon the contemplation that the [ten] directions come only from consciousness. When the conscious mind is perfect and bright, one enters the perfection of the real. One leaves behind reliance on others and attachment to incessant calculating and attains the patience when no dharmas come into being. This is the foremost method. (SS V 111-118)

☞ **Ajita ⟨Bodhisattva⟩, Asaṅga ⟨Bodhisattva⟩, Bodhisattva, Budai ⟨Venerable⟩, Consciousness-Only School, Six Pāramitās—Patience, Vasubandhu ⟨Bodhisattva⟩**

maṇḍala 曼陀羅

Maṇḍala is a Sanskrit word that literally means circle. In Buddhism it usually refers to geometric patterns or images, usually containing circular motifs, that are used for meditation. The two most common types are drawn or painted scrolls and those drawn on the ground, usually with colored pigments. They are used extensively in esoteric Buddhism. *Maṇḍalas* might well be said to be the visual counterpart of mantras.

☞ **cosmogram**
☞ **mantra**

Vajradhātu maṇḍala (see plate 29)

Garbhadhātu maṇḍala (see plate 30)

Mañjuśrī 〈Bodhisattva〉 文殊師利《菩薩》

Bodhisattva Mañjuśrī (see plate 31)

Mañjuśrī is the eldest of the great Bodhisattvas and is foremost in wisdom.

"Mañjuśrī, a Sanskrit word, is interpreted as 'wonderful virtue' or 'wonderfully auspicious.' Of the Bodhisattvas, Mañjuśrī has the greatest wisdom, and so he is known as 'The Greatly Wise Bodhisattva Mañjuśrī.' Among the Bodhisattvas he holds the highest rank, and so he is listed first, before the Bodhisattva Who Observes the Sounds of the World. There are four great Bodhisattvas: Bodhisattva Mañjuśrī, Bodhisattva Who Observes the Sounds of the World [☞Avalokiteśvara], Bodhisattva Universal Worthy [☞SAMANTABHADRA], and Bodhisattva ☞EARTH STORE [Kṣitigarbha].

"Bodhisattva Mañjuśrī dwells in China on Wutai Mountain, where his *bodhimaṇḍa* [☞WAY-PLACE] is located. His efficacious responses are marvelous beyond all reckoning. He became a Buddha long ago and was called Buddha of the Race of Honored Dragon Kings. After becoming a Buddha, he 'hid away the great and manifested the small,' in order to practice the Bodhisattva Way, teach and transform living beings, and help the Buddha [Śākyamuni] propagate the Dharma. His spiritual penetrations and miraculous functions are inconceivable." (DFS II 144-145)

"Bodhisattva Mañjuśrī...is a very special Bodhisattva. When he was born, ten kinds of extraordinary events occurred, which show that he was different from other Bodhisattvas. Mañjuśrī is known for his great wisdom.

"'But the Venerable ☞ŚĀRIPUTRA is also known for his wisdom,' you may ask. 'What is the difference between the two types of wisdom?'

"The wisdom of Śāriputra is provisional wisdom, and the wisdom of Mañjuśrī is real wisdom. The wisdom of Śāriputra is the Hinayana wisdom; the wisdom of Mañjuśrī is the Mahayana wisdom [☞MAHAYANA AND HINAYANA COMPARED].

"What were the ten auspicious signs which manifested at Mañjuśrī's birth?

"1) *The room was filled with bright light*, brighter than the light which could be made by any number of light bulbs. The bright light represented the Bodhisattva's great wisdom.

"2) *The vessels were filled with sweet dew.* Sweet dew is miraculous; drinking it will cure all the sicknesses in the world. Then, instead of having to undergo birth, old age, sickness, and death, you'll only have birth, old age, and death to deal with.

"3) *The seven precious things came forth from the earth.* The seven precious things are gold, silver, lapis lazuli, crystal, mother-of-pearl, red pearls, and carnelian. Why did these treasures appear? Mañjuśrī had cultivated the Six Perfections [☞SIX PĀRAMITĀS] and the Ten Thousand Practices to such a high degree of perfection that in response, wherever he goes, precious gems appear.

"4) *The gods opened the treasuries.* Mañjuśrī Bodhisattva's great spiritual powers caused the earth to open up and expose the many treasuries it contains. This differs from the third, in which the seven precious things well up out of the earth. Here the treasuries were exposed when the earth opened up.

"5) *Chickens gave birth to phoenixes.* Even more unusual than the gods opening the treasuries was the fact that chickens gave birth to phoenixes. Basically, of course, chickens only give birth to chickens. But because Mañjuśrī's birth was such a special occasion, they gave birth to phoenixes.

"6) *Pigs gave birth to dragons.* This is even more unusual than chickens giving birth to phoenixes....

"7) *Horses gave birth to unicorns....*

"8) *Cows gave birth to white* tsai. The white *tsai* is an extremely rare and auspicious animal....It looks like a horse but has the hooves of an ox. It is in a special category all of its own.

"9) *The grain in the granaries turned to gold.* Do you think that is strange? Some of you probably think it is so strange that you don't even believe it. If you don't believe it, it's because you don't understand it. If you don't understand it, it's no doubt because you've never

Bodhisattva Mañjuśrī (see plate 32)

M

encountered such a thing before. And so how could you possibly believe it? However, the world is a very big place and what we have seen and heard is extremely limited. Therefore, it is not strange that there are unusual phenomena which we have not seen or heard. When the grain turned to gold, it could no longer be used as food, but then just a few grains could be exchanged for a lot of food....

"**10)** *Elephants with six tusks appeared.* As we know, elephants usually only have two tusks. At the time of Mañjuśrī's birth, however, they appeared with six. Is that strange or not?

"Those ten special signs appeared at the time of Mañjuśrī's birth and represent Mañjuśrī's rare eloquence in speaking all Dharmas....

"When he speaks the Dharma, Mañjuśrī does not discriminate among the dharmas. Although he does not discriminate among the dharmas, he, nevertheless, does not *not* distinguish all dharmas. The wonder lies right at this point, and that is why he is known as 'wonderful virtue'—Mañjuśrī....

"The six tusks stand for the Six Perfections (☞ SIX PĀRAMITĀS) and the elephants stand for the Ten Thousand Conducts...." (DFS II 144-149)

☞ **Bodhisattva**

---

mantra 咒

Mantras are phrases of sound whose primary meaning or meanings is not cognitive, but on a spiritual level that transcends ordinary linguistic understanding.

"Dharma Master Gushan said, 'The secret mantras in sutras, as a rule, should not be translated. In the past Dharma Masters held various opinions about this, but the ☞ TIANTAI SCHOOL compiled them into four:

"**1)** A mantra contains the names of kings of ghosts and spirits. When you say the king's name, the subjects all obey, due to their respect for their lord. They dare not cause trouble. This is a fortunate benefit for the world.

"**2)** The saying of a mantra is like the secret password of the military. If the reply is correct, there's no further question. If the reply is incorrect, one is punished. This is of benefit to humankind.

"**3)** A mantra is a secret way to stop evil without anybody knowing it. [This is] like a lowly person who goes to another country and passes himself off as a prince. He marries the princess of that country, but he is bad-tempered and hard to attend to. Then somebody comes along who knows him and reveals his disguise. He uses a verse to expose him, which quietly puts him in his place." (SM I 37-38, commentary omitted)

"The verse goes:

> Lacking virtue, you went to another
> country,
> And cheated all the people there.
> Originally you were a poor,
> unfortunate man.
> What right do you have to get so
> angry?" (SM I 38)

"This has the benefit of correcting situations and stopping evil.

"**4)** The mantra is the secret language of all Buddhas, and only the sages know about it. For example, when the king gives the order for *saindhava*, which is really one name for four things: salt, water, a vessel, and a horse, the multitude does not know what he wants. Only the wise officials know. A single phrase of the mantra is filled with many different powers: curing an illness, eradicating offenses, producing good, according with the Way, and entering into the primary truth. Mantras have these four benefits... [which correspond to the four meanings above]." (SM I 38-40, commentary omitted)

Among the better known Buddhist mantras are **1)** *om maṇi padme huṃ* (☞VBS #11 29-31), **2)** the Great Compassion Mantra, and **3)** the Śūraṅgama Mantra.

formula, spell, charm, words with super natural power

☞ **Great Compassion Mantra, Śūraṅgama Mantra, dhāraṇī, Five Types of Buddhist Study and Practice—Esoteric**

Māra 魔

☞ **demons**

meditation 坐禪

A rather vague word in English, meditation is used in the context of Buddhist teachings to indicate the controlling and directing of one's mind inward in the quest for enlightenment. Many different kinds of meditational methods have been taught by the Buddhas and Patriarchs, and meditational practices are found in almost all Buddhist schools. Although meditation can be done while walking, standing, sitting, or lying down, usually emphasis is placed on sitting meditation. The ☞CHAN SCHOOL is most well-known for its single-minded emphasis on direct meditational inquiry. Preliminary meditational practices are usually concerned with the calming and purification of mind and body. Formal stages of meditation prior to enlightenment are discussed in the entries ☞FOUR DHYĀNAS and ☞FOUR FORMLESS REALMS.

Three Prerequisites for Sitting in Meditation

Patience

"What must you be patient with? You must learn to bear the pain in your back and the pain in your legs. When you first begin to sit in Chan meditation, you will experience pain in your back and legs because you are unaccustomed to sitting that way. In the beginning this pain may be hard to bear, so you will have to be patient.

No Greed

"Those who cultivate Chan inquiry should not hope for enlightenment. If you think about how you want to become enlightened, then even if you were meant to get enlightened, that single thought will cover over your enlightenment and prevent it from happening.

"Further, you should not, because of greed, seek speed in your practice. You cannot expect to sit today and get enlightened tomorrow. So many of today's young people are turned upside down, and although they want to do Chan inquiry and study the Buddhadharma, they take drugs, which they say is a way of bringing them enlightenment fast. That is a grave mistake. Not only will such people not get enlightened, the more they study in this way, the more crazy and depraved they become....

"Therefore, I want to stress this: don't try to get off cheap. Don't try to do it fast. Don't think that without putting out any effort you can cash in on welfare. There is nothing of value obtained without doing some work for it.

Perseverance

"You must be constant in your practice of Chan. The best way is to sit in full lotus. This posture is achieved by placing your left ankle onto your right thigh, and then lifting your right ankle onto your left thigh. This posture can quiet your mind. It is your foundation for sitting in Chan. You should train yourself to sit that way. Some of you protest, 'My legs are stiff and I can't sit that way.' Well, then try sitting in 'half-lotus,' which is when your left ankle is on your right thigh. 'But I can't even do that,' some may say. Well, then you'll have to sit in a cross-legged position—in whatever way is possible for you. But you should be working to get into half lotus and eventually into full lotus. Full lotus is the foundation for sitting in meditation. Since it is fundamental, you should work to master it. If you try to build a house on bare ground, the first big rain that comes along will wash it away. The first big wind will blow it down. The same is true for meditation without a foundation. Full lotus is the foundation of Buddhahood. If you want to become a Buddha, first master full lotus.

"Once your legs are in full lotus, you should hold your body erect. Sit up straight and do not lean forward or backward. Keep your spine absolutely straight. Curl your tongue back against the roof of your mouth. If you secrete saliva, you can swallow it. Also people who cultivate Chan should not smoke cigarettes or take drugs; they make your saliva bitter....

"Your eyes are not necessarily open and not necessarily closed. If you leave your eyes open while meditating, it is very easy to have false thinking about what you see. If you completely close your eyes while sitting, it is very easy to fall asleep. And so keeping your eyes half open and half closed is a good way to counteract both problems....

"As to your mind—don't think of anything. Don't have any polluted thoughts. Don't think about what state you are experiencing or hope to experience, and don't think about how you want to get enlightened. The affairs of this world are not that simple. A thief who steals others' money ends up with wealth that is not his own. If you work and earn money, then the wealth you accumulate is your own. The same principle applies to meditation. Don't be greedy for speed, hoping to become enlightened fast. Don't be greedy to get a bargain. If in your cultivation you are greedy for small benefits, then you will never get the big ones." (LY II 90-93)

"Meditation, like all cultivation, must be practiced daily without interruption." (LY II 152)

"When you sit in Chan (meditation), you should not be greedy for the flavor of Chan.... What is the flavor of Chan? It refers to the bliss of the *dhyānas* (☞ FOUR DHYĀNAS). When you have been sitting just about long enough, you start to experience a feeling of comfort and freedom. When that happens, you may feel kind of indolent—like you don't want to move;

you want to just sit there. You become greedy for that feeling of comfort and ease. That's the flavor of Chan. If you become greedy for a state, it is not easy for you to go on and make progress, because you will want to linger there and will get attached to that flavor of Chan. You will keep trying to get back into that state. You will think, 'When am I going to have that kind of state again? In that state there was no self, no others, no living beings, and no life span; no afflictions—no hassles. It was very blissful, very, very comfortable and free. I wonder when I will ever have that experience again.' And you will just sit there waiting for that flavorful experience to recur. And what happens while you wait? You forget all about applying effort—you are no longer able to do the work.

"But people who sit in meditation and want to make progress need to be free of any obstructions or hangups. They can't be seeking anything or be greedy for anything. You can't get excessively happy, or depressed, and you shouldn't have any fear or terror. You should see your body as being the same as empty space and the Dharma Realm. You don't need to be attached to anything. As soon as you become greedy and seek, you fall into a secondary meaning...." (TT 104)

☞ **Chan School, Four Dhyānas, Four Formless Realms, Six Pāramitās—Meditational Concentration, cultivation, enlightenment, lotus posture, mindfulness, samadhi**

merit/merit and virtue 功德

"Wholesome merit and virtue are derived from upholding the Five Precepts and doing the Ten Good Deeds [☞FIVE MORAL PRECEPTS, TEN WHOLESOME DEEDS]. Virtue refers to what is inside, to constantly fortifying oneself with wisdom." (TT 43)

The Sixth Patriarch ☞HUINENG makes the following distinction between the higher practice of merit and virtue and their practice on a lower, worldly level of understanding. He calls the latter 'cultivation of blessings':

> Seeing your own nature is merit, and equanimity is virtue. To be unobstructed in every thought, constantly seeing the true, real, wonderful function of your original nature is called "merit and virtue."
>
> Inner humility is merit and the outer practice of reverence is virtue. Your own nature establishing the ten thousand dharmas is merit and the mind-substance separate from thought is virtue. Not being separate from one's own nature is merit, and the correct use of one's own undefiled (nature) is virtue. If you seek the merit and virtue of the Dharma body, simply act according to these principles, for this is true merit and virtue.
>
> Those who cultivate merit and virtue in their thoughts do not slight others, but always respect them. Those who slight others and do not cut off the 'me' and 'mine' are without merit. One's own inherent nature, vain and unreal, is without virtue, because of the 'me and mine,' because of the greatness of 'self,' and because of the constant slighting of others.
>
> Good Knowing Advisors, continuity of thought is merit, and the mind practicing equality and directness is virtue. Self-cultivation of one's nature is merit, and self-cultivation of the body is virtue.
>
> Good Knowing Advisors, merit and virtue should be seen within one's own nature, not sought through giving and making offerings. That is the difference between blessings and merit and virtue.... (PS 133-137)

☞ **meritorious action, virtue, meritorious qualities**

☞ **blessings, good roots, karma, transference of merit**

Middle Way 中道

The Buddha said: "Those who follow the Way are like pieces of wood in the water which are borne on the current, not touching either shore, and which are not picked up by people, not intercepted by ghosts or spirits, not caught up in whirlpools, and which do not rot. I guarantee that these pieces of wood will certainly reach the sea. I guarantee that students of the Way who are not deluded by emotional desire, nor bothered by myriad devious things, but who are vigorous in their cultivation of the unconditioned, will certainly attain the Way." (S42 55)

These two extremes, monks, should not be followed by one who has gone forth from the life of a householder to the life of a mendicant. Which two? That which is, among sense-pleasures, addiction to attractive sense-pleasure, low, of the common, of the average man, un-Aryan, not connected with the goal, and that which is addiction to self-torment, ill, un-Aryan, not connected with the goal. Now monks, without adopting either of these two extremes, there is a middle course, fully awakened to by the Tathāgata, making for a vision, making for knowledge, which conduces to calming (of passion), to super-knowledge (of the Four Truths), to awakening, to *nirvana*....And what, monks, is this middle course? It is the Aryan eightfold way itself, that is to say: right view, right thought, right speech, right action, right mode of living, right endeavor, right mindfulness, right concentration. (*The Book of the Discipline*, pt. 4, 15; quoted by Jaini in "Śramaṇa Conflict")

What Is the Ultimate Meaning of the Middle Way?

"'Ultimate' means final, 'meaning' means what is fitting, 'middle' means not going to extremes, and 'Way' means practice. One who abides by the Middle does not go too far, nor does he fail to go far enough. When he goes too far he should bring about a lessening, and when he falls short, he should increase. In either case he should avoid falling into ☞EMPTINESS, or grasping at existence. This is what is meant by the Middle Way, the true substance of the principle of True Emptiness. It is also called the Reality-Mark, True Suchness, One's Own Nature, and the ☞BUDDHA-NATURE.

"To put it quite clearly once again, it is like the figure zero which is the sole ancestor of heaven and earth, the father of all Buddhas, the mother of all things, and the source of the most subtle of wonders. Everything in life and death comes from it, and there isn't anything which does not return to it. This is what is meant by the phrase 'True Emptiness is not empty; Wonderful Existence is not existence.' One who understands this can be called a 'person of the Way who is without a mind,' one who has overstepped all categories, who has been released forever from the suffering of the wheel, who roams freely at leisure, and who has ended birth and death—a living dead person." (WM 49-50)

☞ **Way/Path of the Center**
☞ **Four Holy Truths**

mindfulness 念

The ☞FLOWER ADORNMENT SUTRA speaks of these ten aspects of mindfulness:

"mindfulness that is still and quiet,
mindfulness that is pure,
mindfulness that is not turbid,
mindfulness that is bright and penetrating,
mindfulness that is apart from defilement,
mindfulness that is apart from various defilements,
mindfulness that is apart from filth,
mindfulness that is bright and dazzling,
mindfulness that is pleasing, and
mindfulness that is free from obstacles.

"When the Bodhisattvas dwell in these aspects of mindfulness, nothing in the world can disturb or unsettle them. No strange theories can move them. Their good roots from past lives are made pure and they are not defiled by or attached to any dharma in the world. The multitudes of demons and those of external ways cannot destroy them. They can undergo rebirth and receive different bodies without any lapse in memory. They proclaim the Dharma endlessly throughout the past, present, and future." (FAS Ch22 129)

☞ **Four Applications of Mindfulness, recitation of the Buddha's name, meditation, Pure Land School**

moral precepts 戒/戒律

The jeweled precepts with the brilliance of *vajra* are the original source of all Buddhas, the original source of all Bodhisattvas, and the seed of the Buddha-nature. (BNS I 54)

"The world today is filled with terror. People of all races are in a perpetual state of fear, so that they don't feel safe when they walk about; they can't taste the food they eat; and they can't sleep peacefully. What is the principle behind this? Why has such a state appeared? Those who believe in Buddhism should pay particular attention to the principle governing this phenomenon. It is because the evil offenses and evil karma that people are creating are filling up the heavens. Each person keeps creating more ☞KARMA and never makes an attempt to eradicate the karma that they have amassed. Everyone has committed the karma of killing, stealing, sexual misconduct, taking intoxicants, and lying. It is simply because people do not maintain and uphold the precepts which govern these five actions that slowly, bit by bit, the karma accumulates. When the karma from killing living beings becomes great enough, the energy of animosity will completely fill up a great ☞WORLD SYSTEM of a billion worlds." (TT 58)

The Buddha said: "My disciples may be several thousand miles away from me, but if they remember my precepts, they will certainly obtain the fruits of the Way.

"If those who are by my side do not follow my precepts, they may see me constantly, but in the end they will not obtain the Way." (S42 74)

Now it is not thus [by the display of various heavenly offerings], Ānanda, that the Tathāgata is rightly honored, reverenced, venerated, held sacred or revered. But the brother or sister, the devout man or woman, who continually fulfills all the greater and lesser duties, who is correct in life, walking according to the precepts—it is he who rightly honors, reverences, venerates, holds sacred, and reveres the Tathāgata with the worthiest homage. Therefore, O Ānanda, be ye constant in the fulfillment of the greater and of the lesser duties, and be ye correct in life, walking according to the precepts; and thus

Ānanda, should it be taught. (Rhys Davids, tr. *Dialogues of the Buddha* II 150-151)

"'Precepts' refer to rules and regulations. Their purpose is to help us:

Stop evil and avoid misdeeds;
Not do any evil,
But offer up all good conduct.

Precepts include:

The Precept Dharma
The Precept Substance
The Precept Mark

The Precept Dharma includes:

The Five Precepts (for lay people)
The Eight Precepts (for lay people)
The Ten Precepts (for novices)
The Ten Major and Forty-eight Minor Bodhisattva Precepts (for both left-home and lay people)
The 250 Bhikshu Precepts
The 348 Bhikshuni Precepts

"All of those precepts are to tell you not to do any evil but to offer up all good conduct. You should hold the precepts purely and not go against them." (FAS Ch16 33-34)

The Analogy of the Brahma Net

Before the god Brahma, lord of the Brahma Heaven of the pure world of form (☞THREE WORLDS), a circular net curtain is suspended as an adornment. In each hole of the curtain a pearl is found. Each pearl both reflects all other pearls and shines its light on all the other pearls. The result is an incredible display of infinite interreflected light.

The net curtain can be understood analogically. It stands for one's own body and mind. Each hole in the netting represents a particular outflow of one's vital energy. Each pearl represents a moral precept. To the extent that one keeps the moral precepts, the pearls emit light and illuminate one's own body and mind and also those of all other living beings.

Just before the Buddha entered nirvana he said to the Venerable ☞ĀNANDA:

> It may be, Ānanda, that in some of you the thought might arise, "The word of the master is ended, we have no teacher more!" But it is not thus, Ānanda, that you should regard it. The Truths, and the Rules of the Order, which I have set forth and laid down for you all, let them, after I am gone, be teacher for you. (*Dialogues of the Buddha* II 171)

☞ **precepts, moral regulations**
☞ **Five Moral Precepts, faith**

N

Nāgārjuna 〈Bodhisattva〉
龍樹《菩薩》

Nāgārjuna was the Fourteenth Patriarch of the ☞CHAN SCHOOL in India and founder of the Emptiness (Mādhyamika) School of Mahayana Buddhism. He probably lived during the second century C.E. He also is included in the patriarchal lineage of other Buddhist schools.

"The Venerable One was from India. When the Thirteenth Patriarch, in the course of his traveling and teaching, reached the part of India where Nāgārjuna was cultivating, the Venerable Nāgārjuna went out to greet him with these words: 'The deep mountains are so quiet and solitary, the abode of dragons and pythons. How is it that you, who are so virtuous, have strayed so far to come here? What brings you here?' The Patriarch said, 'I am not venerable. I have come to see you, Worthy One.' Nāgārjuna thought to himself, 'The Thirteenth Patriarch is lying when he denies he is venerable.' The Patriarch knew what he was thinking, and Nāgārjuna regretted it, apologizing for being so stupid. The Patriarch immediately transmitted the great Mind-to-Mind Seal to him, and Nāgārjuna and the five hundred who were cultivating the Way with him all received the complete precepts.

the fourteenth patriarch, venerable nagarjuna

"After obtaining the Dharma, the Venerable Nāgārjuna traveled and taught. When he reached southern India, he found the people there preoccupied with the quest for rewards of heavenly blessings and unaware of how to seek the Buddhadharma. The Patriarch told them the meaning of the ☞BUDDHA-NATURE, and how their own natures were endowed with limitless meritorious qualities and blessed rewards. When the multitudes heard that Dharma, they all stopped seeking blessings and turned away from the small to go towards the great. Right where he was sitting, the Patriarch made his body look like the orb of the full moon. The Fifteenth Patriarch-to-be, Kāṇadeva, was in the crowd and remarked, 'The Venerable One is showing us the substance and characteristics of the Buddha-nature.' Nāgārjuna thereupon transmitted the Dharma to Kāṇadeva and entered the Moon's Orb Samadhi, extensively displaying spiritual transformations. Immediately afterwards, he entered cessation.

"His eulogy reads:

> The Buddha-nature in its meaning
> neither exists nor non-exists.
> He made appear Samadhi's Orb,
> a coral moon on high.
> An elder brother in the household,
> he fell not to biases.
> Eyebrows both raised and lowered,
> from one mallet dual sounds..."
> (VBS #100 (Sept. 1978) 2)

This is a summary of the philosophical underpinnings of Nāgārjuna's teachings.

[What follows is] "...a synthetic survey (*saṃkṣepa*) of Nāgārjuna's chief religious and philosophical persuasions.

"The best starting point for such an exposition is the theory of two truths (*satyadvaya*): a relative or conventional truth (*saṃvṛtisatya*) that serves as the means for obtaining the absolute or ultimate truth (*paramārthasatya*).

"The ultimate goal of all endeavors is the highest good of oneself and of others: abolition of rebirth, or nirvana [i.e., enlightenment]. It implies the attainment of Buddhahood, or a twofold body (*kāyadvaya*). This may be considered from four perspectives: **1)** Ontologically: All phenomena (*dharma*) are empty (*śūnya*) since they lack own-being (*svabhāva*), inasmuch as empirically and logically they only occur in mutual dependence (*pratītyasamutpanna*). **2)** Epistemologically: The ultimate truth (*tattva*) is the object of a cognition without an object (*advayajñāna*), and thus only an object metaphorically speaking (*upādāya prajñapti*). **3)** Psychologically: It is the abolition of all the passions (*kleśa*), primarily desire (*rāga*), hatred (*dveṣa*) and delusion (*moha*). **4)** Ethically: It implies freedom from the bonds of karma but subjection to the altruistic imperatives of compassion (*karuṇā*).

"The conventional Buddhist means ([*saṃ*]*vyavahāra*) devised for the fulfillment of this objective may be classified variously, but fit most briefly and comprehensively under the heading of the two accumulations for enlightenment (*bodhisaṃbhāra*): **1)** "Accumulation of merit (*puṇyasaṃbhāra*). This comprises four perfections (*pāramitā*): Liberality (*dāna*) and good morals (*śīla*), which are mainly for the benefit of others, and patience (*kṣānti*) and energy (*vīrya*), which are for one's own good. Their practice presupposes faith (*śraddhā*) in the 'law' of karma and results in the attainment of the physical body (*rūpakāya*) of a Buddha. Along with the pursuit of meditation (*dhyāna*), the fifth *pāramitā*, this constitutes temporal happiness (*abhyudaya*). **2)** "Accumulation of cognition (*jñānasaṃbhāra*). This consists in ecstatic meditation (*dhyāna*) surpassed by insight into the emptiness (*śūnyatā*) of all phenomena (*dharma*), or wisdom (*prajñā*). This is the *ne plus ultra* or ultimate good (*naiḥśreyasa*) of all living beings. It amounts to the attainment of a 'spiritual body' (*dharmakāya*).

"In other words, cognition of emptiness and display of acts of compassion are—to the chosen few—the two means of realizing enlightenment." (Lindtner, Chr. *Master of Wisdom: Writings of the Buddhist Master Nāgārjuna*, xx-xxi).

☞ **emptiness, Bodhisattva**

namo 南無

A grammatical form of the Sanskrit word *namas*, meaning 'bow,' obeisance,' 'reverential salutation,' and often interpreted as meaning 'homage to,' 'devotion to,' or 'take refuge with.'

nirvana 涅槃

> ...the primal pure substance of beginningless *bodhi* nirvana. It is the primal essence of consciousness that can bring forth all conditions. (SS I 180)
>
> The meaning of nirvana is the very Dharma-nature of all Buddhas. (NS Ch3 Pt4)

Nirvana [*nirvāṇa*] is a Sanskrit term [now treated as an English word] that is interpreted in various ways: **1)** cessation, or extinction, referring to the elimination of the afflictions at the time of enlightenment or to the ceasing to be of the *skandhas* (☞ FIVE SKANDHAS) when an enlightened person at death chooses to be reborn no longer; **2)** freedom from desire; and **3)** no longer either coming into being or ceasing to be.

In addition to the above references to enlightenment, in later times the term nirvana came to be used as a polite way of speaking of the death of a monk (Bhikshu) regardless of whether or not he was enlightened and truly entering nirvana.

The most common analogy for nirvana in the Theravada tradition is the going out of a lamp because of its wick and oil being used up:

> "But if someone should ask you, Vaccha: 'This fire in front of you that is extinguished, in what direction has that fire gone from here, east, west, north or south?' What would you answer to such a question?"

"That does not apply, dear Gotama. For that fire that burned because of fuel consisting of straw and wood, has consumed this and not been given anything else and is therefore called 'extinguished through lack of fuel.'"

"Just so the form of the Thus Come One is given up, its root broken, uprooted like a palm, free from further growth or renewed existence in the future. The Thus Come One is free from everything called form, he is deep immeasurable, unfathomable, just like the deep ocean." (Horner, tr. *Majjhima Nikāya* I 486ff)

The Buddha then repeats the whole series of questions and answers, substituting the other four of the Five Skandhas—feeling, cognition, formations, and consciousness—one by one in each successive repetition.

"Most people think that nirvana follows upon death, but actually it is not necessarily an after-death state. It is the certification of the attainment of noumenal being (Ch. *li*). 'Nirvana' is a Sanskrit word, which is interpreted to mean 'neither coming into being nor ceasing to be.' Since there is neither coming into being nor ceasing to be, birth and death have come to an end. One attains nirvana when one is no longer subject to birth and death. However, nirvana does not mean that the Buddha dies. When the Buddha dies, he enters nirvana; he enters the noumenal being of nirvana and verifies its four qualities—permanence, bliss, true self, and purity. Some people who haven't seen things clearly in their study of Buddhism think that nirvana is just death, but nirvana is definitely not death. One who has that view does not understand the principles of Buddhism." (SS I 180-181)

In order to help prevent people from getting attached to the idea of nirvana, the Bodhisattva ☞NĀGĀRJUNA stated:

Saṃsāra [i.e., the stream of conditioned existence] has nothing that distinguishes it from *nirvāṇa*; *nirvāṇa* has nothing that distinguishes it from *saṃsāra*. The limit of *nirvāṇa* is the limit of *saṃsāra*; there is not even the subtlest something separating the two. (*Prasannapāda*, 535, quoted in Robinson, *Early Mādhyamika*, 40)

There are many synonyms for nirvana, as shown by the following passage:

World Honored One, the ground of fruition is *bodhi*, nirvana, true suchness, the Buddha-nature, the *amala*-consciousness, the empty treasury of the Thus Come One, the great, perfect mirror-wisdom. But although it is called by these seven names, it is pure and perfect, its substance is durable, like royal *vajra*, everlasting and indestructible. (SS IV 207)

☞ **cessation, extinction, enlightenment**
☞ **enlightenment**

Nirvana Sutra 涅槃經

There are two sutras having this title, one Mahayana and one Hinayana. Both have the same complete title: *Mahāparinirvāṇa Sutra*. Both sutras recount the events which took place and the teachings of the Buddha which he bestowed immediately prior to his entering nirvana. The perspective and scope of the two works is, of course, radically different. As to length, the Hinayana text is chapter length, while the Mahayana sutra is three volumes in English translation.

no outflows 無漏

☞ **outflows**

Northern Buddhism 北傳佛教

☞ **Mahayana Buddhism**

no self 無我

Mere suffering exists,
  no sufferer is found;
The deeds are, but no doer
  of the deeds is there;
Nirvana is, but not the man
  that enters it;
The path is, but no traveller
  on it is seen.
(Visuddhi Magga XVI, quoted BD 12)

The teaching of no self is one of the most fundamental of the Buddha's teachings. Suffering, the Buddha taught, is caused by our clinging to a self, a permanent sense of identity. Yet the self is not merely the personality, or ego, that identifies itself in terms of social role and interaction. Almost all religions know that self to be illusory. The "self" of "no self" also includes the basic self of our physical being, including our human sexuality, the so-called 'soul' and various other levels of spiritual 'Self.' The 'self' of cosmic consciousness that identifies with the universe—which the Hindus call *ātman*—is also included. Considering any of those as real and permanent is attachment to illusion.

The Buddha declared:

> O bhikkhus, when neither self nor anything pertaining to self can truly and really be found, this speculative view: "The universe is that *ātman* (Soul); I shall be that after death, permanent, abiding, everlasting, unchanging, and I shall exist as such for eternity"—is it not wholly and completely foolish? (Majjhima I 138, quoted in Rahula, *What the Buddha Taught* 59)

Then the World Honored One explained the instability of the self:

"Whatsoever is originated will be dissolved again. All worry about the self is vain; the self is like a mirage, and all the tribulations that touch it will pass away. They will vanish like a nightmare when the sleeper awakes.

"He who has Awakened is freed from fear; he has become a Buddha; he knows the vanity of all his cares, his ambitions, and also of his pains.

"It easily happens that a man, when taking a bath, steps upon a wet rope and imagines that it is a snake. Horror will overcome him, and he will shake from fear, anticipating in his mind all the agonies caused by the serpent's venomous bite. What a relief does this man experience when he sees that the rope is no snake. The cause of his fright lies in his error, his ignorance, and his illusion. If the true nature of the rope is recognized, his peace of mind will come back to him; he will feel relieved; he will be joyful and happy.

"This is the state of mind of one who has recognized that there is no self, that the cause of all his troubles, cares, and vanities is a mirage, a shadow, and dream." (quoted in Lin Yutang, *Wisdom of India and China*, "Buddhism")

"If one says that one has a self-nature (an intrinsic nature of one's own), then one has an attachment. If one thinks that there is no self-nature, then one is without attachment. If one has attachment, then one still has afflictions and ignorance. If one doesn't have any attachments, then one is without afflictions and ignorance. If there are no attachments at all, then there is no place from which afflictions come forth and there is no ignorance. We say: 'Make the self empty'; 'originally there isn't any thing.' That's right, it is empty; however, one still exists as an individual.

If one, in fact, exists here and now and speaks of being 'empty, empty,' while still continuing to exist as an individual, then one is still here. One isn't empty.

"This teaching is to help people get rid of their attachments. Don't be attached to the existence of a self. If you're not, that is emptiness. However, this doesn't mean that your body will disappear, or that your fundamental nature will disappear. One's self-nature should disappear in the sense that it becomes the same substance as empty space. That is basically the way it should be. The fundamental nature is emptiness, and emptiness is the fundamental nature. But if one is still attached to the existence of a fundamental nature, then one cannot unite with empty space, because one has still not broken through that attachment. Why is it that the Buddha's body is like empty space? It is because he has no attachments. The Bodhisattva should also learn about this kind of state of the Buddha. Therefore, don't have any attachments. If one has attachments, then automatically one will give rise to ignorance and afflictions. If one has attachments, there is selfishness, and then one is bound to have afflictions. When one has no attachments and there is no self, then there is no selfishness and there are no afflictions. To be without any afflictions is to see the nature. Those who see the nature know no anxiety, they don't know the meaning of worry." (FAS Ch22 141)

In his *Treatise on Consciousness-Only* Tripiṭaka Master ☞XUANZANG concludes his review of arguments refuting the reality of self in this way:

> The truth is that each sentient being is a continuous physical and mental series which, by the force of vexing passions (*kleśa*) and impure acts, turns from one state of existence (*gati*) to another in cycles of transmigration. Tormented by suffering and disgusted with it, he seeks the attainment of nirvana.
>
> Hence we conclude that there is positively no real ātman; that there are only various consciousnesses which, since before the beginning of time, have followed one another, the subsequent one arising with the disappearance of the antecedent, and thus a continuous series of causes and effects (karmic seeds—actual dharmas—karmic seeds) is formed; and that, by the perfuming energy (*vāsanā*) of false thinking, an image of a pseudo-ātman (of the likeness of an ātman) arises in the consciousness, and it is this pseudo-ātman which the ignorant take for a real ātman. (CWSL, Wei Tat, tr. 27)

☞ **selflessness, not-self, non-ego**

☞ **enlightenment, emptiness, attachment, Five Skandhas, Brahma Net Sutra ⟨Hinayana⟩**

O

offerings 供/供養

"Why should one make offerings to the ☞THREE JEWELS? It is because the Three Jewels provides a place for one to plant ☞BLESSINGS. If you would like to seek blessings, you must perform meritorious acts before the Three Jewels." (DFS II 288)

"One might think, 'Why should one make offerings to the Three Jewels? Wouldn't it be better if the Three Jewels made offerings to me?'

"You may think it's a bargain, but you would really be getting the short end. Why now do you have such poor luck? It's because in the past you didn't make offerings to the Three Jewels. Why are you always short of money—no money for some nice clothes or a decent place to live? It's because you didn't make offerings to the Three Jewels. As a consequence, day by day your blessings grow thinner. If you make offerings to the Three Jewels, your blessings will grow day by day. The Three Jewels is the field...where living beings can plant blessings." (DFS IX 1700-1701)

Fruits, incense, and flowers are offered before Amitābha Buddha.

The Ten Kinds of Offerings

"1) *Incense.* The finest, most expensive incense should be offered to the Buddha. If you were to buy old incense that shopkeepers were about to discard and bring it as an offering to the Buddha, your heart would be lacking in sincerity. On the other hand, if you were to offer *gośīrṣa-candana* (oxhead sandalwood) incense, your gift, involving considerable sacrifice on your part, could be considered sincere. 'Oxhead' incense is often mentioned in the Buddha's teachings. The ☞ŚŪRAṄGAMA SUTRA explains that this incense was so fragrant that it could be detected within a radius of thirteen miles when it was being burned in the city of Śrāvastī during the Buddha's Dharma assemblies. The Brahman woman in the ☞SUTRA OF THE PAST VOWS OF EARTH STORE BODHISATTVA sold her house and sacrificed her wealth in order to make a great offering to Enlightenment Flower Samadhi Self-Existent King Tathāgata. Her sincerity was so great that she sold the very roof over her head in order to make the very best offerings to the Buddha.

"The reward for offering incense to the Buddha is that in the future your body will be fragrant. A rare scent constantly issued from ☞ŚĀKYAMUNI BUDDHA's mouth and from every pore on his body. An ordinary person's body has such a foul odor it can be detected for miles. If you don't believe that, just consider how a police dog is able to trace a human scent at a distance of three to five miles. However, if you make offerings of incense to the Buddha with the hope of gaining a fragrant body, then you have missed the point. You should not seek for it. When your merit and virtue are sufficient, your body will quite naturally be fragrant. The gods, for example, have fragrant bodies because they made offerings of incense to the Buddha in former lives. Until your merit and virtue are sufficient, you will continue to have a common stinking body no matter how much you strive to attain a fragrant odor.

"2) *Flowers.* The finer the flowers that you offer to the Buddha, the greater the merit and virtue you receive from the offering. Do not spend all your money on good things to eat; save a little for an offering to the Buddha. The reward for offerings of flowers is that you will have perfect features and be very beautiful or extremely handsome in your next life. People will fall in love with you at first sight. Women will be strongly attracted to you if you are a man; and men will be unable to resist your beauty if you are a woman. 'That is too much trouble,' you may say. 'I don't want to get involved with that.'

"If you don't want that kind of trouble, so much the better. Śākyamuni Buddha had perfect features as a result of offering incense and flowers to Buddhas in former lives. If you fear the trouble a perfect appearance might bring, you can imitate Patriarch ☞BODHIDHARMA, who had a ragged beard and ugly features! It is up to you. However, if you like it, you can have it that way.

"3) *Lamps.* If you light lamps before the Buddha, in the next life your vision will be clear. You will be able to see things other people cannot see and know things other people cannot know. You will be able to obtain the penetration of the ☞FIVE EYES: the heavenly eye, the Buddha eye, the Dharma eye, the wisdom eye, and the flesh eye....

"4) *Necklaces.* Rare jewels and gems may be placed before the Buddha as offerings.

"5) *Jeweled parasols.* Items used to adorn the Buddha hall are also an acceptable offering.

"6) *Banners and canopies.* Banner made of cloth that has been painted or stitched with adornments, or wooden plaques that have been carved with inscriptions, are offerings appropriate to place before the Buddha. You may also hang canopies like the Great Brahma Heaven King's net canopy, which is circular and adorned with jewels.

"7) *Clothes.* When you make or buy fine clothes, you may place them on the altar before the Buddha prior to wearing them. Only upper garments should be offered. Although the Buddha cannot wear the clothes, the offering is a gesture to express the sincerity of your heart.

"8) *Fruit and food.* Food should be placed before the Buddha prior to being eaten. This offering as well is a gesture of respect.

"9) *Music.* Making temple music includes beating the wooden fish, playing the drum and bell, ringing the small bells, striking the gong, and singing praises. Music such as this is an offering to the Buddha.

"10) *Joined palms.* The tenth kind of offering is simple and does not expend any energy. This is merely placing your palms together as an offering." (VS 105-107)

The merit or blessings derived from an offering depend on a number of factors, including: 1) the sincerity and intentions of the donor, 2) the kind of offering, 3) the recipient, and 4) the result of the offering. In the ☞SUTRA IN FORTY-TWO SECTIONS the Buddha discusses the recipient:

> Giving food to a hundred bad people does not equal giving food to a single good person. Giving food to a thousand good people does not equal giving food to one

person who holds the ☞ FIVE PRECEPTS. Giving food to ten thousand people who hold the Five Precepts does not equal giving food to a single *śrotaāpanna* [Streamwinner, or first stage ☞ ARHAT]. Giving food to a million *śrotaāpanna* does not equal giving food to a single *sakṛdāgāmin* [Once-Returner, or second stage Arhat].

Giving food to ten million *sakṛdāgāmin* does not equal giving food to a single *anāgāmin* [Never-Returner, or third stage Arhat]. Giving food to a hundred million *anāgāmin* does not equal giving food to a single [fourth stage] Arhat.

Giving food to ten billion Arhats does not equal giving food to a single ☞ PRATYEKABUDDHA. Giving food to a hundred billion Pratyekabuddhas does not equal giving food to a Buddha of the three periods of time.

Giving food to ten trillion Buddhas of the three periods of time does not equal giving food to a single one who is without thoughts, without dwelling, without cultivation, and without accomplishment. (S42 25)

☞ **merit, Six Pāramitās—Giving, Sangha—field of blessing**

One Hundred Dharmas 百法

The One Hundred Dharmas are a general categorization of all dharmas according to the ☞ CONSCIOUSNESS-ONLY SCHOOL of the Mahayana. All lists of dharmas are distinction-making for the purpose of breaking attachment to harmful distinctions about our minds and the physical world that are based on attachment to self. Other general categorizations of all dharmas include the ☞ FIVE SKANDHAS and the ☞ EIGHTEEN REALMS. The One Hundred Dharmas make distinctions that are more specific and form the basis for a sophisticated and detailed Buddhist psychology of mind. They include:

11	Form Dharmas (☞ FIVE SKANDHAS—form)
8	Mind Dharmas (☞ EIGHT CONSCIOUSNESSES)
51	Dharmas Interactive with the Mind
24	Dharmas Not Interactive with the Mind
+ 6	Unconditioned Dharmas
100	**Dharmas**

The One Hundred Dharmas are listed individually and discussed in detail in the *Śāstra on the Door to Understanding the Hundred Dharmas* (HD).

☞ **Consciousness-Only School**

One Thousand Hands and Eyes 千手千眼

The Bodhisattva ☞ AVALOKITEŚVARA is often depicted with one thousand hands, each hand containing its own eye, to indicate the vows and powers of the Bodhisattva to see all those suffering in the world and to reach into the world and pull them out of their suffering.

"If you cultivate the ☞ GREAT COMPASSION MANTRA, you can obtain a thousand hands and a thousand eyes.

"But you say, 'I have two hands to pick things up with and two eyes to see things with. This is the scientific age. What possible use would I have for a thousand hands and a thousand eyes?'

"If you don't want them, then don't cultivate the Great Compassion Mantra. However, with a thousand eyes, you can shut your two eyes and give them a rest, and still see things. Isn't that wonderful Dharma?

"A thousand eyes can not only see, but illuminate. Your ordinary eyes can see ten or twenty miles, or with binoculars, perhaps a hundred miles. With a thousand eyes, you can see for a million miles, to the ends of empty space and the ☞DHARMA REALM. You don't even need a television to watch the astronauts walking on the moon. It's so much less expensive than buying a television or photographs, or magazines. Now do you think a thousand eyes are useful?

"Not only that, but with a thousand eyes, you can look out from the back of your head and see what is in front of you. Looking out in front of you, you can see what is behind you. And so the Venerable ☞XUYUN wrote:

"From behind your brains
you can see your face:
You've caught the sparrow hawk.
A full set of eyes at the gate
of the crown:
You've seized a flying bear.

"Most people can't see their own faces, but with a thousand eyes, you can see your own face and you can see behind you. You can even see what's inside your stomach. You can know how many little bugs, lazy bugs, gluttonous bugs, and dead bugs there are in your stomach. From the outside, you can see inside, and from the inside, you can see outside, just as if you were looking through a pane of glass. You can see it all: what your heart looks like and what your stomach is about to say, every movement of those machines inside you. Do you want a thousand eyes or not? Do you still think your two eyes are sufficient? Such is the miraculous function of a thousand eyes.

"What about a thousand hands? If you have only two hands, then when you pick something up in each of them, you can't pick up anything else. With one hand, you can take the thousand dollars; with a thousand hands, you can take a hundred million.

Bodhisattva Avalokiteśvara (see plate 36)

"Now let's divide some apples. You may take as many as you want. Of course, if you only have two hands, you can take only two. If you have a thousand, you can take a thousand. Isn't that useful? But a thousand hands are not for child's play. The reason to have a thousand hands is to save other people. If a thousand people are drowning and you have only two hands, you will only be able to rescue two of them. If you have a thousand hands, you will be able to reach into the water and pull them all out. Is that useful or not?

"A thousand eyes observe,
A thousand ears hear all;
A thousand hands help and support
Living beings everywhere.

"Regardless of what trouble living beings find themselves in, you can save them with your thousand hands and pull them out of the sea of suffering. Without a thousand hands, you can't rescue so many people.

"The Bodhisattva Who Regards the Sounds of the World has a thousand hands, not for stealing things, but for rescuing people. They are not for the purpose of surreptitiously picking a thousand apples. You should be clear about this point.

"Where do the thousand hands and eyes come from? They are born from the Great Compassion Mantra. You must recite the Great Compassion Mantra and cultivate the Great Compassion Dharma of the Forty-two Hands. The last of the forty-two hands is called the "Uniting and Holding, the Thousand Arms Hand." Every time you recite this mantra, your hands increase by forty-two. Recite it once and you have forty-two more hands; recite it again and they increase by forty-two. Recite it a hundred times and you will have 4,200, a thousand times, 42,000, and so forth. It's simply a matter of whether or not you cultivate. But the thousand hands and eyes are not obtained in a day and a night. You must cultivate with effort every single day, never missing a day. If you cultivate daily according to Dharma, you will perfect the inconceivably wonderful function of enlightenment, but if you cultivate today and quit tomorrow, it is of no use at all. In the world, if you want a Ph.D., you have to study for fourteen or fifteen years. How much more effort is needed to study the Buddhadharma! Unless you continually use true, genuine effort, you will have no success...." (DS 2-4)

In the ☞ŚŪRAṄGAMA SUTRA, the Bodhisattva Avalokiteśvara states:

> For example, I may make appear one head, three heads, five heads, seven heads, nine heads, eleven heads, and so forth, until there may be one hundred eight heads, a thousand heads, ten thousand heads, or eighty-four thousand *vajra* heads; two arms, four arms, six arms, eight arms, ten arms, twelve arms, fourteen, sixteen, eighteen arms, or twenty arms, twenty-four arms, and so forth until there may be one hundred eight arms, a thousand arms, or eighty-four thousand *mudrā* arms; two eyes, three eyes, four eyes, nine eyes, and so forth until there may be one hundred eight eyes, a thousand eyes, ten thousand eyes, or eighty four thousand pure and precious eyes, sometimes compassionate, sometimes awesome, sometimes displaying wisdom to rescue and protect living beings so that they may attain great self-mastery. (SS V 178-179)

☞ **Bodhisattva, Avalokiteśvara ⟨Bodhisattva⟩, Dhāraṇī Sutra**

ordination 受具足戒

Ordination as a Buddhist Bhikshu (monk) or Bhikshuni (nun) can be seen both as the culmination of a period of intense preparatory cultivation and as the beginning of a new and fuller life in the Dharma.

The preparatory period begins with Taking ☞REFUGE WITH THE THREE JEWELS, that is, formally becoming a Buddhist and bowing to a teacher. It is followed by stages of learning to live in accord with progressively higher standards of purity and morality as represented by adherence to ☞MORAL PRECEPTS. The taking of the ☞FIVE PRECEPTS is followed by the Eight Precepts and then often the Bodhisattva Precepts (☞BNS). The taking of the novice (*śrāmaṇera*) precepts (☞SV) ushers in a period of a minimum of three years' formal training for becoming a fully-ordained Bhikshu or Bhikshuni.

Ordination itself takes place in a ceremony open only to the Sangha that is presided over by ten elder Bhikshus of high virtue. During the ceremony the 250 Bhikshu precepts (or 348 Bhikshuni precepts) are transmitted.

☞ **refuge with the Three Jewels, Sangha, Bhikshu, Bhikshuni, moral precepts**

outflows 漏

"There are many kinds of outflows. Anger is an outflow, and so is greed. To be deluded is also to have outflows. Having a temper, one has outflows; and if one is a glutton, one has another kind of outflow. Greed for wealth is an outflow, as is greed for forms. Anything which is not proper that you like out of habit is called an outflow.

"Outflows are the root of birth and death. Why can't you end birth and death? Because you have outflows. To be without outflows is to be like a bottle that does not leak—one has to be devoid of all bad habits and faults....Then you are not greedy for wealth or sex or fame or profit. You are not greedy for food or sleep. When you are not greedy for anything, you have penetrated to the state of no outflows.

"Having no outflows is true comfort. When you reach the state of no outflows, then you are genuinely there—you have not run away. You do not run to and from as if engaged in guerrilla warfare. Right now, in a state of outflows, your false thinking is like guerrilla troops. If it isn't going this in direction, it is headed in that direction. One knows not how far you might go! The question always hangs in the air:

"Will the hero be victorious
  or defeated?
Tune in for the next episode.

"If you have no outflows, then your basic nature of true suchness is there—a free and easy presence. If you have outflows, then the truth runs away. What is the truth in people? It is the most valuable thing within your possession. If you let that most valuable thing flow away, if you lose it then you turn into something completely worthless. What is this most valuable thing? It is the collateral for becoming a Buddha, the foundation of becoming a Buddha. If you lose this most valuable thing, then you'll never be able to end birth and death. If you ask how you can stay around and be of worth, how you can be a jewel more valuable than a diamond, you must be without outflows. You have to cut off desire and get rid of emotional love. Although this topic looks really simple, if you have outflows, then what you have that is true has left you and run away." (SM IV 44-45)

"What are outflows? They're just people's bad habits and faults that they've amassed from beginningless time, life after life. That is what is meant by 'all outflows.'

"If you like to drink wine, that's a wine outflow. If you smoke dope, then you have an outflow of smoking dope. People who are greedy for wealth have the outflow of wealth. And those who are greedy for beautiful form have the outflow of beautiful form. Outflows are insatiable. For example, eating is an outflow and wearing clothes is an outflow. When you like to sleep, that's an outflow. Any state that you go along with and end up getting afflicted by is an outflow. If you have thoughts of desire, then you will have a lot of outflows. Outflows are just all our various bad habits and faults. This includes continually breaking the rules and doing things that are not in accord with the Dharma. That's what is meant by outflows.

"Some people hear this explanation of Dharma and give rise to ☞FALSE THINKING. What kind of false thinking? They are opposed to what has just been expressed. They think, 'You say that eating is an outflow, and that wearing clothes is an outflow, and that sleeping is an outflow. Then tell me, what isn't an outflow? Eating is an outflow, but everybody has to eat. Nobody can go without eating. How can we eliminate *that* outflow? Nobody can go without wearing clothes, so, how can we get rid of *that* outflow. Nobody can go without sleep. How can we dispense with *that* outflow. If all those things are outflows, then how can *anyone* be without outflows? If one doesn't eat, one dies. If one doesn't wear clothes, one won't get away with it. If one doesn't sleep, one will soon find it's just as important as eating and wearing clothes. If the outflows we must get rid of are those essential parts of our life, then I definitely object!'

"I agree. There isn't anyone who doesn't need to eat, sleep, and wear clothes! Outflows means overindulgence in these things. For instance, if when you eat, you just eat your fill, then that's okay. You shouldn't pay attention to whether the food is good or bad. The important thing is not to have a lot of false thinking about what you eat, and then you won't have any outflows.

"If, on the other hand, you eat something and then give rise to a lot of false thinking, then you will have an outflow. You think, 'I wonder if what I ate today had any food value. I don't know if I've had enough nourishment or not. Will the things that I've eaten help out my body or not?' On the one hand you eat, and on the other hand you have so much false thinking about it that even if you did eat something nourishing, you'd waste it all by false thinking. You may have put the food in your stomach, but it all flows back out in your false thinking. If, when you eat, you stop when you're full and you don't have any false thinking about whether the food is good or bad, then you're a person of the Way without any thoughts. 'No thoughts' means that you eat and don't have any false thinking. And if you do it in this way, then the nourishment will be endless and boundless. It's just because of your false thinking that all the proteins and vitamins disappear.

"This can be likened to a bowl with water in it. If there aren't any cracks in the bowl then when you put water in it, the water won't run out. It doesn't have any outflows. But if there are cracks, then the water is going to leak out. People's false thoughts are just like cracks in a bowl. If you don't have any false thinking, then you don't leave any cracks for outflows.

"Originally you didn't have any of these false thoughts. Why do you want to create some and start speculating about what the food tastes like and analyzing every bit of it for its vitamin content? No matter how much false thinking you have about what you ate today, by this time tomorrow when it has passed through your body, you certainly won't want to eat it, no matter how good it was before.

"If you don't have any false thinking, then the nourishment will stay in your body and will not flow out. But the more false thinking you have about it, the more of its energy-value you lose in outflows.

"If you wear clothes in order to keep warm, that's okay. But if your objective in wearing clothes isn't to keep warm, but rather to look good and cause others to notice you, then that's an outflow. As soon as someone pays attention to you, an outflow takes place. If you worry about whether your clothes are good or not, and keep wanting to change outfits, then there is an outflow. When you wear clothes you should only wear them to keep warm. Don't have false thinking about them.

"What is the outflow of sleeping like? When it's time to go to sleep, you lie there but you can't go to sleep. Once you start false thinking, sleep runs off and you don't know where to find it. You toss and turn and still you can't go to sleep. Would you call this an outflow or not? It's the outflow of sleep. And if you don't get enough sleep, then the next day you won't have enough energy, because you used it all up false thinking all night.

"Not getting enough sleep is an outflow and getting too much sleep is also an outflow. If you get just the right amount of sleep, then there is no outflow. And so, tell me now, which isn't an outflow? Eating? Sleeping? Wearing clothes? What were you opposing?...

"Not only are eating, wearing, clothes, and sleeping outflows, but whatever you like is an outflow. Your temper is also an outflow. Worry, hate, and desire are also outflows. The seven emotions of happiness, anger, grief, fear, love, hate, and desire are all outflows. But these outflows can be stopped. If you get to the place where you can flow and yet not flow, then you can be said to have no outflows...." (FAS Ch9 10-13)

☞ **contaminations, impurities, influxes, taints, biases**

☞ **ignorance, polluted thoughts**

P

Pali 巴利文

The language of the ☞ THERAVADA Buddhist Canon, Pali was originally a natural, spoken dialect closely related to ☞ SANSKRIT, which was not used for everyday discourse. Pali was not the dialect spoken by the Buddha.

pāramitā 波羅蜜多

"*Pāramitā*, a Sanskrit word, literally means 'having arrived at the other shore.' It means to finish completely whatever you do. If you decide to become a Buddha, then the realization of Buddhahood is *pāramitā*. If you want to go to a university and get a Ph.D., obtaining the degree is *pāramitā*. If you're hungry and want to eat, then when you have eaten your fill, that is *pāramitā*. If you're sleepy, then *pāramitā* is when you lie down and fall asleep. The Sanskrit word *pāramitā* is transliterated into Chinese as *bo luo mi*. *Bo luo* is Chinese for pineapple, and *mi* means 'honey.' And so the fruit of *pāramitā* is said to be sweeter than pineapple or honey." (SS I 9-10)

"What is meant by *pāramitā*? It is a Sanskrit word which in our language means 'having arrived at the other shore,' and is explained as 'being apart from coming into being and ceasing to be.' When one is attached to states of existence, coming into being and ceasing to be arise like waves on water. That is what is meant by 'this shore.' To be apart from states of existence, with no coming into being or ceasing to be, is to be like freely flowing water. That is what is meant by 'the other shore.' Therefore, it is called '*pāramitā*.'" (PS 96)

The most well-known *pāramitās* in Buddhism are the ☞ SIX PĀRAMITĀS and the Ten Pāramitās.

Although the *pāramitās* are usually associated with Mahayana teachings about the practices of the ☞ BODHISATTVA, they are also found in Theravada teachings. The Ten Pāramitās concern the "perfect exercise of the ten principal virtues by a Bodhisattva" (PTSD).

perfection, mastery, supremacy, supreme virtues, completeness, highest state, crossing to the other shore

☞ **Six Pāramitās**

polluted thoughts 妄想

"When it comes right down to it, the Buddhadharma is spoken simply to tell living beings not to have polluted thoughts." (FAS-PI 87)

"Trace the source of your polluted thoughts. For example, if you have polluted thoughts of eating food, it is because you are a gluttonous person. If you have polluted thoughts about sounds, it is because you are greedy to listen to fine sounds. If you have polluted thoughts about sights you see, it is because you enjoy indulging in visual forms. If you have polluted thoughts about bodily contact, it is because you are greedy to experience sensual pleasures. If you have false thoughts about ideas and concepts, it means you are prone to seeking mental dharmas.

"If you are like that, then it means you haven't made it through the gates. You run out the six gates of eyes, ears, nose, tongue, body, and mind. The six sense organs get confused by the six sense objects. But the six sense organs can 'turn' the six sense objects. When that can be done then you are capable of 'not entering' the gates. The Six Sense Objects are: forms, sounds, smells, tastes, objects of touch, and dharmas. When you have passed through the gates, fame and profit won't move you either. You are then not influenced by anything:

> The eyes see shapes and forms,
> But inside there is nothing.
> The ears hear defiling sounds,
> But the mind does not know.

You are no longer turned by false aspects of your environment." (TT 38)

false thinking, (false) discrimination, wild thoughts

☞ **outflows**

prajñā 般若

> Good Knowing Advisors, what is meant by *prajñā*? *Prajñā* in our language means wisdom. Everywhere and at all times, in thought after thought, remain undeluded and practice wisdom constantly; that is *prajñā* conduct. *Prajñā* is cut off by a single deluded thought. By one wise thought, *prajñā* is produced. Worldly men, deluded and confused, do not see *prajñā*. They speak of it with their mouths, but their minds are always deluded. They constantly say of themselves, 'I cultivate *prajñā*!' and though they continually speak of emptiness, they are unaware of true emptiness. *Prajñā*, without form or mark, is just the wisdom-mind.

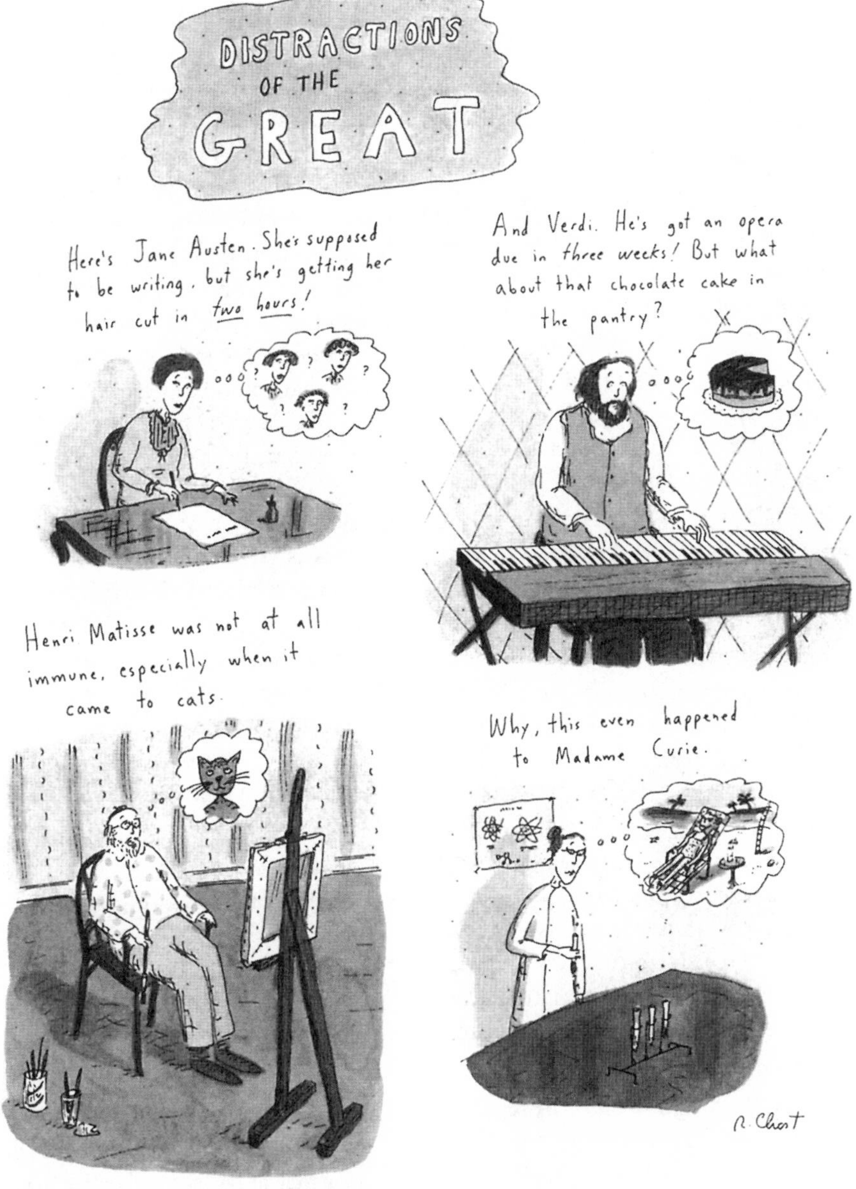
DISTRACTIONS OF THE GREAT
Here's Jane Austen. She's supposed to be writing, but she's getting her hair cut in two hours!
And Verdi. He's got an opera due in three weeks! But what about that chocolate cake in the pantry?
Henri Matisse was not at all immune, especially when it came to cats.
Why, this even happened to Madame Curie.
R. Chast

Examples of polluted thinking

If thus explained, just this is *prajñā*-wisdom. (PS 94-95)

"*Prajñā* is Sanskrit and means, generally, wisdom. Wisdom is a fairly common word. *Prajñā* is a revered term and so it is not translated. It is a miraculous kind of wisdom. Also, it includes several meanings, and [for that reason also] it is not translated. *Prajñā* is of three kinds:

"1) *Literary Prajñā*. This refers to the wisdom contained in the sutras and commentaries spoken by the Buddha. It doesn't refer to ordinary worldly literature. Literary wisdom gives rise to:

"2) *Contemplative Prajñā*. After reading the sutras, one then contemplates and illuminates their meanings through actual practice. This type of *prajñā* then leads one to:

"3) *Real Mark Prajñā*. Real Mark *prajñā* is without a mark. But there is nothing not marked by it. It has no mark, and it is also without the mark of having no mark! The Real Mark is neither existent nor nonexistent. Literary *prajñā* is existent. Contemplative *prajñā* is nonexistent. Real Mark *prajñā* is neither existent nor nonexistent. From existence one penetrates to nonexistence, and from nonexistence one arrives at neither existence nor nonexistence. If you can comprehend the realm of neither existence nor nonexistence, you have attained Real Mark *prajñā*.

"Because *prajñā* has these three meanings, we do not translate it. If you have wisdom, you will have *prajñā*. If you have no wisdom, you're ignorant. Ignorant people lack wisdom. Wise people are devoid of ignorance.

"'I'm worried,' you say, 'because I'm really ignorant. I don't have any *prajñā*.'

"Don't worry. To know that you are ignorant is just the beginning of *prajñā*! It is just to be feared that you don't know that you are ignorant. If you think that you are wise and that you have a lot of *prajñā*, then you *are* ignorant. Why? Because you don't understand yourself. If you understand yourself, you have *prajñā*. If you understand yourself today, then today you have wisdom. If you understand yourself tomorrow, then tomorrow you will have wisdom. If you understand yourself every day, then every day you have wisdom. And so don't be afraid of not having wisdom. Just be afraid that you won't realize that you don't have wisdom! Where does wisdom come from anyway? It comes from ignorance. If you weren't ignorant, you couldn't become wise. If you know that you are ignorant, that means that your wisdom is starting to manifest. It is just that wonderful, that ineffably wonderful. Basically, I can't explain wonderful Dharma to you, but now I see that you have developed to the point that it's okay to tell you. Since we have arrived at the discussion of *prajñā*, you are no doubt wise enough to hear it!" (DFS X 24-25)

✍ **wisdom, gnosis, insight, intuitive knowledge**

☞ **Six Pāramitās—*prajñā* ⟨wisdom⟩, emptiness**

Pratyekabuddha 辟支佛

"The holy sages enlightened to
 conditions
Doze high on mountain peaks alone.
Springtime's flowers wither in the fall
In a cycle of twelve interconnecting
 links.

"*The holy sages enlightened to conditions.* When there is a Buddha in the world, sages are called those 'enlightened to conditions.' When there is no Buddha in the world, they are called 'solitary enlightened ones' or Pratyekabuddhas, because they are able to become enlightened by themselves.

"*Doze high on mountain peaks alone.* They prefer to doze alone in the high desolate mountains. *Springtime's flowers wither in the fall in a cycle of twelve interconnecting links.* In the spring the myriad things are born. Those enlightened to conditions watch the white blossoms open, and in the autumn they see the yellow leaves fall. They awaken to the knowledge that all phenomena are nonexistent. They see that everything naturally gets born and dies, and thus they become enlightened to the twelve links of conditioned coproduction." (TD 29-31)

Sage Enlightened by Conditions, Solitary Enlightened One, Solitary Realizers

☞ **enlightenment**

precepts 戒

☞ **moral precepts**

pure land 淨土

Western Pure Land of Ultimate Bliss (see plate 33)

A pure land is a land in which Buddhas and other pure beings live. It is undefiled by the ☞FIVE TURBIDITIES. The most well-known of the pure lands described by the Buddha is the Land of Ultimate Bliss of ☞AMITĀBHA BUDDHA in the West, which is described in *The Buddha Speaks of* ☞AMITĀBHA SUTRA.

> All beings of this country endure none of the sufferings but enjoy every bliss.... This land of Ultimate Bliss is surrounded by seven tiers of railings, seven layers of netting, and seven rows of trees, all formed from the four treasures.... This Land of Ultimate Bliss has pools of the seven jewels, filled with waters of eight meritorious virtues. The bottom of each pool is pure, spread over with golden sand. On the four sides are stairs of gold, silver, lapis lazuli, and crystal; above are raised pavilions adorned with gold, silver, lapis lazuli, crystal, mother-of-pearl, red pearls, and carnelian. In the pools are lotuses as large as carriage wheels, green colored of green light, yellow colored of yellow light, red colored of red light, white colored of white light, subtly, wonderfully, fragrant and pure.... In that Buddhland there is always heavenly music and the ground is yellow gold. In the six periods of the day and night a heavenly rain of *mandārava* flowers falls, and throughout the clear morning, each living being of that land, with sacks full of the myriads of wonderful flowers, makes offerings to the hundreds of thousands of millions of Buddhas of the other directions. At mealtime they return to their own country, and having eaten, they stroll around.... In this country there are always rare and wonderful varicolored birds: white cranes, peacocks, parrots, and egrets, *kalaviṅkas* and two-headed birds. In the six periods of the day and night the flocks of birds sing forth harmonious and elegant

sounds; their clear and joyful sounds proclaim the Five Roots, the Five Powers, the Seven Bodhi Shares, the Eight Sagely Way Shares, and Dharmas such as those. When living beings of this land hear these sounds, they are altogether mindful of the Buddha, mindful of the Dharma, and mindful of the Sangha.... (AS 109-116)

The Three Sages of the Western Pure Land (see plate 34)

A Buddha's pure land is a world system that has many special characteristics. It is without the three evil destinies of the hells, ghosts, and animals. The earth is level and the land is very beautiful with all kinds of wondrous adornments. Human life is very blissful as in the heavens. Yet, unlike the heavens, everything in a pure land is set up so that living beings there are always mindful of the ☞THREE JEWELS, and they are always able to hear a Buddha and his retinue of Bodhisattvas teaching the Dharma, which they diligently cultivate. All beings born in pure lands eventually become Buddhas themselves in other world systems or they purposely remain as high Bodhisattvas and go to other world systems to help rescue living beings. Once born in a pure land one will never again fall into the three lower realms of existence or retreat from the Buddha's Path.

The Sixth Patriarch (of the Chan School) ☞HUINENG said of the Pure Land:

> Common, deluded people do not understand their own inherent natures and do not know that the Pure Land is within themselves. Therefore, they make vows for the East and vows for the West. To enlightened people all places are the same. As the Buddha said, 'In whatever place one dwells, there is constant peace and happiness.' (PS 143)

The Venerable Master Hsuan Hua commented on the Christian heaven and the Buddhist pure land: "Fundamentally there is no heaven and there is no Pure Land. People imagine a heaven and a heaven exists. They imagine the existence of a Pure land and a Pure Land exists. The Pure Land Dharma-door was spoken by the Buddha in order to teach you to do away with your false thoughts. It is intended to lead you to a realization of the pure, inherently wonderful True Suchness nature. At the ultimate point, when you have no false thoughts or confused ideas, you arrive at the Pure Land. Whoever can do away with their false thoughts can reach the Land of Ultimate Bliss. Whoever cannot do that is still in the Evil World of the Five Turbidities. Heaven is the same. We imagine how fine and wonderful heaven must be, but only on the basis of what we have heard. We also imagine the Pure Land to be as the Buddha said it was. We haven't yet seen it ourselves, except in our imaginations. As I see it, the Pure land Dharma-door is taught only for the sake of causing you to purify your mind. *That* is the Pure Land. If your mind has no confused ideas, *that* is heaven. If you look for it elsewhere, you only show your greed." (*Shambala Review*, v.5, nos.1-2, Winter, 1976, pp. 27-28)

Essay on the Pure Land

With one mind we return our lives to the Land of Ultimate Bliss. With a pure light Amitābha Buddha's vows illumine us, and those kind vows gather us in. Now, with proper mindfulness, we praise the

Thus Come One's name in order to take the path of *bodhi* and to seek rebirth in the pure land. In the past the Buddha vowed, 'If living beings who wish for rebirth in my land and who resolve their minds with faith and joy, even for just ten recitations, are not reborn there, I will not attain the proper enlightenment.' Through mindfulness of the Buddha, we enter the sea of the Thus Come One's vows and receive the power of the Buddha's kindness. Our multitude of offenses is eradicated and our good roots increase and grow. As we approach the end of life, we ourselves will know the time of its coming. Our bodies will be free of illness and pain. Our hearts will have no greed or fondness, and our thoughts will not be upside down, just as in entering *dhyāna*-samadhi. The Buddha and the assembly of sages, leading us by the hand to the golden dais, will come to welcome us. And in the space of a single thought we will be reborn in the Land of Ultimate Bliss. The flower will open, and we will see the Buddha, straightway hear the Buddha vehicle and immediately attain the wisdom of a Buddha. We will take across living beings on a wide scale, fulfilling our *bodhi* vows. All Buddhas of the ten directions and the three periods of time! All Bodhisattvas, Mahāsattvas! *Mahāprajñāpāramitā*! (RH 230-231)

☞ **Buddhaland, Pure Land School, Three Bodies of a Buddha, Buddhaland**

Lotus pool in the Land of Ultimate Bliss (see plate 35)

Pure Land School 淨土宗

☞ **Five Types of Buddhist Study and Practice—Pure Land**

Q

Qingliang Chengguan 〈National Master〉 〈738-840 C.E.〉 清涼澄觀《國師》

"National Master Qingliang of the Tang dynasty in China was a ☞TRANSFORMATION BODY of Flower Adornment Bodhisattva. He is called a transformation body because he specialized in lecturing on the ☞FLOWER ADORNMENT SUTRA and didn't explain other sutras. National Master Qingliang was named Chengguan and his style name was Daxiu. His surname (lay name) was Xiahou. As a layman he associated with scholars. Born during Emperor Xuanzong's reign, during the fifth year of the Kaiyuan period, he was nine feet four inches tall (in the ancient measurements of China), his hands hung down below his knees, and he also had forty teeth. Most of us have thirty-two teeth; the Buddha had forty-two teeth. People with forty teeth are exceptional, and there are very few of them. National Master Qingliang had forty teeth, and eyes which seemed like everyone else's in the daytime, but if you looked at them during the night, you would see that they glowed. What is more, they didn't move; his eyes were fixed, at night they glowed. That was National Master Qingliang.

"During the fourth year of the Qianzhong period (783), he wrote the *Flower Adornment Sutra Commentary and Sub-commentary*, which is the most famous discussion of the *Flower Adornment Sutra* in China. Before he wrote it, he sought the aid of Flower Adornment Bodhisattva. One night he had a dream. He dreamt that all the mountain peaks turned to gold. After he awoke from this dream, he knew that the golden mountain peaks represented light which illumines everywhere, whereupon he wrote his commentary on the *Flower Adornment Sutra*, writing continuously without a break. When most people write articles, they think and then write, think again, and then write some more. But National Master Qingliang wrote continuously because he didn't need to stop and think. He wrote without thinking and completed his commentary in four years. Afterwards, he had another dream, although it is not certain that it was a dream, and so perhaps we should call it an experience; you may say it was a dream or call it an experience. We don't know if it was a dream, but if it wasn't a dream, what was it? It was as if real, and also like a dream. He dreamt that he became a dragon, and then the dragon transformed itself into boundless and measureless tens of millions of dragons, and finally all of them flew off to all the other worlds. He experienced the *Flower Adornment Sutra* in this way, a manifestation of the ☞SIX SPIRITUAL POWERS.

Fourth Patriarch of the Avatamsaka School, National Master Cheng Guan

"National Master Qingliang lived through the reigns of nine emperors and was the teacher of seven. He personally knew nine emperors, of whom seven asked him to be their teacher.

"After he perfected the stillness, he was buried. Later, an elder monk on his way to China from India, met two darkly clad youths on the road. This elder monk was an Arhat, and so he recognized these two young Bodhisattvas and said to them, 'Where are you going?'

"The two youths replied, 'We are going to China to request the molars of Flower Adornment Bodhisattva to take back to India and make offerings to them.' When this Arhat got back to China, he told the emperor about the two darkly clad youths who had come seeking the molars of Flower Adornment Bodhisattva. Thereupon, the emperor had National Master Qingliang's grave opened and found that some of his teeth were missing. These experiences are wonderful and inexpressible. Flower Adornment Bodhisattva had come to China as National Master Qingliang and had these particular characteristics." (UW xx-xxi)

☞ **Huayan School**

R

ranking the teachings 判教

Although the principle is of one flavor, explanations of it can be either shallow or profound. Therefore, they can be divided to indicate whether they are provisional or actual. (FAS-PII(1) 156)

Many schools of Buddhism rank the Buddha's teachings according to their level of profundity. The basic idea is that the Buddha taught people according to their abilities to understand. And as their abilities to understand developed, he taught them more and more profound Dharmas.

One of the most well-known analyses of the Buddha's teachings is that of the Tiantai School, which divides them into Five Periods and Eight Teachings.

"In the first of the Five Periods, the Flower Adornment Period, the ☞FLOWER ADORNMENT SUTRA, a Perfect Teaching, was spoken for twenty-one days, whereas the ☞DHARMA FLOWER and the ☞NIRVANA SUTRAS, which are not nearly so long as the *Flower Adornment Sutra*, together took eight years to speak. The reason is that the *Flower Adornment Sutra* was spoken by the Buddha as Niṣyanda Buddha ☞THREE BODIES OF A BUDDHA], and so it was spoken fast.

"The second was the Āgama Period in which the Store Teaching that provided for the ☞TWO VEHICLES was spoken—the Dharmas of the Four Noble Truths and the Twelve Links of Conditioned Co-production.

"The third was the Expansive Period, an initial door leading from the Theravada through to the Great Vehicle [☞MAHAYANA AND HINAYANA COMPARED], and was called the Connective Teaching. It could connect with the former Store Teaching and with the Prajñā Teaching which followed.

"The fourth was the Prajñā Period, called the Separate Teaching because it is not the same as the previous Connective Teaching, and also not the same as the subsequent Perfect Teaching.

"The fifth, the Dharma Flower and Nirvana Period, is called the Perfect Teaching. It was spoken particularly to liberate those whose dispositions were suited for the Great Vehicle....

"In addition to the four teachings described above, there are four more teachings: **1)** the Sudden Teaching, **2)** the Gradual Teaching, **3)** the Secret Teaching, and **4)** the Unfixed Teaching. The Sudden Teaching refers to sudden and immediate enlightenment. The Gradual Teaching refers to becoming enlightened gradually, little by little. The Secret Teaching means that something is spoken for the other person without the first person knowing it, and something is spoken for the first person without the other person knowing it, both remaining unaware of what the other person knows. The Unfixed Teaching is the Dharma of there being no fixed Dharma. Altogether that makes Eight Teachings...." (FAS-VP 52-53)

☞ **Tiantai School, Huayan School**

rebirth 生/再生

...in the second watch he, whose energy had no peer, gained the supreme divine eyesight [☞ FIVE EYES], being himself the highest of all who possess sight.

Then with that completely purified divine eyesight he beheld the entire world, as it were in a spotless mirror.

His compassionateness waxed greater, as he saw the passing away and rebirth of all creatures according as their acts were lower or higher.

Those living beings whose acts are sinful pass to the sphere of misery, those others whose deeds are good win a place in the triple heaven.

The former are born in the very dreadful fearsome hell [☞ HELLS] and, alas, are woefully tormented with sufferings of many kinds....

In the hells is excessive torture, among animals eating each other, the suffering of hunger and thirst among the *pretas* (i.e., ghosts), among men the suffering of longings.

In the heavens that are free from love the suffering of rebirth is excessive. For the ever-wandering world of the living there is most certainly no peace anywhere.

This stream of the cycle of existence has no support and is ever subject to death. Creatures, thus beset on all sides, find no resting place.

Thus with the divine eyesight he examined the five spheres of life and found nothing substantial in existence, just as no heartwood is found in a plantain-tree when it is cut open. (Aśvaghoṣa, *Acts of the Buddha*, Ch. 14, "Enlightenment")

Ānanda, all beings in the world are caught up in the continuity of birth and death. Birth happens because of their habitual tendencies; death comes through flow and change. When they are on the verge of dying, but when the final warmth has not left their bodies, all the good and evil they have done in that life suddenly and simultaneously manifests. They experience the intermingling of two habits: an abhorrence of death and an attraction to life. (SS VII 95)

"Now let's consider the contents of our past lives. You are thinking, 'I don't believe there are past lives. If I had past lives, why don't I remember them?' Take the dream as a comparison. The day passes and the dream of the night before is forgotten. How much the less can we remember the events of our past lives!...

"You should know that now we too are dreaming. I am telling you right now that you are dreaming, but you can't believe it. Wait until you cultivate, cultivate to understanding, and, 'Ah, everything I did before was all a dream.'" (HS 38)

Out of the horse's belly
  into the womb of a cow:
How many times have you passed
  back and forth through Yama's halls?
First you go for a swing
  by Śakra's palace,
And then plummet back down
  into Sir Yama's pot. (HD 83)

[*NOTE:* Śakra is 'lord of heaven'; Yama is 'king of the nether worlds.']

☞ **reincarnation, transmigration**
☞ **karma, causation, Six Paths of Rebirth**

recitation of the Buddha's name 念佛

The Buddha Amitābha
  is the great Dharma King.
May his Bodhisattvas guide you
  to the Western Land.
Morning and night hold his name;
  with sincerity recite it.

At all times, in contemplation,
think upon it well.
With one mind unconfused,
you'll realize samadhi.
When all creation's emptied,
you'll enter the Lotus Land.
Suddenly you're awakened
to the uncreated;
The Buddha appears in person.
Then wonderful enlightenment
is naturally attained. (LY II 113)

Recitation of the Buddha's name refers to mindful recitation, whether aloud or silently, of the name of a particular Buddha, usually the Buddha Amitābha: "Namo Amitābha Buddha."

"When the water-clearing pearl
is tossed in muddy water,
The muddy water becomes clear.
When the Buddha's name
enters a confused mind,
The confused mind reaches
the Buddha.

"Why should we be mindful of the Buddha? Because we have strong affinities with Amitābha Buddha, who became a Buddha ten *kalpas* ago. Before that he was called Bhikshu Dharma Treasury [Skt. Dharmākara]. At that time he made forty-eight great vows. When making his thirteenth and fourteenth vows he said, 'If the living beings throughout the ten directions say my name and do not become Buddhas, I will not attain the right enlightenment.' In other words, if people who recited his name did not become Buddhas, he would not have become a Buddha. And because of the power of Amitābha Buddha's vows, everyone who recites his name can be reborn in the Land of Ultimate Bliss." (SS V 128)

"Whether one is intelligent, average, or stupid, if one recites the Buddha's name, one will definitely be born transformationally from a lotus in the Land of Ultimate Bliss. One will not pass through a womb but will enter a lotus flower, live in it for a while, and then realize Buddhahood." (AS 21)

"With the Dharma-door of
mindfulness of the Buddha,
One transcends the Three Realms
through the side door
And carries one's karma
into that rebirth.

"What does it mean to transcend the Three Realms (☞THREE WORLDS) through the side door? It's like an insect in a piece of bamboo. If the insect were to gnaw its way out through the length of the bamboo, it would have to go through all the sections; that would take a long time. If the insect were to gnaw a hole in the side of the bamboo instead, it would get out very easily. People who are mindful of the Buddha are like the insect who goes out the side of the bamboo; they escape the Three Realms on a horizontal plane—right at the level where they are. 'And carries one's karma into that rebirth.' The ☞KARMA one carries is former karma, not current karma—it is old karma, not new karma. This means that before you understood the method of being mindful of the Buddha, you created offenses. You can take that karma with you when you go to rebirth in the Pure Land. But don't continue to create bad karma once you know about reciting the Buddha's name, because you can't go there if you are taking that karma along. (SS V 127-128)

"Our recitation is like sending a telegram to Amitābha in the West. At the end of our lives, the Bodhisattvas will guide us to rebirth in the Western Pure Land. Morning and night, in motion and stillness, at all times, you can recite. While moving you can recite and change motion into stillness; when still you can recite and turn the stillness into motion. When there is neither motion nor stillness, your telegram to Amitābha has gotten through and you've received his response.

"If you maintain your recitation with undivided attention morning and night without stopping, you may recite to the point that you don't know that you are walking when you walk, you don't feel thirsty when you are thirsty, and you don't experience hunger when you are hungry; you don't feel cold in freezing weather, and you don't feel the warmth when you are warm. People and dharmas are empty, and you and Amitābha Buddha become one. 'Amitābha Buddha is me, and I am Amitābha Buddha.' The two cannot be separated. Recite single-mindedly and sincerely, without polluted thoughts. Pay no attention to worldly concerns. When you don't know the time and don't know the day, you may arrive at a miraculous state." (LY II 114)

> "The flower opens and one sees the Buddha." (From a Buddhist hymn)

☞ **mindfulness of the Buddha**
☞ **Three Vehicles**

refuge with the Three Jewels 皈依三寶

> This Refuge is peaceful indeed.
> This Refuge is best.
> This Refuge, if taken, frees one
> from all suffering.
> (*Dhammapada* 14:14)

Taking refuge with the Three Jewels is the way one becomes a Buddhist and enters the path to the ending of suffering that comes with full and proper ☞ENLIGHTENMENT. In order to take refuge correctly, one should find a fully ordained ☞BHIKSHU whose daily conduct is fully in accord with the Buddha's teaching and request him to administer the Refuges and to become one's teacher and guide on the Path.

> In taking refuge with the Buddha,
> I vow that living beings
> Will understand the great Path,
> And bring forth the unsurpassed
> resolve (for ***bodhi***).
>
> In taking refuge with the Dharma,
> I vow that living beings
> Will deeply enter the sutra treasury,
> And have wisdom like the sea.
>
> In taking refuge with the Sangha,
> I vow that living beings
> Will unite, forming a Great Assembly,
> In which all will be in harmony.
> (FAS Ch11 116-118)

☞ **Three Jewels**

relics 舍利

'Relics' is a translation of the Sanskrit *śarīra*, which literally means 'body,' but in Buddhist usage most often refers to the sacred relics found in the cremated remains of the Buddha or of a Buddhist monk. After the cremation of the Buddha's body, his relics were distributed and later redistributed by Emperor Aśoka, who built special stupas (Chinese *ta* "pagoda") to house them for worship. Often in the cremated remains of monks who have led extremely pure lives are found *śarīra* of various colors and sizes that sometimes look like effulgent pearls.

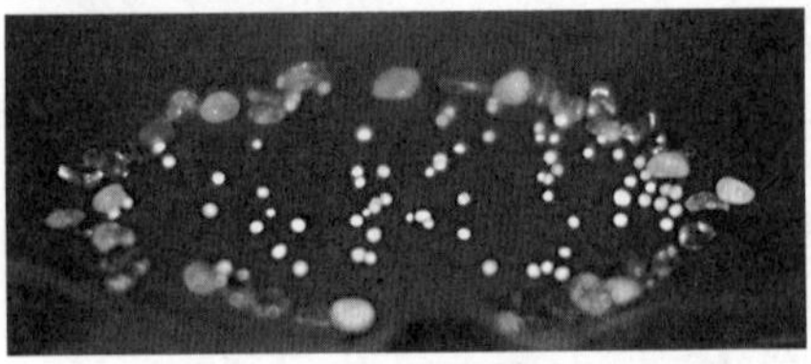

(see plate 27)

Chan Master ☞XUYUN related this experience he had with a relic of the Buddha at Aśoka Monastery:

> Everyday, when visitors came to have a look at the *śarīra*, I always followed them. The visitors' opinions about the relic varied greatly. I had seen it many times; at first it looked to me as of the size of a green bean and of a dark purple color. In the middle of the tenth month, after I had paid reverence to the Mahayana and Hinayana ☞TRIPIṬAKAS, I went again to look and it was the same size as before but like a brilliant red pearl. As I was impatient to see how it would transform itself, I again prostrated myself and felt pains all over my body; the *śarīra* was bigger than a yellow bean, half yellow and half white.
>
> I then realized that its size and color varied according to the visitor's sense organ and its field.... (Luk, *Empty Cloud: The Autobiography of Hsu Yun*)

☞ **remains ⟨holy⟩**
☞ **enlightenment, moral precepts**

repentance 懺悔

I know that my past faults were left uncorrected, yet I know that in the future I may mend my ways. I know that I have not been off the path of confusion for very long, and I am aware of today's rights and yesterday's wrongs. (Tao Yuanming, *Gui qu lai ci* "The Return")

"'Of all bad karma which I have done based on beginningless greed, anger, and delusion, committed by body, mouth, and mind, I now repent and reform.' Greed, anger, and delusion are found at the root of our actions, even those which seem to be motivated by selflessness, love and knowledge. Difficult to understand as this at first seems, it will be born out by sufficient inspection.

"The body, mouth and mind are the vehicles which perform the actions motivated by the three poisons: greed, anger, and delusion. The body is capable of killing, stealing and sexual misconduct. The mouth spews forth false speech, confused prattle, harsh speech, and slander. The mind governs body and mouth through greed, anger, and wrong views. These are called the ten paths of unwholesome conduct, and they constitute the greater part of our conduct. However, they can be transformed into their opposites by our efforts; this is called turning toward the good. To change is simply to repent. Repentance is no emotional outpouring, no futile regret over spilt milk. We regret, we change and that is all there is to it. One gradually learns to stop doing all manner of bad and moves towards all that is good. This is the conduct of the superior person. It is very simply the way by which one begins to leave the confused and troubled state of an ordinary mortal to become a Buddha. It must be done not merely with words and superficial conduct but in the very depths of the mind and consciousness. Therefore, once we begin to put our daily lives in order, we find it necessary to seek out a good advisor. He remonstrates with us and teaches us the proper means of cultivation, and thus we eliminate the accumulated garbage in our minds, stop the deeply ingrained habits which continue to produce ever more garbage, and attain true freedom.

"'Offenses arise from the mind; use the mind to repent. When the mind is forgotten, offenses are no more. Mind forgotten and offenses eradicated, both are empty. This is called true repentance and reform.' The acts of the mind are greed, anger, and delusion. The mind wanders and reels about a universe of its own thinking, planning, scheming, measuring, and calculating. Like a monkey loosed in a grove of ripe fruit trees, the mind clambers on everything, grasping, pulling, and making a general mess. This mad mind directs our daily activities of body and speech; hence all our offenses are ultimately derived from the mind. Everything, in fact, that has name and form, that is labeled and known as distinct from other things, is a product of the mind.

"We must cut off offenses at the root. Thus what we must reform is not merely our behavior but the very depths of our minds. We must take our petty realms of consciousness and expand them until we are capable of including all good deeds as well as bad ones. Reform is in the mind, not in the shallow surface layers of what we know as the thinking mind, but in the deep, hidden wellsprings of consciousness which can only be reached through great effort. When we reach such depths we pass well beyond the limitations of thinking and verbal constructs. This is what is meant by 'mind forgotten.' It is important to understand that this does not imply a simple forgetfulness of our wrong deeds. Rather it is a total passage beyond all normal thought, through which we reach the very source, and there wash off the accumulated dust.

"There are, ultimately, very few who need not listen to the words of the text, for, as it is said:

"The sagely man has few errors;
The superior man changes
his errors;
The petty man hides his errors;
The foolish man sees no errors."
(WM 9-11)

The "Entering the Dharma Realm" chapter of the ☞FLOWER ADORNMENT SUTRA recounts a repentance of the Pure Youth Sudhana [Good Wealth]:

> He remembered how he himself in the past had not practiced bowing and reverence, and he immediately decided that he would practice them with all his might. He further remembered how in the past he had not been pure in body and mind, and he immediately decided that he would concentrate on regulating and cleansing himself. He further remembered how in the past he had created all [sorts of] evil karma, and he immediately decided that he himself would concentrate on avoiding and stopping it.
>
> He further remembered how in the past, he had given rise to all false thoughts, and he immediately decided that he would constantly rectify his thinking. He further remembered how in the past, his cultivation of all practice had only been for the sake of himself, and he immediately decided that he would enlarge the scope of his mind, so that it would universally extend to all conscious beings.
>
> He further remembered how in the past he had intently sought for states of desire, constantly harming and depleting himself, without its having any flavor. And he immediately decided that he would cultivate the Buddhadharma, and nurture all his faculties, and use them to find peace himself.
>
> He further remembered how in the past he had given rise to deviant and distorted reflections. And he immediately decided

that he would produce thoughts of proper views and give rise to the vows of a Bodhisattva. He further remembered how in the past, he had toiled day and night at doing all evil affairs. And he immediately decided that he would bring forth great vigor in accomplishing the Buddhadharmas. He further remembered how in the past he had undergone birth in the Five Destinies without any benefit to himself or to others. And he immediately decided that he wanted to use his body to benefit and aid living beings, accomplish the Buddhadharmas, and attend upon all good knowing advisors.

Upon making such reflections, he became very happy. (EDR VIII 2-4)

The Sixth Patriarch ☞HUINENG explained repentance this way:

What is repentance and what is reform? Repentance is to repent of past errors, to repent so completely of all bad actions done in the past out of foolishness, confusion, arrogance, deceit, jealousy, and other such offenses, that they never arise again. Reform is to refrain from such transgressions in the future. Awakening and cutting off such offenses completely and never committing them again is called repentance and reform.

Common people, foolish and confused, know only how to repent of former errors and do not know how to reform and refrain from transgressions in the future. Because they do not reform, their former errors are not wiped away, and they will occur in the future. If former errors are not wiped away and transgressions are again committed, how can that be called repentance and reform? (PS 178).

Formal repentance is often done publicly, individually before the great assembly, or communally by bowing repentances such as the Great Compassion Repentance or the Repentance before the Ten Thousand Buddhas.

repentance and reform, confession
☞ **One Hundred Dharmas—shame and remorse**

S

Sagely City of Ten Thousand Buddhas
萬佛聖城

A major Buddhist center and pilgrimage site, located in Talmage, California.

The Sagely City of Ten Thousand Buddhas was established in 1976 as the new center for world Buddhism in America. The City was born from the strength, the moral

Entrance (see plate 41)

practice, and the mind-cultivation of the monks and nuns of the Dharma Realm Buddhist Association, which since 1959 has been bringing the genuine teachings of the Buddha to the West.

Guanyin Bodhisattva in the Hall of Ten Thousand Buddhas (see plate 42)

In the beautiful Ukiah valley, 115 miles north of San Francisco, California, sixty-one major buildings are set among orchards, groves, meadows, and farmland on approximately 500 acres. The City includes Dharma Realm Buddhist University, Tathāgata Monastery, Joyous Giving House (convent), the International Institute for the Translation of Buddhist Texts, Instilling Goodness Elementary School and Developing Virtue Secondary School.

In every undertaking at the City of Ten Thousand Buddhas, the intent is to teach the Buddhadharma and to benefit society. All are welcome to come and study, live, work, and practice the Buddha's teachings in harmony. [☞Appendix E]

☞ **Six Principles of the Sagely City of Ten Thousand Buddhas**

Scenes from the Sagely City (see plates 28, 38-43)

Śakra 帝釋

Chief of the gods of the Trayastriṃśa Heaven ['Heaven of the Thirty-three'], one of the Six Desire Heavens.

☞ **Six Desire Heavens, gods**

Śākyamuni 〈Buddha〉 釋迦牟尼《佛》

Śākyamuni Buddha (see plate 37)

The present Buddha of the historical era. According to most, he lived around the sixth century B.C.E. Some traditions place him considerably earlier, some later. His personal name was Siddhārtha, his family name was Gautama. Upon becoming a Buddha he took the name Śākyamuni.

"Śākya [was] the name of the Buddha's clan.... Muni was the Buddha's personal name. It means 'still and quiet' (Ch. *ji mo*). 'Still and unmoving, he is silent.' No words from the mouth, no thoughts from the mind—that is an inconceivable state. The Buddha speaks Dharma without speaking;

he speaks and yet does not speak, does not speak and yet he speaks. This is still and silent, still, still, silent and unmoving, yet responding in accord; responding in accord and yet always, always silent and still. This is the meaning of the Buddha's personal name, Muni. All Buddhas have the title Buddha in common, but only this Buddha has the special name Śākyamuni." (AS 8)

"Why did Śākyamuni Buddha come into the world? Because he saw that all living beings are covered with too much selfishness. He wanted to make it clear to all of us that we shouldn't be so egocentric and only know of ourselves and not know that other people also exist. From selfishness people give rise to strife and kill and mutilate one another. Śākyamuni Buddha saw this situation as something very pathetic; therefore, he came into the world...." (EDR VII 111)

The Life of the Buddha Śākyamuni

The only Buddha to appear in the world in the so-called historical period is the Buddha Śākyamuni. He was born the eldest son of the ruler of a small city state on the border of what is now northern India and Nepal. As a young adult he was struck by the meaninglessness of his life and was moved to give up the kingdom to which he was heir, his parents, wife and young son, and the wealth, pleasures and prerogatives of his position.

As a wandering mendicant he went out into the great forests of northern India in search of a sage to teach him the transcendent path to Reality. In succession he studied with the two greatest meditation teachers of his time and reached those states of cosmic consciousness which they considered true Liberation. After rejecting their ultimacy, he went off to seek his own Path.

First he went to the Himalayas where he meditated for six years while practicing the extreme asceticism of eating only a single grain of wheat and a single sesame seed each day.

> Because I ate so little, all my limbs became like the knotted joints of withered creepers; because I ate so little, my buttocks became like a bullock's hoof; because I ate so little, my protruding backbone became like a string of balls; because I ate so little, my gaunt ribs became like the crazy rafters of a tumble-down shed; because I ate so little, the pupils of my eyes appeared lying low and deep in their sockets as sparkles of water in a deep well appear lying low and deep....But I, even by this procedure, by this course, by this mortification, did not reach the states of further-men or the excellent knowledge and insight befitting the Aryans (i.e., those who are truly noble and holy).... (Chalmers, tr. *Further Dialogues of the Buddha* I 56)

Rejecting such extreme asceticism, the Buddha-to-be made his way down from the mountains, slowly nursed himself back to health, and found an auspicious spot to continue his meditational quest inward. He vowed not to leave that spot, located under a large tree later known as the Bodhi Tree, until he reached his goal. Forty-nine days later, during the second half of the night, he saw a star in the night sky and his last thin strand of attachment was rent asunder. At that moment he became a Buddha, a fully and perfectly enlightened one.

Practicing extreme ascetism (see plate 26)

After remaining seated meditating under the tree for a period of time, he decided to follow that path of those Buddhas who had gone before him and go forth into the world to teach living beings the way to Buddhahood. For forty-nine years he traveled widely in India, together with a great gathering of disciples, teaching all those who sincerely requested instruction. At the end of that period his body died and he was said to have entered ☞ NIRVANA, but for the Buddha at that moment nothing at all really changed.

That is a very brief summary of the important events of the life of the Buddha Śākyamuni. Yet his quest for Buddhahood did not begin with a young prince named Siddhārtha Gautama. The life in which he realized Buddhahood was the culmination of a decision (☞ BODHI RESOLVE) and vows that he made countless lifetimes previously and of intense personal cultivation in each and every lifetime all the way up to that final one over two millennia ago.

☞ **Buddha**

samadhi 三昧/三摩地/定

> When you teach people in the world to cultivate samadhi, they must first of all sever the mind of lust. Therefore, Ānanda, if cultivators of *dhyāna*-samadhi do not eliminate lust, they will be like someone who cooks sand in the hope of getting rice. After hundreds of thousands of aeons it will still just be hot sand. Why? It wasn't rice to begin with; it was only sand. (SS VI 13-14)

> Once your nature is in samadhi and
> the demons are subdued,
> You'll be happy every day.
> If false thoughts do not arise,
> Everywhere you are at peace.
> (FAS Ch11 132)

Samadhi is "a concentrated, self-collected, intent state of mind and meditation, which, concomitant with right living, is a necessary condition to the attainment of higher wisdom and emancipation." (PTSD)

"What is the meaning of proper concentration and proper reception' (i.e., samadhi)? Proper concentration is a state of absorption where the mind is brought into focus which is proper and true and right, not biased or deviant. Proper reception means all that 'comes in'—what you receive at that point—is right and appropriate. But you have to do the cultivation yourself. You can't rely on the Buddhas and Bodhisattvas and expect them to give it to you. If you do the work, then the results are naturally yours." (EDR VII 60)

There are three distinct senses in which the word samadhi is used: **1)** proper concentration, which is a necessary preliminary to the meditative states proper; **2)** a general characteristic of the formal levels of meditational development (☞ FOUR DHYĀNAS, FOUR FORMLESS REALMS), which are entered through one-pointedness of mind; and **3)** enlightened meditational states.

For someone who has the power of samadhi:

> Even when Mount Tai topples over,
> I'm not scared.
> Why? Its toppling over is the same as
> if it hadn't toppled over.
> When a pretty girl appears
> before me, I'm not moved.
> Face to face with her,
> it's as if I wasn't.
> (EDR I 12)

☞ concentration, enstasis, meditative stabilization

☞ Eightfold Path, Six Pāramitās—samadhi, meditation, lotus posture, Three Aspects of Learning to Be Without Outflows, Four Dhyānas, Four Formless Realms

Samantabhadra 〈Bodhisattva〉 普賢《菩薩》

☞ Universal Worthy 〈Bodhisattva〉

saṃsāra 流轉/生死/輪迴

A Sanskrit word meaning 'going or wandering through,' 'undergoing transformation.' It refers to the continuous flowing through the suffering of repeated lives and deaths. It is contrasted with ☞ NIRVANA.

Sangha 僧伽

> Full of hindrances is a household life; it is a path for the grime of passion. Free as the air is the life of him who has renounced all worldly things. How difficult is it for the man who dwells at home to live the higher life in all its fullness, in all its purity, in all its bright perfection. Let me then cut off my hair and beard, let me clothe myself in the orange-coloured robes, and let me go forth from the household life into the homeless state. (Rhys Davids, tr. *Digha-Nikāya* II, 41; v. 1, 62)

> Worthy of honour are they [the Sangha], worthy of reverences, worthy of offerings, worthy of salutations with clasped hands,—a field of merit unsurpassed for the world. (Woodward, F.L. tr. "Itivuttaka: As It Was Said," 179)

Sangha is a Sanskrit word meaning 'community' and in Buddhism refers to the monastic community of monks (Bhikshus) and nuns (Bhikshunis). They are the transmitters of the tradition and the teachers of the lay community. Fully ordained members of the Sangha adhere to a large number of moral precepts, including celibacy, as a guide for their behavior. The Sangha is the third of the ☞ THREE JEWELS.

A distinction can be made dividing Sangha into three types: the Sangha of the Buddhas, the Sangha of the Sages, and the Sangha which is a Field of Blessings.

1 The Sangha of the Buddhas is comprised of all the infinite Buddhas in all world systems.
2 The Sangha of the Sages is comprised of fully enlightened beings, who have been certified as having reached one of the Four Stages of Arhatship, Pratyekabuddhahood, or one of the Bodhisattva stages (☞ ARHAT, PRATYEKABUDDHA, BODHISATTVA).
3 Of the Sangha which is a Field of Blessings the *Six Pāramitās Sutra* says:

> The Sangha is a field of blessings. They are the Bhikshus and Bhikshunis who receive and uphold the moral prohibitions, are learned and wise, and, like trees created by the gods, are able to protect living beings. It is as when thirsty, in need of water in a barren desert, one meets with a heavenly sweet rain in a vast downpour, which is both timely and satisfying. Moreover, it is like the great ocean from which comes all the multitudes of treasures. The Sangha Jewel, as a field of blessings is also like this. It is able to bestow peace and bliss upon all sentient beings. Moreover, this Sangha Jewel is pure and undefiled. It is able to dispel the darkness of living beings' greed, anger, and delusion, as the bright light on the evening of the

> full moon, which all sentient beings gaze upon with awe. It is also like a precious *maṇi* pearl, that can fulfill all the good wishes of sentient beings. (BTTS ms.)

In the Dharma-Ending Age the Buddha predicted that demonic forces would destroy the Buddhadharma by infiltrating the Sangha and undermining it from within. (☞ DHARMA-ENDING AGE—*The Buddha Speaks the Sutra of the Ultimate Extinction of the Dharma*)

community ⟨monastic⟩, Order

☞ **Three Jewels, Bhikshu, Bhikshuni, moral precepts**

Sanskrit 梵文

The classical language of ancient India. In India it functioned as a *lingua franca* in much the same way as Latin did in medieval Europe. In India Buddhist texts were written either in Sanskrit or in closely related 'dialects,' which were natural spoken languages, such as Pali or Buddhist Hybrid Sanskrit.

☞ **Pali**

Śāriputra ⟨Venerable⟩ 舍利弗《尊者》

One of the ten great Arhat disciples of the Buddha who was known for his great wisdom.

"Śāriputra's name is Sanskrit. It means 'son of Śārī [from *śārikā*, a bird with large and beautiful eyes, probably an Indian pelican]'. His mother was named Śārī because her eyes were as keen and beautiful as those of the *śārikā* bird. *Putra* means 'son.' Another explanation of Śāriputra's name is 'body-son,' after the Sanskrit word for body, *śarīra*, because his mother was physically very beautiful. Śāriputra also means 'pearl-son' because his eyes were like pearls and *śarīra* is also the term for the pearl-like relics left after the cremation of a sage (☞ RELICS).

"Śāriputra was the foremost of the *śrāvaka* disciples in wisdom. He wasn't exactly number two when it came to spiritual powers either. His spiritual powers were also great. One time ☞ MAHĀMAUDGALYĀYANA decided to compare his spiritual powers with Śāriputra's. Śākyamuni Buddha had gone elsewhere to speak the Dharma. When he did this, his disciples always went along to hear the Dharma too because they didn't have any tape recorders in those days, and if they missed a lecture they couldn't make it up. That time Śāriputra had entered ☞ SAMADHI. Mahāmaudgalyāyana called to him, but he wouldn't come out of samadhi. 'All right,' said Mahāmaudgalyāyana, 'I'll use my spiritual powers to snap you out of it,' and he applied every ounce of spiritual power he had to get Śāriputra to come out of samadhi, but he couldn't budge even so much as the corner of Shariputra's robe. How great would you say Shariputra's spiritual powers were? Mahāmaudgalyāyana was generally considered foremost in spiritual powers, but he lost to Śāriputra...." (DFS II 108-109)

This is the way Śāriputra first heard of the Buddha and his teaching:

> Sāriputta [i.e., Śāriputra] said to the venerable Assaji [i.e., Aśvajit]: "Your countenance, friend, is serene; your complexion is pure and bright. In whose name, friend, have you retired from the world? Who is your teacher? What doctrine do you profess?"
>
> [Assaji replied]: "There is, friend, the great Samaṇa Sakyaputta [i.e., Śākyamuni Buddha], an ascetic of the Śākya tribe; in His, the Blessed One's, name have I retired

from the world; He, the Blessed One, is my teacher; and His, the Blessed One's, doctrine do I profess."

"And what is the doctrine, Sir, which your teacher holds, and preaches to you?"

"I am only a young disciple, friend; I have but recently received the ordination; and I have newly adopted this doctrine and discipline. I cannot explain to you the doctrine in detail; but I will tell you in short what it means."

Then the paribbājaka [i.e., wandering monk] Śāriputta said to the venerable Assagi: "Well, friend, tell me much or little as you like but be sure to tell me the spirit of the doctrine; I want but the spirit; why do you make so much of the letter?"

Then the venerable Assaji pronounced to the paribbājaka Sāriputta the following text of the Dhamma: "Of all objects which proceed from cause, the Tathāgata has explained the cause, and He has explained their cessation also; this is the doctrine of the great Samaṇa."

And the paribbājaka Sāriputta after having heard this text obtained the pure and spotless Eye of the Truth (that is, the following knowledge): "Whatsoever is subject to the condition of origination is subject also to the condition of cessation." (And he said): "If this alone be the Doctrine the Dhamma), now you have reached up to the state where all sorrow ceases (i.e. Nirvāṇa), (the state) which has remained unseen through many myriads of Kappas [Skt. *kalpa*, i.e.,world-ages] of the past." (Rhys Davids, tr. *Vinaya Texts* I 145-147)

Śāriputra then went to his close friend of many lifetimes, Maudgalyāyana, who also awakened to the teaching. The two then went to leave the home-life under Śākyamuni Buddha.

In the ☞ŚŪRAṄGAMA SUTRA Śāriputra explains the method he used to attain enlightenment:

From distant *kalpas* until the present, my mind and views have been pure. In this way I have undergone as many births as there are grains of sand in the Ganges. As to the various transformations and changes of both the mundane and the transcendental, I am able to understand them at one glance and obtain nonobstruction....

I followed the Buddha and left the home-life. My seeing-awareness became bright and perfect. I obtained fearlessness and became an Arhat. As one of the Buddha's elder disciples, I am born from the Buddha's mouth, transformationally born from the Dharma.

The Buddha asks about perfect penetration. As I have been certified to it, for the mind and the seeing to emit light and for the light to reach throughout knowing and seeing is the foremost method. (SS V 62-65)

The ☞HEART SUTRA and many of the other teachings of the *prajñā-pāramitā* sutras are addressed to Śāriputra in order to get him to turn from the Hinayana to the Mahayana [☞MAHAYANA AND HINAYANA COMPARED].

☞ **Arhat, Mahāmaudgalyāyana ⟨Venerable⟩, Bodhisattva—"The Venerable Śāriputra Tries to Cultivate the Path of the Bodhisattva"**

śarīra/sharira 舍利

☞ relics

śāstra 論

Śāstra is a Sanskrit term that can refer either to a commentary on one of the sutras or to an independent treatise on some aspect or aspects of the Buddhadharma.

"*Śāstras* are discussions. First of all, they tell what is right and what is wrong. Right is right and wrong is definitely wrong. One must not take what is right as wrong, nor should one take what is wrong as right. And so we should discuss things and in this way come to understand them clearly. For people who leave the home-life, cultivation is right and failing to cultivate is wrong.

"The second thing that *śāstras* discuss is what is deviant and what is proper. What is deviant is definitely deviant and what is proper is decidedly proper. You must not take what is deviant and consider it to be proper, nor take what is proper and consider it deviant. That's another reason why there must be discussions.

"The third reason for discussion is to distinguish good and evil. Good is good and evil is evil. You cannot regard what is good as being evil, nor regard what is evil as being good.

"The fourth function of *śāstras* is to discuss cause and effect. A cause is decidedly a cause and an effect is definitely an effect. You can't call a cause an effect, nor an effect a cause. You must make your discriminations clearly.

"The fifth aspect of *śāstras* is to clarify defilement and purity. Defilement is defilement and purity is purity. You must not take defilement to be purity or purity to be defilement. You must not be upside down. And so what *śāstras* do is discriminate these clearly." (HD 7)

✍ **discourse; commentary; treatise, discussion**
☞ **Tripiṭaka, Abhidharma**

Shide 〈Chan Master〉 拾得《禪師》

☞ **Hanshan and Shide 〈Bodhisattvas〉**

Six Desire Heavens 六欲天

The Six Desire Heavens are: **1)** Heaven of the Four Kings, **2)** Heaven of the Thirty-three [Trayastriṃśa], **3)** Suyāma Heaven, **4)** Heaven of Contentment [Tuṣita], **5)** Transformation of Bliss Heaven, and **6)** Heaven of Sovereignty over Others' Transformations.

> In the Heaven of Four Kings
> and the Trayastriṃśa,
> Desire is carried out through
> embracing.
> In the Suyāma Heaven
> they hold hands;
> In the Tuṣita they smile;
> In the Bliss by Transformation
> they gaze;
> In the Sovereignty over Others
> a glance will do.
> (SS VII 206, SPV 54)

Heaven of the Four Kings

Ānanda, there are many people in the world who do not seek what is eternal and who cannot yet renounce the kindness and love they feel for their wives. But they have no interest in deviant sexual activity and so develop a purity and produce light. When their lives end, they draw near the sun and moon and are among those born in the Heaven of the Four Kings. (SS VII 198)

"The Heaven of the Four Kings is located halfway up Mount Sumeru. It is the heaven closest to our human realm. The gods in this heaven have a life span of five hundred [celestial] years. One day and night in that heaven is equivalent to fifty years in the human realm, and so their life span is nine million years if calculated according to our time." (SS VII 199)

"In the east is a king named He Who Maintains the Country [Skt. Dhṛtarāṣṭra]; in the south is a king named Increase and Growth [Skt. Virūḍhaka]; in the west is a king named Wide Eyes [Skt. Virūpākṣa]; and in the north is a king named Much Learning [Skt. Vaiśravaṇa], who is also known as Extensive Renown. The gods in this heaven are half a ☞ *yojana* tall.... Because this heaven is extremely close to us, its inhabitants watch over the affairs of human beings." (SPV 53)

Heaven of the Four Kings

Heaven of the Thirty-three

Those whose sexual love for their wives is slight, but who have not yet obtained the entire flavor of dwelling in purity, transcend the light of sun and moon at the end of their lives and reside at the summit of the human realm. They are among those born in the Trayastriṃśa Heaven. (SS VII 199)

"*Trayastriṃśa* is Sanskrit and means "Heaven of the Thirty-three.' The Lord of the Heaven of the Thirty-three resides above our heads. There are eight heavens in the east, eight in the west, eight in the north, and eight in the south, making thirty-two; the thirty-third is located in the center of the others and is at the peak of Mount Sumeru." (SS VII 201)

"*Trayastriṃśa*, 'Heaven of the Thirty-three,' is not thirty-third in a vertical arrangement of heavens. Vertically it occupies the second position among eighteen heavens. Its name is taken from the fact that it is the central one among a group of heavens located on the same plane, with eight heavens on each of its four sides. The lord of the central heaven, the thirty-third, is named ☞ ŚAKRA or Indra, and in Buddhism he is a protector of the Buddha's Dharma who does not merit a seat but must stand at all Dharma meetings. In the ☞ ŚŪRAṄGAMA MANTRA he is referred to in the phrase, 'Namo Yin Tuo La Ye.'

"The lord of this heaven is the one taken by most people as being God Almighty, ruler of heaven and earth. Although he is extremely powerful and attends to divine matters as well as earthly ones, he is not really different from ordinary people, since he still has sexual desires, and eats, drinks, and sleeps. Although he still has desires, they are far lighter than those of humans, who usually become famished after several days without food, exhausted after a few hours without sleep, and frustrated after a short time without sexual activity. ☞ ŚAKRA can go for one, two, or even three hundred days without eating and can pass a year or so without sleep or sex. Although his desires are light, he has still not eliminated them.

"The Heaven of the Thirty-three is eighty thousand *yojanas* high, and its city, the City of Good View, is made of the seven precious materials and is sixty thousand *yojanas* high. In the center of that city is Śakra's palace, which is made of the most exquisite and valuable gems. Since he is constantly surrounded by such splendor, Śakra has no desire to leave. In fact, he wants all beings to join him in this world, where the life span is a thousand [celestial] years and where one century in the human world is but a day and a night. He extends his hospitality but doesn't know that because of his greed for heavenly delights, even he is doomed." (SPV 25-26)

"At the time of Kāśyapa Buddha, Śakra was a very ordinary and poor woman who saw a temple in ruins and vowed to restore it. Soliciting friends and relatives, she gradually gathered a group of thirty-two women. She herself was the thirty-third. Each of the thirty-three gave as much support as she could muster and with their collective effort they repaired the ruined temple. When each one died she ascended to the heavens and became ruler of her own heaven. The heaven in which Śakra, the former leader of the women, lives, is called the Trayastriṃśa Heaven....

"The thirty-three heavens are merely responses evoked from the ☞KARMA of those thirty-three persons. If it were not for them, there would be no such heavens. Heaven, you see, is merely a spontaneous manifestation of karma and exists only as such. In fact, the heavens are ephemeral, not permanent places of abode, and they should not be considered one's ultimate goal." (SPV 26)

Suyāma Heaven

Those who become temporarily involved when they meet with desire but who forget about it when it is finished, and who, while in the human realm, are active less and quiet more, abide at the end of their lives in light and emptiness where the illumination of the sun and moon does not reach. These beings have their own light, and they are among those born in the Suyāma Heaven. (SS VII 201)

"The Suyāma, "well-divided time," Heaven is a heaven located so high above Mount Sumeru that the light of the sun and moon cannot reach it. It is light there, however, because the gods all emit light. Because there is no light from the sun or moon, time is measured by the opening and closing of lotus flowers; when the lotuses are open, it is day, and when they are closed, night has arrived. The inhabitants of this heaven are two *yojanas* tall and live for two thousand [celestial] years. Throughout all these heavens, height and life span double in each successive heaven." (SPV 53-54)

Heaven of Contentment

Those who are quiet all the time, but who are not yet able to resist when stimulated by contact, ascend at the end of their lives to a subtle and ethereal place; they will not be drawn into the lower realms. The destruction of the realms of humans and gods and the obliteration of *kalpas* by the three disasters will not reach them, for they are among those born in the Tuṣita Heaven. (SS VII 202)

One of the
Four Heavenly Kings

S

"The Tuṣita, or 'contentment,' Heaven is divided into an inner or an outer court. The outer courtyard is subject to destruction by the three disasters of fire, water, and wind, which occur at the end of *kalpas*, but the inner courtyard is not." (SPV 54)

Heaven of Bliss by Transformation

Those who are devoid of desire, but who will engage in it for the sake of their partner, even though the flavor of doing so is like the flavor of chewing on wax, are born at the end of their lives in a place of transcending transformations. They are among those born in the Heaven of Bliss by Transformation. (SS VII 204)

Heaven of Sovereignty over Others' Transformations

Those who have no kind of worldly thoughts while doing what worldly people do, who are lucid and beyond such activity while involved in it, are capable at the end of their lives of entirely transcending states where transformations may be present and may be lacking. They are among those born in the Heaven of the Sovereignty over Others' Transformations. (SS VII 205)

"The gods of the Heaven of Sovereignty over Others' Transformations obtain their bliss through transforming it away from other heavens. [Many of] those who live in this heaven are neither genuine spirits nor immortals but heavenly demons." (SPV 54)

☞ **gods, Six Paths of Rebirth**

Six Pāramitās 六波羅蜜/六度

The Six Pāramitās are: **1)** giving, **2)** moral precepts, **3)** patience, **4)** vigor, **5)** meditational concentration, **6)** wisdom.

Good man, the Bodhisattva, Mahāsattva, takes *prajñā-pāramitā* [the perfection of wisdom] as his mother, clever expedients as his father, *dāna-pāramitā* [the perfection of giving] as his wet-nurse, *śīla-pāramitā* [the perfection of morality] as his foster mother, the *pāramitā* of patience as his adornments, the *pāramitā* of vigor as his nourishment, and *dhyāna-pāramitā* [the perfection of meditational concentration] as the one who cleanses him. (EDR VIII 132)

The Buddha knows the hearts
of living beings,
And each of their different natures.
According with what they
ought to receive,
In that way he speaks the Dharma.
For those who are stingy,
he lauds giving.
For those who break the prohibitions,
he praises the precepts.
For those with much anger,
he praises patience.
For the lazy, he lauds vigor.
For those with scattered minds,
he praises *dhyāna*-concentration.
For the ignorant, he praises wisdom.
(FAS Ch10 ms.)

Giving

The Buddha said:

Wishing to perfect the ☞SIX PĀRAMITĀS, I diligently practiced giving, my mind not begrudging elephants, horses, the seven precious things, countries, cities, wives, children, slaves, servants, even my head, eyes, marrow, brains, body, flesh, hands, and feet—not sparing even life itself. (DFS X 4)

"Giving transforms those who are stingy. Greedy people who can't give should practice giving, for if they do not learn to give, they will never get rid of their stinginess." (AS 4)

There are three major categories of giving: **a)** the giving of wealth, **b)** the giving of Dharma, and **c)** the giving of fearlessness.

There is giving of both "inner and outer wealth. Outer wealth includes one's country, wife, and children. The sutras abound with stories of people giving up their wives and children. A few years ago, a laywoman also resolved to give up her husband, but nobody wanted him! From this you can see that a husband is not that easy to give away. Inner wealth refers to one's own head, brain, eyes, marrow—parts of one's own body." (EDR V 212)

"What is meant by the giving of Dharma? It is to speak the Dharma to benefit living beings, to teach and transform all living beings by explaining the Buddhadharma for them. Of all offerings, the Dharma-offering is supreme...." (DFS II 132)

The first pāramitā is giving to those in need.

Good man, amongst all offerings, the Offering of Dharma is most supreme. This is the offering of cultivating according to the teachings, the offering of benefitting living beings, the offering of gathering in living beings, the offering of standing in for living beings who are undergoing suffering, the offering of diligently cultivating good roots, the offering of not renouncing the karma of the Bodhisattva and the offering of never forsaking the Bodhi mind. (UW 59)

"If someone encounters a frightening experience and you comfort them and deliver them from distress and terror, you have made a gift of fearlessness." (EDR V 215)

Moral Precepts

"The precepts are guides to perfect conduct and eliminate offenses, transgressions, and evil deeds." (AS 4)

"The Perfection of Morality means guarding against offenses in seven departments. The seven divisions are: three of the body and four of the mouth—killing, stealing, and sexual misconduct with the body, and loose speech, lying, harsh speech, and backbiting with the mouth...." (DFS X 5)

☞ **moral precepts, Five Moral Precepts**

Patience

Patience is a priceless gem,
Which few know how to mine;
But if you can master it,
Everything works out fine.
(DFS II 135)

"Patience transforms those who are hateful. If you have an unreasonable temper, cultivate being patient and bearing with things. Don't be an *asura*, a fighter who gets angry all day and is not on speaking terms with anyone unless it's to speak while glaring with fierce, angry eyes. Be patient instead." (AS 4)

"Patience means to bear insult. It means to take what you can't take. For example, if someone hits you or scolds and you don't retaliate in any way, you are being patient. If someone hits you and you kick them right back, you can't call that patience; but if someone hits you on the face and you turn the other cheek, you are practicing patience. Besides, if they just slap one cheek and not the other, the other cheek will get jealous! Not striking back is having patience." (DFS X 5)

The Bodhisattva Maitreya, who will be the next to become a Buddha, excels in the *pāramitā* of patience. For his song on patience, ☞MAITREYA.

Vigor

"There are two types of vigor: physical and mental." (DFS II 135)

"Vigor transforms those who are lazy." (AS 4)

"This means that you finish everything that you start. If you start things with great excitement, but then get tired and quit, you do not have vigor. Completing the job indicates vigor." (DFS X 5)

Meditational Concentration

"*Dhyāna* meditation transforms those who are scattered and confused." (AS 4)

Meditational concentration includes the ☞FOUR DHYĀNAS and the Four Stations of Emptiness.

Wisdom

"*Prajñā*-wisdom transforms those who are deluded; the bright light of wisdom disperses the darkness of delusion." (AS 4)

"With this perfection, one no longer contends or fights. People fight because they lack genuine wisdom, genuine *prajñā*. If one has true wisdom, one won't fight or struggle." (DFS X 6)

For more information on the *prajñā-pāramitā*, ☞PRAJÑĀ, EMPTINESS.

In some sutras a list of ten *pāramitās* is also found. The first six are the same as listed above. They are followed by the *pāramitās* of expedient means, vows, powers, and knowledge.

perfections, mastery, supremacy, supreme virtues, completeness, highest state, crossing to the other shore

☞ **pāramitā, Bodhisattva**

Six Paths of Rebirth 六道輪迴

The Six Paths of Rebirth are: **1)** gods, **2)** humans, **3)** *asuras*, **4)** animals, **5)** ghosts, and **6)** hell-dwellers.

The Six Paths of Rebirth, also called the Six Destinies, refer to the six categories of living beings who are not enlightened. The particular category that one finds oneself reborn in depends upon one's karma at the time of rebirth (☞KARMA, REBIRTH).

The Six Paths of Rebirth are part of the Ten Dharma Realms.

six destinies, six courses of existence

☞ **Ten Dharma Realms, the entries for the individual destinies**

Six Principles of the Sagely City of Ten Thousand Buddhas 萬佛聖城六大宗旨

The Six Principles of the City of Ten Thousand Buddhas are: **1)** no contention; **2)** no greed; **3)** no seeking; **4)** no selfishness; **5)** no seeking personal advantage; and **6)** no lying.

"If each of you can stop all contention, and curb your greed; if you can stop seeking, stop being selfish and wanting self-benefit, and cease being dishonest, then the Proper Dharma will remain long in the world. Why? Because these Six Guiding Principles of the City of Ten Thousand Buddhas are the Proper Dharma. They are simply the Buddha's precepts.

"For example, the first principle, no contention, is the precept against taking life. Why would somebody take another's life? Because of a thought of contention. A verse says:

> Contention breeds an attitude
> of victory and defeat,
> Contrary to the teaching of the Way.
> With a mind full of self and others,
> and beings who pass away,
> What hope do you have
> of accomplishing samadhi?

"If you must be a winner, then someone else must lose. As soon as you contend, you chase away your proper concentration power.

"The second principle, no greed, is the precept against theft. No greed means subduing all thoughts of craving possessions or experiences that do not rightly belong to you. Instead of craving things, people should think, 'If it is not mine, I do not want it.'

"The third principle, no seeking, can counteract promiscuous behavior. The reason why people lose control and want to break the rules is simply because they are seeking something. This impulse to seek and possess is the underlying cause of reckless behavior between men and women.

"The fourth principle is not being selfish. An unselfish individual is incapable of lying. Unselfish people do not even think of cheating others. Why would someone deceive society? Because he wants to siphon off benefits that ought to go to others. This is selfishness in a nutshell: stealing advantages from others.

"Wanting personal advantage seems almost identical with selfishness, but there is a difference: selfishness is an inner disposition, whereas personal advantage is expressed outside. Personal advantage is visible; selfishness is invisible.

"And so the fourth principle, no selfishness, is the precept against telling lies, and the fifth, not wanting personal advantage, is the precept against using intoxicants. Refraining from intoxicants includes not smoking tobacco and not using illegal drugs, as well as not gambling. In general, doing things that exclusively benefit oneself, regardless of their impact on others, is called self-benefit.

"Our job as Buddhist disciples is to look after the interests of all living beings, and to keep the entire world in our purview. Instead of thinking only of our own narrow, tiny sphere, we should reach out to benefit all mankind. Thus, not wanting personal advantage is simply the precept against intoxicants.

"How did the sixth principle come about? For a long time we propagated Five Principles, until we convened the first Board of Directors meeting at Gold Buddha Monastery in Canada. One of the directors exclusively cheated people and habitually told lies. His tactic was to intimidate people, much the same way a terrorist acts. He would approach people and say, 'How did you catch that ghost!' or, 'I see you have got a lot of spirits following you!' or, 'I see you are about to run into some bad trouble.' If asked, he denied accepting or soliciting money. 'I am not interested in making money,' he'd assert. But, all the same, for him to read 'the wind and water' (*feng shui*) of someone's house or land cost at least $500 for the first look. To cure illnesses cost even more. Thus, the sixth principle, no lying, came about.

"I announced at that meeting, 'Anyone who tells lies or cheats people and is discovered by others will be thrown out and never be allowed back in.'

"He spoke right up, 'Oh, I'm afraid I'll be the first one out the door' I answered, 'Now that you know the rules, following them is all that is necessary. After this, stop being dishonest and there's no problem.' And that's how the sixth principle came about.

"If you do not fight and contend, then you will not harm your compassionate nature. When you learn to curb your greed, your righteous and noble qualities shine forth. If you can rest content and not need to seek outside, then you will not violate propriety. By refraining from sexual misconduct, you preserve your very life. Lust harms your life. Being unselfish increases and protects your samadhi. If you are selfish, your concentration-power will scatter and fail. If you have no thought of scheming for self-benefit, you will be replete with wisdom. Wanting personal advantages harms your wisdom. And, if you tell lies, you will undermine your very foundation as a person. Dishonesty will leave you bankrupt—you'll have nothing at all.'

"By casting out these six black clouds that cover over your nature, the inherent and bright virtues of your true nature shine forth. The Six Principles of the Sagely City of Ten Thousand Buddhas are just the Five Moral Precepts in another guise. They are also the heart of the Proper Dharma." (BTTS ms.)

1) no strife, non-contention; 2) no greed/craving/desire, generosity; 3) no grasping/actions based on greed, contentment; 4) unselfishness; 5) incorruptibility, no pursuit of personal advantage; 6) truthfulness, no deceitful speech, no dishonesty, honesty

☞ **Five Moral Precepts, moral precepts, Sagely City of Ten Thousand Buddhas**

Six Spiritual Powers 六神通

The Six Spiritual Powers are: **1)** the spiritual power of the heavenly eye, **2)** the spiritual power of the heavenly ear, **3)** the spiritual power of knowledge of past lives, **4)** the spiritual power of knowledge of the minds of others, **5)** powers derived from a spiritual basis, **6)** the spiritual power of freedom from outflows.

All the gods of the ☞THREE WORLDS have the first five spiritual powers to some degree. ☞GHOSTS and spirits also have some small degree of spiritual power. Those of non-Buddhist religions who cultivate can at the very most only attain the first five. Only one whose enlightenment is certified achieves the sixth, freedom from outflows.

On the level of the ☞ARHAT, the powers are still small. If an Arhat wishes to use one of them, he must first make a point of making himself still, sitting quietly for a while. Only then can he find out what he wishes to know. ☞BODHISATTVAS, however, without wishing, without acting, naturally and at every instant have great spiritual power without measure or limit. This is an inconceivably wonderful fruit of the ☞MAHAYANA.

The Spiritual Power of the Heavenly Eye

"With the heavenly eye one can see the gods and observe all their activities." (AS 5)

"A power that enables one to see an entire world system of a billion worlds as clearly as an apple held in the palm. The Buddha's disciple, the Venerable Aniruddha, was foremost in this power." (SPV 26)

"With it you can see what is inside your own body, all the living beings within you that you must vow to save. Although scientists cannot count the number of living beings inside the human body, if you have the heavenly eye you can see them, count them, and liberate them.... You can even count up the grains of rice you eat. You can see how your meal is being digested in your stomach...." (DFS IV 808-809)

The Spiritual Power of the Heavenly Ear

"With the heavenly ear one can hear the speech and sound of the gods." (AS 5)

"A power by means of which one can hear all the sounds in a world system of a billion worlds, not merely the sounds in the heavens." (SPV 27)

"With the heavenly ear, not only can you hear what the gods are saying, but you can hear all of the little 'bugs' inside of you calling out. You can hear the germs talking, the flowers talking, and the trees talking. Some people say that when you go pick a flower it is afraid and lets out a scream. That's right. 'Oh no! This is it! It's all over. I'm going to die!!!' When you start hearing all these sounds, though, you shouldn't dislike it. You can choose not to listen to them, too. It's up to you. The heavenly eye sees more clearly than an x-ray machine, and the heavenly ear hears more clearly than sonar equipment." (DFS IV 809)

The Spiritual Power of the Knowledge of Past Lives

"A power that enables one to know past events, both good and bad." (SPV 27)

> A ☞ŚRAMAṆA asked: "What are the causes and conditions by which one comes to know past lives and by which one's understanding enables one to attain the Way?"
>
> The Buddha said: "By purifying the mind and guarding the will, your understanding can enable you to attain the Way. Just as when you polish a mirror, the dust vanishes and brightness remains, so too, if you eliminate desire and do not seek (for anything), you can then know past lives." (S42 35)

The Spiritual Power of the Knowledge of the Minds of Others

"A power through which others' thoughts are known before they are even spoken." (SPV 27)

Powers Derived from a Spiritual Basis

This "refers to all kinds of powers of magical transformation. You can be sitting in one place and at the same time go off to New York to play. You can go take a look at things in L.A. It won't take you one second to make your return trip either...." (DFS VII 1296)

[A Bodhisattva who has this power]

> ...can move the great earth. He can make one body into many bodies, and many bodies into one body. He can either disappear or appear. He goes through stone walls and solid mountains as if they were space. In empty space he travels in full lotus, just like a bird in flight. He enters earth as if it were water, and treads upon water as if it were earth. His body puts forth smoke and flames like an immense heap of fire. He further sends down rain just like a mighty cloud. The sun and moon in space have tremendous, awesome might, yet he can touch and rub them with his hand. His body is free and at ease, even up to the world of Brahma.... (FAS Ch26(2) 116)

The Spiritual Power of Freedom from Outflows

☞OUTFLOWS refer to all our faults, especially ignorance and desire, which cause us to expend energy outward as we seek pleasure in external sense-objects.

"To be without outflows is to have no thoughts of greed, anger, delusion, or sexual desire. In general, once one gets rid of all one's bad habits and faults, one has no outflows. Outflows are like water running out of a leaky bottle; at the stage of no outflows the leaks have been stopped up." (AS 6)

Consider a "teacup. Does it have any holes in it, any outflows? It has no outflows, of course, and so it can hold the tea.... Would you say that our bodies have outflows or not? Hah! Our bodies are bottomless pits. You fill your body up today and tomorrow it all runs out....Obviously one's excrement and urine are outflows. They flow out, and we have practically no control over it. Our bodies have nine orifices which constantly secrete impure substances. ...But, these are very common, ordinary outflows and aren't that important. The greatest outflows are the ones you aren't even aware of: greed, anger, delusion, pride, and doubt....In general, outflows are none other than our afflictions...." (DFS VII 1281-1285)

"What are outflows? Do you like to eat? That is an outflow. Do you like to drink coffee? That is an outflow. Women like men; that is an outflow. Men like women; that is an outflow.

"'What can you do that isn't an outflow?' you ask.

"Cultivate! That's simply all there is to it. First and foremost, you have to cultivate. If you cultivate, you can be without outflows. If you do not cultivate, you cannot be without outflows. There's simply no way around it.

"'I'd rather have outflows than cultivate,' you say.

"If that's what you'd like, if it suits you to have outflows, then go ahead and 'flow out.' Let's see where you 'flow out' to. You could flow out and turn into a pig, or a horse, or an ox, or flow out into the hells, into the path of animals, or hungry ghosts. You pick your own path...." (DFS IV 808)

spiritual penetrations, psychic powers, superknowledges, higher or supernatural knowledge, intuition; apperceptions, clarities

☞ **enlightenment, Five Eyes, no outflows**

Sixth Patriarch's Dharma Jewel Platform Sutra 六祖法寶壇經

One of the foremost scriptures of Chan Buddhism, this text describes the life and teachings of the remarkable Patriarch of the Tang Dynasty, Great Master ☞HUINENG, who, though unable to read or write, was enlightened to the true nature of all things.

☞ **Huineng 〈Chan Master/Patriarch〉**

Small Vehicle 小乘

☞ **Mahayana and Hinayana Compared**

Sound Hearer 聲聞

☞ **śrāvaka**

Southern Buddhism 南傳佛教

☞ **Theravada Buddhism**

śramaṇa 沙門

Those who take leave of their families and go forth from the home-life, who recognize their minds and penetrate to their origin, and who understand the unconditioned Dharma, are called *śramaṇas*. Constantly observing the 250 precepts, they enter into and abide in purity. By practicing the four true paths [i.e., ☞FOUR HOLY TRUTHS] they become Arhats. (S42 1)

"*Śramaṇa* is a Sanskrit word that means 'diligently putting to rest.' The *śramaṇa* diligently cultivates precepts, samadhi, and wisdom, and he puts to rest and extinguishes greed, anger, and delusion." (S42 2-3)

Śramaṇa and Bhikshu are synonyms, both appellations for fully ordained Buddhist monks. The Buddha was also called 'the great *śramaṇa*.'

monkhood, religious wanderer or recluse
Bhikshu, Sangha

śrāvaka 聲聞

The *śrāvaka* Sangha,
Both men and women,
Contemplate and practice
the Four Holy Truths,
Concealing the real and
displaying the provisional.
(TD 33)

Śrāvaka is Sanskrit and literally means "one who hears or listens." It is traditionally explained as referring to those who "hear the sound of the Buddha's teaching and awaken to the Way."

"They become enlightened as soon as they hear the Buddha speak the Dharma of the FOUR HOLY TRUTHS. They are one of the TWO VEHICLES. They feel that everything in this world is suffering, empty, without a self, and impermanent, and so are determined to end birth and death. They have the outlook that:

"The Three Realms are like a prison.
Birth and death are like hateful
enemies.

"To them the Desire Realm, the Form Realm, and the Formless Realm seem like a penitentiary, and they detest birth and death. Their attitude is, 'I absolutely must end birth and death, and until I do, I won't rest for even a day.' Therefore, they cultivate all kinds of ascetic practices to cast off birth and death—which is the attachment of Sound Hearers (*śrāvaka*)....

"Sound Hearers are basically Arhats who have certified to the First, Second, Third, and Fourth Fruits. Yet they too fail to recognize the Thus Come One's Treasury, for they only know the emptiness of people, unlike commoners who are attached in every respect to views of self and what belongs to a self saying, 'This is mine; this belongs to me.' Those of the Two Vehicles are not attached to self, but they are attached to dharmas. They don't understand that:

Even dharmas must be renounced,
How much the more non-dharmas.

One has to put down all dharmas, how much more what is not in accord with Dharma. But for them dharmas are not yet empty, and so they still have attachments and are of the SMALL VEHICLE." (FAS-PII(2) 57)

The first *śrāvakas* were the five former companions of the Buddha who became enlighted after hearing the Buddha explain the Four Holy Truths in the Deer Park at Vārāṇasī.

Śrāvaka is often used synonymously with ARHAT.

Four Kinds of Sound Hearers *(Śrāvakas)*

1 Fixed Sound Hearers
2 Sound Hearers of Overweening Pride
3 Sound Hearers Who Have Retreated from the Bodhi Mind
4 Transformationally Responding Sound Hearers

"Because the roots of those in the two categories of the fixed and those of overweening pride have not yet ripened, they cannot become Buddhas.

"Fixed Sound Hearers are simply withered sprouts and sterile seeds and are self-ending Arhats who only know about themselves and do not know about teaching and transforming living beings. Sound

Hearers of Overweening Pride always feel they are higher than anyone else. For example, the five thousand Bhikshus who withdrew when the Buddha spoke the ☞ DHARMA FLOWER SUTRA were all Sound Hearers of Overweening Pride. There are also Sound Hearers who once resolved their minds on Bodhi [☞ BODHI RESOLVE] and practiced the Bodhisattva Way—for awhile. But then they stopped and turned back, like ☞ ŚĀRIPUTRA, who decided to walk the Bodhisattva Path but met someone who wanted his eyes. He concluded it was too hard, and so he gave up his resolve for Bodhi. He brought forth the Bodhi mind 20,000 Buddhas ago, yet to this day he is still a Sound Hearer—one who has retreated from the Bodhi Mind. ...And so cultivation is not easy.

"There are several well-known examples of Transformationally Responding Sound Hearers who

> Conceal their Bodhisattva conduct
> within, and
> Manifest Sound Hearer bodies
> outwardly.

One such is Pūrṇamaitrāyaṇīputra, who, although a Sound Hearer on the outside, inside is walking the Bodhisattva Way. Another is the Venerable ☞ ĀNANDA, who has vowed to go and be the attendant of any of the countless Buddhas who appear in the world. The vow made by Rāhula is that he will be the eldest son for anyone who becomes a Buddha throughout the ten directions and the three periods of time. The roots of the first two categories—Fixed Sound Hearers and Those of Overweening Pride—are not yet mature." (FAS-PII(2) 134-135)

Sound Hearer, Hearer, auditor, listener, disciple

☞ **Arhat**

suffering 苦

Suffering is the first of the ☞ FOUR HOLY TRUTHS. Shouldering the burden of existence on our 'self' is suffering in a comprehensive and all-inclusive way that goes beyond our ordinary ideas about pain. The Sanskrit word *duḥkha* originally meant the friction caused by turning a wheel on its axle. And so it is that there is a basic friction underlying all the activities of our lives. The lists explained below are an aid to understanding some of the important aspects of suffering as it is understood in the light of the Buddha's teachings.

"In this world everything is suffering, and even happiness is not real happiness, but is the cause of suffering. All the dharmas in this world are defiled and impure; the world is all bitter suffering." (UW 87)

Eight Kinds of Suffering

The Suffering of Birth

"The experience of birth is like the experience of a turtle when its shell is ripped off. If you ripped the shell right off of a live turtle, don't you think the turtle would experience a lot of suffering? That's what being born is like. At the moment of birth when one's skin comes in contact with the air for the first time, it is as painful as if being cut by a sharp knife. That's why babies cry.

The Suffering of Old Age

"What's the suffering of being old? One's eyes get blurry, one's ears become deaf, one's teeth fall out, and one's hands and feet can't function properly anymore. And so there is a saying:

> Don't wait until you are old
> to cultivate the Way.

S

The lonely graves are those
of young people.

"When you get old, the things you eat don't seem to have any flavor. When you try to walk, your legs don't want to cooperate. You try to pick things up and your hands don't listen to you. You are tottering and in the decline of old age. The ancients had a poem about old age:

Your skin is wrinkled like a chicken's,
And your hair has turned crane-white.
See how you limp and hobble along?
Gold and jade fill your entire house,
And yet you can't put off
the decrepitude of old age.
Despite thousands upon thousands
of pleasures,
Impermanence finally arrives.
Therefore, the only path
of cultivation
Is to recite 'Amitābha Buddha!'
all the time!...

The Suffering of Sickness

"Being sick is even more suffering! There are many kinds of sickness, but no matter what kind of sickness it is, it is difficult to endure. Even heaven and earth get sick. For instance, when there is a very heavy rainstorm, or lightning and thunder, that's heaven and earth getting angry. Heaven and earth get angry too, and sometimes as a result, humankind is destroyed in the process.

"Sometimes there are earthquakes, which means that the planet is sick. Sometimes there are huge typhoons and tornadoes, which indicate that there is too much hatred around. The ancients said that hurricanes are the result of too much anger and hatred. Now scientists have their own explanation for the existence of hurricanes. But if you have your eyes open, you can see that in the center of a hurricane there are ghosts or spirits or demons who are whipping up the wind. They are whipping up the wind to such velocities that it kills people and in the process destroys trees, homes, and buildings. And all the while, these ghosts are having a grand old time. 'Wow, is this a riot! This is a fantastic amusement!' They kill people as casually as people would kill a mosquito or a fly. For those malevolent beings it seems there's no problem at all, nothing wrong about it. That's because these strange demons and weird ghosts like to harm people and tear them apart. But up to the present, people haven't believed these kinds of principles. They have said it isn't true that malevolent beings instigate storms. Instead they say that hurricanes are precipitated due to a special kind of atmospheric inversion. How often does this sudden atmospheric inversion happen? Out of nowhere, all of a sudden there are clouds and stormy weather. And although science has its own explanation, it is not complete or fully substantiated.

"Suffering in sickness is still not the utmost suffering. The most extreme suffering is the suffering of death.

The Suffering of Death

"When it comes time to die, you'll feel like a calf whose skin is being ripped off. Think about it, if there's a cow and you flay it while it is still alive, how much would it hurt? And so it is very difficult to die. If you don't believe it, you can try it out yourself. You can die and see what it is like. But if you believe it, then don't try it out. It isn't like science where they run experiments on everything. You won't want to experiment with dying. To this day, nobody has yet come up with a method that delivers us from sickness and death and ensures us eternal life.

"Even the Buddha did not invent such a method, but out of great compassion he left us with ☞EIGHTY-FOUR THOUSAND DHARMA-DOORS to teach us how to cultivate. But if you don't cultivate, even the Buddha will have no way to help you.

The Suffering of Being Apart from Those You Love

"Love is the feeling you have toward someone or something you like. When you love someone or something, you want to be together with that person or object all the time. You never want to part from them. However, sometimes circumstances arise in which people must be parted from those that they love and this brings on an acute kind of suffering.

The Suffering of Being Together with Those You Hate

"For example, there is a person whom you absolutely can't stand; you find it so hard to be around such a person that you want to leave him. However, when you deliberately go to another place to get away from him, you run into another person who is exactly like the person whom you couldn't stand. And so that's the suffering of being together with those you hate.

The Suffering of Not Obtaining What You Seek

"Suppose there is something you really want, but circumstances prevent you from getting it for your own. You want it, but you don't get it. No matter what you do, there is no way to fulfill you own wishes. That is the suffering of not obtaining what you seek.

The Suffering of the Scorching Blaze of the Five Skandhas

"The *skandhas* are form, feeling, cognition, formations, and consciousness. They tie you up so you have no freedom. The ☞FIVE SKANDHAS are as severe as a huge blaze. They consume you to the point that you burn to death. And so this is also suffering.

"Now everyone should 'know suffering.' If you know suffering, you can bring forth the ☞BODHI RESOLVE, and end birth and death." (FAS Ch8 11-13)

The *Yogācāryabhūmi-śāstra* also lists 110 kinds of suffering. They are explained briefly in the commentary to the "Four Holy Truths" Chapter of the *Flower Adornment Sutra* (☞FAS CH8 3-5).

ill, pain, misery, unsatisfactoriness, stress

☞ **impermanence, karma, causation, Four Holy Truths**

Śūraṅgama Mantra 楞嚴咒

The Śūraṅgama Mantra is the most powerful mantra in the world. It is contained in the text of the ☞ŚŪRAṄGAMA SUTRA.

"The Śūraṅgama Mantra has a force that upholds heaven and earth and keeps them from becoming extinct. It is that spiritual force which prevents the world from coming to an end.... As long as one person can recite the Śūraṅgama Mantra, the world won't be destroyed and the Dharma won't become extinct. When there is not a single person left who can recite the Śūraṅgama Mantra, the Buddhadharma will die out.

"Heavenly ☞DEMONS and those of outside ways are now spreading rumors that the *Śūraṅgama Sutra* and Mantra are inauthentic. They are simply demons' sons and grandsons sent by heavenly demons and those of outside ways to spread such rumors so as to destroy people's faith in the Śūraṅgama Mantra. If no one believes in the Mantra, then no one will recite it. When no one recites it, the world will quickly be destroyed. Therefore, if you don't want the world to be destroyed, then study and practice the Śūraṅgama Mantra; read and recite the Śūraṅgama Mantra. If you can recite it every day, then in this threatening nuclear age the dangers of nuclear power will not affect you. Therefore, we should singlemindedly read and recite the Śūraṅgama Mantra." (TT 126)

In the *Śūraṅgama Sutra* the Buddha says of the Śūraṅgama Mantra:

> Ānanda, let any living being of any country in the world copy out this mantra in writing on materials native to his region, such as birch bark, *pattra*, plain paper, or white cotton cloth, and store it in a pouch containing incense. If that person wears the pouch on his body, or if he keeps a copy in his home, then you should know that even if he understands so little that he cannot recite it from memory, he will not be harmed by any poison during his entire life. (SS VI 113)

☞ **Śūraṅgama Sutra, mantra, Dharma-Ending Age**

Śūraṅgama Sutra 大佛頂首楞嚴經

The full title of the *Śūraṅgama Sutra* is: *Scripture Explaining the Great Śūraṅgama above the Buddha's Head, the Realization of the Full Meaning of that Hidden Cause of the Tathāgatas, and the Bodhisattvas' Myriad Practices for Attaining It.*

"People who study the Buddhadharma should certainly investigate the *Śūraṅgama Sutra* and gain a thorough understanding of it. The *Śūraṅgama Sutra* is for bringing forth great wisdom. If you want to have right knowledge and right views and open great wisdom, you should certainly understand the *Śūraṅgama Sutra*. The *Śūraṅgama Sutra* breaks up the deviant and reveals the proper. It smashes all the heavenly demons and those of externalist sects and reveals the innate human capacity for right knowledge and right views. But when the Buddhadharma is just about to become extinct, the very first sutra to vanish will be the *Śūraṅgama Sutra.* If we wish to protect and maintain the proper Dharma, we should investigate the *Śūraṅgama Sutra*, come to understand the *Śūraṅgama Sutra*, and protect the *Śūraṅgama Sutra.* When the Buddhadharma is about to become extinct, weird demons and strange ghosts will come into the world, people with deviant knowledge and deviant views. They will be wise to the ways of the world and will be endowed with powers of debate and keen intelligence. They will argue that the *Śūraṅgama Sutra* is spurious—inauthentic—and will tell people not to believe it.

"Why will they say the *Śūraṅgama Sutra* is spurious?

"It is because the *Śūraṅgama Sutra* tells about all their faults. It discusses their kinds of deviant knowledge and deviant views. If the *Śūraṅgama Sutra* remains in the world, no one will believe their deviant views. If there is no *Śūraṅgama Sutra*, then their deviant knowledge and deviant views will succeed in confusing people. Therefore, they argue that the *Śūraṅgama Sutra* is spurious. This is the appearance of demon-kings. Those who study the Buddhadharma should be particularly attentive to this point. They should be particularly careful not to be influenced by the deviant knowledge and deviant views of those demon-kings." (SS II 161-162)

"In this (the Dharma-Ending) age, the Dharma will disappear. The first sutra to disappear will be the *Śūraṅgama Sutra*. That is why those who study the Buddhadharma should first investigate the *Śūraṅgama Sutra*. As long as someone understands this sutra, the Buddhadharma will not become extinct. As long as there is someone who can recite the Śūraṅgama

Mantra (which is part of the sutra), the demon-kings, the heavenly ☞DEMONS and followers of externalist teachings will not dare to come into the world to play their tricks and to make trouble. The Śūraṅgama Mantra is the most miraculous mantra for helping the world. The *Śūraṅgama Sutra* is the primary sutra which protects and supports the Orthodox Dharma." (BRF 18)

☞ **Śūraṅgama Mantra, Dharma-Ending Age**

sutra 經

> The Buddha said: 'One who studies the Buddha's Way should believe in and accord with all that the Buddha says. When you eat honey, it is sweet on the surface and sweet in the center; it is the same with my sutras.' (S42 #39)

The sutras are records of the conversations of the Buddhas and/or the Bodhisattvas or other enlightened disciples of the Buddha.

"The Buddha spoke the sutras to cause all of us living beings

> To go back to the origin and
> return to the source,
> To turn away from confusion and
> take refuge with enlightenment.

That is also:

> To turn our backs
> on the mundane dust
> And unite with enlightenment.

Otherwise, if no living beings listened to the sutras the Buddha spoke, the sutras would be useless. Therefore, if there were no living beings, there would be no sutras; and without sutras, there would be no way to teach living beings to become Buddhas." (FAS-PII(1) 23)

"Sutras provide a road to travel in cultivation. Going from the road of birth and death to the road of no birth and death, the common person penetrates to sagehood—to Buddhahood. One who wishes to walk that road must rely on the Dharma to cultivate. The Dharma is in the sutras." (VS 8)

scripture

☞ **Tripiṭaka, Dharma, and entries for individual sutras**

Sutra in Forty-two Sections 四十二章經

In this sutra, which was the first to be transported from India to China and translated into Chinese, the Buddha gives the most essential instructions for cultivating the Dharma, emphasizing the cardinal virtues of renunciation, contentment, and patience.

Sutra of the Past Vows of Earth Store Bodhisattva 地藏菩薩本願經

This sutra tells how Earth Store Bodhisattva attained his position among the greatest Bodhisattvas as the Foremost in Vows. It also explains the workings of ☞KARMA, how beings undergo ☞REBIRTH, and the various kinds of heavens and ☞HELLS.

☞ **Earth Store ⟨Bodhisattva⟩**

Tathāgata 如來

☞ **Thus Come One**

tathāgatagarbha 如來藏

A Sanskrit word meaning 'treasury of the Thus Come One.'

☞ **Thus Come One**

Ten Dharma Realms 十法界

The Ten Dharma Realms are composed of the four realms of the sages—Buddhas, Bodhisattvas, Pratyekabuddhas, and Arhats—and the Six Paths of Rebirth—gods, humans, *asuras*, animals, ghosts, and hell-dwellers—also known as the Six Mundane Dharma Realms. The ten are described under the individual entries.

The realms other than that of the Buddhas are called the Nine Dharma Realms. "All the living beings of the Nine Dharma Realms are dreaming. The Bodhisattva dreams of seeking the Way of the Buddha above, and of transforming living beings below. He wishes to realize the Way of the Buddha in order to take living beings across, yet it is all in a dream.

"The Condition-Enlightened Ones, the Pratyekabuddhas, are also dreaming. About what? They dream of looking out for themselves alone. Living deep in desolate mountain valleys, they are Arhats who 'comprehend for their own sakes'...'incapable of promoting the common good.' That is also dreaming.

"Hearers, the *śrāvakas*, dream of the one-sided emptiness which is the one-sided truth of nirvana with residue.

"The gods have dreams of happiness and peace; they are at ease and enjoy an especially peaceful, superior and wonderful happiness.

"People dream of seeking fame and fortune. They wish to make a lot of money or to become officials. In their current lives, they are all upside down and take suffering to be happiness. Every day they are busy dreaming of fame and fortune.

"What dream do the *asuras* have? They dream of fighting. For instance, someone going and fighting someone else is an affair of *asuras*. To be an *asura* is to be someone who likes to fight, and to be in the dream of fighting.

"Those in the hells dream of undergoing bitter suffering. Hungry ghosts dream of starving, and animals dream a dream of stupidity.

"Each of the nine Dharma Realms has its own dream. The Buddha, in ultimate nirvana, is the only one who does not dream, and so his realm is called 'ultimate nirvana.'" (HS 104-105)

> To fully understand all Buddhas
> of the three periods of time,
> Contemplate the nature of the
> Dharma Realm:
> Everything is created from the mind
> alone. (FAS Ch20)

☞ **Dharmafields, Dharma-worlds; Dharma-spheres**

☞ **Dharma Realm, Six Paths of Rebirth, Buddha, Bodhisattva, Pratyekabuddha, Arhat**

Ten Grounds/Stages of the Path of the Bodhisattva 菩薩十地

The Ten Grounds of the path of the Bodhisattva are:

1 Happiness
2 Leaving Filth
3 Emitting Light
4 Blazing Wisdom
5 Difficult Conquest
6 Manifestation
7 Traveling Far
8 Not Moving
9 Wholesome Wisdom
10 Dharma Cloud

1. Ground of Happiness

"The Bodhisattva at the very beginning of the Ten Grounds is like an infant who has just left the sagely womb and been born into the lineage of the Tathāgatas. He perfects the conduct of benefitting self and benefitting others, and is certified as to his sagely position. Hence he gives rise to great happiness.

2. Ground of Leaving Filth

"The Bodhisattva becomes replete with pure precepts and renounces all actions that are contrary to morality and comportment. Hence on this ground he leaves the filth of afflictions behind.

3. Ground of Emitting Light

"From supreme samadhi, the wondrous teaching, and four types of *dhāraṇī*, the Bodhisattva gives rise to the Three Wisdoms: the wisdom of hearing, the wisdom of consideration, and the wisdom of cultivation. From the attainment of those kinds of wisdom, he emits a sublime light.

4. Ground of Blazing Wisdom

"On this ground the Bodhisattva achieves a dazzling wisdom light that consumes the tinder of all afflictions. Whereas the former three grounds are still located in the world, this ground marks the beginning of a world-transcending position.

5. Ground of Difficult Conquest

"Upon this ground the Bodhisattva testifies to the interaction between wisdom of relative truth and the nondiscriminating wisdom of absolute truth. Through the mutual and nonobstructive functioning of those two kinds of wisdom, he accomplishes clever expedient means, such as the Five Sciences, to teach living beings. On this level he transcends the world and yet completely accords with the world. Since this is a position that is difficult to surpass, it is called Difficult Conquest.

6. Ground of Manifestation

"The Bodhisattva gives rise to great *prajñā* wisdom through contemplation of the Twelve Links of Conditioned Arising (☞TWELVEFOLD CONDITIONED ARISING) and is no longer caught up in the discrimination of purity and defilement. Thus there is the manifestation of sublime conduct." (EDR V 279-280)

7. Ground of Traveling Far

"This ground is characterized by cultivation that is without an appearance and without effort. Since effortless functioning is accomplished, the Bodhisattva far transcends all the practices of the Two Vehicles. Hence the name 'Traveling Far.'

8. Ground of Not Moving

"As a reward of the Bodhisattva conduct,

the Bodhisattva has now reached the state which is without marks and without interval; hence the name 'Not Moving.' On this ground the Bodhisattva casts off the activities of production within the Three Realms—the realms of desire, form, and formlessness. He also attains the Patience with Non-Production. Through the wisdom of the contemplation of marklessness, he is 'not moved' by any affliction.

9. Ground of Wholesome Wisdom

"The Bodhisattva attains the Four Unobstructed Eloquences and perfects the merit of being a great Dharma Master. He is able to speak Dharma that perfectly suits the potentials of all living beings. Hence on this ground he achieves 'wholesome wisdom.'

10. Ground of the Dharma Cloud

"By this stage the Bodhisattva attains a vast Dharma body. He is full and accomplished, like a huge Dharma cloud that protects all under heaven, and which sends down Dharma rain to nourish all beings. In this way the Bodhisattva benefits sentient creatures in boundlessly inconceivable ways." (EDR VI 280)

☞ **Bodhisattva**

Ten Titles of a Buddha 佛之十號

"Every Buddha has a myriad titles, but people's memories are too poor to remember so many names clearly in a single lifetime. Somewhere in time, the Buddhas of the ten directions and the three periods of time held a meeting and decided they would simplify the myriad titles of a Buddha to one thousand. However, eventually a thousand were still too many, so the Buddhas investigated the question again and further simplified the matter so that each Buddha had one hundred titles. With the passage of time, that again was still too many, and so finally they were reduced to ten titles, which all Buddhas share. Those ten titles are:

1. Thus Come One
2. One Worthy of Offerings
3. One of Proper and Universal Knowledge
4. One Perfect in Clarity and Practice
5. Well Gone One
6. Unsurpassed One Who Understands the World
7. Hero Who Subdues and Tames
8. Teacher of Gods and Humans
9. Buddha
10. World Honored One

"The first title is Thus Come One.

> He has followed the Way that is Thus
> And come to realize Proper
> Enlightenment.

That is one explanation. The ☞VAJRA SUTRA says:

> The Thus Come One does not come from anywhere, nor does he go anywhere; therefore he is called the Thus Come One.

Furthermore, 'Thus' represents noumenon, the basic substance of principle, while 'Come' represents phenomena, the names and characteristics of specifics. Principle and specifics are nondual. The ☞FLOWER ADORNMENT SUTRA takes as its creed the harmony of principle and specifics. The title 'Thus Come One' exemplifies the nonobstruction of noumenon and phenomena.

"The second title is 'One Worthy of Offerings.' The Buddha is one who should receive offerings from the humans and gods of the ☞THREE REALMS, and who deserves the respect and reverence of those in and beyond the world.

"The third title is 'One of Proper and Universal Knowledge.' There is nothing which he does not know and nothing which he fails to understand. His knowledge is both proper and pervasive.

"The fourth title is 'One of Perfect Clarity and Conduct,' for the light of his Four Types of Wisdom is perfect and full: **a)** Wisdom of Successful Performance, **b)** Wonderful Contemplating and Investigating Wisdom, **c)** Impartial Wisdom of the Nature, **d)** Great Perfect Mirror Wisdom.

"The fifth title is 'Well Gone One,' one who has gone to a good place, the very best place.

"The sixth title is 'Unsurpassed One Who Understands the World.' Bodhisattvas are called 'Surpassed Ones,' for there are still the Buddhas above them. A Buddha, however, is unsurpassed. Since he understands all doctrines, both mundane and transcendental, he is one who well understands the world.

"The seventh title is 'Hero Who Subdues and Tames,' one who subdues and tames all the living beings in the world.

"The eighth title is 'Teacher of Gods and Humans.' The Buddha is the master of the gods in the heavens and the people in the world.

"The ninth title is 'Buddha'....

"The tenth title is 'World Honored One.' World Honored One means one who is honored by those in the world and those beyond the world. Those beyond the world have transcended the ☞THREE REALMS...." (FAS Ch7 1-3)

☞ **Buddha, Thus Come One**

Ten Wholesome Deeds 十善

The Ten Wholesome Deeds are abstention from **1)** killing, **2)** stealing, **3)** sexual misconduct, **4)** duplicity, **5)** harsh speech, **6)** lying, **7)** irresponsible speech, **8)** greed, **9)** anger, and **10)** foolishness.

> The Buddha said: 'Living beings may perform ten good practices or ten evil practices. What are the ten? Three are of the body, four are of the mouth, and three are of the mind. The three of the body are killing, stealing, and lust. The four of the mouth are duplicity, harsh speech, lies, and irresponsible speech. The three of the mind are jealousy, hatred, and delusion. Thus these ten are not in accord with the Holy Way and are called ten evil practices. To put a stop to these evils is to perform the ten good practices.' (S42 14)

The ☞FLOWER ADORNMENT SUTRA says this of the Bodhisattva who, by his very nature, practices the Ten Wholesome Deeds.

Abstention from Killing

> By nature he naturally leaves all killing far behind. He does not collect knives or staves. He does not cherish resentment or hatred. He has shame and he has remorse. He is endowed with humaneness and reciprocity. Toward all beings who have a life, he always brings forth thoughts of benefit and kindly mindfulness. This Bodhisattva should not with evil mind even trouble living beings, how much the less give rise to malice and actually kill or harm any whom he realizes are living beings. (FAS Ch26(2) 4)

Abstention from Stealing

> By nature he does not steal. The Bodhisattva is always content with his own

possesions. He is always kind and forgiving towards others and does not wish to encroach upon them. If an item belongs to someone else, he gives rise to the thought that it is someone else's item and would never consider stealing it, down to a blade of grass or a leaf—if not given, he does not take it—how much the less any other of the necessities of life. (FAS Ch26(2) 10)

Abstention from Sexual Misconduct

By nature he does not engage in sexual misconduct. The [married, lay] Bodhisattva is content with his own wife and does not seek the wives of others. Toward the wives and concubines of others, the women protected by others, by relatives of those betrothed, and those protected by the law, he does not even give rise to the thought of greedy defilement, how much the less follow it into action, and how much the less give himself over to what is not the Way. (FAS Ch26(2) 17)

Abstention from Lying

By nature he does not lie. The Bodhisattva always utters true speech, actual speech, and timely speech, to the point that even in a dream, he would never think of wanting to lie, how much the less deliberately commit such violations. (FAS Ch26(2) 20)

Abstention from Divisive Speech

By nature he does not engage in divisive speech. The Bodhisattva, towards all living beings, has no thought of dividing them against each other. He has no thought of troubling or harming. He does not report the speech of one person to break his relationship with a second person, nor does he report the speech of the second person to break his relationship with the first person. If people have not already broken with each other, he does not break them up. If they have already broken with each other, he does not increase the break. He does not enjoy dividing people against each other, nor is he happy when people are divided against each other. He does not utter speech that would divide people against each other, nor does he report speech that would divide people against each other—regardless of whether it is true or false. (FAS Ch26(2) 20-21)

Abstention from Harsh Speech

By nature he does not engage in harsh speech, that is, cruel, malicious speech, coarse, wild speech, speech that brings suffering to others, speech that provokes anger and hatred in others, blunt speech, furtive speech, vile and evil speech, cheap and vulgar speech, speech unpleasant to hear, speech that does not delight the listener, angry hateful speech, speech that burns the heart like fire, speech bound up in resentment, heated, irritating speech, disagreeable speech, displeasing speech, speech that can destroy oneself and others—all such types of speech as those he completely abandons. He always utters kind, encouraging speech, soft and gentle speech, speech that delights the mind, speech pleasant to the listener, speech that makes the listener happy, speech that wholesomely enters into people's hearts, elegant and refined speech, speech agreeable to most people, speech that gladdens most people, and speech that brings joy to body and mind. (FAS Ch26 (2) 25-26)

Abstention from Irresponsible Speech

By nature he does not engage in loose speech. The Bodhisattva always delights in thoughtful, examined speech, in appropriate speech, in true speech, in meaningful speech, lawful speech, speech that accords with principle, skillfully taming and regulating speech, speech which is reckoned and measured according to the time and which is decisive. This Bodhisattva, even when making jokes, always weighs his words, so how much the less would he deliberately pour out scattered and abandoned talk. (FAS Ch26(2) 28)

Abstention from Greed

By nature he does not engage in greed. The Bodhisattva does not covet others' wealth and property, or things owned and used by others. He does not wish for them or seek them. (FAS Ch26(2) 28)

Abstention from Anger

By nature he is free from anger and hatred. The Bodhisattva, towards all living beings, constantly brings forth a mind of kindness, a benefitting mind, a mind of pity and sympathy, a happy mind, a compatible mind, a mind of accepting and gathering them in. He once and for all abandons anger, hatred, resentment, malevolence, rage, and irritation. He is always considerate and cooperative in his conduct, humane, kind, and helpful. (FAS Ch26(2) 29)

Abstention from Foolishness

He is, further, free from deviant views. The Bodhisattva dwells on the Proper Paths. He does not practice astrology or divination. He is not attached to unwholesome precepts. His views are proper and upright. He does not deceive; he does not flatter. He has firm faith in the Buddha, the Dharma, and the Sangha. (FAS Ch26 (2) 29-30)

☞ **good deeds, good acts, good practices; [not to take life, take what has not been given to us, practice sexual misconduct, lie, use harsh speech, engage in idle talk, slander, hold thoughts of covetousness, keep anger and resentment, keep and foster deluded thoughts; to have compassionate caring, generosity, contentment, truthfulness, kindly speech, meaningful speech, harmonious speech, generous thoughts, compassionate thoughts, clear thoughts]**

☞ **moral precepts, Five Moral Precepts**

Theravada Buddhism 南傳佛教

Theravada Buddhism, sometimes referred to as Southern Buddhism, belongs primarily to what the Mahayana calls the Hinayana tradition and is the only so-called Hinayana School to survive to the present. Theravada means 'teachings of the elders' (Skt. *sthavira-vāda*).

Today Theravada Buddhism is found primarily in Sri Lanka, Burma, Thailand, and other countries of Southeast Asia.

☞ **Mahayana and Hinayana Compared**

Thirty-two Major Physical Characteristics of a Buddha 佛三十二相

"Subhūti, what do you think, can the Tathāgata be seen by his physical marks?"

"No, World Honored One, the Tathāgata cannot be seen by his physical marks. And why? It is because the physical marks are spoken of by the Tathāgata as no physical marks."

The Buddha said to Subhūti, "All with marks is empty and false. If you can see all marks as no marks, then you see the Tathāgata." (VS 46)

"Subhūti what do you think, can the Tathāgata be seen by means of the Thirty-two Marks?"

"No, World Honored One, one cannot see the Tathāgata by means of the Thirty-two Marks. And why? The Thirty-two marks are spoken of by the Tathāgata as no Thirty-two Marks; therefore, they are called Thirty-two Marks." (VS 85)

All Buddhas possess these physical characteristics. They are said to be the karmic result of a hundred *kalpas* of cultivation on the ☞ BODHISATTVA PATH.

Thirty-two Major Characteristics

1 level feet
2 thousand-spoked wheel sign on the feet
3 long, slender fingers
4 pliant hands and feet
5 toes and fingers finely webbed
6 full-sized heels
7 arched insteps
8 thighs like a royal stag
9 hands reaching below the knees
10 well-retracted male organ
11 height and stretch of arms equal
12 every hair-root dark colored
13 body hair graceful and curly
14 golden-hued body
15 ten-foot aura around him
16 soft, smooth skin
17 soles, palms, shoulders and crown of head well-rounded
18 area below the armpits well-filled
19 lion-shaped body
20 body erect and upright
21 full, round shoulders
22 forty teeth
23 teeth white, even and close
24 four canine teeth pure white
25 lion-jawed
26 saliva that improves the taste of all food
27 tongue long and broad
28 voice deep and resonant
29 eyes deep blue
30 eyelashes like a royal bull
31 white *ūrṇā* curl that emits light between brows
32 fleshy protuberance on the crown of the head

(including 80 minor characteristics not included here): marks and minor characteristics, subsidiary characteristics, fine marks and special characteristics, magnificent characteristics and subsidiary qualities, hallmarks, attributes

☞ **Buddha, Three Bodies of a Buddha**

Thousand Handed Thousand Eyed Dhāraṇī Sutra 千手千眼陀羅尼經

☞ **Dhāraṇī Sutra**

Three Aspects of Learning to Be Without Outflows 三無漏學

The Three Aspects of Learning to Be Without Outflows are **1)** moral precepts, **2)** samadhi, and **3)** wisdom.

> Diligently cultivate precepts, samadhi, and wisdom;
> Put to rest greed, anger, and delusion.

"Diligently cultivating precepts means putting a stop to evil and avoiding wrongdoing. It is also doing no evil but offering up all good. It means when you recognize your true and actual goal, you should go forward and make courageous progress with vigor, and not change your initial resolution. It also means that you should be firm, sincere, and constant. Your resolve should be solid and firm, it should be sincere, and it should be long-lasting. Constantly and forever one should do no evil and should offer up all good conduct. When you cultivate precepts, you certainly must have patience. That is, you must endure what you cannot endure. In that way the precepts will spontaneously be pure. When the substance of the precepts is pure, then you will be able to give rise to samadhi-power. Samadhi-power means not being moved by outer circumstances. What is meant by wisdom? People with wisdom don't do foolish or upside-down things. They don't do ignorant and afflicted things. That's wisdom.

"If you can diligently cultivate precepts, samadhi, and wisdom, and in turn, put to rest greed, anger, and delusion, then in everything you say and do, you won't calculate for yourself. You should consider the entire world and all of humanity as your responsibility and be concerned about them. Don't be concerned about yourself, and then you won't have any greed. If you make all of humanity your personal responsibility, and set out to benefit each and every person, then you are practicing the Bodhisattva Path. If further you can have no delusion and afflictions, then your anger will be put to rest. Delusion means not recognizing truth and instead doing all kinds of deluded things. If you have no more of all that, then you have put to rest greed, anger, and delusion...." (TT 117)

no outflow studies, kinds of learning that lead to the elimination of outflows

moral precepts, samadhi, prajñā, Three Poisons, outflows

Three Bodies of a Buddha/Three Types of Buddha Bodies 佛之三身

The Three Bodies of a Buddha are **1)** the Dharma body, **2)** the reward body, and **3)** the transformation body (or response body).

"The Dharma body is the principle and nature of Fundamental Enlightenment. The reward body is Perfect Wisdom, or Initial Enlightenment. The transformation body is a compassionate appearance in response to living beings. The Buddha responds to the needs of living beings who are suffering by compassionately appearing in response to them.

"Another way to explain this is that the Dharma body is Vairocana Buddha, which translates as 'All Pervasive Light.' The reward body is Niṣyanda Buddha, which means 'Fulfillment of Purity.' The transformation body is Śākyamuni Buddha, which translates as 'Capable of Humaneness,' and 'Still and Silent.' The three bodies are not one and yet not different. The bodies are one, because there are three bodies. But they are not different, because the three issue from one Buddha. It is because the potentials and conditions of living beings are different that beings see differently. Some see the reward body, others see the response body, and still others see the Dharma body. Again, taking a pearl as an analogy, the Dharma body is the substance of the pearl, which is round and perfect. The reward body is like the pure light emitted by the pearl. The response bodies are like the inter-reflections of pearls—pearl reflected within pearl. Apart from the substance, there is no light. Apart from the light, there is no reflection. The three are one." (BNS I 11)

> If you meet a Good Knowing Advisor, if you listen to the true and right Dharma and cast out your own confusion and falseness, then inside and out there will be penetrating brightness, and within the self-nature all the ten thousand dharmas will appear. That is how it is with those who see their own nature. It is called the clear, pure Dharma body of the Buddha....
>
> What is the perfect, full reward body of the Buddha? Just as one lamp can disperse the darkness of a thousand years, one thought of wisdom can destroy ten thousand years of delusion.
>
> Do not think of the past; it is gone and can never be recovered. Instead think always of the future and in every thought, perfect and clear, see your own original nature. Although good

and evil differ, the original nature is nondual. That nondual nature is the real nature. Undefiled by either good or evil, it is the perfect, full reward body of the Buddha....

What are the hundred thousand myriad transformation bodies of the Buddha? If you are free of any thought of the ten thousand dharmas, then your nature is basically like emptiness, but in one thought of calculation, transformation occurs. Evil thoughts are transformed into hell-beings and good thoughts into heavenly beings. Viciousness is transformed into dragons and snakes, and compassion into Bodhisattvas. Wisdom is transformed into the upper realms, and delusion into the lower realms. The transformations of the self-nature are extremely many, and yet the confused person, unawakened to that truth, continually gives rise to evil and walks evil paths. Turn a single thought back to goodness, and wisdom is produced. That is the transformation body of the Buddha within your self-nature." (PS 188-193)

☞ **Buddha, Thirty-two Major ⟨Physical⟩ Characteristics of a Buddha**

Three Jewels 三寶

The Three Jewels are **1)** the Buddha, **2)** the Dharma, and **3)** the Sangha. The Three Jewels are Buddhism's greatest treasures.

✍ **three gems, three treasures, triple jewel**

☞ **refuge with the Three Jewels, Buddha, Dharma, Sangha**

Three Poisons 三毒

The Three Poisons are **1)** greed, **2)** anger, and **3)** foolishness.

✍ **three basic afflictions: 1) greed/avarice/attraction, 2) hatred/aversion, 3) delusion/ignorance**

☞ **affliction**

Three Refuges 三皈

☞ **refuge with the Three Jewels**

Three Realms 三界

☞ **Three Worlds**

Three Vehicles 三乘

The Three Vehicles are **1)** the Bodhisattva Vehicle, **2)** the Pratyekabuddha Vehicle, and **3)** the Śrāvaka Vehicle.

In the ☞DHARMA FLOWER SUTRA the Buddha reveals that his three teachings—the Śrāvaka Vehicle that leads to Arhatship, the Pratyekabuddha Vehicle that leads to Pratyekabuddhahood, and the Bodhisattva Vehicle that traverses the stages of the Bodhisattva Path—are all provisional, expedient teachings. They lead to fruitions that have no reality in themselves. There is only one reality, and that is Buddhahood.

"It's like taking some milk and dividing it into three different glasses. Three people could each drink one glass, or one person could drink all three glasses, and it would be the same. It's just that if his or her capacity was not that great it might burst his or her stomach. And so the Buddha starts by dividing things up into smaller amounts for you, and when you've polished that much off, he pours you out some more. That's just what's going on." (FAS-PII(1) 249)

☞ **Mahayana and Hinayana Compared, Dharma Flower Sutra, Bodhisattva, Pratyekabuddha, Arhat, śrāvaka**

Three Worlds 三界

The Three Worlds are **1)** the world of desire, **2)** the world of form, and **3)** the formless world. (See chart on next page.)

"The Three Worlds refers to the world of desire, the world of form, and the formless world. Living beings within the world of desire still have desire—greed and lust. Living beings within the world of form do not have such intense desire; however, they still have a physical form and appearance. They are still attached to appearances, and therefore, they are not apart from the marks of self, others, living beings, and lifespans. Living beings of the formless realm are without form or shape, yet they still have consciousness, and they are attached to that consciousness....

"Because living beings within these three worlds are still attached, they cannot get out. Only those who have been certified as having attained the fourth stage of Arhatship can completely escape. But Arhats still belong to the Lesser Vehicle; only Bodhisattvas belong to the Great Vehicle...." (TT 47)

triple world, three realms
Six Paths of Rebirth

Thus Come One 如來

One who seeks me in forms
Or seeks me in sounds
Practices a deviant way
And cannot see the Thus Come One.
(VS 141)

Thus Come One is one of the ☞TEN TITLES OF A BUDDHA. The Sanskrit, *Tathāgata*, can mean both 'thus come' and 'thus gone.' The ☞VAJRA SUTRA says, "The Tathāgata does not come from anywhere, nor does he go anywhere. Therefore, he is called the Tathāgata." (VS 147)

The title Thus Come One refers to a Buddha's Dharma body (☞THREE BODIES OF A BUDDHA). "The Buddha's transformation bodies come and go, but his Dharma body does not. ☞MAITREYA Bodhisattva spoke this verse:

"What comes and goes are the
Buddha's transformation bodies.
The Tathāgata is eternally unmoving.
He is neither the same nor different
From every place within the Dharma
Realm.

"You should know that it is not the Tathāgata who comes and goes; rather the distinctions of our eighth consciousness perceive a coming and a going. When the *Vajra Sutra* tells you not to consider the Buddha as either sitting, lying, coming, or going, it is telling you not to make such distinctions. When you no longer make distinctions, your wisdom can appear...." (VS 149)

Thus Gone One, Thus Come
Buddha

Tiantai School 天台宗

One of the major schools of Buddhism in China, based on the teachings of the ☞DHARMA FLOWER (LOTUS) SUTRA.

Major early patriarchs of the Tiantai School's lineage include:

1 Huiwen (fl. 550 C.E.)
2 Huisi (515-577)
3 Zhiyi (538-597)
4 Guanding (561-632)

The school is named after Mount Tiantai in Zhejiang Province where the third patriarch ☞ZHIYI lived, practiced, and taught.

CHART *of the* THREE WORLDS

World	Division	Sphere of Existence	
FORMLESS WORLD		Heaven of Neither Cognition Nor Non-Cognition	
		Heaven of Nothing Whatsoever	
		Heaven of Boundless Consciousness	
		Heaven of Boundless Space	
WORLD OF FORM	Heavens of the Fourth Dhyāna	5 Heavens of No Return	Ultimate Form Heaven
			Good Manifestation Heaven
			Good View Heaven
			No Heat Heaven
			No Affliction Heaven
		No Thought Heaven	
		Vast Fruit Heaven	
		Love of Blessings Heaven	
		Birth of Blessings Heaven	
	Heavens of the Third Dhyāna	Pervasive Purity Heaven	
		Limitless Purity Heaven	
		Lesser Purity Heaven	
	Heavens of the Second Dhyāna	Light-Sound Heaven	
		Limitless Light Heaven	
		Lesser Light Heaven	
	Heavens of the First Dhyāna	Great Brahma Heaven	
		Ministers of Brahma Heaven	
		Multitudes of Brahma Heaven	

ALL THE GODS IN THE FORM REAL Heavens and, of course, the Formless Realm Heave as well, are without the senses of smell and taste, ar they do not eat, sleep, or have sexual desire. The desir for these things, though, are still latent and they c return to any lower realm of existence in accordan

World	Division	Sphere of Existence
WORLD OF DESIRE	Six Desire Heavens	Heaven of Sovereignty Over Others' Transformatior
		Heaven of Bliss by Transformation
		Tuṣita Heaven
		Suyāma Heaven
		Trayāstriṃśa Heaven
		Heaven of the Four Kings

THE GODS IN THE DESIRE HEAVENS STII have desires connected with the five senses. Yet t happiness they experience is much greater than that the human realm. The human realm compared to ev

World	Sphere of Existence
WORLD OF DESIRE	*Asuras*
	Human beings
	Animals
	Ghosts
	Hell-beings

KEY

1 *kalpa*	=16 million years
1 small *kalpa*	=1000 *kalpas*
1 middle *kalpa*	=20 small *kalpas*
1 great *kalpa*	=4 middle *kalpas*
1 *yojana*	=28 miles

Average Life Span	Average Height	Comments
80,000 great *kalpas* (102.4 quadrillion years)		Beings in the Four Formless Heavens have no bodies. They only have consciousness.
60,000 great *kalpas*		
40,000 great *kalpas*		
20,000 great *kalpas*		
16,000 great *kalpas* (20.48 quadrillion years)	16,000 *yojanas*	The gods of all the other heavens cannot even see the Heavens of No Return, because they are beyond their scope.
8,000 great *kalpas*	8,000 *yojanas*	
4,000 great *kalpas*	4,000 *yojanas*	
2,000 great *kalpas*	2,000 *yojanas*	
1,000 great *kalpas*	1,000 *yojanas*	
500 great *kalpas* (640 trillion years)	500 *yojanas*	These heavens correspond to the state of *dhyāna* meditation called "Ground of the Purity of Casting Away Thought."
500 great *kalpas*	500 *yojanas*	
250 great *kalpas*	250 *yojanas*	
125 great *kalpas*	125 *yojanas*	
64 great *kalpas* (81.92 trillion years)	64 *yojanas*	These heavens correspond to the state of *dhyāna* meditation called "Ground of the Wonderful Happiness of Being Apart from Bliss."
32 great *kalpas*	32 *yojanas*	
16 great *kalpas*	16 *yojanas*	
8 great *kalpas*	8 *yojanas*	These heavens correspond to the state of *dhyāna* meditation called "Ground of Bliss Born of Samadhi."
4 great *kalpas*	4 *yojanas*	
2 great *kalpas*	2 *yojanas*	
3 middle *kalpas*	1-1/2 *yojanas*	These heavens correspond to the state of *dhyāna* meditation called "Ground of Bliss Born of Separation."
2 middle *kalpas*	1 *yojana*	
1 middle *kalpa*	1/2 *yojana*	

ith their karma, once their heavenly life comes to an ɪd. Third and Fourth Stage Arhats and Bodhisattvas ɪve ended these desires at their root.

The comments above describe specific things that ɪppen to a person who enters the levels of *dhyāna* editation that correspond to the Dhyāna Heavens. Also, as a human being, when one enters the First Dhyāna meditation state one can sit for seven days without getting up from one's seat, and without eating, drinking, or sleeping. In the Second Dhyāna one can sit for 49 days. In the Third Dhyāna one can sit for three years. And in the Fourth Dhyāna one can sit for nine years. The happiness experienced in *dhyāna* meditation far surpasses that of the happiness connected with the five senses.

16,000 heaven years (9.2 billion years)	4500 feet	1 day = 1600 human years
8,000 heaven years (2.3 billion years)	3500 feet	1 day = 800 human years
4,000 heaven years (576 million years)	3000 feet	1 day = 400 human years
2,000 heaven years (144 million years)	2250 feet	1 day = 200 human years
1,000 heaven years (36 million years)	1500 feet	1 day = 100 human years
500 heaven years (9 million years)	750 feet	1 day = 50 human years

ɪe lowest Desire Heaven is like a toilet pit. The gods in e first two Desire Heavens fulfill their sexual desire in ɪe same way as those in the human realm. In the ɪyāma Heaven they fulfill it by holding hands. In the Tuṣita Heaven they fulfill it by smiling at each other. In the Heaven of Bliss by Transformation it is fulfilled by mutual gazing. And in the Heaven of Sovereignty Over Others' Transformations it is fulfilled by merely glancing at each other. All the heavens beginning with the Suyāma Heaven and above do not have a sun or moon. The bodies of these gods emit their own light.

In addition to the school's emphasis on the *Dharma Flower Sutra's* teaching about the one Buddha Vehicle that supersedes the teachings of the Three Vehicles, the school is known for its system of ☞RANKING THE TEACHINGS and for its method of sutra exegesis called the Fivefold Esoteric Meaning. The school also emphasized the *zhiguan* or 'calming and contemplation' method of meditation (Skt. *śamatha-vipaśyanā*).

☞ **Five Types of Buddhist Study and Practice—Teachings, Zhiyi ⟨Venerable⟩, Dharma Flower Sutra, ranking the teachings**

time 時

The Buddhist teaching about time is closely linked to the doctrine of ☞IMPERMANENCE. What we see as the passage of time when analyzed in large segments becomes ungraspable when analyzed on the level of single moments of time. Nonetheless, when operating on the ordinary level of discourse, the Buddha taught about the passage of time on both the macrocosmic and microcosmic levels. Just as all beings are born, grow old, get sick and die, so too do entire world systems come into being, achieve stasis, decay, and cease to be. And every moment of thought can also be seen as coming into being, abiding, decaying, and disappearing.

The length of the process on the level of a world system is called a great aeon, or *mahākalpa* in Sanskrit. The length of a *mahākalpa* is calculated as follows: "Starting from a life span of ten years, for every hundred years the age of people increases by one year, and their height increases by one inch. This keeps on increasing until the life span of humans reaches a full 84,000 years. Then this is followed by a process of decrease in the same ratio. For every hundred years, there is a decrease of a year and an inch from the life span and the height of a human being, until his age reaches ten years again. One complete process of increase and decrease makes up one *kalpa*—16,798,000 years. A thousand of these make up one small *kalpa*. Twenty small *kalpas* make up one medium-sized *kalpa*. Four medium-sized *kalpas* make up one great *kalpa* (1,343, 800,000,000 years). Each of the four stages takes up twenty small *kalpas*—twenty *kalpas* for coming into being, twenty *kalpas* for dwelling, twenty *kalpas* for decaying, and twenty *kalpas* for going empty." (EDR I)

"The very first *kalpa* [of a particular world system], of course, begins the cycle of coming into being, stasis, decay, and emptiness. Those four terms are explained as follows. A thousand small *kalpas* together make up a medium-sized *kalpa*. One medium-sized *kalpa* covers a period of coming into being. A period of stasis also spans twenty small *kalpas*, a period of decay is twenty small *kalpas* long, and a period of emptiness is also twenty small *kalpas*.

"'But,' you say, 'I can't possibly conceive of that long a period of time.' Well, if you can't grasp this concept, then I'll shrink the *kalpa* down a bit for you to enable you to understand. Let's discuss the life span of a person. A person's life span extends for several decades, and those years span the time of being born, the time of growing old, the time of sickness, and the time of death. Those four different periods of time are synonymous with the coming into being, stasis, decay, and emptiness of a world system.

"Then you say, 'Well, I still don't understand—I still can't comprehend this idea.' Well, we'll shrink it some more and talk about a single year's time. A year has four seasons: spring, summer, fall, and winter. Spring is the period of coming into being; summer is the period of stasis; fall is the period of decay; and winter is the period of emptiness. Do you see? In the springtime we prepare the fields for planting. The fields are planted with the intention that the plants will come into being. Seeds are planted in the earth, and the summertime, after the seeds have sprouted and the plants are flourishing, is the period of stasis. In the fall the plants reach maturity, and their harvest takes place in the autumn, just as the period of decay sets in. Then, with the coming of winter, after everything that grew from the earth has been harvested, there is a period of emptiness. The principle applies in the same way." (FAS Ch5-6 115-117)

> Suppose, o monks, there was a huge rock of one solid mass, one mile long, one mile wide, one mile high, without split or flaw. And at the end of every one hundred years a man should come and rub against it with a silken cloth. Then that huge rock would wear off and disappear quicker than a *kappa* (i.e., *kalpa*). (SN XV 5, quoted in Trevor Ling, *Dictionary of Buddhism*, 72)

The Buddha also taught that time is relative to our state of mind; it passes more quickly when we are happy and less quickly when we are unhappy. Therefore, passage of time and life span differs on the different paths of rebirth (☞TEN DHARMA REALMS, SIX PATHS OF REBIRTH).

"The Heaven of the Four Kings (☞SIX DESIRE HEAVENS) is the heaven closest to us, located halfway up Mount Sumeru, as explained in the Buddhist sutras. It does not reach the peak of Mount Sumeru. The four great heavenly kings are the eastern heavenly king, the southern heavenly king, the western heavenly king, and the northern heavenly king. The life span of beings in the Heaven of the Four Kings is five hundred years; after five hundred years, they are destined to fall, and the Five Marks of Decay appear [i.e., signs of the impending death of a god]....A day and a night in the Heaven of the Four Kings is equivalent to fifty years among humans. 'How is that the case?' you ask.

"I'll give you an example to help you understand. If we feel very happy on a given day, the day passes without our even being aware of it. We feel the day was very short. All of us are like that. Because it is blissful in the heavens, a day and a night there is equal to fifty years among humans.

"Why is fifty years such a long time in the realm of humans? In the realm of humans there is continual disturbance and affliction, suffering and difficulty, fighting and quarrelling. People are busy from morning to night, and they don't have any idea what they are doing. They are like flies in the air, flying north, south, east, and west without knowing what they are doing. You haven't any bliss here, and so the time is very long.

"Then again, a day and a night among humans is equivalent to fifty years in the hells, because the pain and suffering in the hells is so intense, and so the beings there feel the time is extended. From this you should understand that time is neither short nor long." (SS II 68-69)

According to Mahayana Buddhist teaching, time is fundamentally unreal and is the product of distinction-making in the mind.

> Past thought cannot be got at, present thought cannot be got at, and future thought cannot be got at. (VS 124)

"Earlier a disciple asked me, 'What is time?' I haven't any time. There is no time. Time is just each person's individual awareness of long and short; that is all. If you are happy every day, fifty years can go by and you won't feel it has been a long time. If one's life is very blissful, if one has no worries, anxieties, anger, or afflictions, one's entire life seems but a short time—the blink of an eye. Ultimately, time is nothing more than a distinction based upon each person's awareness.... (SS II 69)

> If 'the present' and 'future' exist presupposing 'the past,' 'the present' and 'future' will exist in 'the past.'
>
> If 'the present' and 'future' did not exist there [in 'the past'], how could 'the present' and 'future' exist presupposing that 'past'?
>
> Without presupposing 'the past' the two things ['the present' and 'future'] cannot be proved to exist.
>
> Therefore, neither present nor future time exist.
>
> In this way the remaining two [times] can be inverted.
>
> Thus one would regard 'highest,' 'lowest' and 'middle,' etc., and oneness and difference.
>
> A non-stationary 'time' cannot be 'grasped;' and a stationary 'time' which can be grasped does not exist.
>
> How, then, can one perceive time if it is not 'grasped?'
>
> Since time is dependent on a thing (*bhāva*), how can time [exist] without a thing?
>
> There is not any thing which exists; how, then, will time become [something]? (Nāgārjuna, "Mūlamadhyamikakārikāḥ," Streng, tr. *Emptiness*)

☞ **world system**

transference of merit 迴向

The practice of transference of merit is a natural and logical development of a fundamental principle of the Path of the Bodhisattva: one uses the benefits that karmically accrue to oneself to benefit others. Transfer of merit means transferring one's own merit to others so that they may benefit from it.

"What does it mean to bring forth a Bodhisattva's mind of transference?

"**1)** He makes transference from himself to others. He transfers his merit and virtue as a universal gift to all living beings in the ☞ DHARMA REALM. He dedicates it to all living beings. If you can have All-Wisdom, then you may be able to see the Buddha. But if you have All-Wisdom, then you should make a vow to use it to make transference to all living beings so that they too will be able to attain All-Wisdom. You should make transference from yourself to them.

"**2)** He makes transference from the cause to the effect. In the future everyone will obtain the fruit of Buddhahood. Now we are cultivating at the level of planting causes. The aim of this transference is to help living beings throughout the Dharma Realm realize the Buddha Way together.

"**3)** He makes transference of the specifics to the principle. We want to dedicate all our specific practices to the still, unsurpassed, and pure substance of all Buddhas.

"**4)** He makes transference from the small to the great. At present the measure of our minds and thoughts is very small. We must make a vow that our minds will pervade the Dharma Realm, fill empty space, and include the ten thousand things. If we are now cultivating the Dharmas of the Small Vehicle, then we should dedicate our practice to the Great Vehicle. There are all kinds of transference." (FAS Ch9 27)

☞ dedication
☞ merit, Six Pāramitās—giving

transformation-bodies 化身

☞ Three Bodies of a Buddha 〈Bodhisattvas also may have transformation-bodies〉

Tripiṭaka 三藏

Tripiṭaka is a Sanskrit word meaning literally 'three baskets.' It refers to the Buddhist canon, which is divided into three portions: sutras, *vinaya*, and Abhidharma. They are sometimes listed as sutras, *vinaya*, and *śāstras*.

"The Sutra Store describes and reveals the study of concentration. The Vinaya Store describes and reveals the study of precepts. And the Śāstra Store describes and reveals the study of wisdom. Sutras, *vinaya*, and *śāstras* correspond to precepts, samadhi, and wisdom, and they eradicate greed, anger, and delusion." (FAS Ch9 185)

☞ Three Storehouses, Three Treasuries
☞ sutra, vinaya, Abhidharma

Tripiṭaka Master 三藏法師

An honorific title used to refer to someone who has fully mastered all three divisions of the Buddhist canon, or Tripiṭaka.

☞ Tripiṭaka

Tuṣita Heaven 兜率天

☞ Six Desire Heavens

Twelvefold Conditioned Arising 十二因緣

The chain of Twelvefold Conditioned Arising consists of **1)** ignorance, **2)** karmic formation, **3)** consciousness, **4)** name and form, **5)** six involvements, **6)** contact, **7)** feeling, **8)** craving, **9)** grasping, **10)** existence, **11)** birth, **12)** old age and death.

"...*ignorance*. Where does it come from? What is its beginning? It cannot be classified as either conditioned or unconditioned but falls between the two... ignorance leads to *karmic activity*.

"Karmic activity is a conditioned dharma, and when it appears, *consciousness*, which makes distinctions about the manifestations of activity, arises. With the making of distinctions the trouble starts.

"*Name and form* are the trouble. Just mentioning them is asking for trouble, because you're bound to say, 'How are name and form troublesome? I don't understand.' Before I said anything, you did not have any problem of not understanding, but once I referred to name and form as trouble, the problem of your not understanding arose and with it the desire to know.

"This quest for knowledge results in the use of the *six organs*, the faculties through which you attempt to achieve understanding. You decide you want to know, and suddenly a visual consciousness appears as do the consciousnesses of the ears, nose, tongue, body, and mind. You think you can gain understanding through the six organs without realizing that the more you 'understand' the more confused you become, and the more confused you are, the less you understand.

"Since you do not understand, you tend toward further involvement, which takes the form of *contact*. You constantly seek encounters, east, west, north, south, above, and below, like a fly madly bouncing off walls. All that results from this desperate attempt to understand is a lot of bruises from all the bumps.

"After the determination to understand sets in and the encounters occur, there is *feeling*. 'OW! It hurts!' you exclaim when you are bumping into things, and 'Boy do I feel good!' when you are not. 'If no one bothers me I'm fine, but I can't stand criticism.' This is where feeling lies. Don't look for it anywhere else.

"Once there is feeling, *love* arises. With love comes hate. You like to get involved in pleasant situations, but you detest painful circumstances. Happiness and unhappiness come from love, and every day the trouble grows.

"Wishing to prolong your contact with the objects of love, you indulge in *grasping*. The reason you clutch at objects of love is that you wish to become one with them. You want them to be inseparable from you, and this grasping leads to *becoming*.

"Your attempt to have them for your own results in further *births*, which lead to *old age and death*. This is the Twelvefold Conditioned Arising." (TD 31)

> And what, brethren, is old age-and-death?
>
> That which, of this and that being, in this and that group, is decay, decrepitude, breaking up, hoariness, wrinkling of the skin, shrinkage of a life-span, over-ripeness of faculties: this is called old age. That which , of this and that being from this or that group, is falling or decease, separation, disappearance, mortality or dying, accomplishment of time: separation of component factors, laying down of the carcass: this is called death. Thus it is this decay and this dying that is called old age-and-death.
>
> And what, brethren, is birth?
>
> That which, of this and that being in this and that group, is birth, continuous birth, descent, reproduction, appearance of component factors, acquiring of sense-spheres. This is called birth.
>
> And what, brethren, is becoming?
>
> Three are these becomings: becoming in kāma (i.e., desire) [-worlds], becoming in rūpa (i.e., form) [-worlds], becoming in arūpa (i.e., formless) [-worlds]. This is called becoming.
>
> And what, brethren, is grasping?
>
> There are these four graspings: grasping of desires, grasping of opinion, grasping of rule and ritual, grasping of soul theory. This is called grasping.
>
> And what, brethren, is craving?
>
> There are these six groups of craving: craving for things seen, for things heard, for odours, for tastes, for things tangible, for ideas. This is called craving.
>
> And what, brethren, is feeling?
>
> There are these six groups of feeling: feeling that is born of eye-contact, feeling that is born of ear-contact, feeling that is born of nose-contact, feeling that is born of tongue-contact, feeling that is born of body-contact, feeling that is born of mind-contact. This is called feeling.
>
> And what, brethren, is contact?
>
> There are these six groups of contact: eye-contact, ear-, nose-, tongue-, body-, mind-contact. This is called contact.
>
> And what, brethren, is sixfold sense?
>
> The sense of eye, ear, nose, tongue, body, mind. This is called sixfold sense.
>
> And what, brethren, is name-and-shape?
>
> Feeling, perception, will, contact, work of mind. This is called name. The four great elements and the shape derived from them. This is called shape. This is the name, this is the shape called name-and-shape.

And what is consciousness?

There are six groups of consciousness:—eye-consciousness, ear-consciousness, smell-, taste-, touch-, and mind-consciousness. This is called consciousness.

And what are activities?

These are the three activities: those of deed, speech, and mind. These are activities.

And what is ignorance?

Nescience concerning ill, its rise, its cessation and concerning the way going to the cessation of ill. This is called ignorance.

So thus, brethren: 'conditioned by ignorance activities, conditioned by activities consciousness,' and so on to 'despair'—such is the uprising of this entire mass of ill.

But from the utter fading out and ceasing of ignorance ceasing of activities, from the ceasing of activities ceasing of consciousness, and so on to 'despair'—such is the ceasing of this entire mass of ill. (Rhys Davids, tr. *Kindred Sayings* II 3-5)

☞ **causes, causes and conditions, conditioned causes, dependent origination, interdependent origination, Conditioned Arising, conditioned co-production, chain of causation, metabolism of kamma, conditioned links**

☞ **causation**

Two Vehicles 二乘

The Two Vehicles are **1)** the ☞PRATYEKABUDDHA VEHICLE, and **2)** the ☞ŚRĀVAKA VEHICLE. The expression Two Vehicles is a common way of referring to those who follow the Hinayana teachings.

☞ **Three Vehicles, Mahayana and Hinayana Compared**

Universal Worthy 〈Bodhisattva〉 普賢《菩薩》

"What is 'Universal'? It means his way pervades everywhere. What does 'Worthy' mean? It means 'his virtue is a sage's virtue.' His conduct is identical to the conduct of the foremost sages.

"There are four great Bodhisattvas. Mañjuśrī Bodhisattva is foremost in wisdom; the Bodhisattva Who Observes the Sounds of the World [☞AVALOKITEŚVARA] is foremost in great ☞COMPASSION; Earth Store [Kṣitigarbha] Bodhisattva is foremost in strength of vows; Universal Worthy [Samantabhadra] Bodhisattva is foremost in practice." (UW 5-6)

Universal Worthy Bodhisattva (see plate 44)

Universal Worthy Bodhisattva
on his six-tusked white elephant
(see plate 45)

Universal Worthy Bodhisattva arose from his seat, bowed at the Buddha's feet, and said to the Buddha, 'I have been a Dharma Prince with as many Thus Come Ones as there are sands in the Ganges. The Thus Come Ones of the ten directions tell their disciples who have the roots of a Bodhisattva to cultivate the Universal Worthy Conduct, which is named after me.

'World Honored One, I use my mind to listen and distinguish the knowledge and views of living beings. In other regions as many realms away as there are sands in the Ganges, if there is any living being who discovers the conduct of Universal Worthy, I immediately mount my six-tusked elephant and create hundreds of thousands of reduplicated bodies which go to those places. Although their obstacles may be so heavy that they do not see me, I secretly rub the crowns of their heads, protect and comfort them, and help them to be successful.' (SS V 65-67)

☞ **Bodhisattva**

upāsaka 優婆塞

A Buddhist layperson.

"An *upāsaka* is a layman and an *upāsikā* is a laywoman. The Sanskrit word *upāsaka* means "man who is close in work." *Upāsikā* means "woman who is close in work," working closely with the Triple Jewel [☞ THREE JEWELS]." (DFS IX 1685)

☞ **layman, layperson**

☞ **upāsikā**

upāsikā 優婆夷

Feminine form of ☞ UPĀSAKA.

V

vajra 金剛

Vajra has two meanings: **1)** An indestuctible substance that is sometimes equated with emptiness, and sometimes used as an adjective to indicate the quality of the substance; **2)** A Dharma-implement.

"*Vajra* is a Sanskrit word that defies translation because of its numerous connotations, but essentially *vajra* is an indestructible substance, usually represented by diamond." (VS 3)

"*Vajra* has three meanings: durable; luminous; and able to cut. *Vajra* is so durable it cannot be destroyed by anything, but can itself destroy everything.

"'If *vajra* breaks up everything, then I won't have anything, and of what use will that be?' you may ask.

"The reason you don't realize Buddhahood is just because you 'have everything.' If you didn't have anything, you could realize Buddhahood. 'Everything' refers to your attachments—all those things you cannot put down....

"Durable *vajra* breaks through thought, but not through no thought. The *vajra* of no thought is durable enough to smash all existing marks—all conditioned marks subject to outflows. No thought can destroy the spiritual penetrations of heavenly demons and those of external ways, because their spiritual penetrations have marks....

"*Vajra* is luminous. Its light can break up all darkness. *Vajra* is able to cut. A sharp knife can sever something with a single slice, while a dull knife saws and saws and still cannot cut through. *Vajra* severs all the deviant knowledge and views of heavenly demons and those of external ways, chops through people's afflictions, and slices through ignorance." (VS 81)

☞ **Vajra Prajñā Pāramitā Sutra**

Vajra ⟨Diamond⟩ Prajñā Pāramitā Sutra 金剛般若波羅密多經

One of the most popular Buddhist scriptures, the *Vajra Sutra* explains how the Bodhisattva relies on the perfection of wisdom to teach and transform beings.

Vasubandhu ⟨Bodhisattva⟩ ⟨fl. 4th cent. C.E.⟩ 世親《菩薩》

The second of three sons, born in Puruṣapura (Peshāwar), India, into the Kauśika family of Indian Brahmins. All three sons were called Vasubandhu and all three became Buddhist Bhikshus. His older brother was known as Asaṅga and his younger brother as Viriñcivatsa. He is known simply as Vasubandhu. In his youth he adhered to the Hinayana teachings of the Sautrāntika School and wrote the *Abhidharmakośa*, perhaps the most well-known of all treatises on the ☞ABHIDHARMA. He was converted to the ☞MAHAYANA by his older brother the Bodhisattva Asaṅga. After his conversion, he wrote many celebrated works on the ☞CONSCIOUSNESS-ONLY SCHOOL of the Mahayana, including the *Twenty Verses on Consciousness-Only* and the *Thirty Verses on Consciousness-Only*.

WORLDLY RELATIVE BODHISATTVA
(VASUBANDHU BODHISATTVA)

Vasubandhu's Conversion

"Asaṅga, teacher of the Law [Dharma], saw that his younger brother was endowed with an intelligence surpassing that of others, his knowledge being deep and wide, and himself well-versed in esoteric and exoteric doctrines. He was afraid that the latter might compose a *śāstra* and crush the Mahayana. He was living then in the Land of the Hero (Puruṣapura) and sent a messenger to Vasubandhu in Ayodhyā with the following message: "I am seriously ill at present. You had better attend to me quickly." Vasubandhu followed the messenger to his native land, saw his brother and inquired what was the cause of his illness. He answered: "I have now a serious disease of the heart, which arose on account of you." Vasubandhu again asked: "Why do you say on account of me?" He answered: "You do not believe in the

Mahayana and are always attacking and discrediting it. For this wickedness you will be sure to sink forever in a miserable life. I am now grieved and troubled for your sake to such an extent that my life will no long survive. On hearing this Vasubandhu was surprised and alarmed and asked his brother to expound the Mahayana for him. He then gave him a concise explanation of the essential principles of the Mahayana. Thereupon the Teacher of the Law (Vasubandhu), who was possessed of clear intelligence and especially of deep insight, became at once convinced that the truth of the Mahayana excelled even that of the Hinayana.

"He then fully investigated, under his brother, the principles of the Mahayana. Soon after he became as thoroughly acquainted with the whole as his brother was. When its meaning was already clear to him, he would meditate on it. From the beginning to the end everything was perfectly in accordance with the truth, there being nothing contradictory to it. For the first time he realized that the Hinayana was wrong and the Mahayana right. If there were no Mahayana, then (he thought) there would be no path (*mārga*) and no fruition (*phala*) of the Tri-yāna [Three Vehicles]. Since he formerly did harm by speaking ill of the Mahayana, in which he then had no faith, he was now afraid that he might fall into a miserable life on account of that wickedness. He deeply reproached himself and earnestly repented of his previous fault. He approached his brother and confessed his error, saying: 'I now desire to make a confession. I do not know by what means I can be pardoned for my former slander.' He said (further): 'I formerly did harm speaking ill (of the truth) by means of my tongue. I will now cut out my tongue in order to atone for my crime.' His brother answered: 'Even if you cut out your tongue a thousand times, you cannot wipe out your crime. If you really want to wipe out your crime, you must find some other means.' Thereupon he asked his brother to explain the means of wiping out the offence. The latter said: 'Your tongue was able to speak very skillfully and effectively against the Mahayana, and thus discredit it. If you want to wipe out your offence, you must now propound the Mahayana equally skillfully and effectively.'" (Takakusu, tr. *The Life of Vasubandhu*, 290-292)

A eulogy says:

> It is difficult to practice two teachings
> at once.
> He elucidated the secret meanings
> of the Compassionate Sage
> In awesome *śāstras* like piled up
> clouds,
> Explaining the untransmitted
> doctrine,
> Revealing the Consciousness-Only,
> Complete in both the Nature and
> Appearance Schools.
> An eternal Dharma lamp,
> He shines upon a million generations.
> (VBS #20 2)

☞ **Asaṅga ‹Bodhisattva›, Consciousness-Only School**

vegetarianism 素食主義

> All beings—human or beast—
> Love life and hate to die.
> They fear most the butcher's knife
> Which slices and chops them
> piece by piece.
> Instead of being cruel and mean,
> Why not stop killing and cherish life?
> (CL I 83)

In Buddhism adhering to a completely vegetarian diet is a natural and logical ramification of the moral precept against the taking of life (☞ FIVE MORAL PRECEPTS). The Bodhisattva Precepts (☞ BRAHMA NET SUTRA) also explicitly forbid the eating of nonvegetarian food and also the eating of garlic, onions, and other related plants.

In the ☞ ŚŪRAṄGAMA SUTRA the Buddha states:

> After my extinction, in the ☞ DHARMA-ENDING AGE, these hordes of ghosts and spirits will abound, spreading like wildfire as they argue that eating meat will bring one to the Bodhi Way.... You should know that these people who eat meat may gain some awareness and may seem to be in samadhi, but they are all great *rākṣasas*. When their retribution ends, they are bound to sink into the bitter sea of birth and death. They are not disciples of the Buddha. Such people as these kill and eat one another in a never-ending cycle. How can such people transcend the ☞ THREE REALMS? (SS VI 20-22)

"Question: When you eat one bowl of rice, you take the life of all the grains of rice, whereas eating meat you take only one animal's life.

"The Master: On the body of one single animal are a hundred thousand, in fact, several million little organisms. These organisms are fragments of what was once an animal. The soul of a human being at death may split up to become many animals. One person can become about ten animals. That's why animals are so ignorant. The soul of an animal can split up and become, in its smallest division, an organism or plant. The feelings which plants have, then, are what separated from the animals's soul when it split up at death. Although the life force of a large number of plants may appear sizeable, it is not as great as that of a single animal or a single mouthful of meat. Take, for example, rice: tens of billions of grains of rice do not contain as much life force as a single piece of meat. If you open your ☞ FIVE EYES you can know this at a glance. If you haven't opened your eyes, no matter how one tries to explain it to you, you won't understand. No matter how it's explained, you won't believe it, because you haven't been a plant!

"Another example is the mosquitoes. The millions of mosquitoes on this mountain may be simply the soul of one person who has been transformed into all those bugs. It is not the case that a single human soul turns into a single mosquito. One person can turn into countless numbers of mosquitoes.

"At death the nature changes, the soul scatters, and its smallest fragments become plants. Thus, there is a difference between eating plants and eating animals. What is more, plants have very short life spans. The grass, for example, is born in the spring and dies within months. Animals live a long time. If you don't kill them, they will live for many years. Rice, regardless of conditions, will only live a short time. And so, if you really look into it, there are many factors to consider, and even science hasn't got it all straight." (BRF 64)

"Mahākāśyapa asked the Buddha, 'Why is it that the Thus Come One does not allow eating meat?'

"The Buddha replied,' It is because meat-eating cuts off the seeds of great compassion." (CL II 5)

☞ **Five Contemplations When Eating, Five Moral Precepts—no killing; liberating living beings, compassion**

(see illustration on page 214)

BIZARRO / By Piraro
Chronicle Features 1985
PIRARO.
"Perhaps THIS will refresh your memory!!"

vinaya 戒/毗奈耶

Vinaya refers to the collected moral regulations governing the life of the Buddhist monastic community, one of the three divisions of the Buddhist canon.

"The *vinaya* includes all the precept-regulations, methods we use to keep watch over ourselves so that it is not necessary for anyone else to keep an eye on us." (SV 10)

According to Buddhist teachings, the monastic regulations contained in the *vinaya* should be read only by fully ordained monks (Bhikshus) and nuns (Bhikshunis). See the story illustrating pure adherence to the *vinaya* under FAITH.

☞ **moral precepts, Sangha, Tripiṭaka**

Vinaya School 律宗

The Vinaya School in China was founded by Vinaya Master Daoxuan (596-667 C.E.). Its roots go back to the time of the Buddha and the Venerable Upāli, who was foremost among the Buddha's disciples in practicing the regulations for personal conduct laid down by the Buddha.

☞ **moral precepts, Five Types of Buddhist Study and Practice—moral regulations**

vows 願

"The power of vows eradicates heavy karma, wipes away all illnesses of mind and body at their karmic source, subdues demons, and can move gods and humans to respect....

"One must make great vows. A cultivator is like a person who wants to cross the sea. The great vows of a cultivator are like a boat which can carry him or her from birth and death across the sea of suffering to the other shore of ☞NIRVANA. The mind which makes great vows must be solid and durable. It must be permanent and unchanging. It must be indestructible. It must be like ☞VAJRA." (UW 153-154)

"Vows are very important. But you can't make someone else's vows. You can't say, "I will make ☞AVALOKITEŚVARA BODHISATTVA's ten vows, or ☞UNIVERSAL WORTHY BODHISATTVA's ten vows, ☞AMITĀBHA's forty-eight vows, or Medicine Master's twelve vows. Those are *their* vows. You can't just copy them. You must make your own vows. You could make vows even greater than those of Amitābha Buddha or Avalokiteśvara Bodhisattva, but they must be your own. You aren't them!

"'Well,' you might argue, 'suppose I am a transformation of Amitābha Buddha? What is wrong with making his vows then?'

"Even if you are, you are still just a transformation; you aren't the original. You have to make new vows. It is like metal which was one thing and then got melted down into something else. Perhaps you were a metal sculpture of a turtle, and now you've turned into a train. You can't be a turtle again, not even if you want to. I won't argue with you about whether or not you are Amitabha's ☞TRANSFORMATION BODY, but you still need to make brand new vows, no old ones.

"There are some old vows which everyone can make; they are standard vows that every Bodhisattva makes, and that's all right:

> I vow to save the boundless
> numbers of beings.
> I vow to cut off the inexhaustible
> afflictions.
> I vow to study the endless
> Dharma-doors.
> I vow to realize the supreme
> Buddha Way.

"When Amitābha Buddha was at the level of planting causes, he was a Bhikshu by the name of Fazang [Skt. Dharmākara]. He made forty-eight vows which he used to cultivate in every lifetime. He made those vows in every life for who knows how many great aeons before he became a Buddha and created the Land of Ultimate Bliss. You should make vows right at the beginning when you start cultivating. Even if you are an old-timer and have been cultivating for quite a while, you should make solid vows. Perhaps some of you have been planting Buddha-seeds throughout many lifetimes, many aeons. And now as a result you have encountered this opportunity. You are able to put all of your energy into practicing the Buddhadharma.

"Write out your vows. You can write them just how you want them. Perhaps: **1)** I vow to save all ants. **2)** I vow to save all mosquitoes. **3)** I vow to save all hopeless cases. Of course, I'm joking. But one of my disciples did make a vow to become a Buddha in the northern continent of Uttarakuru [☞ WORLD SYSTEMS]. Why did he do that? Because right now there is no Buddha there. When he gets there, because there are no Buddhas there, he will be worshipped exclusively for sure! Not much competition! I was quite pleased with that vow; it is very special, and so I made a vow that I would guarantee that he fulfills that vow. Everything in the world can change. There's nothing fixed. If someone makes a vow to go somewhere and become a Buddha, a Buddha will, in the future, appear in that place. No one ever made a vow to become a Buddha in Uttarakuru before, and so there is no Buddhadharma there right now.

"Once you have made your vows, even if you would like to slack off in your cultivation, you won't dare, because you made the vows to cultivate! Vows are extremely important." (DFS VII 1195-1197)

☞ **Earth Store ⟨Bodhisattva⟩**

W

Way 道

☞ **Middle Way**

Way-place 道場

A Way-place is a place where one cultivates the Way, or one's spiritual Path. The original Way-place was the spot under the Bodhi tree where the Buddha became fully enlightened. The term 'Way-place' includes monasteries and other auspicious sites where people, either singly or together, put the Buddhadharma into practice

platform, terrace, seat of enlightenment, spot under Bodhi tree, any place for cultivation of the Path

world systems 世界

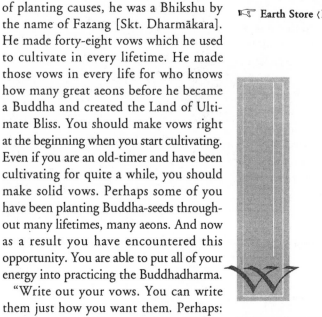

The Buddha taught that the Earth is not the center of the universe and is not the only planet with intelligent life. He taught that there are an infinite number of world systems, that some of those worlds are inhabited by intelligent life, and that on some of those worlds other Buddhas also teach the Buddhadharma.

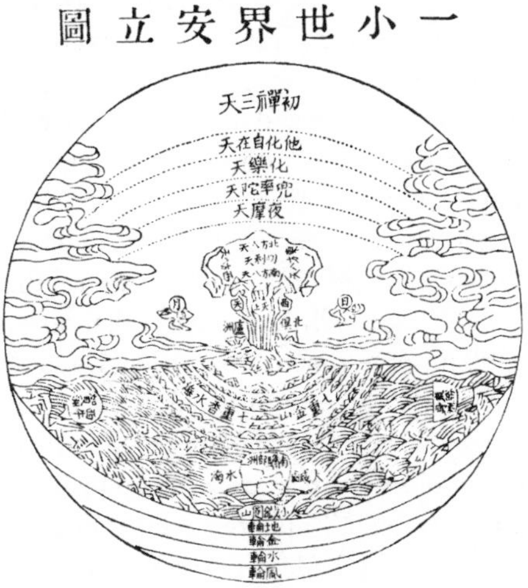

Chinese woodblock depiction of a world system

Description of a World System

"One sun, one moon, one Mount Sumeru, and one set of four great continents is what is called 'a set of four continents under heaven,' that is, a world system. In our world system, a smaller version of the larger whole, Asia could be called Southern Jambudvīpa. Probably America is equivalent to Eastern Pūrvavideha, Europe to Western Aparagodānīya, and the Soviet Union to Northern Uttarakuru. However the Buddhist sutras say that the inhabitants of Northern Uttarakuru do not see the Buddha, do not hear the Dharma, and do not see members of the Sangha. They say that when it is daytime in Southern Jambudvīpa, it is nighttime in Northern Uttarakuru. Every world system has these four great continents, and perhaps sometimes the directions of the four can be different. Don't get attached to it." (EDR VIII 215-216)

A thousand world systems of four great continents, etc. comprise a 'small world system.' A thousand small world systems comprise a medium-sized world system, and a thousand medium-sized world systems comprise a great world system of a billion worlds, or literally a thousand times a thousand times a thousand worlds (Skt. *tri-sahasra-mahā-sahasra-loka-dhātu*).

In the ☞FLOWER ADORNMENT SUTRA the Buddha taught that the universe of world systems is shaped like a great lotus flower and that world systems are arrayed within it in petal-like tiers. Our world system, called the Sahā World, is located on the thirteenth tier.

According to Buddhist teachings this planet we live on is not unique in supporting intelligent life, is not the center of the universe, and is not the only world on which Buddhism is taught and practiced.

> The world systems are spoken of by the Tathāgata as no world systems; therefore, they are called "world systems." (VS 80)

☞ **time, cosmology**

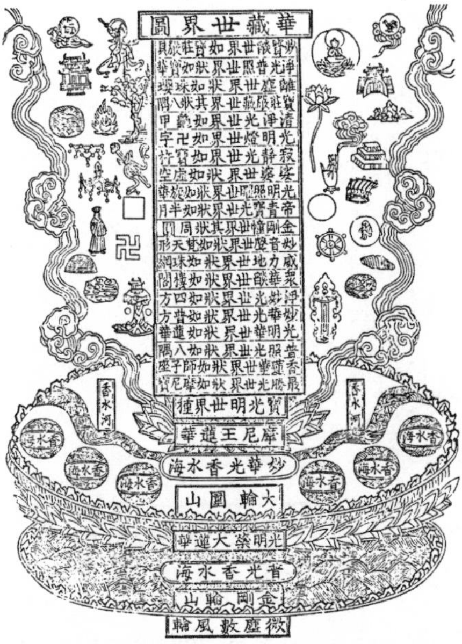

Chinese woodblock chart of the Flower Treasury World System (showing the name and shape of the world on each tier)

W

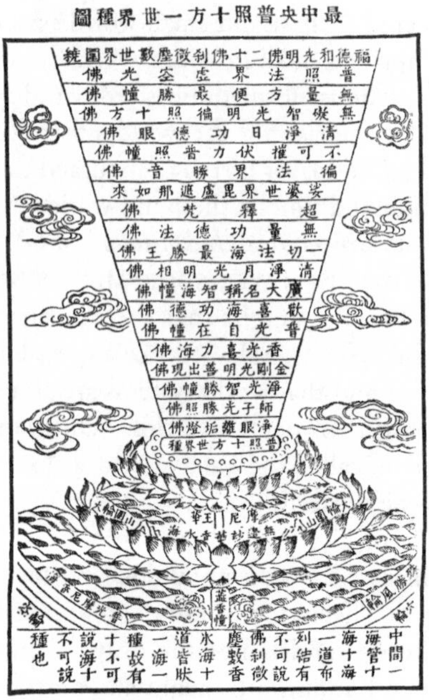

Chinese woodblock chart of the
Flower Treasury World System
(showing the name of the Buddha in each world)

X

Xuanzang ⟨Tripiṭaka Master⟩ ⟨596-664 C.E.⟩ 玄奘《三藏法師》

Xuanzang was a great enlightened master, translator, and founder of the ☞ CONSCIOUSNESS-ONLY SCHOOL in China.

"This Bhikshu's contributions to Buddhism have been exceptionally great. It can be said that from ancient times to the present, there has never been anyone who can compare to this Dharma Master in his achievements. His worldly name was Cha. His father was an official, but a poor one. Why did he end up a poor official? It was because he didn't take bribes. He wasn't after the citizens' money nor that of the government. He wasn't like people today who hold office and always feel they are earning too little money so that on top of their government salary they force the citizens to give them their hard-earned money as well. Dharma Master Xuanzang's father didn't want money. He remained a poor official all his life. Even though he was poor, he had a virtuous nature and because of that he had two sons who left the home-life, lectured sutras, and were adept cultivators of the Way.

"Dharma Master Xuanzang left the home-life at the age of thirteen and commenced his study of the Buddhadharma. During those early years of study, if there was a Dharma Master lecturing a Buddhist text, no matter who the Dharma Master was or how far away the lecture was being held, he was sure to go to listen, whether it was a ☞ SUTRA lecture, a ☞ ŚĀSTRA lecture or a ☞ VINAYA lecture. He went to listen to them all. Wind and rain couldn't keep him away from lectures on the ☞ TRIPIṬAKA, to the point that he even forgot to be hungry. He just ate the Dharma, taking the Buddhadharma as his food and drink. He did this for five years and then took the Complete Precepts.

TANG DYNASTY
TRIPITAKA MASTER XUAN-CHUANG OF
CI-EN TEMPLE

"However, the principles lectured by the Dharma Masters he heard were all different. They all explained the same sutras in very different ways—each with his own interpretation. And there was a big difference between the lectures of those with wisdom and those without wisdom. But Dharma Master Xuanzang had not yet really become enlightened, and he didn't have the Selective Dharma Eye, and so how could he know whose lectures to rely on? At that time he vowed to go to India, saying, 'The Buddhadharma has been transmitted from India, and so there is certainly true and genuine Buddhadharma to be found in India.'

"Thereupon, he wrote a request for permission to go to India to seek the Dharma and presented it to the emperor. Emperor Taizong of the Tang Dynasty did not grant his wish, but Dharma Master Xuanzang, who had already vowed to go, said, 'I would prefer to disobey the son of Heaven and have my head cut off than not to go and seek the Dharma.' And so he returned to the monastery and began to practice mountain-climbing. He piled chairs, tables, and benches together to simulate a mountain and practiced jumping from one piece of furniture to the next. This was his method of practicing mountain-climbing. From morning till night he leaped from table to chair. Probably there weren't any big mountains where he lived, and so he had to practice in the temple. All the young, old, and older novices wondered what he was up to, jumping on furniture all day long instead of reciting sutras or cultivating. He didn't tell anyone that he was training to climb the Himalayas, and so most people thought he was goofing off. Eventually he trained his body so that it was very strong, and then when he was physically able, he started his trip through Siberia.

"On the day of his departure, when Emperor Taizong learned he intended to go even without imperial consent, the emperor asked him, 'I haven't given you permission and you still insist on going. When will you be back?'

"Dharma Master Xuanzang replied, 'Look at this pine tree. The needles are pointing toward the west. Wait until those needles turn around and face east. That is the time when I will return.' He didn't say how many years that would be. And so he set out. At that time there were no airplanes, steamboats, buses, or trains. There were boats, but they were made of wood and not too sturdy. Besides, since he didn't have imperial permission, he probably could not have gotten the use of a boat anyway. And so he traveled by land through many countries, from the Siberian area of the Russian border to India. He was gone for more than a decade. When he reached India, he didn't know the language at all. But bit-by-bit he studied Sanskrit and listened to many Dharma Masters lecture the Buddhadharma. Some people say this took him fourteen years. Others say it took nineteen. In general he went through a great deal of suffering and difficulty to study the Buddhadharma and then when he'd completed his studies, he returned to China.

"When his return was imminent, the needles on the pine tree turned to the east. As soon as the emperor saw that the pine needles were indeed pointing east, he knew that Dharma Master Xuanzang was coming back and he sent out a party of officials to the western gate to welcome him and escort him back. When they reached the gate, there indeed, was Dharma Master Xuanzang returning.

"Dharma Master Xuanzang then concentrated on translating the sutras and other works that he had brought back with him. He translated from Sanskrit into Chinese. At the time when he was translating the *Mahāprajñāpāramitā-sūtra*, within one single year, the peach trees blossomed six times. That was a sign of the auspiciousness of the *Mahāprajñāpāramitā-sūtra* and its importance to all of us. The fact that it was being translated moved even the wood and plants to display their delight.

"Dharma Master Xuanzang translated a great many sutras. While in India, he bowed to the Buddha's ☞ŚARĪRA and bones. He saw where the Buddha in a previous life had given up his eyes, and went to the place where the Buddha in a previous life had practiced the conduct of patience, and went to the place where the Buddha in a previous life had given up his life for the sake of a tiger. He also went to see the Bodhi tree under which the Buddha realized the Way. He went to all of those places celebrated in Buddhism. These pilgrimages are another indication of the extent of his true sincerity. While in India, whenever he met Dharma Masters, he never looked down on them, no matter how little they may have cultivated. He was extremely respectful. He wasn't the least bit arrogant or haughty. When he finished his studies, many Small Vehicle Dharma Masters and masters of externalist ways came to debate with him, but

Tripiṭaka Master Xuanzang bringing sutras from India back to China (see plate 46)

none was able to defeat him.

Dharma Master Xuanzang is known as a Tripiṭaka Master. The Tripiṭaka includes the Sutra Treasury, the Śāstra Treasury, and the Vinaya Treasury. He was honored with this title because he understood all three Treasuries without obstruction....

"As to his name, Xuan means 'esoteric and wonderful.' He was esoteric in the sense that none could really understand him. Zang means 'awe-inspiring.' He was awe-inspiring in that he could do what others could not do. He was an outstanding person among his peers...." (HD 15-17)

The Master's name has also been transliterated as follows: Hsuan-tsang, Sywan-Dzang, Yuan Chwang, etc.

☞ **Consciousness-Only School**

Xuyun 〈Chan Master〉 虛雲《禪師》

Chan Master Xuyun

Almost universally acknowledged as the greatest enlightened master of modern times, Chan Master Xuyun, also spelled 'Hsu Yun', ("Empty Cloud") (1840-1959) revitalized the Chan School in China and retransmitted all five of the authentic Chan lineages.

In the winter of his fifty-sixth year, "on the third evening of the eighth week of the (meditation) session, after six hours of sitting in meditation, the attendant made his rounds, filling up the tea cups. The Master's hand was burned by spilled boiling water, and his cup fell to the floor. At the sound of the crash, the root of his doubt was instantly severed. He was joyous beyond words at having fulfilled his lifelong ambition. It was as if he had just awakened from a dream, and he observed the conditions of the past unravel. If he had not fallen into the river and become gravely ill, if he had not met good advisors who plied him with both adversity and felicity, how would this present experience have been possible? The Master's verse of explanation says:

"A cup fell down and struck the floor;
The sound of the crash
was distinctly heard.
Emptiness was pulverized,
And the mad mind stopped
on the spot." (PB I 104)

In the final year of his life, the Venerable Master Xuyun composed the following verse:

This crazed fellow—
Where does he come from?
For no reason he sticks out his neck
During the Dharma-Ending Age.
Lamenting that the Sagely Path hangs
by a precarious thread,
He cares not for his own affairs—
for whom does he worry?
On a lonely mountain peak
He sends down bait and tackle
to catch a carp.
Plummeting down to the great
ocean bed,
He stokes the flames to fry a sea
bubble.
Not finding one who "knows his
sound,"
He sighs in sorrow,
Yet his laughter
pierces the void!
Scold him, he
doesn't gripe.
Ask him: why
don't you put it
down?
"When will the
masses' suffering
come to an end?
That's when I will
rest!"
(PB II, preface)

☞ **Chan School**

Chan Master Xuyun (left) with Master Hua

Yogācāra 瑜伽宗

☞ **Consciousness-Only School**

yojana 由旬

A measure of length, about seven English miles.

Z

Zen 禪

☞ **Chan School**

Zhiyi 〈Venerable〉 〈538-597 C.E.〉 智顗《法師》

The third patriarch of the Chinese Tiantai School of Mahayana Buddhism, which is based on the teachings of the ☞ DHARMA FLOWER (LOTUS) SUTRA.

Third patriarch of the Tian-tai school, Great Master Zhi-zhe

"When Great Master 'Wise One' [Zhiyi] went to pay his respects, Great Master [Hui] Si, [the second Tiantai patriarch], said to him, 'Oh, so you have come. We listened to the *Dharma Flower Sutra* together on Vulture Peak at the time of Śākyamuni Buddha.' As soon as Great Master 'Wise One' heard that, he realized, 'Yes, that's right. We did investigate the *Dharma Flower Sutra* together at the time of Śākyamuni Buddha.'

"Afterwards, Great Master 'Wise One' had a state. He was reading the *Dharma Flower Sutra* and reached the section in which Medicine King Bodhisattva burns his body as an offering to the Buddha, the passage that reads: 'This is true vigor. This is called a true offering of Dharma.' He suddenly entered samadhi, right while reading the text, and was able to see the Dharma Flower Assembly on Vulture Peak with Śākyamuni Buddha still speaking the Dharma and the multitudes of Bodhisattvas, Sound Hearers, and those of the ☞ EIGHTFOLD DIVISION listening to the *Dharma Flower Sutra.*" (FAS-PII(2) 3)

The Venerable Master Zhiyi is not only considered one of the truly great enlightened Buddhist masters of China, but also is well known for his clear and systematic explanations of Buddhist meditational practices and doctrinal systems.

☞ **Tiantai School, Dharma Flower 〈Lotus〉 Sutra**

APPENDICES

A Additional Reference Material for Entries 224
B The Buddhist Text Translation Society 238
C Comparative Tables of Romanization: Pinyin / Wade-Giles / Yale 240
D Sanskrit Pronunciation Guide 245
E The Venerable Master Hsuan Hua Brings the Dharma to the West 246
F On Translating Buddhist Texts and Speaking the Dharma 257
G The Eighteen Great Vows of Venerable Master Hsuan Hua 265

BIBLIOGRAPHIES

Bibliography of BTTS Publications in English 267
Bibliography of Cited Non-BTTS Publications 270

INDICES

Index of Sanskrit Terms 273
Index of Pali Terms 277
Index of Chinese Terms (Pinyin) 279
DRBA Branch Monasteries 283

The reference material for each entry includes the following sections:

1 CH lists one or more Chinese equivalents, giving the romanization in pinyin followed by the characters.

2 SKT lists one or more Sanskrit equivalents.

3 PALI lists one or more Pali equivalents.

4 REF References to the topic which can be found in Buddhist Text Translation Society publications.

NOTES:

* While general terms in English are often given in the plural, e.g. **demons**, they are sometimes expressed in Sanskrit or Pali using the singular or stem form. Some Sanskrit and Pali plurals are cited in stem form and others are not.
* Not every Sanskrit, Pali, or Chinese citation is the exact equivalent of the English term, but is given with the intention of providing the closest relevant term in those languages.

A

abbot 方丈
CH *fang zhang* 方丈, *zhu chi* 住持
SKT *vihārasvāmin*

Abhidharma 阿毗達摩
CH *a bi da mo* 阿毗達摩, *lun* 論
SKT *abhidharma*
PALI *abhidhamma*
REF FAS-PII 97-108.

Amitābha (Buddha) 阿彌陀(佛)
CH *a mi to fo* 阿彌陀(佛) (Jap. 'amida')
SKT *amitābha* (*amitāyus*)
REF AS 10-11, 20; UW 28-29, 131-135, 215-217; SM IV 53; SM V 10-11.

Amitābha Sutra 阿彌陀經
CH *(fo shuo) a mi to jing* (佛說)阿彌陀經
SKT *sukhāvatī-vyūha-sūtra*
REF AS.

Ānanda (Venerable) 阿難(尊者)
CH *a nan (zun zhe)* 阿難(尊者)
SKT *ānanda*
PALI *ānanda*
REF FAS-PI (Seventh Door, ms.); AS 91-92; SS I 24-26; DFS II 124; DFS VIII 1500-1510.

anuttara-samyak-saṃbodhi 阿耨多羅三藐三菩提
CH *a nou duo luo san miao san pu ti* 阿耨多羅三藐三菩提, *wu shang zheng deng zheng jue* 無上正等正覺
SKT *anuttarasamyak-saṃbodhi*
PALI *anuttarasammā-sambodhi*
REF FAS Ch16, 22; DFS IV 519; DFS VII 1305.

Arhat 阿羅漢
CH *a luo han* 阿羅漢
SKT *arhat, arhant, arhanta*
PALI *arahat*
REF DFS VII 1371-2, 1449-50; DFS X 52; TT 47; EDR II 57-58; FAS Ch16 28-31; SS I 107-109; AS 66; VBS #196 4-5.

Asaṅga (Bodhisattva) 無著(菩薩)
CH *wu zhao* 無著
SKT *asaṅga*
REF HD 9-12; UW 1-3.

asaṅkhyeya/asaṃkhyeya 阿僧祇
CH *a seng qi* 阿僧祇
SKT *asaṅkhyeya, asaṃkhyeya*
PALI *asankheyya*

asura 阿修羅
CH *a xiu luo* 阿修羅
SKT *asura*
PALI *asura*
REF TD 42-44; SS IV 239-242, V 135, VII 239-243; TT 47, 57-58; VBS (May 1970) 34-37.

attachment 執著
CH *zhi zhao* 執著
SKT *abhiniveśa*

PALI *abhinivesa*
REF EDR II 131-132.

Avalokiteśvara (Bodhisattva)
觀世音 (菩薩)
CH *guan yin* 觀音, *guan shi yin* 觀世音, *guan zi zai (pu sa)* 觀自在 (菩薩)
SKT *avalokiteśvara*

avīci hell 阿鼻地獄
CH *a bi di yu* 阿鼻地獄, *wu jian di yu* 無間地獄,
SKT *avīci naraka/niraya*
PALI *avīci niraya*

B

Baozhi (Chan Master)
寶誌 (禪師)
CH *bao zhi* (*chan shi*) 寶誌 (禪師)
REF DFS IX 1708-1710.

Bhikshu 比丘
CH *bi qiu* 比丘
SKT *bhikṣu*
PALI *bhikkhu*
REF EDR I 166-167; FAS Ch11 106-116; FAS Ch16 30-31; SS I 63-64; SS V 148-149; DFS II 181, 345; DFS IX 1683-1685.

Bhikshuni 比丘尼
CH *bi qiu ni* 比丘尼
SKT *bhikṣuṇī*
PALI *bhikkhuni*
REF See references for Bhikshu.

blessings 福報
CH *fu* 福, *fu bao* 福報
SKT *puṇya[-phala]*
PALI *puñña*
REF S42 23-27; DFS 1080-1081; UW 77; PS 133-134, 194.

bodhi 菩提
CH *pu ti* 菩提
SKT *bodhi*
PALI *bodhi*
REF SS I 180-181; SS III 135-137, 196-197; FAS Ch24 63.

Bodhidharma (Patriarch)
菩提達摩 (祖師)
CH *pu ti da mo (zu shi)* 菩提達摩 (祖師)
SKT *bodhidharma*
REF VBS #169 (June, 1984), pp. 1-3, 12; PS 8-16; SS VII 54-55.

Bodhi resolve (bringing forth)
發菩提心
CH *fa pu ti xin* 發菩提心
SKT *bodhicittotpāda*
REF "Essay on Exhortation to Bring Forth the Bodhi Resolve" BTTS ms.; FAS Ch6 178-179, Ch17; EDR VIII 67-102.

Bodhisattva 菩薩
CH *pu sa* 菩薩, *pu ti sa duo* 菩提薩馱
SKT *bodhisattva*
PALI *bodhisatta*
REF HS 95-97, DFS II 301-2; DS 5-6;TD 27-29; HD 13; EDR II 70-72; UW 25-26; FAS-PI 51-54 ; FAS Ch9 44-45; FAS Ch 11 39; SS I 107; SS VI 48-55; AS 98-99.

bowing 禮拜
CH *bai* 拜, *li bai* 禮拜, *ding li* 頂禮
SKT *vandana*
PALI *vandana*
REF WM 38-39; SV 57; UW 18-25; PDS "Seven Types of Bowing: What Happens When People Bow"; WOH; TS.

Brahma Net Sutra 梵網經
CH *fan wang jing* 梵網經 (a) T. 21, (b) T. 1484
SKT *brahmajāla-sūtra* (not extant)
PALI *brahmajāla-sutta*
REF (b) BNS 2 vols.

Budai (Venerable)
布袋 (和尚)
CH *bu dai (he shang)* 布袋 (和尚)

Buddha 佛
CH *fo* 佛, *fo tuo* 佛陀, *fo tuo ye* 佛陀耶
SKT *buddha*
PALI *buddha*
REF LY I 13, DFS VI 1124-5, 1131; TD 26-27; VS 141-142; DFS Ch2, 8,9; UW 25-26; FAS Ch24 20-22ff, 58-60; FAS-PI 149-150, 155; FAS Ch7 3-5, 14-15, 33-34; SS II 166-167; AS 2-5.

Buddhaland 佛土
CH *fo du* 佛土
SKT *buddhakṣetra*
PALI *buddhakhetta*

Buddha-nature 佛性
CH *fo xing* 佛性
SKT *buddhatā, buddhabhāva, buddhatva*
PALI *buddhatā, buddhabhāva, buddhatta*
REF SS IV 108ff; DFS V (Ch4 'Belief and Understanding'); NS.

Buddhism/Buddhadharma
佛教/佛法
CH *fo jiao* 佛教, *fo fa* 佛法
SKT *buddhadharma*
PALI *buddhadhamma*
REF FAS Ch9 93; "The Kennedys Request a Lecture,"

VBS, May 1970, 30-38; FAS-PII 129; PS 121.

Buddhist sects 宗派

CH *zong pai* 宗派

C

causation 因緣

CH *yin yuan* 因緣
SKT *hetu-pratyaya*
PALI *hetu-paccaya*
REF DFS V 936-939; CL II 27 (=SPV Ch5); FHS I 22-32 (The Buddha Speaks the Sutra on Cause and Effect); BRF 52; SPV 128-9; EDR II 123, 130-131 (Nāgārjuna); WM 41, 47-49; SS VII; TT 33-35, 131 par 1; SM I 95; EDR VI 215; FAS Ch7 11; FAS Ch22 "Second Ground"; SS II 47 (finger pointing at the moon), 112 (par 2); AS 30.

certification 證/證明/證得

CH *zheng* 證, *zheng ming* 證明, *zheng de* 證得
SKT *prāpti sakṣat-kṛti*

Changren (Chan Master) 常仁 (禪師)

CH *chang ren* (*chan shi*) 常仁（禪師）
REF RL I; VBS #201, 15; WM 14-41.

Changzhi (Chan Master) 常智 (禪師)

CH *chang zhi* (*chan shi*) 常智（禪師）

Chan School 禪宗

CH *chan zong* 禪宗
REF LY II 14-17; WM 70-73; SE 65-70.

compassion 慈悲

CH *ci bei* 慈悲
SKT *maitrī, karuṇā*
PALI *mettā, karuṇā*
REF AS7-8.

Consciousness-Only School 唯識宗

CH *wei shi zong* 唯識宗
SKT *vijñānavāda* (*yogācāra*)
REF HD; FAS-PII(2) 79-89; "The Transformation of Consciousness into Wisdom: the Path of the Bodhisattva according to the *Cheng Weishi Lun*, VBS #176, 177, 178 (Jan.-Mar. 1985).

cosmology 宇宙論

CH *yu zhou lun* 宇宙論
REF FAS Ch5; SPV 53-60, 139-143.

creation (world and humans) 生

CH *sheng* 生, *sheng zao* 生造
SKT *jāti*
PALI *jāti*
REF TD; TT 51-53, 149-151; FAS Ch24 116-120; SS IV 13 ff; *Nirvana Sutra* lecture, 8-18-85; VBS #95, 25-28.

cultivation 修行

CH *xiu xing* 修行
SKT *caryā, bhāvanā*
PALI *cariya, bhāvanā*
REF EDR VII 152-153; FAS Ch15 30ff; FAS Ch5-6 89-90; TT 43.

D

Daosheng (Venerable) 道生 (法師)

CH *dao sheng* (*fa shi*) 道生（法師）
REF WM 71-73, VS 151-152; FAS-PII(2) 145-149.

demons 魔

CH *mo* 魔, *mo luo* 魔羅
SKT *māra*
PALI *māra*
REF SS I 175; SS VIII; UW 122-123, 206-207; TT 66; Unpublished lecture by Ven. Master Hua, July 29, 1985; *Venerable Master Hua's Talks on Dharma* III 107-113; Lethcoe, Nancy. "Māra, Buddhas, and Bodhisattvas." VBS #14 (May, 1971) 22-25; #16 (July, 1971) 36-38; #18 (Sept., 1971) 23-26.

Devadatta 提婆達多

CH *ti po da duo* 提婆達多
SKT *devadatta*
PALI *devadatta*
REF DFS X (Ch12 "Devadatta"); FAS-PII(3) 78-79; VBS #196 4-5; VBS #197 4-5.

dhāraṇī 陀羅尼

CH *tuo luo ni* 陀羅尼
SKT *dhāraṇī*
REF DS 1, 73.

Dhāraṇī Sutra 陀羅尼經

CH *tuo luo ni jing* 陀羅尼經
SKT *dhāraṇī-sūtra*
REF DS.

Dharma/dharma 法

CH *fa* 法
SKT *dharma*
PALI *dhamma*
REF FAS-PII(1) 97-99; FAS PII(2) 100; FAS Ch15 1-2 VBS #179 6-7; DFS I 14ff 28, 30, 31, 7, 8; DFS II 132 DFS I 39; HS 51; HD 26.

Dharma-door 法門
CH *fa men* 法門
SKT *dharma-mukha dharma-paryāya*
PALI *dhamma-pariyāya*

Dharma-Ending Age 末法時代
CH *mo fa shi dai* 末法時代
SKT *saddharma-vipralopa-kāla, saddharmasya antardhāna-kāla-samaya*
PALI *saddhammassa-antaradhāna*
REF BRF 17-19; SE 62-64; UW 135; SS I xiv-xvi; VBS #152 (Jan. 1983) "Buddha Speaks the Sutra of Changes to Come" (T. 395).

Dharma Flower (Lotus) Sutra 法華經
CH *fa hua jing* 法華經, *miao fa lian hua jing* 妙法蓮華經, T. 262.
SKT *saddharmapuṇḍarīka-sūtra*
REF DFS.

Dharma Master 法師
CH *fa shi* 法師
SKT *dharma-bhāṇaka, dharma-kathika, upādhyāya*
PALI *dhamma-bhāṇaka, dhamma-kathika, upajjhāya*
REF DFS I 66.

Dharma-protector 護法
CH *hu fa* 護法
SKT *dharma-pāla*
PALI *dhamma-pāla*

Dharma Realm 法界
CH *fa jie* 法界
SKT *dharma-dhātu*
PALI *dhamma-dhātu*
REF TD 57-61; EDR I 218.

Dharma-transmission 傳法
CH *chuan fa* 傳法

E

Earth Store (Bodhisattva) 地藏（菩薩）
CH *di zang (wang) pu sa* 地藏（王）菩薩
SKT *kṣitigarbha*
REF SPV, TT 136.

Eight Consciousnesses 八識
CH *ba shi* 八識
SKT *aṣṭa-vijñānāni*
REF HD 30-33; EDR IV 26-28; VBS #331-342 (Dec. 1997-Nov. 1998) "Verses Delineating the Eight Consciousnesses."

Eighteen Realms 十八界
CH *shi ba jie* 十八界
SKT *aṣṭādaśa-dhātavaḥ*
PALI *aṭṭhārasa-dhātuyo*
REF HD 31; HS 56-59; PS 334-335.

Eightfold Division of Ghosts and Spirits 天龍八部
CH *tian long ba bu* 天龍八部, *ba bu zhong* 八部眾, *long sheng ba bu* 龍神八部
SKT *devanāgayakṣa-gandharvāsuragaruḍakinnara-mahoraga*
REF DFS IV 562, VII 1233-1235, 1254-1257, IX 1675-1678.

Eightfold Path 八正道
CH *ba zheng dao* 八正道, *ba sheng dao* 八聖道
SKT *(ārya) aṣṭāṅgika-mārga*
PALI *(ariyo) aṭṭangika-maggo*
REF HS 87-88, DFS IV 663-670; AS 125-128.

Eight Winds 八風
CH *ba feng* 八風
REF HS 18-20; FAS Ch26 II 158.

Eighty-eight Deluded View-points 八十八品見惑
CH *ba shi ba pin jian huo* 八十八品見惑, *ba shi ba pin jian fen* 八十八品見分
SKT *darśana-heya*
REF HS 123-124; S42 8.

Eighty-four Thousand Dharma-doors 八萬四千法門
CH *ba wan si qian fa men* 八萬四千法門
SKT *catvāry-aśītidharma-skandhasahasrāṇi*
PALI *caturāsīti sahassāni dhammā*
REF TT 107-108.

Eighty-one Cognitive Delusions 八十一品思惑
CH *ba shi yi pin si huo* 八十一品思惑
SKT *bhāvanā-mārga-prahātavya-kleśa, bhāvanā-heya*
REF HS 123-124.

Eleven Benefits from Making Images of Buddhas 造像十一種功德
CH *zao xiang si yi zhong gong de* 造像十一種功德

emptiness 空
CH *kong* 空, *shun ruo duo* 舜若多
SKT *śūnyatā*
PALI *suññatā*
REF HS 21-23, 57; FAS-PII (2) 93-94, 102, 106; FAS-PII (3) 68-69; PS Ch2.

enlightenment 悟

CH *wu* 悟, *jue wu* 覺悟, *kai wu* 開悟

SKT *bodhi*

PALI *bodhi*

REF SS I 38-39; SS VI 48-55; DFS IV 519; EDR I 96; FAS-VP 40; FAS-PII(1) 232-234.

expedient Dharmas 方便法

CH *fang bian fa* 方便法, *quan qiao fang bian* 權巧方便

SKT *upāya-kuśala/kauśalya*

PALI *upāya-kosalla*

REF EDR V 79-80, 220-221; FAS Ch15 46ff (Dwelling in the Endowment of Skill-in-Means); SS V 194.

F

faith 信

CH *xin* 信

SKT *śraddhā*

PALI *saddhā*

REF WM 53-54; FAS-PI 184; FAS-PII(1) 139-140; FAS Ch11 184, Ch22 4-6; AS 24; HD 44.

filial piety (respect for all) 孝/孝道

CH *xiao* 孝, *xiao dao* 孝道

REF FHS I 1, 8, 63, 65, 68; FHS II 17, 30, 81-109; SPV 9, 18-20, 22-23, 80, 88, 103-4; UW 115-116; BNS 60.

Five Contemplations when Eating 食存五觀

CH *shi cun wu guan* 食存五觀

REF SV 54-56.

Five Desires 五欲

CH *wu yu* 五欲

SKT *pañca-kāma-guṇāḥ*

PALI *pañca-kāma-guṇā*

REF S42 47, 48-54, 57, 62-63, 61; FAS Ch11 99.

Five Eyes 五眼

CH *wu yan* 五眼

SKT *pañca-cakṣus*

PALI *pañca-cakkhūni*

REF SPV 69-70; SM II 89-90; SM III 35, 84-85; VS 106-107, 122-123; AS 6-7.

Five Moral Precepts 五戒

CH *wu jie* 五戒

SKT *pañca-śīlāni*

PALI *pañca-sīla*

REF BRF 59-61; DFS II 211; DFS V 902-3; S42 75-76 (precepts); TT 58; SV 14-29; BNS I 73-97; FAS Ch26(2) 4, 10, 17, 20, 25-26, 28.

Five Skandhas 五陰/五蘊

CH *wu yin/wu yun* 五陰/五蘊

SKT *skandha, pañcopādāna-skandha*

PALI *panc'upādāna-kkhandha*

FORM:

CH *se/shai* 色

SKT *rūpa*

PALI *rūpa*

FEELING:

CH *shou* 受

SKT *vedanā*

PALI *vedanā*

COGNITION:

CH *xiang* 想

SKT *saṃjñā*

PALI *saññā*

FORMATIONS:

CH *xing* 行

SKT *saṃskārāḥ* (pl.)

PALI *sankhārā*

CONSCIOUSNESS:

CH *shi* 識

SKT *vijñāna*

PALI *viññāṇa*

REF HS 24-28, 41-48; LY II 103-104, 223-225; SS III 4-24; SS VIII.

Five Turbidities 五濁

CH *wu zhuo* 五濁, *wu zhuo e shi* 五濁惡世

SKT *pañca-kasāya*

PALI *pañca-kasāya*

REF DFS III 425; SPV 32-3; SS III 205-207; SS IV 144-151, 256-257; AS 149-150.

Five Types of Buddhist Study and Practice 五大宗

CH *wu da zong* 五大宗, *wu jiao* 五教

TEACHINGS:

CH *jiao zong* 教宗

MORAL REGULATIONS:

CH *lü zong* 律宗

SKT *vinaya*

PALI *vinaya*

ESOTERIC:

CH *mi zong* 密宗

SKT *tantra, mantrayāna, vajrayāna*

MEDITATION:

CH *chan zong* 禪宗 [Jap. *zen*]

SKT *dhyāna*

PALI *jhāna*

PURE LAND:

CH *jing du zong* 淨土宗

REF FAS Ch26 II 113-114; WM 16-19, 70-77; RH 230-231; VBS #12 (March, 1971) 32ff; VBS #185, 186 "Pure Land Dharma Door," Oct.-Nov. 1985.

Flower Adornment Sutra
[大方廣佛] 華嚴經

CH *hua yan jing* 華嚴經, *da fang guang fo hua yan jing* 大方廣佛華嚴經

SKT *avataṃsaka-sūtra, mahāvaipulya-buddhāvataṃsaka-sūtra*

REF The BTTS has published the FAS in four different series: (1)FASP and FASVP, (2)FAS, (3)EDR, (4) UW. For general comments, see EDR VII 13-14; FAS-VP xv-xvi.

Four Applications of Mindfulness
四念處

CH *si nian chu* 四念處

SKT *smṛtyupasthāna, catvāri-smṛtyupasthānāni*

PALI *satipaṭṭhāna*

REF HS 88; VBS #11 19-24; DFS IV 608, 760ff; DFS V 940-943; FAS-PII(1) 59-65; AS 56-59.

Four Dhyānas 四禪

CH *si chan* 四禪, *si jing lü* 四靜慮

SKT *dhyāna, catur-dhyāna*

PALI *jhāna*

REF SS VII 207-229; LY II 75-6; DFS IV 706ff; SPV 55-60; DFS X 5-6; TT 104-107; EDR I 225; EDR VIII 13-14; FAS-PII 29-30; FAS Ch26(2) 109-112; SS I 15.

Fourfold Assembly 四眾

CH *si zhong* 四眾, *si zhong di zi* 四眾弟子

SKT *catasraḥ-parṣadaḥ*

PALI *catur-parisā*

Four Formless Realms 四無色界

CH *si kong chu* 四空處, *si wu se/shai jie* 四無色界, *si wu se/shai ding chu* 四無色定處

SKT *catur-arūpyabrahmaloka*

REF SS VII 229-238; DFS IV 708; SPV 60; DFS X 6; EDR I 225; FASP II 29-30; FAS Ch26(2) 109.

Four Great Elements 四大

CH *si da* 四大

SKT *mahābhūta*

PALI *mahābhūta*

REF HD 64; SS IV 22-25, 144, 148.

Four Great Vows 四弘誓願

CH *si hong shi yuan* 四弘誓願

SKT *catvāri-mahā-praṇidhāna*

REF DFS IV 788-795; LY I 17; PS 178-182.

Four Holy Truths 四聖諦

CH *si di* 四諦, *si sheng di* 四聖諦

SKT *ārya-satyāni, catvāry-ārya-satyāni*

PALI *ariya-sacca, catur ariya-saccāni*

SUFFERING:

CH *ku* 苦

SKT *duḥkha*

PALI *dukkha*

ORIGINATION:

CH *ji* 集

SKT *samudaya*

PALI *samudaya*

CESSATION:

CH *mie* 滅

SKT *nirodha*

PALI *nirodha*

PATH:

CH *dao* 道

SKT *mārga*

PALI *magga*

REF DFS III 504; HS 68-70, 78-84; FASP II(2) 45-47; FAS Ch8 (esp. pp. 1-3—Four Holy Truths Chapter); TD 13-14; VBS #206 6.

Four Unlimited Aspects of Mind
四無量心

CH *si wu liang xin* 四無量心

SKT *catvāry-apramāṇāni, brāhma-vihāra*

PALI *appamaññā, brahma-vihāra*

KINDNESS:

CH *ci* 慈

SKT *maitrī*

PALI *mettā*

COMPASSION:

CH *bei* 悲

SKT *karuṇā*

PALI *karuṇā*

JOY:

CH *xi* 喜

SKT *muditā*

PALI *muditā*

EQUANIMITY:

CH *she* 捨

SKT *upekṣā*

PALI *upekkhā*

G

Gautama/Gotama (Buddha)
瞿曇 (佛)

CH *ju tan (fo)* 瞿曇 (佛), *qiao da mo* 喬答摩

SKT *gautama*

PALI *gotama*

ghosts 鬼

CH *gui* 鬼, *e gui* 餓鬼

SKT *preta*

PALI *peta*

REF SS VII 155-175, SPV 65-6; TD 50-52; HD 83-84; EDR III 26-27; PS 83; SS VII 155-176.

God 上帝/天主
CH *shang di* 上帝, *tian zhu* 天主
SKT *īśvara*
PALI *issara*
REF FAS Ch14 (lecture Oct. 5-6, 1975).

gods 天人
CH *tian* 天, *tian ren* 天人, *shen* 神
SKT *devāḥ, devaputrāḥ*
PALI *devā, devaputta*
REF SPV 209-10; UW 220-224; FASP II(2) 141-144; FAS Ch11 69-72; SS VII 198-238.

gongfu (kungfu) 功夫
CH *gong fu* 功夫

Good and Wise Advisor 善知識
CH *shan zhi shi* 善知識
SKT *kalyāṇamitra*
PALI *kalyāṇa-mitta*
REF LY I 50-2; PS 112-114; EDR II xii-xiv, 2-3, 6-7, 83-84; FAS Ch24 42-43; PB I (intro pp:); EDR IV 113; EDR V 69-71; EDR VI 82-83; EDR VII 11, 142ff-155; "What Is a Good Advisor?" *Venerable Master Hua's Talks on Dharma* VIII 75-79; VBS #198 2.

good roots 善根
CH *shan gen* 善根
SKT *kuśala-mūlāni*
PALI *kusala-mūla*
REF VS 50; DFS Ch3 753.

Great Compassion Mantra 大悲咒
CH *da bei zhou* 大悲咒
SKT *mahākāruṇā-dhāraṇī, mahākāruṇikahṛdaya-dhāraṇī*
REF TT 133; DS 30-39, 40-43, 60-66, 135ff; *Great Compassion Mantra Verses; Dharma Talks in Europe* 76-83.

H

Hanshan and Shide (Bodhisattvas) 寒山拾得 (大士)
CH *han shan shi de (da shi)* 寒山拾得（大士）
REF UW 139-141; VBS #27 1, #17 37, #28 1, #60 70-73 ("Poetry of Shih-Te" by James M. Hargett), #200 11.

Heart Sutra 心經
CH *bo re bo luo mi duo xin jing* 般若波羅蜜多心經
SKT *prajñā-pāramitā-hṛdaya-sūtra*
REF HS.

hells 地獄
CH *di yu* 地獄
SKT *naraka, niraya*
PALI *naraka, niraya*
REF SPV 84-6, 141-3; TD 52-54; FASVP 24; SS VII 109-155.

Huayan School 華嚴宗
CH *hua yan zong* 華嚴宗 [Jap. Kegon]
REF FASP.

Huineng (Chan Master/ Patriarch) 惠能 (禪師/祖師)
CH *hui neng (chan shi/zu shi)* 惠能（禪師/祖師）
REF PS; VBS #174 1.

I

ignorance 無明
CH *wu ming* 無明
SKT *avidyā*
PALI *avijjā*
REF DFS III 374.

impermanence 無常
CH *wu chang* 無常
SKT *anitya*
PALI *anicca*
REF TT 110, 111 (2 verses); SS II 24-36 (text only); NS Ch. 2 Pt. 1 24-25 and lectures.

K

kalpa 劫
CH *jie* 劫, *jie bo* 劫波
SKT *kalpa*
PALI *kappa*

karma 業
CH *ye* 業
SKT *karma*
PALI *kamma*
REF FHS I 22-32 (Sutra o Cause and Effect in the Thre Periods of Time); SPV 101-102 SS I 172-173; SS II 139-159.

Kumārajīva (Tripiṭaka Master) 鳩摩羅什 (三藏法師)
CH *jiu mo luo shi (san zan fa shi)* 鳩摩羅什（三藏法師
SKT *kumārajīva*
REF DFS I 57-66; VS 12 13; BNS I 36-37; AS 44-48 VBS #23 1; RHS 26-42.

L

liberating living beings 放生
CH *fang sheng* 放生
REF FHS I 27; DFS I 1601-2; CL II 15, 59 (= BN 20th minor); BNS I 162-5 FAS Ch8 76-77; RH 186-19 Hsuan Hua (Ven. Master

"Developing our Compassion by Liberating Living Beings," PDS (May 1985); "To Atone for Killing Karma Liberate the Living Instead," VBS #147 (Aug. 1982) 13-17.

lineage 宗派/法脈
CH *zong pai* 宗派, *fa mai* 法脈

living beings 眾生
CH *zhong sheng* 眾生, *you qing* 有情
SKT *sattva*
PALI *satta*
REF EDR V 136-7; VS 40-41; SS IV 36-38; SS VI 165-180; UW 7-8; FASVP 60-61; DFS IV 789-790.

lotus posture 雙跏趺坐
CH *shuang jia fu zuo* 雙跏趺坐, *jie jia fu zuo* 結跏趺坐, *lian hua zuo* 蓮花坐
SKT *padmāsana*
REF TD 63-67; FAS Ch11 127-131, 244-245; SS I 98-99; LY I 70-75; DFS IX 1716-17, 1722-1727.

love 愛/貪愛/愛欲
CH *ai* 愛, *tan ai* 貪愛, *ai yu* 愛欲
SKT *tṛṣṇā*
PALI *taṇhā*
REF S42 40, 48; FAS Ch9 32-34.

M

Madhyamaka/Mādhyamika 中觀論(派)
CH *zhong guan lun (pai)* 中觀論(派)
SKT *madhyamaka[-śāstra]/ mādhyamika*

mahā 摩訶
CH *mo he* 摩訶
SKT *mahā*
PALI *mahā/maha*

Mahākāśyapa (Venerable) 摩訶迦葉 (尊者)
CH *mo he jia she (zun zhe)* 摩訶迦葉(尊者)
SKT *mahākāśyapa (sthavira)*
PALI *mahākassapa (thera)*
REF AS 75-80; DFS V 869-872; DFS VI 1105-1116; EDR I 220; SS IV 198, 202; SS V 39-43; VBS #165 (Jan. 1984) 1.

Mahāmaudgalyāyana (Venerable) 摩訶目犍連 (尊者)
CH *mo he mu jian lian (zun zhe)* 摩訶目犍連(尊者)
SKT *mahāmaudgalyāyana (sthavira)*
PALI *mahāmoggallāna (thera)*
REF DFS V 872; DFS VI 1146-1162; EDR I 220; SS V 86-89; SS VII 86-87; AS 73-75.

Mahāsattva 摩訶薩
CH *mo he sa* 摩訶薩
SKT *mahāsattva*
PALI *mahāsatta*

Mahayana and Hinayana Compared 大乘小乘比較
CH (a) *da cheng* 大乘 (b) *xiao cheng* 小乘
SKT (a) *mahāyāna* (b) *hīnayāna*
REF LY I 146-7, 150; FAS Ch3 (Mahayana); FAS-PII (1) 116-120; EDR I 198-199 (verse); SV 6-7.

Maitreya (Bodhisattva) 彌勒 (菩薩)
CH *mi lei/le (pu sa)* 彌勒(菩薩)
SKT *maitreya*
PALI *metteyya*
REF DFS II 156, 351ff; DFS IX 1584-87; AS 103-105; EDR VII 135; EDR VIII 19; SS V 111-119; VBS #172 10.

maṇḍala 曼陀羅
CH *man tuo luo* 曼陀羅
SKT *maṇḍala*
PALI *maṇḍala*

Mañjuśrī (Bodhisattva) 文殊師利 (菩薩)
CH *wen shu shi li (pu sa)* 文殊師利(菩薩)
SKT *mañjuśrī*
REF DFS II 144 ff; FAS Ch 9 8-10; EDR I 161ff, 226-228; AS 99-103.

mantra 咒
CH *zhou* 咒
SKT *mantra, dhāraṇī*
PALI *manta*
REF HS 109-110, 116; SM I 37-40; RH.

meditation 坐禪/禪
CH *zuo chan* 坐禪, *chan* 禪
SKT *dhyāna, bhāvanā*
PALI *jhāna, bhāvanā*
REF PDS (May 1985) 2 "The Chan Practice…," TT 104ff; LYII 74ff; VBS #205ff "Chan Talks" series.

merit/merit and virtue 功德
CH *gong de* 功德
SKT *puṇya, puṇya-guṇa*
PALI *puñña*
REF PS 132-137; UW 9-10, 32, 76; TT 43.

Middle Way 中道

CH *zhong dao* 中道

SKT *madhyama-pratipad*

PALI *majjhima-paṭipadā*

REF WM 49; S42 55, 67.

mindfulness 念

CH *nian* 念

SKT *smṛti, anusmṛti*

PALI *sati, anussati*

REF FAS Ch22 (Treasury of Mindfulness).

moral precepts 戒/戒律

CH *jie* 戒, *jie lü* 戒律

SKT *śīla, śikṣāpada*

PALI *sīla, sikkhāpada*

REF SV; BNS I & II; TT 117, 132; FAS Ch16 33-35; FAS Ch11 27; FAS Ch22 15-27; FAS Ch26(2) 5-6; SS I 12, 47; SS III 109; SS VI 9; SS VII 107-108; S42 76.

N

Nāgārjuna (Bodhisattva) 龍樹 (菩薩)

CH *long shu (pu sa)* 龍樹（菩薩）

SKT *nāgārjuna*

REF FASVP 101-102.

namo 南無

CH *na(n) mo* 南無

SKT *namas*

PALI *namo*

nirvana 涅槃

CH *nie pan* 涅槃, *ni huan* 泥洹

SKT *nirvāṇa, mahāparinirvāṇa*

PALI *nibbāna, mahāparinibbāna*

REF VS 429 (4 kinds); UW 157; DFS II 315-316 (3 kinds); DFS VII 1356 (2 kinds); SS I 180-181; SS IV 138-139, 244-245.

Nirvana Sutra 涅槃經

SKT *Mahāparinirvāṇa-sūtra*

PALI *Mahāparinibbāna-suttanta*

REF NS (ms).

no self 無我

CH *wu wo* 無我

SKT *anātman*

PALI *anatta*

REF FAS Ch22 141.

O

offerings 供/供養

CH *gong* 供, *gong yang* 供養

SKT *pūjā*

PALI *pūjā*

REF DFS II 288-289; DFS IX 1700-1701; VS 105-107; S42 23-27; UW 55-68, 142-144; *Nirvana Sutra* lecture on October 27, 1985 by Ven. Master Hua.

One Hundred Dharmas 百法

CH *bai fa* 百法

SKT *śata-dharmāḥ*

PALI *sata-dhamma*

REF HD, esp. 5, 26-29; HS 50; FASP II(3) 44ff.

One Thousand Hands and Eyes 千手千眼

CH *qian shou qian yan* 千手千眼

SKT *sahasrabhujasahasranetra*

REF *Great Compassion Dharma Transmission Verses*; DS 2-5, 24-25; SS V 178-179; VBS #197 3.

ordination 受具足戒

CH *shou ju zu jie* 受具足戒

SKT *upasaṃpadā*

PALI *upasampadā*

REF FAS Ch16 36-37.

outflows 漏

CH *lou* 漏

SKT *āsrava*

PALI *āsava*

REF AS 125; SM IV 44-45; FAS Ch9 10-15.

P

Pali 巴利文

CH *ba li wen* 巴利文, *ba li yu* 巴利語

SKT *pāli*

PALI *pāli*

pāramitā 波羅蜜多

CH *bo luo mi (duo)* 波羅蜜（多）, *du* 度

SKT *pāramitā, pāramī*

PALI *pāramitā, pārami*

REF PS 96-97; VS 7; SM II 8; SS I 9-10.

polluted thoughts 妄想

CH *wang xiang* 妄想

SKT *parikalpa, vikalpa*

PALI *parikappa, vikappa*

REF PS 98-99, 192-193; TT 38; FASP I 87.

prajñā 般若

CH *bo re* 般若

SKT *prajñā*

PALI *paññā*

REF PS 94-96; DFS X 24-25.

Pratyekabuddha 辟支佛

CH *bi zhi fo* 辟支佛, *du jue/jiao* 獨覺, *yuan jue/jiao* 緣覺

SKT *pratyekabuddha, pratyayabuddha*
PALI *paccekabuddha*
REF TD 29-31, DFS II 300-301; FASP II(2) 57-58.

pure land 淨土
CH *jing du* 淨土
SKT *sukhāvatī*
REF PS 140-145; FASP I 116ff.

Q

Qingliang Chengguan (National Master) 清涼澄觀（國師）
CH *qing liang cheng guan (guo shi)* 清涼澄觀（國師）
REF UW xx-xxi, xxiii; FASVP 15-18; FASP I 221-230; VBS #35 1.

R

ranking the teachings 判教
CH *pan jiao* 判教
REF FASVP 51-54; FASP II (1) 156ff; FASP II(2) (entire volume); FASP III (entire volume); BNS I 34-35; *Dharma Talks in Europe* 9ff.

rebirth 生/再生
CH *sheng* 生 *zaisheng* 再生
SKT *jāti, pratisaṃdhi*
PALI *jāti, paṭisandhi*
REF CL II 81; HS 38; FAS Ch16 44; SS IV 34-36; SS VII 96-97.

recitation of the Buddha's name 念佛
CH *nian fo* 念佛
SKT *buddhānusmṛti*
PALI *buddhānussati*
REF LY I 1-47; LY II; CPL; AS; FAS Ch22 56; EDR IV 152-153; SS V 126-129; PDS May, 1985, "Reciting the Name of Guanshiyin Bodhisattva"; *"Nian fo fa men,"* unpublished lecture, December 16, 1985; *Venerable Master Hua's Talks on Dharma* III 2-41.

refuge with the Three Jewels 皈依三寶
CH *gui yi san bao* 皈依三寶
SKT *tri-śaraṇa*
PALI *ti-saraṇa*
REF PS 184-187; UW 13; FAS Ch11 116-118; *The True Meaning of Taking Refuge* (entire volume).

relics 舍利
CH *she li* 舍利
SKT *śarīra*
PALI *sarīra*
REF HS 120.

repentance 懺悔
CH *chan hui* 懺悔
SKT *vipratisāra, deśanā, kṣamāpaṇa, kaukṛtya*
PALI *vippaṭisāra, desanā, khamāpanā, kukkucca*
REF PS 120, 176-178; WM 9-11; UW 30-31, 144-145; TT 87-96 (verse of repentance of Universal Worthy Bodhisattva); EDR VIII 2-4, 69-73; FASP II(3) 9-10; FAS Ch22 29-34 ("Treasury of Shame"), 35-41 ("Treasury of Remorse"); RH ("Repentance before the Eighty-Eight Buddhas").

S

Sagely City of Ten Thousand Buddhas 萬佛聖城
CH *wan fo sheng cheng* 萬佛聖城

Śakra 帝釋
CH *di shi* 帝釋, *shi jia po* 釋迦婆, i.e., *yin tuo la* 因陀羅 (Indra)
SKT *śakra*
PALI *sakka*

Śākyamuni (Buddha) 釋迦牟尼（佛）
CH *shi jia mou ni (fo)* 釋迦牟尼（佛）
SKT *śākyamuni*
PALI *sakyamuni*
REF SM VI (ms.); DFS VII, XIV (Ch20), III 319; EDR VII 111; AS 8.

samadhi 三昧/三摩地/定
CH *san mei* 三昧, *san mo di* 三摩地, *ding* 定
SKT *samādhi*
PALI *samādhi*
REF TT 127-8; EDR I 12; EDR VII 60; FAS Ch11 131-133; SS II 121-122; SS VI 13-14.

saṃsāra 流轉/生死/輪迴
CH *liu zhuan* 流轉, *sheng si* 生死, *lun hui* 輪迴
SKT *saṃsāra*
PALI *saṃsāra*

Sangha 僧伽
CH *seng qie* 僧伽
SKT *saṅgha, saṃgha*
PALI *sangha*
REF DFS IV 666-667; PDS "The So-Called Lay Sangha in America."

Sanskrit 梵文
CH *fan wen* 梵文, *fan yu* 梵語
SKT *saṃskṛta*

Śāriputra (Venerable) 舍利弗 (尊者)
CH *she li fu (zun zhe)* 舍利弗 (尊者), *she li zi* 舍利子
SKT *śāriputra (sthavira)*
PALI *sāriputta (thera)*
REF AS 69-71; HS 33-34, 120-121; DFS Ch2 107-109; EDR I 219; SS V 62-64.

śāstra 論
CH *lun* 論
SKT *śāstra*
REF HD 6-8.

Six Desire Heavens 六欲天
CH *liu yu tian* 六欲天
SKT *ṣaṭ kāmāvacarā devalokāḥ*
REF SS VII 198-207; SPV 25-26, 53-55.

Six Pāramitās 六波羅蜜/六度
CH *liu bo luo mi* 六波羅蜜, *liu du* 六度
SKT *ṣaṭ pāramitā*
PALI *pāramitā, pārami*
REF LY II 2-3; HS 90-1; DFS II 131 ff, 242-254, 350-353; DFS X 5-32, 41-43; EDR V 72-79; 212-220; EDR VIII 132-133, 140-141 (patience); FASP II(1) 112-115; FASP II (2)36-40; VS 94ff, 102 (photo) (patience—King of Kalinga); S42 38-39 (patience); TT 143-144 (patience); SS I 6-17; AS 4; FAS Ch15 31-33; FAS Ch11 16-27, 31-39, 75-78, 81-83; FAS Ch22 53-96 (Treasury of Giving).

Six Paths of Rebirth 六道輪迴
CH *liu dao lun hui* 六道輪迴, *liu qu* 六趣
SKT *ṣaḍ-gatyāḥ*
REF SS V 135; HD 83; TD 39-54; VBS #206 7.

Six Principles of the Sagely City of Ten Thousand Buddhas 萬佛聖城六大宗旨
CH *wan fo sheng cheng liu da zhong zhi* 萬佛聖城六大宗旨
REF *Talks on Dharma by the Venerable Master Hua* VIII 107-127; "Chan Talks #1, VBS #205 (June, 1987) 15, 19; "Chan Talks #9," VBS #211 (Dec. 1987) 13-14.

Six Spiritual Powers 六神通
CH *liu shen tong* 六神通
SKT *abhijñā, ṣaḍ-abhijñāḥ*
PALI *abhiññā, chaḷabhiññā*
REF SPV 26-27; DFS IV 808-815; DFS VII 1292-1297; (outflows) DFS VII 1283-86; S42 35-36 (knowledge of past lives); HS 18; AS 5-6; FAS Ch26 (2) 116-118.

Sixth Patriarch's Dharma Jewel Platform Sutra 六祖法寶壇經
CH *liu zu fa bao tan jing* 六祖法寶壇經
REF PS.

śramaṇa 沙門
CH *sha men* 沙門
SKT *śramaṇa*
PALI *samaṇa*
REF SV 44; DS 9; S42 1, 3, 10; EDR I 159.

śrāvaka 聲聞
CH *sheng wen* 聲聞
SKT *śrāvaka*
PALI *sāvaka*
REF DFS II 299; TD 33; S42 1, 3-9; FASP II(1) 115-116; FASP II(2) 57, 134-135.

suffering 苦
CH *ku* 苦
SKT *duḥkha*
PALI *dukkha*
REF UW 87-88; FASP II(1) 99-101; FAS Ch8 3-13; FAS Ch15 36-37; VBS #206 6.

Śūraṅgama Mantra 楞嚴咒
CH *leng yan zhou* 楞嚴咒
SKT *śūraṅgama-mantra*
REF SS VI 89-91; 91-103 (text); 113; TT 124-126; SM I (intro), 32-33, 97-101; SM III 34.

Śūraṅgama Sutra 大佛頂首楞嚴經
CH *da fo ding shou leng yan jing* 大佛頂首楞嚴經, 10 rolls (T. 845). Translated into Chinese by Paramiti and others in 705 C.E.
SKT *śūraṅgama-sūtra*
REF SS I-VIII; BRF 18-19; *A Sure Sign of the Proper Dharma.*

sutra 經
CH *jing* 經, *jing dian* 經典
SKT *sūtra*
PALI *sutta*
REF SPV 21; HS 11-12; VS 8; S42 80; FASVP 37-38; FASP II(1) 7-26; AS 12-14.

Sutra in Forty-two Sections 四十二章經
CH *si shi er zhang jing* 四十二章經
REF S42.

Sutra of the Past Vows of Earth Store Bodhisattva 地藏菩薩本願經
CH *di zang pu sa ben yuan jing* 地藏菩薩本願經
SKT *kṣitigarbha-bodhisattva-pūrvapraṇidāna-sūtra* (no longer extant)
REF SPV.

T

tathāgatagarbha 如來藏
CH *ru lai zang* 如來藏
SKT *tathāgatagarbha*

Ten Dharma Realms 十法界
CH *shi fa jie* 十法界
REF TD; HS 104-5; TT 46-49; FASVP 23-27; VBS #206 4.

Ten Grounds/Stages of the Bodhisattva Path 菩薩十地
CH *pu sa shi di* 菩薩十地
SKT *daśabhūmayaḥ*
PALI *dasabhūmi*
REF FAS Ch26(1), Ch26(2); EDR V 279-280; EDR VI 278; SS VII 62-69; "Transformation of Consciousness into Wisdom," VBS #176 22; VBS #177 15; VBS #178 14.

Ten Titles of a Buddha 佛之十號
CH *fo zhi shi hao* 佛之十號
REF FAS Ch7; SPV 121-123

Ten Wholesome Deeds 十善
CH *shi shan* 十善
SKT *daśa-kuśala-karma-patha, daśa-kusalāni*
PALI *kusala-kamma-patha*
REF S42 14-15; DFS X 6; FAS Ch26(2) 4-35.

Theravada Buddhism 南傳佛教
CH *nan chuan fo jiao* 南傳佛教, *shang zuo bu* 上座部
SKT *sthavira-vāda*
PALI *theravāda*

Thirty-two Major Physical Characteristics of a Buddha 佛三十二相
CH *fo san shi er xiang* 佛三十二相
SKT *dvātriṃśan mahāpuruṣalakṣaṇa, dvātrimśad varalakṣaṇa*
PALI *dvattiṃsa mahāpurisalakkhaṇa*
REF EDR I 189-190; EDR VI 212-213, 215; VS 85-86.

Three Aspects of Learning to Be without Outflows 三無漏學
CH *san wu lou xue/xiao* 三無漏學
REF TT 117ff.

Three Bodies of a Buddha/Three Types of Buddha Bodies 佛之三身
CH *fo zhi san shen* 佛之三身
SKT *trikāya*
PALI *tikāya*
REF PS 188-194; FASP II(3) 74-75; BNS I 11; EDR I 14; FAS Ch24 50-51. VBS #196 6.

Three Jewels 三寶
CH *san bao* 三寶
SKT *triratna, ratna-traya*
PALI *tiratana, ratana-ttaya*

Three Poisons 三毒
CH *san du* 三毒
SKT *akuśala-mūlā*
PALI *akusala-mūlā*
REF PS 4; TD 5-14.

Three Vehicles 三乘
CH *san cheng* 三乘
SKT *triyāna*
REF FASP II(1) 248-250.

Three Worlds 三界
CH *san jie* 三界
SKT *triloka, tridhātu*
PALI *tiloka*
REF TT 47; EDR VIII 218-219; FASP II(2) 139-141.

Thus Come One 如來
CH *ru lai* 如來
SKT *tathāgata*
PALI *tathāgata*
REF DFS IV 540; VS 141ff; EDR VIII 217-218; TD 26.

Tiantai School 天台宗
CH *tiantai zong* 天台宗 [Jap. *tendai*]
REF DFS I 1-11; FASP II(1) 196-197.

time 時
CH *shi* 時
SKT *kāla*
PALI *kāla*
REF TT 6; EDR I 28-29; UW 219-220, 222; FAS Ch5-6 115-117; FAS Ch9 147-148; SS II 68-69; SS IV 147, 165-167; VS 124.

transference of merit 迴向
CH *hui xiang* 迴向
SKT *pariṇāmana*
PALI *pariṇāmana*
REF UW 38-39; FAS Ch9 26-28; EDR IV (Ten Transferences); FAS Ch25; RH 71, 82, 146-157, 158-162; SS VII 50-59 (Ten Transferences).

transformation bodies 化身

CH *hua shen* 化身

SKT *nirmāṇakāya*

Tripiṭaka 三藏

CH *san zang* 三藏

SKT *tripiṭaka*

PALI *tipiṭaka*

REF HS 13, VS 11;UW 3; FASP II(1) 109-111; FAS Ch9 185.

Tripiṭaka Master 三藏法師

CH *san zang fa shi* 三藏法師

SKT *tripiṭaka-ācārya*

PALI *tipiṭaka-ācariya*

Twelvefold Conditioned Arising 十二因緣

CH *shi er yin yuan* 十二因緣

SKT *dvādaśāṅga nidāna, dvādaśāṅga pratītyasamutpāda*

PALI *nidāna, paṭicca-samuppāda*

REF HS 61-65; SS IV 32-35; TD 31; FAS Ch26 "Fifth Ground" 52ff, "Sixth Ground" 70-89; TD 9-10; AS 3.

Two Vehicles 二乘

CH *er cheng* 二乘

SKT *dviyāna*

U

Universal Worthy (Bodhisattva) 普賢(菩薩)

CH *pu xian (pu sa)* 普賢（菩薩）

SKT *samantabhadra*

REF UW 5; SS V 65-68.

upāsaka 優婆賽

CH *you po sai* 優婆賽, *jin shi nan* 近事男

SKT *upāsaka*

PALI *upāsaka*

upāsikā 優婆夷

CH *you po yi* 優婆夷, *jin shi nü* 近事女

SKT *upāsikā*

PALI *upāsikā*

V

vajra 金剛

CH *jin gang* 金剛

SKT *vajra*

PALI *vajira*

REF VS 3, 81.

Vajra (Diamond) Prajñā Pāramitā Sutra 金剛般若波羅密多經

CH *jin gang bo re bo luo mi duo jing* 金剛般若波羅密多經, *jin gang jing* 金剛經

SKT *vajra-prajñā-pāramitā-sūtra*

REF VS.

Vasubandhu (Bodhisattva) 世親菩薩

CH *shi qin (pu sa)* 世親菩薩, *tian qin (pu sa)* 天親菩薩

SKT *vasubandhu*

REF HD 9-12; UW 1-3; VBS #20 1-2.

vegetarianism 素食主義

CH *su shi zhu yi* 素食主義

REF FASP II 29-31; FAS Ch11 214-224; FAS Ch22 59-63; DFS 789-791; LY I 112-114, 116-118; BNS I (Third Minor Precept) 118-119, BRF 63-65; CL I 1-4, 83; CL II 1-3, 5, 7, 9, 63 (= BNS third minor), 142-144; SS III 78-79; SS IV 40-42; SS VI 20-23; SS VII 4-8; BNS I 120-122 (5 allium); DFS IV 790-792; PDS (Dec. 1984) 2, "Verses on a Simple and Practical Way to be Kind to Other Living Beings."

Vinaya 戒/毗柰耶

CH *jie* 戒, *pi nai ye* 毗柰耶

SKT *vinaya*

PALI *vinaya*

REF FASP II(1) 77-78, 86-96; SV 10.

Vinaya School 律宗

CH *lü zong* 律宗

vows 願

CH *yuan* 願

SKT *praṇidhāna*

PALI *paṇidhāna*

REF DFS VII 1195-1197; UW xiii; FAS Ch22 154.

W

Way-place 道場

CH *dao chang* 道場

SKT *bodhimaṇḍa*

PALI *bodhimaṇḍa*

REF SS VI 70-77.

world systems 世界

CH *shi jie* 世界

SKT *lokadhātu*

PALI *lokadhātu*

REF EDR VI 206-210, 260-261; EDR VIII 215-216; FAS Ch5(1) 14, 102, 107, 109; FAS Ch5-6 frontis., 48.

X

Xuanzang (Tripiṭaka Master) 玄奘(三藏法師)

CH *xuan zang (san zang fa shi)* 玄奘（三藏法師）

REF HS 13-14; HD 15-19; FASP II(2) 80, 82.

Xuyun (Chan Master) 虛雲 (禪師)

CH *xu yun (chan shi)*
虛雲（禪師）
REF PB I and II; VBS #17 (Aug. 1971) 1-2.

Y

yojana 由旬

CH *you xun* 由旬
SKT *yojana*
PALI *yojana*

Z

Zhiyi (Venerable) 智顗 (法師)

CH *zhi yi (fa shi)* 智顗（法師）
REF FASP II(2) 1-4; DFS I 1, 15, 17-18, 35, 53, 55; VBS #129 (Feb. 1981) 1.

When Buddhism first came to China from India, one of the most important tasks required for its establishment was the translation of the Buddhist scriptures from Sanskrit into Chinese. This work involved a great many people, such as the renowned monk National Master Kumārajīva (5th century C.E.), who led an assembly of over 800 people who worked on the translation of the Tripiṭaka (Buddhist Canon) for over a decade. Because of the work of individuals such as these, nearly the entire Buddhist Tripiṭaka of over a thousand texts exists to the present day in Chinese.

Now the banner of the Buddha's teachings is being firmly planted in Western soil, and the same translation work is being done from Chinese into English. Since 1970, the Buddhist Text Translation Society (BTTS) has been making a paramount contribution toward this goal. Aware that the Buddhist Tripiṭaka is a work of such magnitude that its translation could never be entrusted to a single person, the BTTS, emulating the translation assemblies of ancient times, does not publish a work until it has passed through four committees for primary translation, reviewing, editing, and certification. The leaders of these committees are Bhikshus (monks) and Bhikshunis (nuns), who have devoted their entire lives to the study and practice of the Buddha's teachings. For this reason, all of the works of the BTTS put an emphasis on what the principles of the Buddha's teachings mean in terms of actual practice, rather than in terms of intellectual conjecture.

To date, in addition to publishing over one hundred volumes of Buddhist texts in Chinese, the Society has published more than one hundred volumes of English, French, Spanish, Vietnamese, and Japanese translations of Buddhist texts, as well as bilingual (Chinese and English) editions. Audio and video tapes in several languages are currently being produced, so that people may hear and see the Dharma and cultivate accordingly. The monthly journal *Vajra Bodhi Sea,* which has been in circulation for nearly thirty years, has been published in bilingual (Chinese and English) format in recent years.

All those who aspire to devote themselves to the work of translating and publishing Buddhist texts should uphold the Eight Guidelines of the Buddhist Text Translation Society:

1 A volunteer must free him/herself from the motives of personal fame and profit.

2 A volunteer must cultivate a respectful and sincere attitude free from arrogance and conceit.

3 A volunteer must refrain from aggrandizing his/her work and denigrating that of others.

4 A volunteer must not establish him/herself as the standard of correctness and suppress the work of others with his or her fault-finding.

5 A volunteer must take the Buddha-mind as his/her own mind.

6 A volunteer must use the wisdom of Dharma-Selecting Vision to determine true principles.

7 A volunteer must request Virtuous Elders in the ten directions to certify his/her translations.

8 A volunteer must endeavor to propagate the teachings by printing sutras, *śāstra* texts, and *vinaya* texts when the translations are certified as being correct.

APPENDIX C

Comparative Tables of Romanization: Pinyin/Wade-Giles/Yale

Pinyin, Wade-Giles, and Yale are three common systems of romanization for Chinese words. Pinyin is used in this book, except for some proper names which retain familiar romanizations.

PY	WG	YALE
a	a	a
ai	ai	ai
an	an	an
ang	ang	ang
ao	ao	au
ba	pa	ba
bai	pai	bai
ban	pan	ban
bang	pang	bang
bao	pao	bau
bei	pei	bei
ben	pen	ben
beng	peng	beng
bi	pi	bi
bian	pien	byan
biao	piao	byau
bie	pieh	bye
bin	pin	bin
bing	ping	bing
bo	po	bwo
bu	pu	bu
ca	ts'a	tsa
cai	ts'ai	tsai
can	ts'an	tsan
cang	ts'ang	tsang
cao	ts'ao	tsau
ce	ts'e	tse
cen	ts'en	tsen
ceng	ts'eng	tseng
cha	ch'a	cha
chai	ch'ai	chai
chan	ch'an	chan
chang	ch'ang	chang
chao	ch'ao	chau
che	ch'e	che
chen	ch'en	chen
cheng	ch'eng	cheng
chi	ch'ih	chr
chong	ch'ung	chung
chou	ch'ou	chou
chu	ch'u	chu
chuai	ch'uai	chwai
chuan	ch'uan	chwan
chuang	ch'uang	chwang
chui	ch'ui	chwei
chun	ch'un	chwun
chuo	ch'o	chwo
ci	tz'u	tsz
cong	ts'ung	tsung
cou	ts'ou	tsou
cu	ts'u	tsu
cuan	ts'uan	tswan
cui	ts'ui	tswei
cun	ts'un	tswun
cuo	ts'o	tswo
da	ta	da
dai	tai	dai
dan	tan	dan
dang	tang	dang
dao	tao	dau
de	te	de
dei	tei	dei
deng	teng	deng
di	ti	di
dian	tien	dyan
diao	tiao	dyau
die	tieh	dye
ding	ting	ding
diu	tiu	dyou
dong	tung	dung
dou	tou	dou
du	tu	du
duan	tuan	dwan
dui	tui	dwei
dun	tun	dwun
duo	to	dwo
e	e	e
ei	ei	ei
en	en	en
er	erh	er
fa	fa	fa
fan	fan	fan
fang	fang	fang
fei	fei	fei
fen	fen	fen

PY	WG	YALE
feng	feng	feng
fo	fo	fwo
fou	fou	fou
fu	fu	fu
ga	ka	ga
gai	kai	gai
gan	kan	gan
gang	kang	gang
gao	kao	gau
ge	ke	ge
gei	kei	gei
gen	ken	gen
geng	keng	geng
gong	kung	gung
gou	kou	gou
gu	ku	gu
gua	kua	gwa
guai	kuai	gwai
guan	kuan	gwan
guang	kuang	gwang
gui	kuei	gwei
gun	kun	gwun
guo	kuo	gwo
ha	ha	ha
hai	hai	hai
han	han	han
hang	hang	hang
hao	hao	hau
he	he	he
hei	hei	hei
hen	hen	hen
heng	heng	heng
hong	hung	hung
hou	hou	hou
hu	hu	hu
hua	hua	hwa
huai	huai	hwai
huan	huan	hwan
huang	huang	hwang
hui	hui	hwei
hun	hun	hwun
huo	huo	hwo
ji	chi	ji
jia	chia	jya
jian	chien	jyan
jiang	chiang	jyang
jiao	chiao	jyau
jie	chieh	jye
jin	chin	jin
jing	ching	jing
jiong	chiung	jyung
jiu	chiu	jyou
ju	chü	jyu
juan	chüan	jywan
jue	chüeh	jywe
jun	chün	jyun
ka	k'a	ka
kai	k'ai	kai
kan	k'an	kan
kang	k'ang	kang
kao	k'ao	kau
ke	k'e	ke
ken	k'en	ken
keng	k'eng	keng
kong	k'ung	kung
kou	k'ou	kou
ku	k'u	ku
kua	k'ua	kwa
kuai	k'uai	kwai
kuan	k'uan	kwan
kuang	k'uang	kwang
kui	k'uei	kwei
kun	k'un	kwun
kuo	k'uo	kwo
la	la	la
lai	lai	lai
lan	lan	lan
lang	lang	lang
lao	lao	lau
le	le	le
lei	lei	lei
leng	leng	leng
li	li	li
lia	lia	lya
lian	lien	lyan
liang	liang	lyang
liao	liao	lyau
lie	lieh	lye
lin	lin	lin
ling	ling	ling
iu	liu	lyou

PY	WG	YALE
lo	lo	lo
long	lung	lung
lou	lou	lou
lu	lu	lu
lü	lü	lyu
luan	luan	lwan
lüe	lüeh	lywe
lun	lun	lwun
luo	luo	lwo
ma	ma	ma
mai	mai	mai
man	man	man
mang	mang	mang
mao	mao	mau
me	me	me
mei	mei	mei
men	men	men
meng	meng	meng
mi	mi	mi
mian	mien	myan
miao	miao	myau
mie	mieh	mye
min	min	min
ming	ming	ming
miu	miu	myou
mo	mo	mwo
mou	mou	mou
mu	mu	mu
na	na	na
nai	nai	nai
nan	nan	nan
nang	nang	nang
nao	nao	nau
ne	ne	ne
nei	nei	nei
nen	nen	nen
neng	neng	neng
ni	ni	ni
nian	nien	nyan
niang	niang	nyang
niao	niao	nyau
nie	nieh	nye
nin	nin	nin
ning	ning	ning
niu	niu	nyou
nong	nung	nung
nou	nou	nou
nu	nu	nu
nü	nü	nyu
nuan	nuan	nwan
nüe	nüeh	nywe
nuo	no	nwo
nuo	no	nwo
ou	ou	ou
pa	p'a	pa
pai	p'ai	pai
pan	p'an	pan
pang	p'ang	pang
pao	p'ao	pau
pei	p'ei	pei
pen	p'en	pen
peng	p'eng	peng
pi	p'i	pi
pian	p'ien	pyan
piao	p'iao	pyau
pie	p'ieh	pye
pin	p'in	pin
ping	p'ing	ping
po	p'o	pwo
pou	p'ou	pou
pu	p'u	pu
qi	ch'i	chi
qia	ch'ia	chya
qian	ch'ien	chyan
qiang	ch'iang	chyang
qiao	ch'iao	chyau
qie	ch'ieh	chye
qin	ch'in	chin
qing	ch'ing	ching
qiong	ch'iung	chyung
qiu	ch'iu	chyou
qu	ch'ü	chyu
quan	ch'üan	chywan
que	ch'üeh	chywe
qun	ch'ün	chyun
ran	jan	ran
rang	jang	rang
rao	jao	rau
re	je	re
ren	jen	ren
reng	jeng	reng
ri	jih	r

PY	WG	YALE
rong	jung	rung
rou	jou	rou
ru	ju	ru
ruan	juan	rwan
rui	jui	rwei
run	jun	rwun
ruo	jo	rwo
sa	sa	sa
sai	sai	sai
san	san	san
sang	sang	sang
sao	sao	sau
se	se	se
sen	sen	sen
seng	seng	seng
sha	sha	sha
shai	shai	shai
shan	shan	shan
shang	shang	shang
shao	shao	shau
she	she	she
shei	shei	shei
shen	shen	shen
sheng	sheng	sheng
shi	shih	shr
shou	shou	shou
shu	shu	shu
shua	shua	shwa
shuai	shuai	shwai
shuan	shuan	shwan
shuang	shuang	shwang
shui	shui	shwei
shun	shun	shwun
shuo	shuo	shwo
si	ssu	sz
song	sung	sung
sou	sou	sou
su	su	su
suan	suan	swan
sui	sui	swei
sun	sun	swun
suo	so	swo
ta	t'a	ta
tai	t'ai	tai
tan	t'an	tan
tang	t'ang	tang
tao	t'ao	tau
te	t'e	te
teng	t'eng	teng
ti	t'i	ti
tian	t'ien	tyan
tiao	t'iao	tyau
tie	t'ieh	tye
ting	t'ing	ting
tong	t'ung	tung
tou	t'ou	tou
tu	t'u	tu
tuan	t'uan	twan
tui	t'ui	twei
tun	t'un	twun
tuo	t'o	two
wa	wa	wa
wai	wai	wai
wan	wan	wan
wang	wang	wang
wei	wei	wei
wen	wen	wen
weng	weng	weng
wo	o	o
wo	wo	wo
wu	wu	wu
xi	hsi	xyi
xia	hsia	sya
xian	hsien	syan
xiang	hsiang	syang
xiao	hsiao	syau
xie	hsieh	sye
xin	hsin	syin
xing	hsing	sying
xiong	hsiung	syung
xiu	hsiu	syou
xu	hsü	syu
xuan	hsüan	sywan
xue	hsüeh	sywe
xun	hsün	syun
ya	ya	ya
yan	yan	yan
yang	yang	yang
yao	yao	yau
ye	yeh	ye
yi	i	yi
yin	yin	yin

PY	WG	YALE
ying	ying	ying
yong	yung	yung
you	yu	you
yu	yü	yu
yuan	yüan	ywan
yue	yüeh	ywe
yun	yün	yun
za	tsa	dza
zai	tsai	dzai
zan	tsan	dzan
zang	tsang	dzang
zao	tsao	dzau
ze	tse	dze
zei	tsei	dzei
zen	tsen	dzen
zeng	tseng	dzeng
zha	cha	ja
zhai	chai	jai
zhan	chan	jan
zhang	chang	jang
zhao	chao	jau
zhe	che	je
zhei	chei	jei
zhen	chen	jen
zheng	cheng	jeng
zhi	chih	jr
zhong	chung	jung
zhou	chou	jou
zhu	chu	ju
zhua	chua	jwa
zhuai	chuai	jwai
zhuan	chuan	jwan
zhuang	chuang	jwang
zhui	chui	jwei
zhun	chun	jwun
zhuo	cho	jwo
zi	tzu	dz
zong	tsung	dzung
zou	tsou	dzou
zu	tsu	dzu
zuan	tsuan	dzwan
zui	tsui	dzwei
zun	tsun	dzwun
zuo	tso	dzwo

The following pronunciation guide for Sanskrit is provided, since the romanization of Sanskrit terms is not always close to the actual pronunciation.

Simple Sounds

a	as the 'a' in about
ā	as the 'a' in 'father'
i	as the 'ee' of 'teen' said fast
ī	as the 'ee' of 'teen'
u	as the 'oo' in 'moon' said fast
ū	as the 'oo' in 'moon'
ṛ	as 'ri' said fast with tongue tip curled back
ṝ	as 'ri', tongue tip curled slightly back
ḷ	tongue as before, say l

Complex Sounds

e	as in 'day'; is really a + i said together fast
ai	as in 'aisle'; ā + i together
o	as in 'go'; is a + u said fast
au	as in 'out'; made up of ā + u

Letters Between Consonants and Vowels

ḥ	a kind of puff of air; only found at the end of words
ṃ	nasalizes the vowel before it

Consonantal Sounds

ka karma	**kha** backhand	**ga** game	**gha** tag hard	**ṅa** Saṅgha
ca chart	**cha** catch hat	**ja** jar	**jha** page half	**ña** manual

NOTE: For the first row below, curl tip of tongue slightly back against the ridge behind the upper front teeth. Touch tongue quickly against the teeth to say the second row below.

ṭa tame	**ṭha** at heart	**ḍa** day	**ḍha** had half	**ṇa** name
ta tame	**tha** at heart	**da** day	**dha** had half	**ṇa** name
pa pain	**pha** haphazard	**ba** bag	**bha** grab hard	**ma** magic
ya yard	**ra** 'r' ***(with tongue as above)***	**la** land	**va** valor	
śa shame	**ṣa** ***(German 'ich' or Chinese 'hsien')***	**sa** same	**ha** harvest	

- By Ronald B. Epstein -

LAYING THE FOUNDATION

1. The Origins of the Master's Mission to the West

The Venerable Master's vision was as vast as the Dharma Realm, and he taught and transformed all beings without regard to path of rebirth, country, ethnic origin, religion, and so forth. There are two countries, however, where he had special affinities in this life: China and United States. Although the majority of his disciples are Chinese, history will probably remember him primarily for his work in bringing the teachings of the Buddha to the people of the West.

The story begins in rural Manchuria (northeast China) at his mother's grave site. The Master, then in his late teens or early twenties, was observing the Chinese filial practice of three years' mourning. As a novice Buddhist monk, he did it in a uniquely Buddhist way by building a meditation hut of sorghum thatch and sitting in continuous meditation there. One day he saw the Venerable Master Huineng, the Sixth Patriarch in China of the Chan (Zen) Lineage, walk into his hut. The Patriarch spoke with him for a long time. The Master remembered him saying:

> In the future you can go to America to teach and transform living beings: The five schools will divide into ten. Ten will become a hundred and than a thousand, until they are endless... countless like the sands of the Ganges... the genuine beginning [of Buddhism] in the West.

That was part of the Patriarch's instruction to the Master in which he told him that he should leave China and spread the Dharma in the West. Afterwards the Master got up to accompany the Patriarch out of the hut. Only after the Patriarch had disappeared did the Master remember that the Patriarch had entered nirvana long ago (in 713 C.E.).

Despite knowing from this initial vision of the Sixth Patriarch that he would eventually go to the West to propagate the Dharma, the Master had little contact with Westerners until he moved to Hong Kong in 1949. There he had his first substantial experiences with Western culture.

After his Dharma-lineage predecessor, the Venerable Chan Master Xuyun (1840-1959), entered nirvana and the Master completed the proper ceremonies in his memory, he felt that conditions had ripened for pursuing his Dharma mission in the West. Several of his lay disciples from Hong Kong had already gone to the United States to study.

In November 1960 the Master went to Australia to investigate the conditions for the growth of Buddhism there. He spent a difficult year there and then returned to Hong Kong briefly. In 1958 a branch of the Buddhist Lecture Hall had already been established in San

Francisco by his disciples there. In response to their invitation, the Master decided to go to San Francisco and arrived there early in 1962. At the small Chinatown temple, he lectured on the *Amitābha Sutra*. During that period various Americans who were interested in Zen, such as Richard Baker, former Abbot of the San Francisco Zen Center, visited the Master.

In the fall of 1962 the Cuban missile crisis broke out. Wishing in some measure to repay the benefit that he had received from living in the United States, and seeing clearly the catastrophic threat imposed by the missiles in Cuba, the Venerable Master embarked on a total fast for thirty-five days, during which he took only water. He dedicated the merit of his sacrifice to end the hostilities.

2. The Monk in the Grave Period

In 1963, because some of the disciples there were not respectful of the Dharma, he left Chinatown and moved the Buddhist Lecture Hall to a first-floor flat on the corner of Sutter and Webster Streets on the edge of San Francisco's Fillmore District and Japantown. The Master's move marked the beginning of a period of relative seclusion during which he called himself "a monk in the grave." It lasted until 1968. He later continued to refer to himself in that way and wrote the following poem:

> Each of you now meets
>   a monk in the grave.
> Above there is no sun and moon,
>   below there is no lamp.
> Affliction and enlightenment—
>   ice is water.
> Let go of self-seeking and
>   renounce all that is false.
> When the mad mind ceases,
>   enlightenment pervades all.
> Enlightened, attain the bright
>   treasury of your own nature.
> Basically, the retribution body
>   is the Dharma body.

It was at that Sutter Street location that the Master first started having regular contact with young Americans who were interested in meditation. Some came to his daily, public meditation hour from seven to eight every evening, and a few Americans also attended his sutra lectures. He lectured there on the *Amitābha Sutra*, the *Diamond Sutra*, the *Heart Sutra* with his own verse commentary, on his own commentary to the *Song of Enlightenment*, and also on portions of the *Lotus* (*Dharma Flower*) *Sutra*.

In July of 1967 the Master moved back to Chinatown, locating the San Francisco Buddhist Lecture Hall in the Tianhou Temple, the oldest Chinese temple in America. There he lectured on the Verses of the Seven Buddhas of Antiquity and "Universal Door" Chapter of the *Lotus* (*Dharma Flower*) *Sutra*.

On Chinese New Year's Day in 1968, the Master made two important pronouncements to a small gathering. First he predicted that in the course of the year the lotus of American Buddhism would bloom. At that time there was still little outward sign of the influx of young Americans that would begin that spring.

Secondly, noting the great fear among large segments of the community that there would be an earthquake in the spring of that year, he declared that as long as he was in San Francisco, he would not permit earthquakes large enough to do damage or cause injury or death to occur. Every subsequent Chinese New Year he would renew his vow. When the San Francisco earthquake of 1989 occurred, the Master was out of the country in Taiwan.

In the spring of 1968 a group of university students at the University of Washington in Seattle wrote to the Master and requested that the Master come to Seattle to lead a weeklong meditation session. The Master had Nancy Dana Lovett, a disciple, write for him to Ron Epstein, another disciple who was a member of the Seattle group, to tell the group that he could not come to Seattle, because if he left San Francisco, there would be an earthquake. He suggested that they come to the Buddhist Lecture Hall in San Francisco instead. The group went and that spring both a Buddha-recitation session and a Chan (Zen) meditation session, each a week long, were held. About thirty people attended.

3. The 1968 Śūraṅgama Sutra Summer Lecture and Cultivation Session

At the conclusion of the spring sessions, the Master suggested to several of the participants that a three-month lecture and cultivation session be held during the summer months. About thirty people decided to attend. During that 98-day session, the Master lectured on the *Śūraṅgama Sutra* twice a day, and near the end of the session three and even four times a day, to explain the entire sutra. The lectures were also open to the general public. The session itself started at six every morning and officially ended at nine in the evening. In addition to the sutra lectures, the schedule consisted of alternate hours of meditation, study, and discussion, so there was very little free time.

Although those who attended were of varied age and background, the majority were young Americans of college age or in their middle or late twenties. Most had had little or no previous training in Buddhism; however, several had studied Buddhism at the undergraduate level and some at the graduate level. A few had also had a little previous experience with meditation. The handful who had some competency in Chinese provided translations, which started out on a rather rudimentary level and became quite competent during the course of the summer.

Events of special note that took place during the session included two refuge ceremonies, at which most of the regular participants became formal disciples of the Master, and a precept ceremony late in the summer in which almost all the disciples took vows to follow moral precepts of varying numbers, including some or all of the Five Moral Precepts up to the Ten Major and Forty-eight Minor Bodhisattva Precepts. One participant took the vows of a novice monk. The Master's teachings that summer specially emphasized the moral precepts as a foundation for the spiritual life. In this way he used them as an effective antidote against the proclivities of the popular culture for drug experience and sexual promiscuity.

4. Five Americans Leave the Home-Life

Soon afterwards four other Americans, three of whom had also participated in the summer session, left the home-life. In December of 1969 the five, three men and two women, received full ordination at Haihui Monastery near Keelung, Taiwan, and became the first Americans to do so. They were Bhikshus (monks) Heng Ch'ien, Heng Ching, and Heng Shou, and Bhikshunis (nuns) Heng Yin and Heng Ch'ih.

5. The Master's Plan for American Buddhism

With the founding of a new American Sangha, the Master was then ready to embark on an incredible building program for American Buddhism. The Venerable Master has explained that his life's work lay in three main areas: 1) bringing the true and orthodox teachings of the Buddha to the West and establishing a proper monastic community of fully ordained monks and nuns (Sangha) here; 2) organizing and supporting the translation of the entire Buddhist canon into English and other Western languages; and 3) promoting wholesome education through the establishment of schools and universities.

ESTABLISHING A BUDDHIST SANGHA IN THE WEST

1. The First Ordination Ceremonies in the West

Because of the increasing numbers of people who wished to leave the home-life to become monks and nuns under the Master's guidance, in 1972 the Master decided to hold at Gold Mountain Dhyāna Monastery the first formal, full ordination ceremonies for Buddhist monks and nuns to be held in the West. He invited virtuous elder masters to preside with him over the ordination platform. Two monks and one nun received ordination. Subsequent ordination platforms have been held at the Sagely City of Ten Thousand Buddhas in 1976, 1979, 1982, 1989, 1991, 1992, 1995, 2000, and 2002, and progressively larger numbers of people have received full ordination. Over two hundred people from countries all over the world were ordained under him.

2. The Master as Reformer

The Master was determined to transmit the original and correct teachings of the Buddha to the West and was outspoken about not infecting Western Buddhism with corrupt practices that were widespread in Chinese Buddhism. While encouraging his disciples to learn the ancient traditions, he cautioned them against mistaking cultural overlay and ignorant superstition for the true Dharma. He encouraged them to understand the logical reasons behind the ancient practices.

Among the reforms that he instituted were the following: he reestablished the wearing of the precept sash (*kaṣāya*) as a sign of a member of the Sangha; he emphasized that the Buddha instructed that monks and nuns not eat after noon and encouraged his Sangha to follow the Buddha's practice, which he followed, of eating only one meal a day at noon; he also encouraged them to follow his example in the practice of not lying down at night, which was also recommended by the Buddha. In the early days at Tianhou Temple in San Francisco's Chinatown, some of the disciples, in order to train themselves in this practice, found appropriate-sized packing crates abandoned in the streets and modified them so that they could sit in them at night and keep themselves from stretching out their legs. The Master also criticized the current Chinese practice among many Buddhist lay people of taking refuge with many different teachers, and he himself would not accept disciples who had previously taken refuge with another monk.

Some of the Master's American disciples were initially attracted to the Master and Buddhism because of their interest in extraordinary spiritual experiences and psychic powers. Many of them were trying to understand remarkable experiences of their own, and many with special psychic abilities were naturally drawn to the Master. Clearly recognizing the danger of the popularity of the quest for special experiences in American culture, the Master emphasized that special mental states can be a sign of progress in cultivation but can also be very dangerous if misunderstood. He taught about the Buddha's monastic prohibitions against advertising one's spiritual abilities and made clear that spiritual abilities in themselves are not an indication of wisdom and do not insure wholesome character.

Generally speaking, the Master was concerned with the pure motivation of those who left the home-life under him and did not want the American Sangha to be polluted by those who had ulterior, worldly reasons for leaving the home-life. To that end he established these fundamental guidelines for monastic practice:

Freezing to death, we do not
  scheme.
Starving to death, we do not beg.
Dying of poverty, we ask for
  nothing.
According with conditions,
  we do not change.
Not changing,
  we accord with conditions.
We adhere firmly
  to our three great principles.
We renounce our lives
  to do the Buddha's work.
We take the responsibility
  to mold our own destinies.
We rectify our lives
  as the Sangha's work.
Encountering specific matters,
  we understand the principles.
Understanding the principles,
  we apply them in specific matters
We carry on the single pulse of the
  patriarchs' mind-transmission.

In addition he summarized the standards of counduct that he upheld throughout his life for all his disciples, both Sangha members and lay people, in Six Great Guidelines: not contending, not being greedy, not seeking, not being selfish, not pursuing personal profit, and not lying.

One of the Master's more remarkable endeavors in the area of monastic reform was his attempt to heal the two-thousand-year-old rift between Mahayana and Theravada monastic communities.He encouraged cordial relations between the Sanghas, invited distinguished Theravada monks to preside with him in monastic ordination ceremonies, and initiated talks aimed at resolving areas of difference.

3. Founding of the Sino-American Buddhist Association and the Dharma Realm Buddhist Association

The Master felt that one of the marks of decay of proper monastic practice in China had been the gradual shift of emphasis from large monastic training monasteries to small individual temples, each with one or two monks or nuns free to do more or less whatever they pleased. In order to insure that tendency for laxity of practice did not take hold in the West, the Master wished to unite all his Sangha members and lay people under a single organization, that could both help to maintain uniform pure standards of couduct for members of the Sangha and discourage the making of offerings to individuals instead of to the Sangha as a whole. In order to strengthen central organization and in recognition of his growing number of American disciples, in December, 1968 the Buddhist Lecture Hall was expanded into the newly incorporated Sino-American Buddhist Association. As that organization became more international in scope, in 1984, the name of the organization was officially changed to the Dharma Realm Buddhist Association.

4. Monasteries and Temples Founded by the Master in the West.

With the large influx of Americans wishing to study the Dharma, the small Tianhou Temple was quickly outgrown, and in 1970 the Association moved to a large three-story brick building, which was remodelled to become Gold Mountain Dhyāna Monastery. In 1976 the Master established the Sagely City of Ten Thousand Buddhas, which now encompasses almost five hundred acres of land at Wonderful Enlightenment Mountain in northern California. Among the many other temples, monasteries, and retreat centers established by the Master are Gold Wheel Monastery in Los Angeles, Long Beach Monastery in Long Beach, California, Gold Buddha Monastery in Vancouver, Gold Summit Monastery in Seattle, Avatamsaka Monastery in Calgary, the Berkeley Buddhist Monastery and Institute of World Religions, and the Administrative Headquarters and International Translation Institute, both in Burlingame, California.

TEACHING THE DHARMA AND TRANSLATING THE BUDDHIST CANON

1. What the Master Taught

In retrospect, the vigor, depth and breadth of the Master's efforts in teaching in the West are nothing short of incredible. In his early days of teaching Westerners, he often had little or no help. He cooked, taught them to cook, sat with them in meditation and taught them to sit, entertained them with Buddhist stories, and taught them the rudiments of Buddhadharma and Buddhist courtesy and ceremony. He gave lessons in Chinese and in Chinese calligraphy, and taught the fundamentals of the pure Buddhist lifestyle.

As his Western students progressed in their understanding and practice, he did not slack off in the least. He continued not only to lecture daily on the sutras, but to give various other classes. He lectured on the four major Mahayana sutras, completing the *Śūraṅgama Sutra*, the *Lotus* (*Dharma Flower*) *Sutra*, and the *Avataṃsaka Sutra*, and finishing a substantial portion of the *Nirvana Sutra*. He also lectured on the *Heart Sutra*, the *Diamond* (*Vajra*) *Sutra*, the *Sixth Patriarch's Platform Sutra*, the *Earth Store Sutra*, the *Song of Enlightenment* and a host of other Buddhist works.

He also trained a whole staff of translators and taught many disciples how to lecture on the sutras themselves. In almost every formal teaching situation, in order to train his disciples, he would first ask them to speak and only speak himself after they had had the opportunity.

The Master's teaching methods included yearly sutra lecture and cultivation sessions modeled on the first Śūraṅgama Sutra Session. He laid down vigorous standards for meditation and recitation sessions, giving frequent instructuctional talks during the sessions. He explained the importance of the Buddhist Dharmas of repentance and encouraged the bowing of the Great Compassion Repentance, the Great Repentance Before the Ten Thousand Buddhas, and other repentance ceremonies.

Much of the Master's most important teaching took place outside of his formal Dharma lectures. For the Master, every situation was an opportunity for teaching, and he paid little attention to whether the recipients of instruction were formal disciples. For him every worldly encounter, whether with disciples or politicians or realtors, was an opportunity to help people become aware of their faults and change them and to develop their inherent wisdom. The Master was always open, direct, and totally honest with everyone in every situation. He treated everyone equally, from the President of the United States to little children. Everything he did was to benefit others and never for himself.

2. Traveling to Spread the Dharma in the West

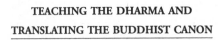

Whenever and wherever he was respectfully invited to speak the Dharma, the Master always tried his best to oblige, even if it was at the cost of his own physical wellbeing. In addition to his almost continual traveling in the United States and Canada to lecture and several major trips to Asian countries, the Master also visited South America and Europe.

In 1973 the Master traveled to Brazil, Argentina, Paraguay and other countries in South America. His main purpose was to establish affinities with the people, and so he spent much time while there, reciting mantras of great compassion and transferring the merit to the local people.

In 1990 at the invitation of Buddhists in many countries of Europe, the Master took a large delegation there on a Dharma tour, knowing full well that, because of his ill health at the time, the rigors of the trip would shorten his life span. However, as always the Master considered the Dharma more important than his very life. Among the countries visited were England, France, Belgium, Germany, and Poland.

3. The Buddhist Text Translation Society and Vajra Bodhi Sea

In 1970 the Master founded the Buddhist Text Translation Society with the eventual goal of translating the entire Buddhist Canon into English and other languages of the West. The Master saw clearly that reliable translations into English with readable and understandable commentaries were essential to the understanding and practice of the Buddhadharma by Westerners. To date the Buddhist Text Translation Society has published over a hundred volumes, and the work of translating Buddhist scriptures, many with the Master's own commentaries, is ongoing.

Also in 1970 the Master founded *Vajra Bodhi Sea*, a monthly journal of orthodox Buddhism. It has been published continuously ever since. Initially in English, it now appears in a bilingual Chinese-English format.

PROMOTING EDUCATION

The Master felt that one of the weaknesses of Buddhism in China was that it did not give high priority to education and failed to develop a widespread network of Buddhist schools and universities. In order to begin to remedy that situation in the West, the Venerable Master founded Dharma Realm Buddhist University, primary and secondary schools, and developed financial aid programs for needy and deserving students.

The Master taught that education is the best national defense. He counseled that in elementary school children should be taught filial respect, in secondary school love of country and loyalty to it, and at the university level students should learn not only professional skills but a sense of personal responsibility for improving the world they live in.

The Master balanced tradition with educational innovation. He pioneered what he called the development of each individual's inherent wisdom, and he was always ready to employ new ways of teaching. For example, he wrote several songs in English himself and encouraged his disciples to use that medium for teaching the Dharma.

1. Dharma Realm Buddhist University

In 1976 the Master established Dharma Realm Buddhist University with its main campus at the Sagely City of Ten Thousand Buddhas. Its main goals are to provide education to all the peoples of the world by explaining and propagating the Buddha's teachings, developing straightforward minds, benefitting society, and enlightening all beings. The University currently offers undergraduate and/or graduate degrees in Buddhist Study and Practice, Translation of Buddhist Texts, Buddhist Education, and Chinese Studies. In his final instructions, the Master indicated that special attention should be paid to the fulfillment of his vision for the University.

Over the years many well-known professors from American universities, including Edward Conze, P. Jaini, David Ruegg, Henry Rosemont, Jr. and Jacob Needleman to name just a few, came to pay their respects to the Master and to listen to his teachings. He was also invited to lecture at various universities, including Stanford, Berkeley, University of Washington, University of Oregon, UCLA, University of California at Davis, University of Hawaii, and San Francisco State University.

2. Sangha and Laity Training Programs

In 1982 the Master established the Sangha and Laity Training Programs. The Laity Training Program emphasizes Buddhist Studies and Practice for lay people in a monastic setting with an emphasis on moral discipline. The Sangha Training Program emphasizes religious practice, monastic discipline, and temple management. Through these programs the Master has been able to train fully qualified and committed staff for the various programs and activities of the Dharma Realm Buddhist Association.

3. Instilling Goodness and Developing Virtue Schools

At the suggestion of Carol Ruth Silver, who was then a San Francisco Supervisor, the Master founded Instilling Goodness School in 1976. In addition to nurturing the roots of goodness and virtue in the young children, the school was devoted to quality education. It promoted a bilingual Chinese-English curriculum and taught the fundamentals of both Western and Chinese cultural heritages. Principal Terri Nicholson and her staff taught the first classes in the furnished basement of the International Institute for the Translation of Buddhist Texts on Washington Street in San Francisco. The school moved to the Sagely City of Ten Thousand Buddhas in 1978. Developing Virtue Secondary School opened its doors in 1980, and a separation into boys' and girls' schools occurred in 1981.

4. The Master's Ecumenical Teaching

In consonance with his Dharma Realm vision, the Master often said that Buddhism was too limiting a label for the Buddha's teaching and often referred to it as the teaching of living being. Just as he was critical of sectarian divisions within Buddhism as not being in the true spirit of the Dharma, he felt that people should not be attached to interreligious distinctions either, that it is important for people of all religions to learn from the strengths of each religious tradition. To make that vision a reality, he invited his good friend Paul Cardinal Yu Bin, the Catholic cardinal of Taiwan, to join him in establishing a World Religions Center at the Sagely City of Ten Thousand Buddha and to be its first director. He suggested that the cardinal be a "Buddhist among the Catholics" and that he himself would be a "Catholic among the Buddhists." Unfortunately the cardinal's untimely death delayed the plans for the Center, which in 1994 opened in Berkeley as the Institute of World Religions.

The Master also directed Dharma Realm Buddhist University to host a World Religions Conference in 1987 at the Sagely City of Ten Thousand Buddhas. Also in 1987 the Master gave a major address at the Third International Buddhist-Christian Dialogue Conference in Berkeley. Once the Master was invited to give a eulogy at Grace Cathedral in San Francisco. In 1989 the Master was invited to the Quaker Retreat Center at Pendle Hill, Pennsylvania to give a series of talks, and in 1992 he was the guest speaker at the yearly Vedanta Society gathering at Olema, California. Also worthy of mention is the ongoing friendship that the Master had with Father John Rogers, Catholic Chaplain of Humboldt State University.

THE MASTER'S ENDURING LEGACY FOR THE WEST

Throughout his life the Venerable Master was widely known for his selfless humility and his compassion for all living beings. He worked tirelessly and without regard for his own health and welfare to dissolve the boundaries of ignorance that obstruct true self-understanding. He constantly worked for peace and harmony throughout the world on all levels, between people, between species, between religions, and between nations. Although his mission has been to the Dharma Realm, in this brief account we have tried to focus on his contributions to Buddhism in the West. In this light, we conclude with a brief overview.

When the first Chan (Zen) Patriarch Bodhidharma came to China, although Buddhism had arrived several centuries earlier, most people in China were still confused about the central meaning of the Buddha's teaching and could not distinguish what was true from what was false, what was superficial from what was essential. Patriarch Bodhidharma cut through that confusion and taught people to illuminate their own minds, see their true natures, and become Buddhas. The Venerable Master Hsuan Hua came to the West about a hundred years after Buddhism's first introduction here. When he arrived there was much genuine interest but also tremendous confusion and misunderstanding. Teaching that Buddhism flourishes only in countries where the Sangha is strong and pure, the Master established a reformed monastic community and emphasized the importance of moral precepts both for Sangha and laity. Understanding the practical and pragmatic nature of the American character, he emphasized vigorous and proper meditation practice in the spirit and lineage of Patriarch Bodhidharma, so that the eternal truths of the Buddha's teachings could be directly and personally experienced. Seeing clearly the dangers of widely prevalent wrong notions about the Buddha's teachings, he explained the major scriptures in a clear and simple manner while bringing out their contemporary, practical relevance. Then he worked to make those teachings available in English so that they would be accessible to Westerners. And finally, he chose to live and teach in the West so that every day he provided a living, breathing manifestation of the true meaning of the Buddha's teachings. In that way he touched and profoundly transformed the lives of countless Westerners and planted the seeds of *bodhi* (enlightenment) in their hearts.

Certainly our personal cultivation is extremely important. If we can cultivate and realize enlightenment, of course we will be able to help Buddhism in a great way. Even so, this is only a temporary contribution. If we can translate the sutras into the languages of every country and deliver the Buddhadharma into every person's heart, that is a lasting achievement.

- Master Hua

Today's highly developed material civilization and extravagant material lifestyle are unprecedented in the history of human-kind. However, if we contemplate the global picture, we see that the sufferings of living beings have only increased. Wars, famines, droughts, and other human calamities and natural disasters are occurring everywhere. The nations of the world invest great amounts of money and employ endless strategies in an attempt to solve these problems, but they can only provide temporary relief. They have no way to remove the ultimate cause of human suffering.

The Venerable Master once said:

Now it can be said that the world has gone bad. The only thing that can save the world is the Buddhadharma. If people can understand the Buddhadharma, the evils of these times be averted. If people don't understand the Buddhadharma, then I am afraid this world will soon be destroyed.

If we translate the Buddhadharma into English, if everyone understands the Buddhadharma, if everyone knows better than to be lazy, and if people resolve to cultivate, then the end of the world will be very far away in the future, perhaps even great eons away. As soon as the great Dharma Wheel of the Buddhadharma is set in motion, even the sun will be pulled in and won't be able to set, so there won't be any final day. The countries of the world have all sought to emulate Western science and technology. And yet, in recent years many Westerners, wishing to regulate their minds, have sought out Buddhism. However, teachers who are grounded in the orthodox Buddhist tradition were hard to find, and there were the barriers of language and culture.

In his youth, the Master had already begun to study how to make the Buddhist teachings available to all parts of the world in order to help the world. The Master said:

When I became a monk, I wanted to find out why such a perfect teaching as Buddhism was studied by so few people in the world. After looking into it, I discovered that the reason Buddhism has not spread throughout the world is because we, the disciples of the Buddha, have not translated the Buddhist scriptures into the languages of each and every nation. If we can make the Buddhist scriptures accessible, translating them into as many languages as we are able, Buddhism will become a universal teaching even without our wishing it. So, I made a vow when I left the home-life that, even though I don't know any other language, as long as I'm alive, I will see to it that the Buddhist scriptures are translated into the languages of the world. That's my vow. I'm willing to exhaust my abilities to promote this work.

The transmission of the Buddhadharma from India to China was made possible through the valiant and tireless efforts of generations of high Sanghans and Patriarchs to obtain the sutras and to translate them. Due to their efforts, the people of China have had the opportunity to understand the subtle, wonderful, and inconceivable Buddhadharma. Just as the Master said:

> For everything we understand in a sutra, we should give great thanks to the translator. If he had never existed, we would be unable to see the sutra or even to hear its name. If that were the case, how would we be able to cultivate according to the methods prescribed in it? It would be impossible to find its path of cultivation. Therefore, we should be grateful to the people who translated the sutras, since from that time up to the present moment, every generation has benefited from their compassionate contribution. The merit of translating sutras is inconceivable. It is extremely vast. Now it is up to you to translate the sutras into Western languages. The merit derived by the people who take part in this work will be without limit, for it will benefit not only their own lives, but will be cause for the gratitude of generations of people in the West. Everyone can be included in the work of translation; I hope no one will fall behind. You should quickly learn Chinese and translate the sutras into English. Everyone should be eager to make a contribution to the people of the West.

With his vision for the future, the Master clearly saw the key to saving the world. That's why he made the vast vow of translating the Buddhist canon. However, the work of translating sutras is extremely difficult. In the past, the emperors and ministers of China used the country's resources to accomplish this task. In the West, the situation differs. The Master said in the early 1970's when very few Buddhist canonical texts existed in English:

> I dare not bring up this matter of translation with anyone, because as soon as I mention it, everyone feels overwhelmed by the immensity of the task. Everyone is frightened, because this is something that has never been done before, something that nobody dares to do. The human resources, financial resources, and various conditions required by this project are not simple matters. As of now, no one dares to take on this responsibility. Even among my disciples who have taken refuge with me, there is no one who truly understands the importance of this undertaking.

The Master, with his courageous spirit, took this monumental task upon himself. He said,

> The work of translating the sutras is sacred work, and it will last for endless generations. We are common people doing the work of sages. Not only is this our duty, it is also very meaningful, for we can benefit others and establish merit. In the past, the kings and emperors used their

imperial authority and the strength of the government to carry out the translation of the sutras. Now we are merely using our strength as ordinary citizens. We must first lay a foundation. We must first gather strength among the people.

Even so, the Master never thought of himself as having initiated some greatly meritorious endeavor. Instead, he said,

> I'm just a worker who sweeps the ground and levels the road for everyone. In the future, there will be others who can lay the gravel and pour on the asphalt. Right now, we can do the work that nobody wants to do, the work that no one dares to do. Bit by bit, we will open up paths that lead into Buddhism.

The Master also told disciples,

> We cannot be negligent in doing this work. We must do our best to carry out our real responsibilities. However much we can do, we should do that much. Let's keep pressing forward and working. We should take Buddhism as our own responsibility. The propagation of the Buddhadharma should be our personal duty in life.

The translation of sutras has such great significance, and yet, how can a person who doesn't even know English or any language other than Chinese manage to translate the Chinese sutras into other languages? The Master said:

> I have vowed to do this work. Even though I don't know any other language, I'm bold enough to want to translate the sutras. The mere thought of wanting to do this has already made the Buddhas happy. Even a person like me, who doesn't know any other language, wants to do this work, how much more should people who do know other languages honestly devote themselves to carrying out this task.

Actually, the Master was extremely thorough and clear in his understanding of the principles and methodology of sutra translation. Of the three principles of accuracy, elegance, and clarity of meaning, accuracy is foremost. The Master said,

> In translating the sutras, nothing is more important than accuracy. The translation cannot be at odds with the original text. When translating someone else's work, you must translate that person's words faithfully. You cannot add your own ideas. If the grammar is awkward, you may smooth it out, but there is no need to add your own interpretations.

The Master explained the sutras in simple terms for the sake of beginners, as well as to allow translators to learn from them, gain a basic knowledge of the Buddhadharma, and cultivate accordingly. The Master wasn't attached to his own words. He modestly said,

> You can use my kindergarten-level explanations if you want. Since we are just beginning, we should first lay a firm foundation. After that, we can expand our scope and translate other things.

The translation of the Buddhist canon is an endeavor that may take a hundred years or a thousand years. From his standpoint as a trailblazer, the Master said,

> In our present translations, it will be enough if the meaning is clear and understandable. We shouldn't embellish our work so that it is as beautiful as

embroidery. As long as it's passable, that's enough.

When the Buddhist Text Translation Society was established, the Master set up Four Committees to govern the translation process: **1**) Primary Translation Committee, **2**) Reviewing Committee, **3**) Editing Committee, and **4**) Certifying Committee. Since 1972, the Buddhist Text Translation Society has been publishing translations of Buddhist texts.

ON SPEAKING THE DHARMA

The Master said:

I may go without eating for days, but I cannot go without speaking the Dharma for even a single day. My vow is that as long as I have one breath left, I will lecture on the sutras and speak the Dharma. Only when I have no more breath will I stop speaking. As long as there's a single person who wants to hear me speak the Dharma, I will speak. Even if no human beings are listening. I will still lecture to the ghosts, spirits, and other supernatural beings.

The Master said:

You can go anywhere in the world and you won't find a place where lectures on the sutras and talks on Dharma are given every day. It doesn't matter whether any people come to listen or not, the lectures go on. That's because we want to do our best to turn the Dharma wheel. We want to do all we can to propagate the Buddhadharma.

The Dharma is spoken to enable beings to recognize the truth. Therefore, each Way-place includes in its daily schedule a time for giving or listening to lectures on the sutras. "The waters of the Ganges River flow day after day; the Dharma of the Sagely City of Ten Thousand Buddhas is spoken day after day."

In the early period the Master used a method called "Developing Inherent Wisdom" to train the fourfold assembly of disciples on an equal basis. They would take turns to request the Dharma, give lectures, and evaluate lectures. The Master also regularly held classes on "Matching Couplets" to help his disciples activate the wisdom in their own natures.

The Master would always choose the appropriate Dharma to speak to the people he was addressing. To ordinary people, he spoke of being content with their work and fulfilling their basic duties. To students, he spoke of filial piety, fraternal respect, loyalty, trustworthiness, propriety, righteousness, incorruptibility, and a sense of shame; of cherishing oneself, loving one's family, and serving the country. To professors and university presidents, he spoke of educating for the sake of education. To political leaders, he spoke of moral probity and cherishing the people as if they were one's own children. The Master didn't want personal fame. Because he wished to train other people, he never went to give a lecture alone. Rather, he would always bring a delegation of disciples on trips to study and learn in various countries.

When the Master left Hong Kong and came to America in 1962, his first task was to lecture on the sutras and speak the

Dharma. The Master lectured on the *Vajra Sutra*, the *Heart Sutra*, the *Sixth Patriarch's Sutra*, the *Earth Store Sutra*, the *Śūraṅgama Sutra*, the *Dharma Flower Sutra*, the *Flower Adornment [Avataṃsaka] Sutra*, and even on such short texts as the *Sutra of the Eight Awakenings of Great People*, the *Sutra of the Buddha's Final Teaching*, the *Sutra in Forty-two Sections*, the *Song of Enlightenment*, and others. The Master was lecturing on the sutras almost every single day. He spoke Dharma and explained sutras countless times. Everything he said was for the sake of helping humankind and keeping this world from being destroyed. The following talk, given on February 9, 1985 at the University of British Columbia in Vancouver, is considered to an important one because in it, the Master makes several predictions.

THE FUTURE OF HUMANKIND

- By Master Hua -

In this era, when technology and materialism flourish, we want to take a careful look at the thinking of the times and ask ourselves whether or not this is a good age to live in. Science has made great advances in technology and that certainly counts as good. But we should also realize the truth in the saying, "Anything taken to the ultimate point transforms into its opposite."

In the case of technological advances, good things also beckon misfortune. Let's look at television; for example, I know people will object to my analysis of the TV, saying, "Dharma Master, you're being reactionary. You're out of step with the times." Nonetheless, in my opinion, the television is a menace to human life. The television is consuming humankind. Did you know that? Look at children these days. Instead of doing their homework, they sit in front of the TV set. They're glued to the screen, and it consumes their very life-force. The children might as well be dead, because they will never learn the basic principles of being good people. They only learn how to stare at the television.

And what does the TV teach them? Every kind of strange and freakish behavior you can imagine. They learn precious little of value. The kids very quickly learn to enact the evil and harmful lessons they watch. In no time at all, they learn all the bad things that people can do.

Before television came into the world, radio consumed people's vital energy. People used to stick a radio in their ear and completely forgot everything else. Radios made us forget about eating, sleeping, and the ordinary events of life. Now the television has confused us to the point of not knowing whether we're coming or going.

Computers have followed along right after the television. In Chinese, the word for computer translates literally into "electric brain." In the future there will be electric eyes, as well as electric ears, electric tongues, electric noses and electric bodies. Every one of the six organs will have disposable modules, likes cassettes, and will gain an electric boost. Eyes, ears, nose, tongue, body, and mind will be computerized. Even the mind will tie in organically with "know-it-all computer memory banks." Is this a good time to be a person? On the contrary, this is a dark age in human history.

In this benighted era, our wisdom has been stolen away by material things. Nobody has any natural wisdom to speak of. Our inherent brightness has been replaced by products and goods. And once we substitute things for wisdom, then people will grow up blank, like idiots. Wisdom will become outmoded. People will no longer serve any useful function. Mark my words: in the future, people will become obsolete. Would you say this is a serious problem or not? Pay attention! People will soon be rendered useless!

For instance, some unethical scientists now are busy inventing miraculous monsters. You say it's human? It's not really human. You say it's an animal? It's not exactly an animal either. Since they graft human genes onto animal bodies and alter human genes with animal strains, this mutual genetic modification produces a mutant hybrid that resembles neither parent.

Now people can be born with horns, or elephant-like trunks. In my opinion, a human born with a nose like a pachyderm is more a goblin than a person. These goblins and freaks are all within the realm of possibility today.

Furthermore, the range of technology has grown out of control. Within the next two centuries, telephones and the like will be totally obsolete. Televisions and computers will have disappeared. Every person's physical body will contain the capabilities of these machines. Nobody will have to bother dialing a telephone or punching a touch-tone. A person will only need to beam out the number of the desired party from his own built-in phone, with its antennae located in the eyebrows, perhaps, or from his hair, and the other person will receive the call the same built-in way. "Hello! Good morning!" That's how easy it will be to place a phone call.

Somebody may be thinking at this point, "Dharma Master, that's the craziest talk I've ever heard."

Well, I ask you to consider this. How many people would have believed you if five hundred years ago you had said, "In five hundred years, there will be airplanes, television, and radios?" Everyone would have considered you insane. But all these inventions are commonplace now.

Why do I mention this topic in the first place? Because we should recognize that advances in science and in material benefits are not necessarily good for humanity in the long run. They are incomplete, imperfect benefits. Wisdom, on the other hand, is a universal benefit for the whole world. Thinking and attitudes born of morality and virtue are thoroughly good for us all. The Buddha's four measureless attitudes of kindness, compassion, joy, and equanimity are beneficial to all creatures. When we adopt such attitudes, we can put technology to work for us. There's no fear that we will forget the fundamental aspects of humanity: our own bodies for example. But, if we do not nurture such virtues, then in the future we will forget entirely how people are supposed to act. We will all become like animals. I'm not kidding.

That's how the world turns. Good taken to the ultimate point becomes bad. Evil, once it reaches an extreme, turns into good. A person who is totally destitute can suddenly strike it rich, while rich people can lose every penny overnight. Once born, we are tiny infants, but we grow up, grow old, get sick, and die. The cycle of creation and destruction rolls on in the world. It is a natural process of cyclical change and transformation. If we recognize the human condition, then getting rich won't appeal to us any longer. And if we should lose our wealth, then we will see things according to the proverb:

> The superior person, even in
> poverty, maintains his integrity.
> The petty person stops at nothing
> to strike it rich.

It is most important in this day and age where insanity often reigns supreme not to go crazy, and not to forget what it means to be human. We must keep in mind what our purpose for being is. When speaking of the meaning of human life, I can say frankly that the most beneficial things I have run across in my entire life are the Six Principles of the City of Ten Thousand Buddhas.

The first of these is to refrain from fighting. This rule applies unilaterally. I will not contend with anybody. No matter what criticism you give me, I will accept it without reservation. Call me what you will: a cat? Fine, I'm a cat. Call me a dog? Okay, I'm a dog. However you perceive me in your mind, that's what I am. Do you see me as a Buddha? I'm a Buddha. Do you see me as a Bodhisattva? That's what I am. Everything is made from the mind alone. "I am whatever you conceive me to be."

For my own part, I have my goals and purposes for being a person. What are they? Foremost is not contending with people, no matter who they may be. You may call me what you please, and I will wear that label. I will acknowledge the name. That will be who I am. I won't contend with you.

The second principle is to refrain from greed. Whatever you own is yours. I don't want it. However, anything of mine that you want, I will give to you. I actually will hand it over.

The third is to refrain from seeking, which means not looking for opportunities to make a killing, or to score a fat profit. Far too many people in the world fight for advantages. If we understand the principle of not seeking, and resting content, with few desires, then we won't contend with people anymore. Someone who grasps this point truly understands the Six Guiding Principles.

Why shouldn't we seek? It's because we don't want to be selfish. Selfishness is the only reason a person would seek for things. With no self, there's no reason left to seek. And free of selfishness, one won't run after personal benefits. These two of the Six Principles are interrelated.

The last one is to refrain from lying. The only reason a person would lie is out of fear; he's afraid of losing his selfish advantages. This fear moves him to criticize everybody else, saying, "All of you are wrong. I'm the only one who's right. "Why does he feel this way? Because he fears he'll lose his benefits to other people. Someone who didn't hanker after personal profits would have no reason to tell a lie. In the final analysis, what's a lie worth, anyway? If you can truly understand these Six Guiding Principles, then you know what it means to be a person.

If you don't understand the Six Principles, then you're simply running in lockstep with the rat-race of this mad age. As long as you flow with the tide of insanity, you're just another madman, as crazy as the next person.

That's my message for you all today. I hope the young people among you who hear me won't go insane. The elderly among you should even more keep a grip in your sanity. The little children here can learn along with the adults. Learn how not to go crazy. I always say, "Everything's okay, no problem!" There's a bit more to add here. Don't get scared when you hear me call television, radios, and computers man-eating goblins. No need to be afraid. My hope is that you will clearly recognize these things for what they are. Once you recognize them, then electric gadgets lose their power to confuse you. That's enough to know. But if you're confused by them, then they can gobble you down.

The same principle applies to beauty. If the sight of a pretty figure has the power to confuse you, then you've been swallowed by a man-eater. If the sight of money confuses you, then you've just been devoured by a man-eater. If your purpose is to establish a big reputation and fame confuses you, then you've just be swallowed by the goblin of fame. If good food confuses you, although you feel you've just enjoyed a tasty dish, in fact, the food has eaten you. The food has eaten your spiritual soul, your Dharma-body. It has eaten up your wisdom, and left you as deluded as can be.

If sleep keeps you in a stupor for several centuries, and when you finally wake and see by your wrist watch that it's already half-past noon, and if then, you simply roll over and go back to sleep, then you've been devoured by sleep. Get the point?

1 I vow that as long as there is a single Bodhisattva in the three periods of time throughout the ten directions of the Dharma Realm, to the very ends of space, who has not realized Buddhahood, I too will not attain the right enlightenment.

2 I vow that as long as there is a single Pratyekabuddha in the three periods of time throughout the ten directions of the Dharma Realm, to the very ends of space, who has not realized Buddhahood, I too will not attain the right enlightenment.

3 I vow that as long as there is a single *śrāvaka* in the three periods of time throughout the ten directions of the Dharma Realm, to the very ends of space, who has not realized Buddhahood, I too will not attain the right enlightenment.

4 I vow that as long as there is a single god in the Three Realms who has not realized Buddhahood, I too will not attain the right enlightenment.

5 I vow that as long as there is a single human being in the worlds of the ten directions who has not realized Buddhahood, I too will not attain the right enlightenment.

6 I vow that as long as there is a single *asura* who has not realized Buddhahood, I too will not attain the right enlightenment.

7 I vow that as long as there is a single animal who has not realized Buddhahood, I too will not attain the right enlightenment.

8 I vow that as long as there is a single hungry ghost who has not realized Buddhahood, I too will not attain the right enlightenment.

9 I vow that as long as there is a single being in the hells who has not realized Buddhahood, I too will not attain the right enlightenment.

10 I vow that as long as there is a single god, immortal, human, *asura*, air-bound or water-bound creature, animate creature or inanimate object, or a single dragon, beast, ghost, or spirit, and so forth, of the spiritual realm that has taken refuge with me and has not realized Buddhahood, I too will not attain the right enlightenment.

11 I vow to fully dedicate all blessings and bliss that I myself ought to receive and enjoy to all living beings of the Dharma Realm.

12 I vow to fully take upon myself all the sufferings and hardships of all the living beings in the Dharma Realm.

13 I vow to manifest innumerable bodies as a means to gain access into the minds of living beings throughout the universe who do not believe in the Buddhadharma, causing them to correct their faults and tend toward wholesomeness, repent of their errors and start anew, take refuge in the Triple Jewel, and ultimately realize Buddhahood.

14 I vow that all living beings who see my face or even hear my name will bring forth the Bodhi resolve and quickly realize Buddhahood.

15 I vow to respectfully observe the Buddha's instructions and cultivate the practice of eating only one meal per day.

16 I vow to enlighten all sentient beings, universally responding to the multitudes of differing potentials.

17 I vow to obtain the five eyes, the six spiritual powers, and the freedom of being able to fly in this very life.

18 I vow that all of my vows will certainly be fulfilled.

Conclusion:

I vow to save the countless living beings.

I vow to eradicate the infinite afflictions.

I vow to study the innumerable Dharma-doors.

I vow to realize the unsurpassed Buddha Way.

NOTE: Books without listed authors are either sutras without commentaries or books authored or compiled and edited by BTTS. Some of the multivolumed sutra commentaries have not yet been completed. The number of volumes listed indicates the number published to date.

The Buddha Speaks the Brahma Net Sutra. Talmage, 1982.

Cherishing Life, 2 vols. Talmage, 1983.

City of 10,000 Buddhas Daily Recitation Handbook. 2nd printing: Talmage, 1982.

Filiality: The Human Source, 2 vols. Talmage, 1983.

Heng Ju and Heng Yo (Bhikshus). *Three Steps One Bow.*

Heng Sure and Heng Ch'au (Bhikshus). *News from True Cultivators,* 2 vols. Talmage, 1983.

____________. *With One Heart Bowing to the City of Ten Thousand Buddhas,* 9 vols. San Francisco and Talmage, 1979-1983.

Hsu Fa (Dharma Master), comm. / Hua (Tripiṭaka Master), verses & subcomm. *Shurangama Mantra,* 5 vols. Talmage, 1981-1985.

[Hsuan] Hua (Ch'an/Tripiṭaka Master). *Buddha Root Farm.* San Francisco, 1976.

____________, comm. *Dhāraṇī Sutra: The Sutra of the Vast, Great, Full, Unimpeded Great Compassion Heart Dhāraṇī of the Thousand-Handed, Thousand-Eyed Bodhisattva Who Regards the World's Sounds.* San Francisco, 1976.

Dharma Talks in Europe: Given by the Venerable Master Hua in 1990. Burlingame, 1998.

____________, comm. *A General Explanation of the Buddha Speaks of Amitābha Sutra.* San Francisco, 1974.

____________, comm. *A General Explanation of the Buddha Speaks the Sutra in Forty-two Sections.* San Francisco, 1977.

____________, comm. *A General Explanation of the Vajra Prajñā Pāramitā Sutra.* San Francisco, 1974.

____________. *Great Compassion Mantra Verses.* Burlingame, 2000.

____________. *Great Compassion Dharma Transmission Verses of the Forty-two Hands and Eyes.* Talmage, 1983.

___________, comm. *(Great Means Expansive Buddha) Flower Adornment Sutra,* 28 vols. Talmage, 1981-1984.

___________, comm. *The Heart of Prajñā Pāramitā with Verses Without a Stand and Prose Commentary.* San Francisco, 1980.

___________. *Herein Lies the Treasure Trove,* vol. 1. Talmage, 1983.

___________. *Listen to Yourself; Think Everything Over,* 2 vols. Talmage, 1978, 1983.

___________. *A Pictorial Biography of the Venerable Master Hsu Yun,* 2 vols. Talmage, 1983, 1985.

___________. *Pure Land and Ch'an Dharma Talks.* San Francisco, 1974.

___________. *Records of High Sanghans,* vol. 1. Talmage, 1983.

___________, comm. *Shurangama Sutra,* 7 vols. Talmage, 1977-1981.

___________, comm. *The Shurangama Sutra, Volume 8: The Fifty Skandha-Demon States.* Burlingame, 1996.

___________, comm. *The Shurangama Sutra: Great Strength Bodhisattva's Perfect Penetration through Mindfulness of the Buddha. Burlingame,* 1997.

___________, comm. *The Sixth Patriarch's Dharma Jewel Platform Sutra.* San Francisco, 1977.

___________. *A Sure Sign of the Proper Dharma,* Proper Dharma Series No. 2. Burlingame, 1995.

___________. *Sutra of the Past Vows of Earth Store Bodhisattva: The Collected Lectures of Tripitaka Master Hsuan Hua.* NY, 1974.

___________. *The Ten Dharma Realms Are Not Beyond a Single Thought.* San Francisco, 1976.

_________. *The True Meaning of Taking Refuge,* Proper Dharma Series No. 4. Burlingame, 1996.

___________. *Water Mirror Reflecting Heaven.* Talmage, 1982.

___________, comm. *The Wonderful Dharma Lotus Flower Sutra,* 10 vols. San Francisco, 1977-1982.

Hui Seng (Elder Master)., comm. *The Buddha Speaks the Brahma Net Sutra.* 2 Pts. Talmage, 1981.

Human Roots: Buddhist Stories for Young Readers, 2 vols. Talmage, 1982, 1983.

Lien-ch'ih Chu-hung (High Master) / Hua (Tripiṭaka Master), comm. *A General Explanation of 'The Essentials of the Śrāmaṇera Vinaya' and 'Rules of Deportment'.* San Francisco, 1975.

Open Your Eyes Take a Look at the World: Journals of the Sino-American Buddhist Association Dharma Realm Buddhist University Delegation to Asia. San Francisco, 1979.

Records of the Life of the Venerable Master Hsuan Hua, vol. 1. San Francisco, 1973; rpt. Talmage, 1981.

Records of the Life of Ch'an Master Hsuan Hua, Pt. II. San Francisco, 1975.

Sutra of the Past Vows of Earth Store Bodhisattva. Talmage, 1982.

Vajra Bodhi Sea: A Monthly Journal of Orthodox Buddhism. San Francisco, 1970-present.

Vasubandhu (Bodhisattva) / Hua (Tripiṭaka Master), comm. *Shastra on the Door to Understanding the Hundred Dharmas.* Talmage, 1983.

Venerable Master Hua's Talks on Dharma. (English/Chinese) 9 vols. Burlingame, 1994-2001.

Yung Chia (Great Master) / Hua (Tripiṭaka Master), comm. *Song of Enlightenment.* Talmage, 1983.

Aśvaghoṣa. Buddhacarita or Acts of the Buddha, 2 vols. Johnston, E.H., trans. and ed. Panjab University Oriental Publications vols. 31-32. 1936; rpt. Delhi: Motilal Banarsidass, 1972.

Chalmers, Lord, tr. *Further Dialogues of the Buddha.* 2 vols. London: Oxford University Press, 1926-27.

Conze, Edward, tr. *Buddhist Texts Through the Ages.* 1954; rpt. New York: Harper, 1964.

____________. *The Large Sutra on Perfect Wisdom, with the Divisions of the Abhisamayālaṅkāra.* Berkeley: University of California Press, 1975.

____________. "Prasastrasena's Ārya-Prajñāpāramitā-hṛdaya-ṭīkā." *Buddhist Studies in Honour of I.B. Horner.* Cousins, L. et. al., eds. Dordrecht-Holland: Reidel, 1974, pp. 51-61.

Demieville, Paul, ed. *Hôbôgirin, dictionaire encyclopédique du bouddhisme d'après les sources chinoises et japonaises.* Tokyo: Maison Franco-Japanaise, 4 vols. 1929-1967.

Dhammapada.

Elder, Joseph Walter, ed. *Chapters in Indian Civilization.* Rev. ed. Dubuque, Iowa: Kendall/Hunt Pub. Co., 1970.

Hirschfield, Jane with Aratani, Mariko, tr. *The Ink Dark Moon: Love Poems by Ono no Komachi & Izumi Shikibu.* New York: Scribner, 1988.

Hopkins, Jeffry. *Meditation on Emptiness.* London: Wisdom Publications, 1983.

Horner, I.B. [Isaline Blew], tr. *The Book of the Discipline.* 5 vols. London: Pali Text Society, 1949-1951.

__________. "Mahavagga." *The Book of the Discipline,* vol. 4. London: Pali Text Society, 1951.

__________. *The Collection of the Middle Length Sayings (Majjhima-Nikāya).* Pali Text Society Translation Series, No. 29-31. London: Luzac and Co., Ltd., 1954-1959.

Hsüan-tsang. *Ch'eng Wei-shih Lun; The Doctrine of Mere-Consciousness.* Translated from Chinese by Wei Tat. Hong Kong: Ch'eng Wei-shih Lun Publication Committee, 1973.

Hsueh-tou, 980-1052. *Blue Cliff Records 3 vols. Cleary,* Thomas and J.C., trs. Boulder, CO: Shambhala, 1977.

Jones, J.J., tr. *The Mahāvastu.* 3 vols. 1949; rpt. London: Pali Text Society, 1973.

Jaini, P.S. "Śramaṇa Conflict," *Chapters in Indian Civilization,* vol. 1. Elder, ed. Dubuque, Iowa: Kendall-Hunt, 1970, pp. 39-82.

Keyes, Charles F. and Daniel, E. Valentine, eds. *Karma: An Anthropological Inquiry.* Berkeley: University of California Press, 1983.

Lamotte, Étienne, tr. *Le traité de la grande vertu de sagesse de Nāgārjuna (Mahāprajñāpāramitāśāstra).* Louvain-La-Neuve: Université de Louvain, Institut orientaliste, 1981.

Lin, Yutang, ed. *The Wisdom of China and India.* New York: Random House, 1942.

Lindtner, Chr. *Master of Wisdom: Writings of the Buddhist Master Nāgārjuna.* Berkeley, California: Dharma Publishing, 1986.

Ling, T.O. *A Dictionary of Buddhism.* New York: Scribners, 1972.

Luk, Charles, tr. *Ch'an and Zen Teaching,* Series One. London: Rider, 1960.

____________. *Empty Cloud: The Autobiography of Hsü Yün.* Rochester: Empty Cloud Press, 1974. [See also Xu Yun. *Empty Cloud: the Autobiography of the Chinese Zen Master Xu Yun.* Luk, Charles, ed. Revised and edited by Richard Hunn. Longmead, Shaftsbury, Dorset: Element Books, 1988.]

Malalasekera, G.P., ed. *Dictionary of Pali Proper Names,* 2 vols. London, 1937-38.

____________. *Encyclopedia of Buddhism,* 3 vols. (more forthcoming) Ceylon: Government of Ceylon [Sri Lanka], 1961-1971.

Rahula, Walpola. *What the Buddha Taught.* Rev. ed. New York: Grove Press, 1974.

Rhys Davids (Mrs) [Caroline A.F.], tr. *The Book of Kindred Sayings (Sanyutta-Nikāya),* 4 vols. London: Pali Text Society, 1917-1927.

____________. *Psalms of the Early Buddhists I, Psalms of the Sisters.* London: Pali Text Society, 1909.

Rhys Davids, T.W. & C.A.F., tr. *Dialogues of the Buddha (Digha-Nikāya),* 3 vols. London: Pali Text Society, 1899-1921.

Rhys Davids, T.W. and Oldenberg, Hermann, tr. *Vinaya Texts.* 3 vols. Delhi: Motilal Banarsidass, 1974.

Rhys Davids, T.W., and Stede, W., eds. *Pali Text Society's Pali-English Dictionary.* London, 1921-25.

Robinson, Richard H. *Early Mādhyamika in India and China.* Madison: University of Wisconsin Press, 1967.

Shambala Review, v.5, nos.1-2, Winter, 1976, p. 26.

Snyder, Gary, tr. *Riprap, and Cold Mountain Poems.* San Francisco: Four Seasons Foundation, 1969.

Streng, Frederick J. *Emptiness: a Study in Religious Meaning.* Nashville: Abingdon Press, 1967.

Takakusu, J., tr. "The Life of Vasubandhu by Paramartha (499-569 CE)." *T'oung Pao,* Ser. II, vol. 5 (1904), pp. 269-296.

Takakusu, J. & Watanabe, K. eds. *Taisho shinshu Daizokyo,* 85 vols. Tokyo: Taisho Issaikyo Kankokai, 1924-1932.

Vasubandhu, fl. 4th-5th cent. *Abhidharmakośa,* v.1. Jha, Subhandra, tr. n.p.:Kashi Prasad Jayaswal Research Institute, 1983.

Watson, Burton, tr. *Cold Mountain: 100 Poems by the T'ang Poet Han-Shan.* 1962; rpt. New York: Columbia University Press, 1970.

Woodward, F.L., tr. "Itivuttaka: As It Was Said." *The Minor Anthologies of the Pali Canon,* Part II. London: Geoffrey Cumberlege, Oxford University Press, 1948.

Yamamoto, Kosho, tr. *Mahayana Mahāparinirvāṇa-sutra: a Complete Translation from Classical Chinese Language in 3 Volumes.* Oyama, Japan: Karinbunko, 1973.

Yu, Chun-fang. *The Renewal of Buddhism in China: Chu-hung and the Late Ming Synthesis.* New York: Columbia University Press, 1981.

Numbers in **bold** refer to illustrations.

A

abhidharma 2, 211, 224
abhidharmakośa 2, 10, 211
abhidharma-piṭaka 2
abhijñā 234
abhiniveśa 224
abhyudaya 146
advayajñāna 145
āgama 165
ajātaśatru 3, 52, 53
ajita 2, 134, 135
akuśala-mūlā 235
ālaya 62-63, 100
amala 147
amitābha **3**, 4, 32, 93, 110, **162**, 166, 168, 224
amitābha-sūtra 3, 161, 224
amitāyurdhyāna-sūtra 3
amitāyus 93, 224
anāgāmin 8, 70, 152
ānanda **4**, 44, 57, 59, 93, 106, 117, 143, 144, 189, 224
anātman 232
aniruddha 108, 185
anitya 230
anusmṛti 232
anuttara-samyak-saṃbodhi 5, 6, 22, 31, 93, 224
arhant 224
arhanta 224
arhat 6, **7**, **8**, 57, 58, 70, 74, 75, 133, 175, 185, 203, 224
ārya aṣṭāṅgika-mārga 227
ārya-prajñā-pāramitā-hṛdaya-ṭīkā 89
ārya-satyāni 229
asaṃkhyeya 5, 10, 32, 224
asaṅga 9, 135
asaṅkhyeya 10, 21, 224
aśoka 168
āsrava 232
aṣṭādaśa-dhātavaḥ 227
aṣṭa-vijñānāni 227
asura **11**, 45, 65, 70, 92, 182, 194, 224
aśvaghoṣa 166
aśvajit 176
ātman 62, 148
avalokiteśvara **12**, **24**, 54, 108, 123, 152, **153**, 154, **162**, **172**, 209, 225
avataṃsaka-sūtra 10, 12, **94**, **95**, **96**, 229
avīci-naraka/niraya 12, 58, 225
avidyā 230

B

bhagavān 57
bhāvanā 226, 231
bhāvanā-heya 227
bhāvanā-mārga-prahātavya-kleśa 227
bhikṣu 6, 13, 59, 78, 92, 99, 144, 146, 154-155, 168, 175, 225
bhikṣuṇī 59, 92, 99, 144, 154, 175, 225
bhūmi 10
bīja 62
bimbisāra 52
bodhi 16, 21, 22, 33, 92, 125, 146, 147, 163, 225, 228
bodhicittotpāda 225
bodhidharma 16, 17, **18**, 19, 20, **21**, 39, 40, 151, 225
bodhimaṇḍa 92, 136, 236
bodhisaṃbhāra 146
bodhisattva 22-26, 57, 58, 61, 74, 75, 82, 94, 122, 143, 144, 175, 225
brahma **106**, 144
brahmajāla-sūtra **30**, 225
brahmaloka 40, 70
brahma-vihāra 229
buddha **3**, **31**, **32**, 74, 115-116, 150, **173**, 225
buddhabhāva 225
buddhadharma 154, 225
buddhakṣetra **161**, 225
buddhānusmṛti 233
buddhatā 225
buddhatva 225

C

caitta 62
caryā 226
catasraḥ-parṣadāḥ 229
catvāri-smṛtyupasthānāni 229
catur-ārūpyabrahmaloka 229
catvary-aśītidharmaskandhasahasrāṇi 227
catur-dhyāna 229
catvāry-ārya-satyāni 229
catvāri-mahāpraṇidhānāni 229
catvāry-apramāṇāni 229

D

dāna 146
darśana-heya 227
daśabhūmayaḥ 235
daśa-kuśala-karma-patha 235
daśa-kuśalāni 235
deśanā 233
devadatta 52-53, 226
devāḥ 41, 64, 230
devaputrāḥ 230
devanāgayakṣagandharvāsura-garuḍakinnaramahoraga **64**, 227
dhāraṇī 53, 92, 139, 195, 226, 231

dhāraṇī-sūtra 54, 108, 226
dharma 145, 226
dharma-bhāṇaka 227
dharma-dhātu 227
dharmākara 4, 167, 216
dharma-kathika 227
dharmakāya 146
dharma-mukha 227
dharma-pāla 227
dharma-paryāya 227
dhṛtarāṣṭra 179
dhūta 130
dhyāna 4, 8, 39, 41, 66, 67, 70, 93, 98, 99, 139, 140, 141, 146, 163, 174, 181, 228, 229, 231
dhyāna-sūtra 100
duḥkha 189, 229, 234
dvādaśāṅga nidāna 236
dvādaśāṅga pratītyasamutpāda 236
dvātrimśad-varalakṣaṇa 235
dvātriṃśan-mahāpuruṣalakṣaṇa 235
dveṣa 146
dviyāna 236

G

gandharva 64
garbhadhātu maṇḍala **136**
garuḍa 64, 65
gāthā 111
gati 149
gautama **31, 32**, 103, **173**, 174, 229
gośīrṣa-candana 150

H

hetu-pratyaya 226
hīnayāna 2, 9, 31, 133, 137, 165, 177

I

icchantika 48-50
īśvara 230

J

jambudvīpa 4, 43, 82
jāti 226, 233
jñānasaṃbhāra 146

K

kāla 235
kalaviṅka 161
kalpa 5, 10, 32, 36, 45, 80, 89, 91, 116, 129, 135, 167, 177, 180, 204, 230
kalyāṇamitra 230
kāṇadeva 145
karma 117-120, 167, 230
karuṇā 42, 146, 226, 229
kāśyapa 39, **129**, 130, 231
kāśyapa buddha 81, 180
kaukṛtya 233
kauśika 9
kāyadvaya 145
kinnara 64
kleśa 146, 149
kṣamāpaṇa 233
kṣānti 146
kṣatriya 16
kṣitigarbha 61, 136, 209, 227
kṣitigarbha-bodhisattva-pūrvapraṇidāna-sūtra 235
kolita 131
kumārajīva **120**-122, 230
kumārāyaṇa 120-121
kuśala-mūlāni 230
kuśinagara 57

L

lokadhātu 236

M

madhyamaka[-śāstra] 129, 231
madhyama-pratipad 232
mādhyamika 91, 129, 231
magadha 129
mahā 129, 231
mahābhūta 229
mahābrahmā devarājā 40
mahākalpa 204
mahākāruṇā-dhāraṇī 230
mahākāruṇika-hṛdaya-dhāraṇī 230
mahākāśyapa 40, 41, **129**-131, 213, 231
mahāmaudgalyāyana 119, 120, **131**-132, 176, 231
mahāparinirvāṇa 232
mahāparinirvāṇa-sūtra 131, 132, 147, 232
mahāprajñāpāramitā-sūtra 41, 220
mahāsattva 132, 231
mahāvaipulya-buddhāvataṃsaka-sūtra 229
mahāvastu 46
mahāyāna 2, 31, 64, 132, 133-134, 137, 165, 177, 185, 212, 231
mahoraga 64, 65
maitreya 10, 30, 58, 130, **134, 135**, 183, 231
maitrī 42, 226, 229
manas 62, 63, 100
maṇḍala 47, **136**, 231
mandārava 161
maṇi 176
mañjuśrī **136, 137**, 138, 231
mantra 138, 139, 231
mantrayāna 228
māra 13, 14, 32, 50, 51, 131, 226
mārga 212, 229

mleccha 128
moha 146
muditā 229
mudrā 154
mūlamadhyamaka-kārikāḥ 73

N

nāga 64
nāgārjuna 71, 73, 95, 144, **145**, 147, 232
naiḥśreyasa 146
namas 146, 232
naraka **112**, **113**, 230
nerañjarā 51
nidāna 236
nigrodha 51
niraya **112**, **113**, 230
nirmāṇakāya 236
nirodha 229
nirvāṇa 21, 30, 56, 57, 142, 146-147, 174, 215, 232
nirvāṇa-sūtra 50, 147, 165, 232
niṣyanda 165

O

oṃ maṇi padme huṃ 139

P

padmāsana 231
pāli 157, 232
pañca-cakṣus 81, 228
pañca-kāma-guṇāḥ 81, 228
pañca-kaṣāya 89, 228
pañca-śīlāni 83, 228
pañcopādāna-skandha 85, 228
paramārtha 10
paramārthasatya 145
pāramī 232
pāramitā 22, 24, 91, 135, 137, 146, 157, 175, 181, 232, 234
parikalpa 232
pariṇāmana 235
pattra 192
piṇḍola 9
pippala 129
prajñā 2, 40, 72, 111, 146, 158, 160, 165, 183, 195, 233
prajñapti 146
prajñā pāramitā 85, 111, 181
prajñā-pāramitā-sūtra 177
prajñā-pāramitā-hṛdaya-sūtra 230
prajñātāra 16
praṇidhāna 236
prāpti sākṣāt-karoti 226
prasannapāda 147
prasenajit 115-116
pratisaṃdhi 233
pratītyasamutpanna 145
pratyayabuddha 233
pratyekabuddha 7, 57, 58, 72, 74, 152, 160, 175, 233
pratyutpanna-samādhi 58
pravāraṇa 132
preta 4, 103, 166, 230
prīti 98
pudgala 89
pūjā 149, 232
puṇya 141, 232
puṇya-guṇa 141, 232
puṇya[-phala] 14, 225
puṇyasaṃbhāra 146
pūrṇamaitrāyaṇīputra 47, 189
puruṣa 89
puruṣapura 9
pūrvavideha 9, 217

R

rāga 146
rākṣasa 23, 128, 213
ratna-traya 202, 235
rūpa 228
rūpakāya 146

S

ṣaḍ-abhijñāḥ 234
saddharmapuṇḍarīka-sūtra **59**, 227
saddharmasya antardhāna-kāla-samaya 227
saddharma-vipralopa-kāla 227
ṣaḍ-gatyaḥ 234
sahasrabhujasahasranetra 232
saindhava 138
śakra 166, 172, 179, 233
sakṛdāgāmin 8, 70, 152
śākyamuni 3, 21, **31**, **32**, 52, 53, 78, 120, 124, **129**, 134, 150, 151, **173**, 174, 233
samādhi 4, 98, 174, 233
samantabhadra-bodhisattva 136, **209**, **210**, 236
śamatha-vipaśyanā 204
saṃgha 175, 234
saṃjñā 87, 228
saṃkṣepa 145
saṃsāra 147, 175, 233
saṃskārāḥ 228
saṃskṛta 176, 234
samudaya 229
saṃvṛtisatya 145
saṃvyavahāra 146
saṅgha 175, 234
saptadaśabhūmi-sūtra 10
śārikā 176
śāriputra 24-26, 120, 131, 137, 176, **177**, 189, 234
śarīra 127, **168**, 178, 220, 233
sarvāstivāda 9
śāstra 2, 152, 178, 207, 211, 212, 234
śata-dharmāḥ 232
ṣaṭ kāmāvacara devalokāḥ 234
ṣaṭ pāramitā 234
sattva 124, 231
satyadvaya 145
sautrantika 211

siddhārtha 172
śikṣāpada 232
śīla 143, 146, 232
skandha 47, 55, 63, 72, 85, 86, 89, 99, 146, 191, 228
smṛti 232
smṛtyupasthāna 229
śraddhā 146, 228
śramaṇa 15, 57, 58, 96, 186, 187, 234
śrāmaṇera 74, 92, 154
śrāmaṇerika 92
śrāvaka 9, 187, 188, 194, 202, 209, 234
śrāvastī 74, 150
śrotaāpanna 7, 8, 152
sthavira-vāda 199, 235
stūpa 127, 128, 168
sukha 98
sukhāvatī 3, 233
sukhāvati-vyūha-sūtra 224
sumeru 29, **43**, 179, 180, 217 **śūnya** 145
śūnyatā 71, 146, 227
śūraṅgama-mantra 52, 179, 191-192, 234
śūraṅgama-sūtra 4, 44-45, **47-48**, 51, 58, 74, 75, 93, 130, 135, 150, 154, 191, 192-193, 213, 234
sūtra 193, 234
suyāma 178, 180
svabhāva 71, 145

T

tamālapattracandana 132
tantra 228
tathāgata 57, 83, 93, 142, 143, 177, 195, 203, 235
tathāgatagarbha 194, 235
tattva 145
trayastriṃśa 172, 178, 179
tridhātu 235
trikāya 235
triloka 235
tripiṭaka 2, 169, 207, 218, 236
tripiṭaka-ācārya 236
triratna 235
tri-sahasra-mahā-sahasra-loka-dhātu 217
tri-śaraṇa 168, 233
triyāna 202, 212, 235
tṛṣṇā 231
tuṣita 9, 32, 178, 180, 181

U

ullambana 132
upādhyāya 59, 227
upāsaka 68, 74, 92, 99, 210, 236
upasaṃpadā 232
upāsikā 92, 99, 210, 236
upāya-kuśala/kauśalya 76, 228
upekṣā 229
uttarakuru 217

V

vaidehī 3
vairocana 12
vaiśravaṇa 179
vajra 72, 115, 143, 147, 154, 210, 236
vajradhātu maṇḍala **136**
vajra-prajñā-pāramitā-sūtra 34, 72, 203, 211, 236
vajrayāna 228
vandana 26, 225
vārāṇasī 188
vāsanā 149
vasubandhu 2, **211**, 236
vedanā 228
vicāra 98
vihārasvāmin 224
vijñāna 62, 228
vijñānavāda 134, 226
vikalpa 232
vimalakīrti 2
vinaya 94, 207, 215, 218, 228, 236
vinayapiṭaka 72
vipaśyin 129
vipratisāra 233
viriñcivatsa 9, 211
virūḍhaka 179
virūpākṣa 179
vīrya 146
vitarka 98
vyavahāra 146

Y

yakṣa 14, 64
yama 166
yogācāra 9, 91, 134, 191, 221, 226
yojana 132, 179, 180, 222, 237

Numbers in **bold** refer to illustrations.

A

abhidhamma 2, 211, 224
abhinivesa 224
abhiññā 234
akusala-mūlā 235
ānanda **4**, 44, 57, 59, 93, 106, 117, 143, 144, 189, 224
anatta 232
anicca 230
anussati 232
anuttarasammāsambodhi 6, 224
appamaññā 229
arahant 224
arahat 224
ariya-sacca 229
ariyo aṭṭangika-maggo 227
asankheyya 10, 224
āsava 232
assaji 174
asura **11**, 45, 65, 70, 92, 182, 194, 224
aṭṭhārasa-dhātuyo 227
avīci niraya 12, 58, 225
avijjā 230

B

bhāvanā 226, 231
bhikkhu 13, 225
bhikkhunī 14, 225
bodhi 16, 21, 22, 33, 92, 125, 146, 147, 163, 225, 228
bodhimaṇḍa 92, 136, 236
bodhisatta 22-26, 57, 58, 61, 74, 75, 82, 94, 122, 143, 144, 175, 225
brahmajāla-sutta 30, 225
brahma-vihāra 229
buddha **3**, **31**, **32**, 74, 115-116, **150**, **173**, 225
buddhabhāva 225
buddhadhamma 154, 225
buddhakhetta **161**, 225
buddhānusatti 233
buddhatā 225
buddhatta 225

C

cariya 226
cattāri ariya-saccāni 229
caturāsīti sahassāni dhammā 227
catur parisā 229
chaḷabhiññā 234

D

dasabhūmi 235
desanā 233
devā 230
devadatta 52-53, 226
devaputta 230
dhamma 226
dhamma-bhāṇaka 227
dhamma-dhātu 227
dhamma-kathika 227
dhamma-pāla 227
dhamma-pariyāya 227
dukkha 189, 229, 234
dvattiṃsa mahāpurisalakkhaṇa 235

G

gotama **31**, **32**, 103, 147, **173**, 174, 229

H

hetu-paccaya 226

I

issara 230

J

jāti 226, 233
jhāna 228, 229, 231

K

kāla 235
kalyāṇa-mitta 230
kamma 117-120, 230
kappa 204, 205, 230
karuṇā 42, 146, 226, 229
khamāpanā 233
khandha 228
kukkucca 233
kusala-kamma-patha 235
kusala-mūla 230

L

lokadhātu 236

M

magga 229
mahā/maha 129, 231
mahābhūta 229
mahākassapa 231
mahāmoggallāna **131**, 132, 231
mahāparinibbāna 232
mahāsatta 132, 231
majjhima 148
majjhima-nikāya 147
majjhima-paṭipadā 232
maṇḍala 47, **136**, 231
manta 138, 139, 231
māra 13, 14, 32, 50, 51, 131, 226
mettā 42, 226, 229
metteyya **134**, **135**, 231

muditā 229

N

namo 146, 232
naraka **112**, **113**, 230
nibbāna 146, 232
nidāna 236
niraya 230
nirodha 229

P

paccekabuddha 160, 233
pāli 157, 232
pañca-cakkhūni 81, 228
pañca-kāma-guṇā 81, 228
pañca-kasāya 89, 228
pañca-sīla 83, 228
panc'upādāna-kkhandha 85, 228
paṇidhāna 237
paññā 158, 233
pārami 232, 234
pāramitā 157, 232, 234
paribbājaka 177
parikappa 232
pariṇāmana 235
paṭicca-samuppāda 236
peta 103, 230
pūjā 149, 232
puñña 14, 141, 225, 232

R

ratana-ttaya 202, 235
rūpa 228

S

saddhā 228
saddhammassa-antaradhāna 227
sakka 172, 233
sakyamuni **31**, **32**, 52-53, 129, **173**, 233
samādhi 174, 233
samaṇa 187, 234
saṃsāra 175, 233
samudaya 229
sangha 175, 234
sankhārā 228
saññā 228
sāriputta 176, **177**, 234
sarīra 127, **168**, 233
sata-dhamma 232
sati 232
satipaṭṭhāna 229
satta 124, 231
sāvaka 188, 234
sikkhāpada 232
sīla 143, 146, 232
suññatā 71, 146, 227
sutta 193, 234

T

taṇhā 231
tathāgata 57, 83, 93, 142, 143, 177, 195, 203, 235
theravāda 26, 146, 157, 199, 235
tikāya 201, 235
tiloka 203, 235
tipiṭaka 207, 236
tipiṭaka-ācariya 207, 236
tiratana 202, 235
ti-saraṇa 168, 233

U

upajjhāya 59, 227
upāsaka 68, 74, 92, 99, 210, 236
upasaṃpadā 232
upāsikā 92, 99, 210, 236
upāya-kosalla 76, 228
upekkhā 229

V

vaccha 146
vajira 210, 236
vandana 26, 225
vedanā 228
vikappa 232
vinaya 94, 207, 215, 218, 228, 237
viññāṇa 228
vippaṭisāra 233
visuddhi magga 148

Y

yojana 132, 179, 180, 222, 237

Numbers in **bold** refer to illustrations.

A

a bi da mo 阿毗達磨 2, 224
a bi di yu 阿鼻地獄 12, 225
a luo han 阿羅漢 6, 7, **8**, 224
a mi tuo (fo) 阿彌陀 (佛) **3**, **162**, 224
a mi tuo jing 阿彌陀經 3, 224
a nan (zun zhe) 阿難 (尊者) 4, 224
a nou duo luo san miao san pu ti 阿耨多羅三藐三菩提 6, 224
a seng qi 阿僧祇 10, 224
a xiu luo 阿修羅 11, 224
a yi duo (pu sa) 阿逸多 (菩薩) 2
ai 愛 128
ai yu 愛欲 128

B

ba bu zhong 八部眾 **64**, 227
ba feng 八風 67, 227
ba li wen 巴利文 2, 232
ba li yu 巴利語 157, 232
ba sheng dao 八聖道 227
ba shi 八識 62, 227
ba shi ba pin jian fen 八十八品見分 227
ba shi ba pin jian huo 八十八品見惑 69, 227
ba shi yi pin si huo 八十一品思惑 70, 227
ba wan si qian fa men 八萬四千法門 69, 227
ba zheng dao 八正道 65, 227
bai 拜 26, 225
bai fa 百法 232
bao zhi (chan shi) 寶誌 (禪師) 12, **13**, 225
bei 悲 42, 229
bi qiu 比丘 13, 225
bi qiu ni 比丘尼 14, 225
bi zhi fo 辟支佛 160, 233
bo luo mi (duo) 波羅蜜 (多) 157, **182**, 232
bo re 般若 158, 233
bo re bo luo mi duo xin jing 般若波羅蜜多心經 111, 230
bu dai (he shang) 布袋 (和尚) **30**, **31**, 225

C

chan 禪 4, 39, 41, 60, 93, 98, 99, 124, 140, 231
chan hui 懺悔 233
chan shi 禪師 37, 226
chan zong 禪宗 39, 226, 228
chang ren (chan shi) 常仁 (禪師) 37, **38**, 226
chang zhi (chan shi) 常智 (禪師) 38, 226
cheng wei shi lun 成唯識論 2
ci 慈 229
chuan fa 傳法 60, 227

D

da bei zhou 大悲咒 108, 230
da cheng 大乘 109, 231
da fang guang fo hua yan jing 大方廣佛華嚴經 **94**, 229
da fo ding shou leng yan jing 大佛頂首楞嚴經 192, 234
dao 道 216, 229
dao chang 道場 22, 216, 236
dao sheng (fa shi) 道生 (法師) 48, **49**, 226
di shi 帝釋 172, 233
di yu 地獄 **112**, **113**, 230
di zang pu sa ben yuan jing 地藏菩薩本願經 136, 235
di zang (wang) pu sa 地藏 (王) 菩薩 **61**, 227
ding 定 174, 233
ding li 頂禮 26, 225
du 度 232
du jue/jiao 獨覺 233

E

e gui 餓鬼 114, 230
er cheng 二乘 209, 236

F

fa 法 33, 53, 54, 55, 226
fa hua jing 法華經 **59**, 128, 227
fa jie 法界 60, 227
fa mai 法脈 124, 231
fa men 法門 55, 227
fa pu ti xin 發菩提心 21, 225
fa shi 法師 59, 226, 227
fan wang jing 梵網經 30, 227
fan wen 梵文 176, 234
fan yu 梵語 234
fang bian fa 方便法 76, 227
fang sheng 放生 **122**, 231
fang zhang 方丈 **2**, 224
fo 佛 **3**, **31**, **32**, 103, **173**, 227
fo du 佛土 32, **161**, **162**, **163**, 225

fo fa 佛法 33, 225
fo jiao 佛教 33, 225
fo san shi er xiang 佛三十二相 199, 235
(fo shuo) a mi tuo jing (佛說)阿彌陀經 3, 224
fo tuo 佛陀 225
fo tuo ye 佛陀耶 225
fo xing 佛性 33, 225
fo zhi san shen 佛之三身 201, 235
fo zhi shi hao 佛之十號 196, 235
fu 福 14, 225
fu bao 福報 225

G

gong 供 149, 232
gong de 功德 141, 232
gong fu 功夫 107, 230
gong yang 供養 149, **150**, **151**, 232
guan shi yin 觀世音 **12**, **24**, 123, **153**, 225
guan yin 觀音 **172**, 225
guan zi zai (pu sa) 觀自在 (菩薩) 225
gui 鬼 103, 230
gui yi san bao 皈依三寶 168, 233

H

han shan (da shi) 寒山 (大士) **109**, **111**, 230
hu fa 護法 60, 227
hua shen 化身 207, 236
hua yan jing 華嚴經 12, 94, **95**, **96**, 229
hua yan zong 華嚴宗 113, 230
hui neng (chan shi/zu shi) 慧能 (禪師/祖師) 113, **114**, 230
hui xiang 迴向 206, 235

J

ji 集 229
jie 劫 116, 204, 230
jie 戒 143, 161, 215, 232, 236
jie bo 劫波 230
jie jia fu zuo 結跏趺坐 **125**, 231
jie lü 戒律 143, 232
jin gang 金剛 210, 236
jin gang bo re bo luo mi duo jing 金剛般若波羅蜜多經 211, 236
jin gang jing 金剛經 236
jing 經 193, 234
jing dian 經典 234
jing du 淨土 **161**, **162**, **163**, 233
jing du zong 淨土宗 93, 228
jiao zong 教宗 228
jin shi nan 近事男 236
jin shi nü 近事女 236
jiu hua shan 九華山 **61**
jiu mo luo shi (san zang fa shi) 鳩摩羅什 (三藏法師) **120**, 230
ju tan (fo) 瞿曇 (佛) **31**, **32**, 103, **173**, 229
jue wu 覺悟 74, 228

K

kai wu 開悟 74, 228
kong 空 71, 227
ku 苦 189, 229

L

leng yan jing 楞嚴經 192, 235
leng yan zhou 楞嚴咒 191, 235
li bai 禮拜 26, 225
lian hua zuo 蓮花坐 231
liu bo luo mi 六波羅蜜 157, 181, 234
liu da zhong zhi 六大宗旨 183, 234
liu dao lun hui 六道輪迴 175, 183, 234
liu du 六度 181, 234
liu qu 六趣 234
liu shen tong 六神通 185, 234
liu yu tian 六欲天 178, 234
liu zhuan 流轉 175, 233
liu zu fa bao tan jing 六祖法寶壇經 187, 234
long sheng ba bu 龍神八部 **64**, 227
long shu (pu sa) 龍樹 (菩薩) 144, **145**, 232
lou 漏 147, 155, 233
lü zong 律宗 215, 228, 236
lun 論 178, 234
lun hui 輪迴 175, 183, 233

M

man tuo luo 曼陀羅 **136**, 231
mi lei/le (pu sa) 彌勒 (菩薩) **134**, **135**, 231
mi zong 密宗 76, 228
miao fa lian hua jing 妙法蓮華經 **59**, 128, 227
mie 滅 229
mo 魔 50, 226
mo fa shi dai 末法時代 55, 227
mo he 摩訶 129, 231
mo he jia she (zun zhe) 摩訶迦葉 (尊者) **129**, 231
mo he mu jian lian (zun zhe) 摩訶目犍連 (尊者) **131**, 231

mo he sa 摩訶薩 132, 231
mo lo 魔羅 226

N

na(n) mo 南無 146, 232
nan chuan fo jiao 南傳佛教 199, 235
ni huan 泥洹 232
nian 念 142, 232
nian fo 念佛 166, 233
nie pan 涅槃 146, 232
nie pan jing 涅槃經 147, 232

P

pan jiao 判教 165, 233
pi nai ye 毗柰耶 215, 236
pu sa 菩薩 2, 9, 12, 22, 61, 134, 136, 144, 175, 195, 209, 211, 225
pu sa shi di 菩薩十地 195, 225
pu ti 菩提 16, 21, 225
pu ti da mo (zu shi) 菩提達摩 (祖師) 16, **18**, **21**, 225
pu ti sa duo 菩提薩馱 225
pu xian (pu sa) 普賢 (菩薩) 175, **209**, **210**, 236

Q

qian shou qian yan 千手千眼 152, 153, 232
qiao da mo 喬答摩 229
qing liang cheng guan (guo shi) 清涼澄觀 (國師) **164**, 233
quan qiao fang bian 權巧方便 228

R

ru lai 如來 194, 235
ru lai zang 如來藏 194, 235

S

san bao 三寶 168, 202, 235
san cheng 三乘 202, 235
san du 三毒 202, 235
san jie 三界 202, **203**, 235
san mei 三昧 174, 233
san mo di 三摩地 174, 233
san wu lou xue/xiao 三無漏學 200, 235
san zang 三藏 207, 236
san zang fa shi 三藏法師 120, 207, 218, 236
se/shai 色 228
seng qie 僧伽 175, 234
sha men 沙門 187, 234
shan gen 善根 108, 230
shan zhi shi 善知識 107, 230
shang di 上帝 104, 230
she 捨 229
she li 舍利 233
she li fu (zun zhe) 舍利弗 (尊者) 176, **177**, 234
she li zi 舍利子 127, **168**, 169, 176, 177, 220
shen 神 230
sheng 生 44, 166, 226, 233
sheng si 生死 175, 233
sheng wen 聲聞 111, 187, 188, 234
sheng zao 生造 226
shi 時 204, 235
shi 識 228
shi ba jie 十八界 63, 227
shi cun wu guan 食存五觀 80, 228
shi de (chan shi) 拾得 (禪師) 109, **110**, **111**, 178, 230
shi er yin yuan 十二因緣 207, 236
shi fa jie 十法界 194, 235
shi jia po 釋迦婆 233
shi jie 世界 **43**, **217**, **218**, 236
shi jia mou ni (fo) 釋迦牟尼 (佛) **31**, **32**, **129**, **172**, **173**, 233
shi qin (pu sa) 世親 (菩薩) **211**, 236
shi shan 十善 197, 235
shou 受 228
shou ju zu jie 受具足戒 154, 232
shuang jia fu zuo 雙跏趺坐 **125**, 231
shun ruo duo 舜若多 227
si chan 四禪 98, 229
si da 四大 **87**, 100, 229
si di 四諦 101, 229
si hong shi yuan 四弘誓願 101, 229
si jing lü 四靜慮 98, 229
si kong chu 四空處 103, 229
si nian chu 四念處 97, 229
si sheng di 四聖諦 102, 229
si shi er zhang jing 四十二章經 193, 235
si wu liang xin 四無量心 103, 229
si wu se/shai ding chu 四無色定處 99, 229
si wu se/shai jie 四無色界 99, 229
si zhong 四眾 99, 229
si zhong di zi 四眾弟子 99, 229
su shi zhu yi 素食主義 212, 236

T

tan ai 貪愛 128, 231
tian 天 104, 106, 230
tian long ba bu 天龍八部 **64**, 227
tian qin (pu sa) 天親 (菩薩) **211**, 236
tian ren 天人 106, 230
tian tai zong 天台宗 203, 235
tian zhu 天主 104, 230

ti po da duo 提婆達多 52, 226
tuo luo ni 陀羅尼 53, 226
tuo luo ni jing 陀羅尼經 54,226

W

wan fo sheng cheng 萬佛聖城 **171**, **172**, 183, 233, 234
wang xiang 妄想 79, 158, **159**, 232
wei shi zong 唯識宗 42, 226
wei tuo 韋馱 **59**
wen shu shi li (pu sa) 文殊師利(菩薩) **136**, **137**, 231
wu 悟 74, 228
wu chang 無常 115, 230
wu da zong 五大宗 90, 228
wu guan 五觀 80, 228
wu jian di yu 無間地獄 225
wu jiao 五教 90, 228
wu jie 五戒 83, 143, 228
wu ming 無明 115, 230
wu shang zheng deng zheng jue 無上正等正覺 6, 224
wu wo 無我 148, 232
wu yan 五眼 81, 228
wu yin 五陰 85, 228
wu yu 五欲 81, 228
wu yun 五蘊 85, 228
wu zhao 無著 9, 224
wu zhuo 五濁 89, 228
wu zhuo e shi 五濁惡世 228

X

xi 喜 229
xiang 想 228
xiao 孝 79, 228
xiao cheng 小乘 231
xiao dao 孝道 79, 228
xin 信 77, 228
xing 行 228
xiu xing 修行 48, 226
xu yun (chan shi) 虛雲(禪師) **220**, **221**, 237
xuan zang (san zang fa shi) 玄奘(三藏法師) **218**, **220**, 237

Y

ye 業 117, 230
yin tuo la 因陀羅 233
yin yuan 因緣 35, 226
you po sai 優婆塞 236
you po yi 優婆夷 236
you qing 有情 231
you xun 由旬 222, 237
yuan 願 215, 236
yuan jue/jiao 緣覺 233
yu zhou lun 宇宙論 **43**, 226

Z

zai sheng 再生 166, 233
zao xiang si yi zhong gong de 造像十一種功德 70, 227
zheng 證 226
zheng de 證得 37, 226
zheng ming 證明 226
zhi yi (fa shi) 智顗(法師) **222**, 237
zhi zhao 執著 224
zhong dao 中道 142, 216, 232
zhong guan lun (pai) 中觀論(派) 129, 231
zhong sheng 眾生 124, 231
zhou 咒 138, 231
zhu chi 住持 224
zong pai 宗派 34, 124, 226, 231
zuo chan 坐禪 **139**, 231

Dharma Realm Buddhist Association
The City of Ten Thousand Buddhas
4951 Bodhi Way, Ukiah, CA 95482 USA

T (707) 462-0939
F (707) 462-0949
HP www.drba.org
E cttb@jps.net

Buddhist Text Translation Society
4951 Bodhi Way, Ukiah, CA 95482 USA

HP www.bttsonline.org

Instilling Goodness Elementary & Developing Virtue Secondary Schools
4951 Bodhi Way, Ukiah, CA 95482 USA

T (707) 468-3896 (girls)
(707) 468-1138 (boys)
E instillgood@drba.org

Dharma Realm Buddhist University
4951 Bodhi Way, Ukiah, CA 95482 USA

T (707) 468-9112
E drbu@drba.org

Institute for World Religions
(Berkeley Buddhist Monastery)
2304 McKinley Avenue, Berkeley, CA 94703 USA

T (510) 848-3440
E paramita@drba.org

The City of the Dharma Realm
1029 West Capitol Avenue
West Sacramento, CA 95691 USA

T (916) 374-8268
E drbacdr@jps.net

Gold Mountain Monastery
800 Sacramento Street
San Francisco, CA 94108 USA

T (415) 421-6117
F (415) 788-6001
E drbagmm@jps.net

Gold Wheel Monastery
235 N. Avenue 58
Los Angeles, CA 90042 USA

T (323) 258-6668
E drbagwm@pacbell.net

Gold Buddha Monastery
248 East 11th Avenue, Vancouver B.C., V5T 2C3 CANADA

T (604) 709-0248
E drbagbm@mdi.ca

Gold Summit Monastery
233 1st Avenue W., Seattle, WA 98119 USA

T (206) 284-6690
F (206) 284-6918

Gold Sage Monastery
11455 Clayton Road, San Jose, CA 95127 USA

T (408) 923-7243
F (408) 923-1064
E drbagsm@jps.net

The International Translation Institute
1777 Murchison Drive
Burlingame, CA 94010-4504 USA

T (650) 692-5912
F (650) 692-5056
E drbaiti@jps.net

Long Beach Monastery
3361 East Ocean Boulevard
Long Beach, CA 90803 USA

T (562) 438-8902
E drbalbsm@aol.com

Blessings, Prosperity, & Longevity Monastery
4140 Long Beach Boulevard
Long Beach, CA 90807 USA

T (562) 595-4966

Avatamsaka Hermitage
11721 Beall Mountain Road
Potomac, MD 20854-1128 USA

T (301) 299-3693
E drbaah@aol.com

Avatamsaka Monastery
1009 4th Ave. S.W., Calgary, AB T2P OK8
Canada

T (403) 234-0644
E ava@nucleus.com

Dharma Realm Buddhist Books Distribution Society
11th Floor, 85 Chung-hsiao E. Road, Sec. 6,
Taipei, Taiwan, R.O.C.

T (02)2786-3022
F (02)2786-2674
E drbbds@ms1.seeder.net

Amitabha Monastery
7 Su-chien-hui, Chih-nan Village,
Shou-feng, Hualien County,
Taiwan, R.O.C.

T (03) 865-1956
F (03) 7980-1272

Prajna Guanyin Sagely Monastery
Batu 5-1/2 Jalan Sungai Besi,
Salak Selatan, 57100 Kuala Lumpur, Malaysia

T (03) 7982-6560
F (03) 7980-1272
E shengh@pd.jaring.my

Deng Bi An Temple
161 Jalan Ampang, 50450 Kuala Lumpur,
Malaysia

T (03) 2164-8055
F (03) 2163-7118

Buddhist Lecture Hall
31 Wong Nei Chong Road, Top Floor,
Happy Valley, Hong Kong

T (2) 2572-7644

$21.95